The Contingent Valuation of Natural Parks

NEW HORIZONS IN ENVIRONMENTAL ECONOMICS

Series Editors: Wallace E. Oates, *Professor of Economics, University of Maryland, USA* and Henk Folmer, *Professor of General Economics, Wageningen University and Professor of Environmental Economics, Tilburg University, The Netherlands*

This important series is designed to make a significant contribution to the development of the principles and practices of environmental economics. It includes both theoretical and empirical work. International in scope, it addresses issues of current and future concern in both East and West and in developed and developing countries.

The main purpose of the series is to create a forum for the publication of high quality work and to show how economic analysis can make a contribution to understanding and resolving the environmental problems confronting the world in the twenty-first century.

Recent titles in the series include:

Environmental Co-operation and Institutional Change
Theories and Policies for European Agriculture
Edited by Konrad Hagedorn

Valuing Environmental and Natural Resources
The Econometrics of Non-Market Valuation
Timothy C. Haab and Kenneth E. McConnell

Controlling Global Warming
Perspectives from Economics, Game Theory and Public Choice
Edited by Christoph Böhringer, Michael Finus and Carsten Vogt

Environmental Regulation in a Federal System
Framing Environmental Policy in the European Union
Tim Jeppesen

The International Yearbook of Environmental and Resource Economics 2002/2003
A Survey of Current Issues
Edited by Tom Tietenberg and Henk Folmer

International Climate Policy to Combat Global Warming
An Analysis of the Ancillary Benefits of Reducing Carbon Emissions
Dirk T.G. Rübbelke

Pollution, Property and Prices
An Essay in Policy-making & Economics
J.H. Dales

The Contingent Valuation of Natural Parks
Assessing the Warmglow Propensity Factor
Paulo A.L.D. Nunes

Environmental Policy Making in Economics
with Prior Tax Distortions
Edited by Lawrence H. Goulder

Recent Advances in Environmental Economics
Edited by Aart de Zeeuw and John A. List

Sustainability and Endogenous Growth
Karen Pittel

The Contingent Valuation of Natural Parks

Assessing the Warmglow Propensity Factor

Paulo A. L. D. Nunes

Senior Economist, Faculty of Economics,
Free University Amsterdam, The Netherlands
Visitor in Centre for Economic Studies,
Catholic University Leuven, Belgium
Research Leader, Centre of Excellence for Sustainable
Development in the Mediterranean Coastal Areas, University
of Venice, Italy

NEW HORIZONS IN ENVIRONMENTAL ECONOMICS

Edward Elgar
Cheltenham, UK • Northampton, MA, USA

Published by
Edward Elgar Publishing Limited
Glensanda House
Montpellier Parade
Cheltenham
Glos GL50 1UA
UK

Edward Elgar Publishing, Inc.
136 West Street
Suite 202
Northampton
Massachusetts 01060
USA

A catalogue record for this book
is available from the British Library

Library of Congress Cataloguing in Publication Data
Nunes, Paulo, 1970-
  The contingent valuation of natural parks : assessing the warmglow propensity factor / Paulo Nunes.
      p. cm.–(New horizons in environmental economics)
  Includes bibliographical references and index.
  1. Contingent valuation. 2. Parks–Economic aspects. I. Title. II. Series.

  HB846.55 .N86 2002
  333.78'3–dc21

                                                        2002018856

ISBN 1 84064 945 3
Printed and bound in Great Britain by MPG Books Ltd, Bodmin, Cornwall

CONTENTS

LIST OF FIGURES

LIST OF TABLES

LIST OF ABBREVIATIONS AND SYMBOLS

Abbreviations

AIC	Akaike information Criteria
ANP	Alentejo Natural Park
	(Parque Natural do Sudoeste Alentejano e Costa Vicentina)
BV	Bequest nalue
CERCLA	Comprehensive Environmental Response, Compensation and Liability Act
CESOP	Survey Research Department of the Portuguese Catholic University
	(Centro de Estudos e Sondagens de Opinião Pública da Universidade Católica)
CI	Confidence interval
CS	Consumer surplus
CV	Contingent valuation
D/K	Do not know
DC	Dichotomous choice (double-bounded)
DUV	Direct use value
EO	Executive Order
EPA	Environmental Protection Agency
HC	Hicksian compensating
HE	Hicksian equivalent
ICN	Portuguese National Institute for the Conservation of the Nature
	(Instituto de Conservação da Natureza)
INE	Portuguese National Bureau of Statistics
	(Instituto de Nacional de Estatística)
IRS	Personal Income Tax
IUV	Indirect use value
Ln N	Log-likelihood for log-normal distribution
LR	Likelihood ratio est
MARN	Portuguese Ministry of Environment and Natural Resources
	(Ministério do Ambiente e Recursos Naturais)
MRS	Marginal rate of substitution
N/A	No answer
NCO-94	National Classification of Occupations
NNV	Norwegian Association for the Protection of Nature
NOAA	National Oceanic and Atmospheric Administration
NUV	Non-use value
OE	Open ended
OV	Option value
PSUs	Primary sampling units
qL	Quasi linear preferences structure
Quercus	Portuguese Association for Nature Conservation

RA	Recreation area
RDUs	Residential dwelling units
SMC	Square multiple correlation
TAX	National Park Tax scheme
TEV	Total economic value
TC	Travel cost
TIOLI	Take-it-or-leave-it
WA	Wilderness area
WTA	Willingness to accept
WTP	Willingness to pay
WTP_{RA}	Willingness to pay for the protection of the recreation areas
WTP_{WA}	Willingness to pay for the protection of the wilderness areas
$WTP_{(WA+RA)}$	Willingness to Pay for the protection of both recreation and wilderness areas
WWF	Worldwide Fund for Nature
UV	Use value
VC	Voluntary contribution scheme
XV	Existence value

Symbols

Chapter 1

V	Utility function
x	Private good
q	Quantity of the environmental attribute (e.g. number of recreational areas)
z	Quality of environmental attribute (e.g. level of biological diversity)
p	Price of q
M	Money income
$v(.)$	Indirect utility function
$e(.)$	Expenditure function
$\pi \;(1-\pi)$	Probability of saying 'yes' (probability of saying 'no')
F	Distribution prior
G	Cumulative distribution function
η , ϖ	Error term

Chapter 2

v	Indirect utility function
j	Indexes the individual consumers
b_j	Maximum willingness to pay of individual consumer j
c_j	Cost written in the survey instrument as presented to the j respondent.

Chapter 3

f_u	Use motivation function
f_{nu}	Non-use motivation function
f_{wg}	Warmglow motivation function
$\mathbf{d}^j$	Vector of psychological characteristics of the consumer j
$\mathbf{h}^j$	Vector of socio-economic characteristics of the consumer j
J	Consumers in the economy
M^j	j exogenous income
Y^j	Quantity of tradable private goods (standard numeraire)
p	price of a unit of q
θ	Warmglow motivation coefficient (when assumed as a linear function)
ρ	Use motivation coefficient (when assumed as a linear function)
τ	Nonuse motivation coefficient (when assumed as a linear function)
q^j	j contribution for the environmental protection plan
$\bar{q}$	Sum of contributions from all other consumers
Q	Environment protection plan for the Natural Area
B_u	Use characteristic
B_{nu}	Non-use characteristic
B_{wg}	Warmglow characteristic
$\pi(.)$	Marginal willingness to pay
$\hat{B}_u(.)$	Use restricted demand function
$\hat{B}_{nu}(.)$	Non-use restricted demand function
$\hat{B}_{wg}(.)$	Warmglow restricted demand function
$\tilde{B}_u(.)$	Use unrestricted demand function
$\tilde{B}_{nu}(.)$	Nonuse unrestricted demand function
$\tilde{B}_{wg}(.)$	Warmglow unrestricted demand function
$\tilde{p}_u$	Virtual price of the use characteristic
$\tilde{p}_{nu}$	Virtual price of the nonuse characteristic
$\tilde{p}_{wg}$	Virtual price of the warmglow characteristic
$\tilde{M}$	Virtual income
$C_{i,k}$	Compensated price term (1st term of the Slutsky equation)

Chapter 9

b_i	Initial bid (as stated in the survey instrument)
b_h	Higher bid
b_l	Lower bid
π_{YY}	Probability of saying 'yes' to the initial bid and 'yes' to the higher bid (or simply, the probability of saying 'yes/yes')
π_{YN}	Probability of saying 'yes/no'

π_{NY}	Probability of saying 'no/yes'
π_{NN}	Probability of saying 'no/no'
$F(.)$	Cumulative distribution function of the WTP
r_{nn}^{i}	'no/no' binary indicator variable
r_{ny}^{i}	'no/yes' binary indicator variable
r_{yn}^{i}	'yes/no' binary indicator variable
r_{yy}^{i}	'yes/yes' binary indicator variable
β	Location parameter for log-normal distribution
σ	Scale parameter for log-normal distribution

Chapter 10

m	Attitudinal items (as stated in the survey instrument)
$av_{m,j}$	Response of the j respondent to the m item (observable variable)
$\overline{av}_{m,j}$	sample response average to the m item
$f_{u,j}$	j use motivational factor score (unobservable variable)
$f_{nu,j}$	j nonuse motivational factor score (unobservable variable)
$f_{wg,j}$	j warmglow motivational factor score (unobservable variable)
$\lambda_{m,u}, \lambda_{m,nu}, \lambda_{m,wg}$	Loading coefficients associated with the m item
$\phi_{m,j}$	Error term
av	Matrix giving the answers of the respondents on the 26 attitudinal items
f	Matrix of factor scores
Λ	Matrix of factor loadings
Ξ	Matrix of residual terms
Ω	Co-variance matrix of residual terms
h_m^2	Communality term $\left(\lambda_{m,u}^2 + \lambda_{m,nu}^2 + \lambda_{m,wg} \right)$
ω_m	Specific variance term
$\hat{f}_l$	Vector with all the individual observations for the level of motivation l
x_k	Vector with the all individuals for the socio-economic characteristic k
u_l	Vector with disturbance terms
a's	Coefficients to be estimated

Chapter 11

α_{WA}^{j}	Individual marginal willingness to pay for the protection of the WA
α_{RA}^{j}	Individual marginal willingness to pay for the protection of the RA
ε	Disturbance term
d_{WA}, d_{RA}	Dummy variables
δ_{wg}	Warmglow effect parameter
δ_u	Use effect parameter
δ_{nu}	Non-use effect parameter

PREFACE

Putting a monetary value on environmental goods and services is widely accepted among economists. Two major categories of valuation techniques are available to us that are capable of putting an economic value on such commodities. On the one hand, there is the revealed preferences method, which is based on the available market information (for example, travel cost, hedonic price, averting behaviour, production cost or productivity method). On the other hand, there is the stated preferences method that is based on survey-constructed information (for example, contingent valuation, contingent ranking, allocation games). In recent decades the number of publications in the domain of stated preferences methods, and in particular in contingent valuation (CV) method, have grown incredibly. For example, the scientific programme of last year's World Conference of the Environmental and Resources Economists contained 58 CV papers, representing about 80 % of the papers in the valuation sessions. This represents an increase of about 280 % with respect to the CV presentations held in 1996 during Lisbon's 7th Annual Conference of the European Association of Environmental and Resource Economists. The 'popularity' of the CV method is related to the following historical benchmarks:

- the re-interpretation in 1989 of the Comprehensive Environmental Response, Compensation and Liability Act, also referred as CERCLA. This US government decision expressed not only the legitimacy of non-use values as a component of the total resource value but also granted equal standing to stated and revealed preference evaluation techniques (USDI 1989)

- the valuation study in 1992 of the loss of passive use values arising from injuries to natural resources caused by the *Exxon Valdez* oil spill in Prince William Sound in the State of the Alaska, considered as the 'road map' by many CV researchers (Carson *et al.* 1992)

- more recently, in 1993, a panel of experts, including the Nobel Laureate Kenneth Arrow, provided positive counsel to the National Oceanic and Atmospheric Administration (NOAA) concerning the application and validity of the CV: 'the Panel concludes that well conducted CV studies can produce estimates reliable enough to be the starting point of a judicial process of damage assessment, including lost passive values'. (NOAA 1993)

On theoretical and methodological grounds, the contingent valuation method presents general advantages that also contributed to its increased use for the valuation of environmental goods and services. In particular:

- the survey instrument, and respective scenario description, are highly suited for public decision making, namely when evaluating different policy options under consideration. This reflects the flexibility that we have in designing the protection scenarios, and respective states of the environmental good, even if they lie outside the present institutional arrangements or levels of provision (Hanley 1988; Pearce and Markandya 1989; World Bank 1990; Portney 1994; Hanley and Spash 1993)

- the CV has an important role in the monetary valuation of environmental goods since it is the only technique able to assess non-use benefits, that is, benefits which are associated with no behavioural market trace (Mitchell and Carson 1989; Carson 1991; Mitchell and Carson 1993; Navrud and Strand 1992; Portney 1994)

- the CV method carries with it the advantage that specific methodological tests can be explored so as to investigate the validity of the stated responses. As a matter of fact, this domain has received much of the research attention from CV practitioners, given the interest in checking the methodological validity of the survey instrument and respective estimation results (Loomis 1989 and 1990; Loomis *et al.* 1993; Carson and Mitchell 1993; Desvousges *et al.* 1993; Hoevenagel 1992; Hoevenagel 1994 and 1996; Diamond *et al.* 1993; Wiestra 1996).

Nevertheless, the CV technique has been the target of diverse critiques. As a matter of fact, well-known scholars such as Jerry Hausman, Peter Diamond, William Desvousges and Paul Milgrom express their doubts with respect to the suitability of CV results for inclusion in benefit cost analyses (Hausman 1993; Hausman *et al.* 1993; Diamond *et al.* 1993; Diamond 1996; Desvousges *et al.* 1993; Desvousges *et al.* 1993a; Milgrom 1993). These authors raise a well-known question: 'is a number better than no number?' (Diamond and Hausman 1994). The scepticism is particularly strong when the CV application is addressed to measure non-use values. According to Milgrom, for non-use values, as measured by survey methods, to be consistent with economic theory 'it would be necessary for respondent's individual existence values to reflect only their own personal economic motives and not altruistic motives, or a sense of duty, or moral obligation' (1993, p. 431). Most of the critiques have their origin in the valuation embedding frequently arising in CV estimations. We illustrate the embedding problem with the following experiment:

> Group 1: willingness to pay X for the protection plan A;
> Group 2: willingness to pay Y for the protection plan B;
> Group 3: willingness to pay Z for the protection plans A and B.

Embedding is present when $X + Y > Z$, which thus implies the rejection of the adding-up valuation hypothesis. This situation can be explained in terms of:

- warmglow effect. The authors view CV responses as a way to signal non-economic considerations, especially the pleasure derived from giving to good causes or simply from concern over the environment. Kahneman and Knetsch (1992) argue that the stated bids are based on the 'moral satisfaction' of giving. If this moral satisfaction presents rapidly diminishing marginal utility with respect to the size of the gift, then we may expect that respondents will bid about the same for obtaining moral satisfaction. Bearing on our illustration, we would have $X = X' + C$; $Y = Y' + C$ and $Z = Z' + C$ where C is the value attached to the warmglow of giving and $Z' \equiv X' + Y'$. Then the sum of the individual protection plans will be $Z' + 2C$, which is greater than $Z = Z' + C$, the value of the two protection plans jointly;

- ignoring substitution and income effects. If the benefits of providing different public goods are each independently estimated in a partial equilibrium framework (Hoevenagel 1994), then summing independent values, X and Y, overestimates the total benefits, Z, of the provision by ignoring substitution and income effects;

- mental models. This third explanation constitutes a psychological view of the stated valuation responses and arises from research of the many statements of the individuals participating in focus groups and individual debriefings. More recently, verbal protocols allow the researchers to register how respondents think while they fill in the questionnaire and answer the elicitation question (Schkade and Payne 1993; Schkade and Payne 1994; Hutchinson *et al.* 1995). These views, called 'mental models' by psychologists, often exhibit a part–whole interpretation bias, that is, the respondent values much more than the researcher intended to value: when the respondent is asked the value of partial (and independent) provisions of a public good, for example X and Y, such an individual *corrects* the 'foolish' question asked by a 'silly' researcher and provides a value for the total provision of the public good, Z. Thus the three values, X, Y and Z, are nearly the same, so the sum of the mean values from groups 1 and 2 will exceed the mean value of group 3.

In this monograph, we are particularly interested in modelling warmglow and explore the empirical validity of the respective valuation transmission effect, that is, we test whether warmglow is an underlying driving force of the individual CV responses. If the empirical evidence does not reject the warmglow valuation transmission effect hypothesis, then we propose to assess its magnitude in the valuation function. The ultimate goal is to disentangle the warmglow from the original WTP mean estimates and compute a *dry* WTP, that is, free from any warmglow. In order to test the empirical validity of such a conjecture, we conducted a national CV application so as to measure the use and non-use benefits of the *Parque Natural do Sudoeste Alentejano e Costa Vicentina* in Portugal.

The first part of this work deals with the modelling of individual consumer preferences. First, we explore the joint characteristic product model so as to analyse the individual consumer contributions to the protection of the Natural Area. In this context, the individual's own contributions are interpreted in terms of the characteristics that they generate. We assumed that the financial contributions to the protection of the Natural Area generate a flow of public characteristics: the use and non-use characteristics. The use characteristic refers to the set of recreational possibilities that the individual consumer is able to enjoy whenever visiting the Natural Area. The non-use characteristic is associated with the Natural Area function of wildlife diversity protection and the guarantee of non-extinction of some species. The warmglow value component has to do with the gain in utility associated with the feeling of well-being associated with the act of contributing to good causes. Second, we develop the concept of consumer motivations that are responsible for setting the relationship between the goods and characteristic space dimensions. In the analytical model formulation we identify the 'use/recreation', 'warmglow' and 'non-use/existence' motivations. Finally, we explore the comparative static properties of the consumer's own contributions.

The second part deals with the development of the contingent valuation survey instrument and its application to the Alentejo Natural Park in Portugal. First, interdisciplinary discussions involving different specialists were used in order to achieve credible and accurate policy scenario descriptions. We also made extensive use of focus groups and pre-testing which help in crafting the language and visual aid applied in the survey instrument. Second, we selected personal interviews and worked with the double dichotomous elicitation question format. In the final survey we used 28 versions involving the use of different protection programmes, payment vehicles, survey information levels and elicitation bid cards. As far as the protection programmes are concerned, we took into account three scenario descriptions. We refer to the protection of the Recreational Areas (RA) of the Alentejo Natural Park from tourism development; the protection of the Wilderness Areas (WA) of the Alentejo Natural Park from tourism development, and the protection of both the Wilderness Areas and Recreational Areas (WA + RA) of the Alentejo Natural Park from tourism development.

The third part contains the analysis of the data collected by the national CV application. First, we made use of non-parametric formal test procedures and investigated the stated willingness to pay (WTP) responses across the two payment vehicles and across the two survey information levels. The test results indicated that the stated WTP distribution in the scenario where the respondent is informed about government expenditures in keeping the Natural Park free from any commercial development is not statistically different from the WTP distribution in the scenario where the respondent is not provided with such information. This test was interpreted as a clear rejection of the hypothesis of a starting point bias, that is, the hypothesis that the indication of how much money is spent may be used by the respondent as a 'clue' about the Park monetary valuation is rejected. As far as the inference analysis of the payment vehicles is concerned, the test results confirmed that in the voluntary contribution scheme, free-riding is present in respondents' contribution behaviour, though it is hardly statistically significant. Both non-parametric test results were interpreted as important indicators confirming the validity of our contingent valuation experiment and, in this way, guaranteed the quality of the proposed questionnaire as a value measurement instrument.

Second, we assessed the total economic value of the three protection programmes. The estimated WTP for preventing the WA and the RA from commercial development was approximately 148 million euro and 114 million euro, respectively. In contrast, the WTP for the two programmes jointly was estimated to be 140 million euro. Therefore, and if we admit that the Government intends to pursue a policy action which is characterized by the partial commercial development of the Alentejo Natural Park, then the valuation results clearly indicate that Portuguese households prefer to keep the WA of the Alentejo Natural Park always protected and also not to introduce commercial development in the RA. This is a very important result since it reiterates the importance of the non-use value component of the Alentejo Natural Park, which can only be assessed with the use of the contingent valuation technique.

Third, we tested whether the warmglow valuation transmission mechanism is present in the respondent's stated WTP responses, that is, we tested the premise that the financial contribution, by itself, also constitutes a source of well-being to the individual respondent. With the help of factor analysis we operationalize the individual warmglow motivation and introduce such a latent variable in the multivariate regression of the WTP responses. The estimation results confirmed that the warmglow motivation factor is statistically robust across all the WTP functions and thus confirmed the empirical validity of the warmglow valuation transmission mechanism in the stated WTP responses. Finally, we proposed the estimation of a *dry* WTP measure, that is, a WTP measure that is free from a general feeling of well-being or satisfaction generated by the act of giving. We verified that the *dry* WTP was much lower than the original estimates, and unlike the original estimates, the *dry* WTP estimates do not violate the adding-up property, that is, the $WTP_{WA}^{dry} + WTP_{RA}^{dry} = WTP_{(WA+RA)}^{dry}$ proposition is no longer rejected. However, a question now remains: which measure should be taken into account in cost–benefit   analysis and policy formulation? Should we use the original WTP estimates or, on the contrary, should we correct for warmglow? We showed a strong conviction that the survey responses do reflect true WTP responses – the empirical results confirm the validity of the proposed impure public good model formulation and – in this way, the original WTP responses constituted correct information to be used in the estimation of the demand for the public good.

Several persons contributed to the successful realisation of this work. To all of them I would like to express my sincere gratitude. I would especially like to mention Erik Schokkaert and Stef Proost, at Catholic University Leuven (Belgium), John Loomis, at Colorado State University (USA), Marno Verbeek, at Rotterdam University (The Netherlands), Clara Duarte, at Lisbon New University (Portugal), and a number of anonymous reviewers who read through parts of the manuscript and made corrections and suggestions. Special thanks go to Richard Carson, at University California San Diego (US), William Green, at New York University (US) and to Olvar Bergland, at Agriculture University Norway, for helping me to cope with important estimation difficulties. Of course I retain sole responsibility for any remaining errors.

Paulo Augusto Lourenço Dias Nunes

Amsterdam

To Laura
and to Rubens
who is disappointed because he cannot read it.

PART I
Economic Valuation, Warmglow and Preference Modelling

Chapter

1

VALUES, VALUATION METHODS AND CONTINGENT VALUATION: AN OVERVIEW

1.1 Introduction

One of the central themes in the field of environmental economics is the valuation of environmental resources, usually within the framework of cost–benefit analysis or natural damage assessment. Environmental resources such as natural parks, wildlife diversity, clean air and clean water are public goods that have an economic value, but there is no relevant market where their value is expressed. Conceptually, the total economic value of an environmental resource consists of its use value and non-use value. Use values relate to the individual's present and future use/consumption of the environmental resource. Non-use values relate to the individual's willingness to pay even if the consumer makes no use of the resource and has no intention of making use of it.

The monetary value assessment of the total economic value of an environmental resource requires the use of special valuation tools. Contingent valuation (CV) is one of the valuations tools suggested in the literature (Mitchell and Carson 1989). The CV method involves the use of questionnaires to elicit individual willingness to pay (WTP) for the specified environmental quality change. The CV method turns out to be a very important valuation technique since it is often the only technique available for assessing benefits, mainly because CV is the only method capable of shedding light on non-use values.

The present chapter contains five sections. Section 1.2 presents and discusses the concept of total economic value of an environmental asset. Section 1.3 reviews the different valuation methods available to put a monetary value on environmental resources as a non-market good. Section 1.4 focuses on the contingent valuation (CV) and respective state-of-art research work guidelines. Finally, section 1.5 presents the link of CV valuation answers to standard economic theory.

1.2 The concept of total economic value

The concept of total economic value of an environmental resource has its foundations in welfare economics: the basic premise of economic valuation of any environmental resource is its effect on the well-being of the individuals who make up the society. Therefore, if society wishes to make the most in terms of individuals' well-being maximisation, the issue of the monetary assessment of the total economic value of an environmental resource is a key issue in terms of policy decisions. Conceptually, the total economic value (TEV) of an environmental resource consists of its use value (UV) and non-use value (NUV) (Pearce and Moran 1994) – see Table 1.1.

Table 1.1: Classification of values of an environmental asset

TOTAL ECONOMIC VALUE	USE VALUES	direct use value	recreation benefits e.g. sight-seeing, fishing, swimming
		indirect use value	ecosystem functional benefits e.g. watershed protection, timber production
		option value	safeguard of use benefits e.g. future pharmaceuticals, future visits
	NONUSE VALUES	bequest value	legacy benefits e.g. habitat conservation for future generations
		existence value	existence benefits e.g. knowledge of continued protection of wildlife diversity

Adapted from Pearce and Moran (1994)

Use values are what they seem to be: values arising from the actual use/consumption made of the environmental resource (Pearce and Moran 1994). Use values are further divided into direct use values (DUV), indirect use values (IUV) and option values (OV). Since we focus on the value assessment of the benefits[1] derived from the protection of a Natural Park, in particular the Alentejo Natural Park, the direct use value refers to the various forms of recreation possibilities available to the Park's visitors; the indirect use value refers to benefits deriving from ecosystem functions such as the Park's role in protecting the soil from erosion or protecting the watershed; the option value refers essentially to the individual's willingness to pay for the preservation of the Natural Park against some (subjective) probability that the individual will make use of it at a future date (Randall 1991). The conservation of a Natural Park has, however, impacts on the well-being of the individuals that are not directly associated with recreational consumption. These are referred to in the literature as the non-use values, that is, anthropocentric values which are not associated with current or expected use/consumption of the environmental resource (Carson *et al.* 1992). The non-use values are usually divided between the bequest value (BV) and the existence value (XV). The bequest value refers to the benefit accruing to any individual from the knowledge that others might benefit from the Park in the future; the existence value refers to the benefit derived simply from the knowledge of continued protection of the Natural Park. The origin of the concept of

---

[1] Since benefits are valued in terms of their effect on individuals' well-being, the terms *economic value* and *welfare change* can be used interchangeably.

existence value is attributed to John Krutilla who suggested that people may still value a resource even if they do not use it (Krutilla 1967). Thus in total we have:

$$TEV = UV + NUV = (DUV + IUV + OV) + (XV + BV)$$

The non-use values have typically a public good character for which no market price is available to disclose accurate monetary valuation. The lack of such market price information may convey the impression that benefits of conservation policies are unimportant, when compared to the market priced allocation alternatives (for example, urbanisation and tourism development). As a consequence, most of the time policy makers have based their decisions on an undervaluation of the environmental resources that has thus resulted in a misallocation of scarce environmental resources. The monetary assessment of the use and non-use benefits involved with the conservation policy is, therefore, an important step in policy decisions about environmental resources use. The money value assessment of such environmental assets requires special tools. These are discussed in the following section.

1.3 Monetary valuation methods

Various valuation methods are available to put an economic value on environmental commodities. Freeman (1979), for example, classifies the valuation methods into methods based on non-market data and methods based on market data. The latter category is divided into methods in which the environmental commodity indirectly creates well-being by being an input factor in the production of market goods, and into methods in which the environmental commodity directly creates well-being, by being an argument in the individual's utility functions. Pearce and Markandya (1989), however, classify the valuation methods that reveal people's preferences as direct, and methods that rely on a dose-response (for example, production cost techniques) as indirect. Finally, Mitchell and Carson (1989) label all valuation methods that reveal people's preferences as behavioral-linkage methods.

Since almost every author who deals with valuation of environmental commodities defines his or her own classification, our categorisation of the valuation methods will not be an exception to the rule. We distinguish two groups of valuation methods: the direct and indirect or dose response valuation methods – see Table 1.2. The dose response methods have in common that they put a price on environmental commodities without retrieving people's preferences for these commodities. The production cost techniques, an example of the dose response methods, calculate the monetary value of the negative effects of, say, air pollution on buildings, by using a production cost technique and multiply the increased maintenance and repair activities by some maintenance and repair prices (Feenstra 1984). Another example of the dose response methods is when researchers use the production factor technique to estimate the economic value of, say, cleaner soil, through the increased agricultural output by using a demand and supply model (Smith 1991). Conversely, the direct methods rely on individual preferences. On the basis of the process by which these methods retrieve individuals' preferences, these methods are further divided into 'revealed preference' methods and 'stated preference' methods. Whereas economists who use revealed preference valuation methods have to carry out estimation exercises bearing in mind the existent data, economists who use stated preference valuation methods have to collect their own data by means of questionnaires. Therefore, the use of interdisciplinary teams has become very important in CV research: economists work closely with experts from other disciplines such as market research, survey

Table 1.2: A classification of valuation methods

DIRECT METHODS		INDIRECT METHODS
Revealed Preference Methods	Stated Preference Methods	Dose Response Methods
• travel cost method • hedonic price method • averting behavior	• contingent valuation • contingent ranking • pairwise comparison • allocation games	• production cost • production factor

research, sociology and psychology in order to improve the methodology and, in this way, the quality of the value measurements (Carson *et al.* 1992; NOAA 1993; Gregory *et al.* 1993). In contrast, revealed preference methods have remained an exclusive valuation tool for economists.

The group of revealed preference valuation methods consists of three methods: the travel cost method, the hedonic price method, and the averting behavior method (Braden and Kolstad 1991). The common underlying feature is a dependency on a relationship between a market good and the environmental commodity. For example, when using the travel cost method, researchers estimate the economic value of recreational sites by looking at the costs of the trips made by the visitors to these sites (Bockstael *et al.* 1991). When using the hedonic price method to estimate the economic value of an environmental commodity, say, cleaner air, the researchers explore the analysis of house prices and surrounding air characteristics (Palmquist 1991). Researchers who use the averting behavior method try to estimate the economic value of environmental quality on the basis of expenditures made to avert or mitigate the adverse effects of pollution (Cropper and Freeman 1991).

The group of stated preference valuation methods all use the survey method. The underlying feature is the use of the questionnaire to ask directly the individuals to state their economic values for environmental commodities (Mitchell and Carson 1989). However, this method encompasses different versions, such as the contingent valuation, contingent ranking, pairwise comparison, and allocation games (Hoevenagel 1994). The differences between the various versions of the survey method relate to the way in which the economic values are elicited. For example, whereas the contingent valuation method asks respondents to express directly their preferences in monetary terms for some defined environmental good, the contingent ranking method asks the respondent to rank a number of described alternatives (Bergland 1997). The pairwise comparison is closely related to the contingent ranking method, yet respondents are asked to compare a series of pairs of alternatives. Finally, in an allocation game respondents are asked to allocate a fixed budget among a set of environmental goods. This method is used more particularly in experimental economics (Brookshire 1997).

Today, the contingent valuation (CV) method is one of the most used techniques for valuation of environmental goods. This is partly due to the advantages of CV compared to the revealed preference methods and the other stated preference methods. First, the CV method gives, and contrary to the other stated preference methods – immediately an answer to the typical problem in environmental valuation: the monetary assessment of respondents' preferences. This information plays a crucial role in the determination of the economic value of the environmental good and it can be directly used in cost–benefit exercises, an important tool in policy making. Second, the CV method is, and contrary to the other revealed preference methods, the only valuation technique which is capable of shedding light on the monetary valuation of the non-use values, that is, the benefit value component of the environmental commodity which is not directly associated with its direct use or consumption. These values are characterized by having no behavioral market trace. Therefore, economists cannot glean information about these values relying on market-based valuation approaches. For environmental resources such as Natural Parks, which play an important role in guaranteeing the protection of local wildlife diversity, the non-use value component may account for the major part of the conservation benefits.[2] Ignoring such values will be responsible for a systematic bias in the estimation (an underestimation) of the total benefits associated with the preservation of the Natural Park. Third, CV brings with it the advantage that environmental changes may be valued even if they have not yet occurred (*ex ante* valuation). This implies that the CV method can be a useful advisory tool for policy decision making. Fourth, and as a result environmental changes may be valued even if they have not yet occurred, CV offers a greater potential scope and flexibility than the revealed preference methods since it is possible to specify different states of nature (policy scenarios) that may even lie outside the current institutional arrangements or levels of provision (Hoehn and Randall 1989). Furthermore, the constructed nature of the CV method permits the testing of various methodological issues concerning the measurement validity of the individual's stated valuation responses. Indeed, part of this research work is concerned with the validity of CV responses. We start, however, with a brief overview of the CV method and the linkage of respondents' valuation answers to standard economic theory.

1.4 The contingent valuation methodology

Contingent valuation method is a stated preference valuation method that uses questionnaires to ask directly individuals to state their preferences for environmental commodities. Mitchell and Carson defined the method as follows:

'The CV method uses survey questions to elicit people's preferences for public goods by finding out what they are willing to pay (WTP) for specified improvements in them. The method thus aims at eliciting their WTP in dollar amounts. It circumvents the absence of markets for public goods by presenting consumers with hypothetical markets in which they have the opportunity to buy the good in question. The hypothetical market may be modelled after either a private goods' market or a political market. Because the elicited WTP values are contingent upon the hypothetical market described to the respondents, this approach came to be called the contingent valuation method.' (Mitchell and Carson 1989, p. 2-3)

The typical CV survey consists of three sections (Mitchell and Carson 1989; NOAA 1993). The first section is characterized by a description of the environmental change as conveyed by the policy formulation and a description of the contingent market. The policy formulation involves describing the availability (or quality) of the environmental commodity in both the 'reference state' (usually the *status quo*) and 'target state' (usually depicting the policy action). Since all monetary transactions occur in a social context, it is also crucial to define the contingent market – usually rather unfamiliar to the respondents – by stating to the respondent both the rules specifying the conditions that would lead to policy implementation

---

[2] These areas are most of the time closed to the general public. No commercial development, roads or other infrastructures are allowed here. The objective is to protect the natural habitat conditions and its wildlife diversity.

as well the payment to be exacted from the respondent's household in the event of policy implementation.

The second section of the CV instrument is where the respondent is asked to state his or her monetary valuation for the described policy formulation. This part is the core of the CV survey instrument. The major objective of this section is to obtain a monetary measure of the maximum willingness to pay that the individual consumers are willing to pay for the described environmental policy action.

The third section of the CV instrument is a set of questions that collect socio-demographic information about the respondents. The answers to these questions help to better characterize the respondent's profile and are used to understand the respondent's stated WTP responses. The third section finishes with follow-up questions. The follow-up questions are answered by the interviewers after they have left the respondent. The goal is to assess whether the respondents have (well) understood the CV survey in general, and the valuation question in particular.

1.4.1 Some historical benchmarks in the CV research path

The first published CV reference dates from 1947 (Ciriacy-Wantrup 1947), and is an article published in the *Journal of Farm Economics*.[3] The study focuses on the valuation of the economic effects of preventing soil erosion. The author suggested that one way to obtain information on the demand for these favourable effects would be to ask individuals how much they would be willing to pay for successive increments. However, no empirical valuation was attempted. The first CV design and implementation only occured two decades later when Robert Davis assessed the economic value of the recreational possibilities of the Maine Woods by exploring the survey technique (Davis 1963). Davis simulated a market behavior situation by putting the interviewer in the 'position of a seller who elicits the highest possible bid from the users of the services being offered'.

Since these early beginnings, the CV method has been used to measure the benefits of a wide range of environmental goods including recreation, amenity value, scenery, forests, wetlands, wildlife, air and water quality (Mitchell and Carson 1989). However, early CV studies were related to species valuation such as waterfowl in North America (Hammack and Brown 1974), Canadian geese (Bishop 1980), whooping cranes (Stoll and Johnson 1984) and the option and existence values for grizzly bear and bighorn sheep populations (Brookshire *et al.* 1983). More recently, there has been a trend to conducting CV studies not only to value environmental goods, but also to investigate the various methodological issues involved in the valuation exercise (Hausman 1993; Pethig 1994; Harrison and Kriström 1995; Jakobsson and Dragun 1996). During these decades, the CV method has gone through several phases, emerging from the academy into the rough and tumble of the outside world. Strong development stimulus was given by the Reagan Executive Order 12291, introduced in 1981; the re-interpretation of CERCLA, in 1989; the *Exxon Valdez* damage assessment, in 1992; and, more recently, the NOAA panel.

1.4.1.1 Reagan Executive Order and the re-interpretation of CERCLA

The Reagan Executive Order 12291, introduced in 1981, constitutes a strong stimulus for the development of the monetary valuation methods of environmental commodities. In concrete terms, the Executive Order stipulated that all federal regulations on environmental policy should be submitted to a cost–benefit analysis. All regulations, including both the

---

[3] Nowadays the *American Journal of Agricultural Economics*.

promulgation of new regulations and the review of existing ones, would only be carried out if a positive present value for the society could be achieved. Therefore, the social benefits had to be monetized. The flexibility and generality of the CV method's application was the main reason why this valuation method received most of the EPA's 'demands' in the monetary assessment of the social costs and benefits associated with the new regulations on environmental policy. Thus, the appearance of Executive Order 12291 had a major impact on the development of the CV method.

Another important benchmark in the CV method is the District of Columbia Court of Appeals reinterpretation in 1989 of the US Comprehensive Environmental Response, Compensation and Liability Act of 1980 (USDI 1989). This governmental decision expressed not only the legitimacy of non-use values as a component of the total resource value, but also granted equal standing to stated and revealed preference evaluation techniques. Since then, the CV technique is widely used by academic institutions as well as by governmental agencies as a crucial tool in cost benefit analysis and damage cost assessment.[4]

1.4.1.2 The *Exxon Valdez* report

Another important benchmark in the history of the CV research was the massive oil spill due to the grounding of the oil tanker *Exxon Valdez* in Prince William Sound in the northern part of the Gulf of Alaska on March 24, 1989. This was the largest oil spill from a tanker in US history: more than 1 300 kilometres of coastline were affected and almost 23 000 birds were killed (Carson *et al.* 1992). After the oil spill, the State of Alaska commissioned various studies to identify the physical damage to natural resources. The follow-up economic damage assessment studies also take into account, in addition to water purification costs, economic losses such as the decrease in revenue from recreation and fisheries. Moreover, the State of Alaska appointed an interdisciplinary group of CV researchers to design and implement a national CV study to measure the loss of non-use values to US citizens as a result of the oil spill. This study constitutes one of the major contingent valuation applications and represents an important methodological reference for all contingent valuation researchers' work. The loss of non-use values resulting from the *Exxon Valdez* oil spill is estimated at 2.8 billion dollars. However, anticipating these high financial consequences, Exxon commissioned a group of researchers to verify whether non-use values could be accurately measured by means of CV. The main argument of critics of CV is that the method is not capable of resulting in valid and reliable monetary measures of nonuse values. Hausman's well-know argument 'is some number better than no number' fully expresses the scepticism toward the CV method. Therefore, according to Hausman, assessments of lost non-use values by means of the CV method should not be used in court; in the following chapter we discuss in detail Hausman's critique.

---

[4] Carson *et al.* (1994b) list an extensive bibliography of works related to the CV method: major organizations across the world such as the World Bank (1990), Resources for the Future (for example, Mitchell and Carson 1989; Smith 1993; Smith 1994), Organization for Economic Co-operation and Development (for example, Pearce and Markandya 1989) as well as US agencies such as the US Environmental Protection Agency (for example, McClelland *et al.* 1992) represent important CV work. More recently, Navrud (1999) catalogues the European CV applications.

1.4.1.3 The NOAA Panel

More recently, a panel of experts, with the Nobel Laureates Kenneth Arrow and Robert Solow as chairmen,[5] provided advice to the National Oceanic and Atmospheric Administration (NOAA) on the following question:

'is the contingent valuation method capable of providing estimates of lost non-use or existence values that are reliable enough to be used in the natural resource damage assessments?'

The final advice of the NOAA panel may be summarized by the following sentence:

'the Panel concludes that well conducted CV studies can produce estimates reliable enough to be the starting point of a judicial process of damage assessment, including lost passive values.' (Federal Register, vol. 58, no. 10, p. 4610)

This conclusion cheered all researchers who wish to use contingent valuation. However, the Panel was rather prudent with its conclusion and qualified its statement by establishing a set of guidelines, recommended for all future CV applications, concerning the design and execution of the survey instrument. The six most important guidelines, also well-known as the six pillars of the NOAA (NOAA 1993), are summarized as follows:

1) CV experiments should rely on face-to-face interviews rather than telephone interviews, and whenever this is not possible (especially because of the high costs associated with personal interviews) telephone interviews are preferable to mail surveys;
2) CV experiments should elicit the respondent's WTP to prevent a future incident rather than WTA for an incident already occurred;
3) CV experiments should use a dichotomous choice referendum elicitation format, that is, respondents should be asked how they would vote (for or against) upon a described environmental quality change. The main reason for the dichotomous choice is that such a take-it-or-leave-it survey valuation question is more likely to reflect the real world market decisions which individuals are confronted with. Moreover, the dichotomous choice referendum reveals itself to be less vulnerable to strategic bidding behavior than, for example, the open-ended elicitation format;
4) CV experiments should contain an accurate and understandable description of the programme or policy under consideration and the associated environmental benefits in each of the two scenarios, that is, with and without the policy. Interdisciplinary work with other research areas, namely the biological sciences, is here recommended;
5) CV experiments should include reminders of the substitutes for the commodity in question as well as its budget. In a context where the respondents are being asked how they would vote on a financial contribution to protect a natural area, the respondents should be reminded of the existence of the other areas that exist. Moreover, the respondent should be reminded that such a contribution would reduce the amount of money that he or she has available to spend on other things. The major idea here is to make such a (hypothetical) valuation exercise resemble as closely as possible an actual market transaction;
6) CV method experiments should include a follow-up section at the end of the questionnaire to be sure if the respondents understood (or not) the choice that they were asked to make.

---

[5] In addition to Arrow and Solow, the panel included Edward Leamer, Roy Radner, Howard Schuman and Paul Portney.

According to the Panel, this set of guidelines contributes to guaranteeing the quality of the CV survey as a measurement instrument and the validity of the respective monetary measures for cost–benefit analysis and damage cost assessments.

1.5 CV theoretical underpinning

Neo-classical theory attempts to model the demand for goods given certain assumptions. The central assumption pertains to the behavioural characteristics of the individual, that is, the consumer. The theory assumes that consumers act rationally (Freeman 1979; Hanley and Spash 1993). This behavioural premise implies two things. First, individual consumers have coherent preferences over the different states of the world. These states can be defined so broadly that they can encompass the distribution of private goods and services, or the provision of public goods such as environmental quality. Second, when making choices among alternative states of the world, the individual does this on the basis of his or her preferences, choosing the state that is most preferred. The underlying intuition that one can draw from the rationality premise is that if an outside observer knew the preferences of any given individual as the individual knows them, that knowledge could be used to explain human behaviour as it relates to choices.

It is important, however, to see that the prior 'rationality' does not mean 'unbounded rationality' (Kopp *et al.* 1997): surely there are cognitive constraints to any respondent's ability to make complex choices such as the economic valuation of environmental changes (seldom thought of in monetary terms). The important thing is that the respondent answers to the CV questionnaire in general, and to elicitation questions in particular, in a manner consistent with the respondent's preferences. In empirical terms, the rationality premise can be used to form prior expectations regarding the relationship between the respondent's stated valuation responses and the respondent's attributes/preferences as reported in the CV questionnaire. For example, it is possible to explore formal analysis, including statistical testing, and assess whether such human behaviour premises hold. In this context, if we find that self-characterized 'strong environmentalist' respondents were willing to pay less, *ceteris paribus*, than 'anti-environmentalist' respondents, then some doubts may be raised about the reliability of the final CV estimation results.

In the following sub-section, we show how the behavior of CV respondents can be analysed with standard microeconomic models of choice and explore the demand for environmental quality with respect to alternative measures for assessing welfare changes.

1.5.1 The basic model

The present section draws on the theoretical perspective initially provided by Schultze, d'Arge and Brookshire (1981) and more recently explored by Braden, Kolstad and Miltz (1991). A basic postulate is that individuals make welfare-optimizing consumption decisions. These decisions are captured in the consumer demand functions with respect to available goods and services. Environmental attributes enter those demands. For some environmental goods, such as visits to a Natural Park, the consumer exercises direct choice over the amount consumed (assuming that the commodity is available). To illustrate this setting, we consider an individual whose utility function has the following form:

$$V = V(x, q, z) \qquad (1.1)$$

where x is the consumption of the private good, q the quantity of the environmental attribute and z the quality of that attribute.[6] For example, q could represent the number of recreational sites and z the level of biological diversity. We assume that all commodities, including the environmental attribute, have prices. Moreover, we assume that x is a composite private good whose price is normalized to one, and p is the price associated with q, and that p is fixed. We also assume that the consumer exercises direct choice over q but not over z. The consumer maximizes utility subject to a budget constraint:

$$p.q + x \leq M \qquad (1.2)$$

where M is money income. Assume non-satiation, that is, assume that the consumer uses the available budget fully. For a particular level of M and z, the consumer solves:

$$\underset{\{x,q\}}{Max} \ V(x,q,z) \qquad (1.3)$$

$$s.t.$$

$$p.q + x = M$$

$$q, x \geq 0$$

yielding some level of utility, V^*, and an optimal consumption bundle, (q^*,x^*), both of which are functions of p, M and z. To investigate a change in z, holding utility constant, we proceed to the total differentiation of $V(x^*,q^*,z)$ and $p.q^* + x^* = M$. Formally, we have:

$$dV = \frac{\partial V}{\partial q} dq + \frac{\partial V}{\partial z} dz + \frac{\partial V}{\partial x} dx \qquad (1.4)$$

and

$$dM = qdp + pdq + dx \qquad (1.5)$$

We focus on how changes in q and z can be compensated by changes in M. Thus, we let $dV = 0$. The assumption of fixed prices means that $dp = 0$, so the first term in (1.5) drops out. Rearranging (1.4) − (1.5), we get:

$$-dx = \frac{\partial V / \partial q}{\partial V / \partial x} dq + \frac{\partial V / \partial z}{\partial V / \partial x} dz \qquad (1.6)$$

and

$$-dx = pdq - dM \qquad (1.7)$$

Now let z be the attribute for which a change is contemplated. Setting equal the right-hand sides of the expressions (1.6) − (1.7) gives:

---

[6] This framework can be easily generalized to the case where x, q and z are vectors.

$$\frac{\partial V/\partial q}{\partial V/\partial x}dq + \frac{\partial V/\partial z}{\partial V/\partial x}dz - pdq = -dM \qquad (1.8)$$

Equation (1.8) establishes that the monetary payment must equal the difference between the personal worth of the change in quantity and quality, the first two terms on the left-hand side, and the change in the expenditure on q, the last term on the left-hand side. A fundamental condition in consumer theory is the consumers that make welfare-optimizing consumption decisions equate the marginal rate of substitution to the ratio of product prices. In the present case, p is normalized with respect to the price of composite commodity x:

$$\frac{\partial V/\partial q}{\partial V/\partial x} = p \qquad (1.9)$$

Substituting (1.9) into (1.8) and cancelling the terms results in:

$$\frac{\partial V/\partial z}{\partial V/\partial x} = -\frac{dM}{dz} \qquad (1.10)$$

that is, the marginal rate of substitution between z and x must equal the change in income that will keep utility constant as z changes.[7] That income change is the 'price' that reflects the consumer's maximum willingness to pay (WTP) to avoid an undesirable change in z.[8] In other words, the theoretical economic measure of welfare change, as described by (1.10), is the payment that will make a consumer indifferent between having and not having a particular change in the quality or quantity of the environmental attribute. This is the measure of welfare change that CV researchers look for through the use of direct questioning.

1.5.2 Measures of welfare change

The literature suggests three alternative measures that can be used to assess the magnitude of the welfare change as described by (1.10). The first measure is the change in the consumer's surplus, a concept whose origin can be traced back through Alfred Marshall to Dupuit (Marshall 1920; Dupuit 1844). The other two measures of welfare change, respectively the Hicksian compensating measure and the Hicksian equivalent measure, are theoretical refinements of the ordinary consumer's surplus (Hicks 1943).

1.5.2.1 Consumer's surplus

Dupuit (1844) described consumer's surplus as being the difference between the price actually paid when purchasing a commodity and the (subjective) price the consumer would have been

---

[7] dz may be interpreted as an outcome of the introduction of a set of new environmental regulations that increase (or decrease) the protection of biological diversity and its natural habitats.

[8] This interpretation assumes that the benchmark is the level of welfare with the change. If, however, the changes are being compared with the status quo (without the change in z), then we are measuring the willingness to be compensated to live with the change.

willing to pay. Therefore, the consumer's surplus is measured by the area under the ordinary demand curve but above the horizontal price line. Welfare measures, assessed in terms of changes in the consumer's surplus, can be defined for either changes in quantities or changes in prices. Clearly, lowering (raising) the purchasing price will increase (decrease) the consumer surplus. As Dupuit (ibid., p. 29) stated:

'Hence the saying that we shall often repeat because it is often forgotten: the only real utility is that which people are willing to pay for. We see that in general the relative or definitive utility of a product is expressed by the difference between the sacrifice that the purchaser would be willing to make in order to get it and the purchase price that he has to pay in an exchange. It follows that anything that raises the purchase price diminishes the utility and to the same extent, anything that depresses the price increases the utility in the same manner.'

As far as changes in the quantities are concerned, increasing (decreasing) the amount of quantities consumed will increase (decrease) the consumer's surplus. Nevertheless, the marginal willingness to pay diminishes as more units of the commodity are consumed. The reason for diminishing marginal WTP is that the extra satisfaction derived from a good declines the more of it an individual consumes.

1.5.2.2 Hicksian compensating and Hicksian equivalent measures

Before introducing the Hicksian compensating and the Hicksian equivalent as alternative welfare measures of welfare change, we return to the model as presented in the last section and investigate the welfare change associated with a non-marginal decrease in the quality level of the environmental attribute, z. This environmental change may be interpreted as the introduction of a set of new regulations designed to allow urbanization in the protected areas. In the original situation, that is, before the setting of the new regulations policy, the individual consumer faces a particular quality level of the environmental attribute. Let us denote such a level by z^0. For an environmental quality level z^0, and given an amount M of monetary income, the consumer solves (1.3) yielding an optimal consumption bundle (q^0, x^0) and the utility level $V^0 = V(q^0, x^0, z^0)$. Inserting the demand functions in the utility function gives the indirect utility function $V(q^0(p, M, z^0), x^0(p, M, z^0), z^0) = v(p, M, z^0)$. Inverting the indirect utility function for the term M yields the expenditure function on market goods required to achieve utility level V, given p and z^0. This is $e(p, M, z^0)$. Table 1.3 summarizes the notation.

The Hicksian compensating measure

This welfare measure equals the compensating payment, that is, an offsetting change in income, necessary to make the individual indifferent between the original situation (status quo) and the new environmental regulation policy (after the environmental quality change). In terms of the indirect utility function, the Hicksian compensating variation (HC) is the solution to:

$$v(p, M, z^0) = v(p, M + HC, z^1) = V^0 \qquad (1.11)$$

that is, the HC measures what must be paid to the individual to make that person indifferent to the new environmental quality level. In other words, if the new regulation is adopted, the individual's income could be increased by the amount of HC and that person would still be as well off as in the original situation. Alternatively, HC can also be defined in terms of the

Table 1.3: Summary of the results

	Original situation	New regulation
Environmental attribute quality	z^0	z^1
Utility level	V^0	V^1 with $V^0 > V^1$
Indirect utility function	$v(p, M, z^0)$	$v(p, M, z^1)$
Expenditure function	$e(p, z^0, V^0)$	$e(p, z^1, V^1)$

expenditure function. In terms of the expenditure function, HC is the difference between the expenditures required to sustain utility level V^0 at the new environmental quality level, that is:

$$HC = e(p, z^1, V^0) - e(p, z^0, V^0) \tag{1.12}$$

$$= e(p, z^1, V^0) - M$$

Since spending M at the new environmental attribute quality level yields a lower level of utility, V^1, we can also write:

$$M = e(p, z^1, V^1) \tag{1.13}$$

and by substitution

$$HC = e(p, z^1, V^0) - e(p, z^1, V^1) \tag{1.14}$$

that is, although the HC is defined in terms of V^0, it also measures the amount of money required to raise the utility from V^1 to V^0 at the new quality level of the environmental attribute.

The Hicksian equivalent

This measure asks what change in income (given the original quality level) would lead to the same utility change as the change in the quality of the environmental attribute. In terms of the indirect utility function, the Hicksian equivalent (HE) is the solution to:

$$v(p, M, z^1) = v(p, M - HE, z^0) = V^1 \tag{1.15}$$

that is, the HE measures the income change equivalent to the welfare lost due to the decrease in the quality of the environmental attribute. In other words, and if we admit that the implied property rights are assigned to the change and not to the *status quo*, the HE translates the maximum amount that the individual would be willing to pay to avoid the changes in the quality level of the environmental attribute. The HE can also be defined in terms of the expenditure function. It is the difference between the expenditures required to sustain utility level V^1, at the original environmental quality level:

$$HE = e\big(p,z^0,V^0\big) - e\big(p,z^0,V^1\big) \qquad (1.16)$$

$$= M - e\big(p,z^0,V^1\big)$$

Substituting (1.13) into (1.16), we get:

$$HE = e\big(p,z^1,V^1\big) - e\big(p,z^0,V^1\big) \qquad (1.17)$$

that is, although the HE is defined in terms of the monetary equivalent of a change from V^1 to V^0, it can also be measured by the change in the expenditure function associated with the environmental quality changes (given the utility level V^1).

These two Hicksian welfare measures can also be interpreted in terms of the implicit rights and obligations associated with alternative environmental quality levels. The HC carries with it implicitly the assumption that the individual has the right to the original environmental quality level in case of environmental quality deterioration. In contrast, the HE contains the assumption that the individual has an obligation to accept the decrease in the quality in the environmental attribute and thus will have to make a payment if the new quality level is not to be attained. Based on the interpretation of the two measures, we are able to argue that the choice between them is, basically, an ethical one, that is, one that depends on the value judgement as to which underlying distribution of property rights is more equitable (Krutilla 1967). The results are summarized in Table 1.4.

Table 1.4: Hicksian welfare measures and the property rights distribution

Attribute quality	Hicksian equivalent (HE) measure: implied property rights in the change	Hicksian compensating (HC) measure: implied property rights in the status quo
Increase	WAC to forgo	WTP to obtain
Decrease	WTP to avoid[9]	WAC to accept

1.5.2.3 A comparison of the three measures

Willig (1976) offered rigorous derivations of expressions relating compensating variation, consumer surplus and equivalent variation. Willig's bounds for the calculus of the different welfare magnitudes are based on the fact that the differences between the three measures of welfare change arise from the income elasticity of the demand for the good in question and the size of the change in real income brought with the change. For most realistic cases, the differences among these measures appear to be small and almost trivial when compared, for example, with the errors in the estimation of the parameters of demand functions by econometric models (Freeman 1991). Nevertheless, the differences among the three measures can be shown with the help of Figure 1.1, where the case of a change in the quality of environmental the attribute is plotted.

---

[9] The preferred welfare measure according to the suggestions of the NOAA panel (1993).

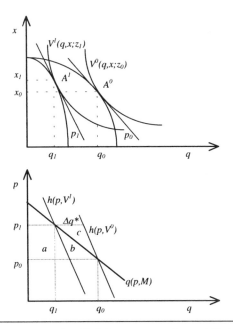

Figure 1.1: Consumer surplus, Hicksian compensating and Hicksian equivalent

We assume that the quality of environmental attribute changes from z^0 to z^1 (for example, a set of new regulations designed to allow urbanization in a natural forest area). Such an environmental quality decrease is graphically represented by a contraction in the consumption possibility set. We assume that the consumption possibility set will shrink along the horizontal axis indicating a higher loss in terms of nature related recreation possibilities q – with the new regulation there are fewer natural recreation sites available – when compared to the consumption of the private good, x (see top of Figure 1.1). At the new allocation A^1, where the V^1 indifference curve is tangent to the new consumption possibility frontier (and equal to the price ratio p^1), we can verify that the individual consumption of natural recreational areas is lower than before: $q^0 < q^0$. However, we assume that a decrease in the quality of the environmental attribute will be associated with an additional consumption of the private good, x, which can be interpreted as a possible 'off-setting' consumption effect towards the forgone nature-related recreation possibilities. In other words, if a natural forest area is urbanized, resulting in $(z^0 \rightarrow z^1)$, it more difficult (and expensive) to enrol in nature-related recreation possibilities and thus people may refrain from their nature-related recreation consumption, traduced in $(q^0 \rightarrow q^1)$, that, in turn, may set some money free and so probably people now go to the cinema more often, will visit zoos or buy nature-related books $(x^0 \rightarrow x^1)$. But, in the end, they are less 'happy' than before, that is, $V^1 < V^0$. At the bottom of Figure 1.1 we plot the ordinary and compensated demand curves. These are assumed to be linear. They are respectively denoted by $q(.)$ and $h(.)$. As seen before, the consumer's surplus (CS) is measured by the area under the ordinary demand curve above the price line. So the change in individual welfare, measured in terms of the loss of the consumer's surplus, is the area $a + b$, that is:

$$CS = a + b \qquad (1.18)$$

The welfare change associated with the same environmental quality change can be also measured in terms of the Hicksian variation and the Hicksian compensating. These are represented in Figure 1.1 by:

$$HE = a + b + c \qquad (1.19)$$
$$= CS + c$$

$$HC = a \qquad (1.20)$$
$$= CS - b$$

The errors in using CS to approximate HE and HC are equal to the areas b and c respectively. Therefore, the factors influencing the size of the approximation error can be analysed by examining the determinants of the areas a and b. If we focus, for example, on the Hicksian compensation, we may rewrite (1.20) as follows:

$$HC - CS = -b \qquad (1.21)$$
$$= -\frac{1}{2}\Delta p.\Delta q *$$

where $\Delta q *$ is the income effect on the quantity demanded of q associated with increasing the income sufficiently to hold utility at V^0. Let $\Delta M *$ represent this income change. By definition, $\Delta M *$ is the HC. We also know that, by definition, the income elasticity of demand is:

$$E_M = \frac{\Delta q}{\Delta M}\frac{M}{q} \qquad (1.22)$$

rearranging this expression in terms of $\Delta q *$ and $\Delta M *$, and substituting into (1.21), we get:

$$HC - CS = -\frac{\Delta p.q.E_M.HC}{2M} \qquad (1.23)$$

In general, for small changes in p, $\Delta p.q \cong CS$.[10] Substituting this in (1.23), and dividing both sides by HC gives:

$$\frac{HC - CS}{HC} \cong -\frac{E_M}{2}.\frac{CS}{M} \qquad (1.24)$$

that is, the approximation error in using CS to approximate HC, measured in percentage terms, is proportional to the income elasticity of demand and the weight of the consumer surplus relative to the consumer's income. Naturally, if the income elasticity of the demand for q is zero, the income differences will have no effect in the purchase of q. The HC and the HE

---

[10] This is strictly true for the linear demand curve when q is evaluated at the mid-point between q^0 and q^1.

would be exactly equal, and they could both be measured by the area under the ordinary demand curve without any measurement error.

1.5.3 Operationalization of the welfare change derived from the CV responses: an overview of the statistical model specifications

The CV method is a direct valuation method where the individual expresses directly his or her preferences, in monetary terms, for the described environmental change to be delivered by the proposed policy action. The principal idea underlying this method is that individual consumers have not only defined preferences over the described environmental good, but also are capable of transforming these preferences into monetary units (d'Arge 1985). From a welfare-theoretic point of view, the CV methodology denotes a set of procedures used to generate, through direct questioning, estimates of the Hicksian measures of welfare change. The respondents' answers provide directly the information that the CV researcher is looking for. Conversely, the researcher may choose to present a given price bid to the respondent and ask whether he or she is willing to pay this amount for the described environmental change as proposed by the policy action. Since the respondent's WTP is not known to the researcher, the researcher uses the respondent's no and yes responses to the elicitation as an indicator of the range of WTP. With such information the researcher is able to infer the sample mean (or median) WTP. This valuation scheme has been originally proposed by Bishop and Heberlein (1979) and more recently explored by Michael Hanemann (1984) and Trudy Cameron (1988).

1.5.3.1 Bishop and Heberlein's approach

Bishop and Heberlein (1979) use the respondents yes–no answers upon each bid amount and calculate the proportion of yes answers to each bid b_k according to the following form:

$$\ln\left(\frac{\pi}{1-\pi}\right)_k = \alpha + \beta \ln(b_k) + \varepsilon_k \tag{1.25}$$

where π is the proportion of yes to bid b_k and ε_k the error term. In the final estimation's results, it is expected to find $\beta < 0$, that is, that the probability of saying yes to the provision of the public good decreases, *ceteris paribus*, when one increases the bid amount stated in the CV survey, thus confirming the usual downwards sloped inverse demand curve.

1.5.3.2 Michael Hanemann's approach

Michael Hanemann (1984), in a widely cited paper, provides a utility theoretic interpretation of Bishop and Heberlein's argument. The key equation in Hanemann's theoretic interpretation is the following:

$$\Pr(yes) = \Pr(WTP > b) = 1 - G_{WTP}(b) = F_\eta(\Delta v) \tag{1.26}$$

where $G_{WTP}(b)$ is the cumulative distribution function (cdf) of the WTP and Δv is the utility difference between the state with, Q^1, and without the nature protection programe, Q^0, that is, $\Delta v \equiv v\,(p,\,M - HE,\,Q^1) - v\,(p,\,M,\,Q^0)$. Since the preferences of any given individual are not observed to the CV researcher, then Δv is only known to the researcher up to a random error term, η, given the assumed distributional prior, F.

1.5.3.3 Trudy Cameron's approach

More recently, Trudy Cameron (1988) proposed an alternative statistical model specification of the respondent's stated WTP answers. Rather than looking at utility differences, Cameron focuses directly on the cost function; this approach is also referred to in the literature as the 'dual' version of Hanemann's utility difference. Let HE represent the Hicksian equivalent measure defined as $\Delta e \equiv e\ (p,\ z^1,\ V^1) - e\ (p,\ z^0,\ V^1)$. The individual consumer only accepts paying b if $WTP \geq b$, that is:

$$\Pr(yes) = \Pr(WTP > b) = 1 - G_{WTP}(b) = F_{\varpi}(\Delta e) \tag{1.27}$$

where F denotes the assumed distributional prior and ϖ the random error term. Independently of the statistical model specification used, it is clear how the CV method is linked to standard microeconomic theory and how the data on the respondents' responses can be used in a direct and efficient way to trace out welfare changes associated to different states of the world and, in this way, enable the monetary estimation of a welfare-improving policy.

1.6 Conclusions

An environmental resource asset, such as the conservation of a natural area, provides a wide range of benefits. Generally speaking, the conservation benefits are classified in terms of the natural area's provision of use and non-use service flows. The use benefits, as the name suggests, refer to a set of recreational possibilities that individuals are able to experience when visiting the natural area, such as hiking or simply enjoying the aesthetic satisfaction of being in a natural environment. The non-use benefits refer to the set of activities not necessarily associated with any human use that the natural area is also able to provide, for example, areas closed to the general public and created to guarantee the protection of local biodiversity in their natural habitat. Different valuation instruments are available to the researcher to assess such conservation benefits. CV is an important valuation technique and since it is the only one capable of assessing the value of the non-use benefits, which are characterized by having no behavioural market trace. Therefore, economists cannot glean information regarding these values by merely relying on market-based valuation approaches. Today the CV method is a well-known benefit valuation technique of non-market goods and services and is widely used within the framework of cost–benefit analysis or natural damage assessment. The CV method consists of implementing a market with the help of a survey directed to the individual consumer. The principal idea underlying this method is that individuals not only have preferences defined over the described environmental good, but also are capable of transforming these preferences into monetary units.

Chapter

2

Evaluating CV Measurement Validity: Separating the Light from the Heat

2.1 Introduction

The CV method is the subject of strong critiques, especially as a non-use value measurement instrument. The embedding phenomenon is one of such critiques (Hausman 1993). According to Hausman, the empirical evidence supports an (in)variability of CV estimates much larger than can be explained by reference to 'plausible economic effects', that is, substitution effects, income effects and changes in the composition of the choice set. The term 'embedding' was first used by Kahneman (1986) to refer to the situation(s) where, even though the CV survey format was originally designed to distinguish two or more, environmental policies, the CV estimates state that respondents are willing to pay essentially the same amount for each policy. Later, Kahneman and Knetsch (1992) offered an explanatory hypothesis of the embedding effect. According to them embedding has its roots in consumer behaviour and the embedding effect signals the fact that CV responses reflect not only that individuals want more of the environmental resource described, but also 'a purchase of moral satisfaction', that is, a feel of well-being associated with the act of contributing to good causes.

The present chapter contains three sections. Section 2.2 presents potential measurement bias involved with the use of the CV method, discusses the associated implications in terms of value estimations, and suggests possible precautionary survey design measures so as to minimize the likelihood of measurement bias. Section 2.3 reviews the major critique presented to CV: the embedding valuation effect. This critique is supported by well-known scholars such as Jerry Hausman, Peter Diamond, William Desvousges and Paul Milgrom, who express their doubts with respect to the suitability of CV results for inclusion in cost–benefit analyses. Finally, section 2.4 focuses on Kahneman and Knetsch's explanatory hypothesis of the presence of embedding. According to Kahneman and Knetsch, embedding is an issue related to consumer behaviour and not a problem of survey design.

2.2 CV survey instrument and potential measurement bias

Throughout the survey instrument design process, the researcher makes important decisions involving a range of theoretical and operational issues. The different choices will be reflected in the final format of the survey instrument. The use of different formats of the survey instrument, when applied to the same environmental change, will eventually make it impossible to find a unique value estimate. However, the researcher's task in applied CV work is not to find *the* unique estimate of some change in amenities, since an individual's valuation is conditioned on the choice of the valuation context, but to determine the value of the change *contingent* upon (1) an accurate description of the amenities levels associated with the proposed policy formulation, and (2) an appropriate specification of the policy decision rule and the respective definition of the individual payments in the event of implementation (Mitchell and Carson 1993). In order to achieve (1) and (2), the researcher needs to make important decisions involving major theoretical and operational issues conditioning the survey design. We discuss issues with respect to (a) the level of information conveyed in the survey, (b) the potential strategic bidding behavior, and (c) the hypothetical nature of the contingent market. These issues are reviewed and discussed in the following sections.

2.2.1 Information

In 'standard' private market exchanges, an individual evaluates the alternative market prospects, given previous experience and market information. The nature of the CV application, in terms of policy choice appraisal, makes the value formulation problem more difficult relative to ordinary market decisions (Mitchell and Carson 1993). First, in CV, an individual formulates a valuation given the experience and the information provided by the contingent market, that is, as described in the survey instrument. Second, CV is usually applied to assess the monetary valuation of alternative protection choices that, most of the time, are unfamiliar to citizens. However, these are precisely the cases where the lack of public information for policy choice is the greatest. Third, the time devoted to contingent choices may be more limited than in market situations. This time constraint occurs for two reasons: (a) the research strategy may seek to reduce data collection costs by limiting the time devoted to gathering each set of observations; (b) the respondent may choose to limit the time resources devoted to value formulation. Therefore, the value formulation process in the contingent market is subject to sources of error. Information errors may arise as complex information is communicated to the respondents and may be left uncorrected due to time constraints on review or repetition. Thus the time-constrained process of communicating complex information is an important source of error in the value formulation process.

The question is then: what is the level of information it is necessary to provide in the survey instrument? How much information should be provided in a CV questionnaire so that respondents are able to make a valid value formulation? This question does not have a straightforward answer. On one hand, enough information must be provided to enable the respondents to make sound choices (Fischhoff and Furby 1988). Naturally, it is easier to make a valuation of a 'red car' if information is also available about the brand, its age, mileage, and so on, than to make a valuation of a 'red car' without such additional information. Most probably, one could expect that such 'variations' in the information set would be associated with different value estimates. Empirical evidence from CV studies supports this assertion. Samples, Dixon and Gowen (1986) tested the proposition that an individual's reported WTP to preserve a particular species would be significantly influenced by information about the species and its endangered status. The test results confirmed that the estimated values of wildlife conservation were indeed dependent on the level of information conveyed. Hanley, Spash and Walker (1995) found that the WTP to preserve biodiversity increases significantly as the level of information provision increases, but at a decreasing rate: 'what is out of sight, is out of mind' (Tversky and Kahneman 1973; Woo 1996). But, on the other hand, the need for information must be balanced with the need for surveys to be a reasonable length and easily comprehensible. If enough information is required to communicate alternative policy formulations that, most of the times are unfamiliar to citizens, too much information will drive the respondent's attention away. The challenge is, therefore, to reach an appropriate level of information. This involves two tasks: an accurate description of the environmental changes associated with the proposed policy formulation as well as an accurate description of the contingent market.

2.2.1.1 Description of the environmental change with the proposed policy

As far as the description of the policy formulation is concerned, the CV researcher has, in the first place, to identify the set of environmental attributes to which the policy formulation is addressed and, in the second place, to measure the respective levels in each of the two states, that is, measure and describe the levels of the identified environmental attributes in the 'reference state' and in the 'target state'. At this stage it is crucial to work together in a multidisciplinary team, making the best use of the scientific information available. This work goes usually hand-in-hand with the use of focus groups: small groups of citizens, from all educational levels and varied life experiences, who are invited to discuss the degree of understanding of the material it is proposed to use in the description of the public policy. Their comprehension feedback is crucial since it is very important that all the individuals potentially affected by the change in public policy are able to understand the described contingent market. Therefore, careful wording has to be provided without making the questionnaire so complex that understanding it would be beyond the ability, or interest, of many respondents. Finally, the CV survey communicates the policy formulation as much as possible in visual form, making use of photos, images and computer manipulated images: this makes it possible for the respondent to better 'visualise' the range of changes involved.

2.2.1.2 Description of the contingent market

The description of the contingent market is very important in guaranteeing a successful valuation exercise and, in this way, can produce estimation results that can be interpreted in economic terms (Carson *et al.* 1999). The description of the contingent market involves two major design tasks. The CV researcher has not only to make clear the social context that involves the hypothetical transaction, but must also identify the circumstances under which the environmental change is made available to the respondents.

First, the CV researcher has to choose the payment mechanism and the number of the years involved in the transaction. This means that the respondent must be informed both about the way in which the described environmental changes are financed and about the number of years over which payments are to be collected. The best recommendation is to choose a plausible payment vehicle, that is, one that is perceived as a likely way to pay the environmental change. This improves the credibility of the contingent market: if the respondent finds the payment vehicle believable, *ceteris paribus*, he or she takes the choice situation more seriously.

Second, before being asked to report his/her monetary valuation, the respondent has to be informed how the survey results are likely to be used. This involves describing to the respondent the capacity of the government in providing the described environmental service(s) as well as the ability of the government to (coercively) collect the payment for the described environmental service(s). The underlying idea is to make the respondents take care about the policy outcomes described in the survey instrument as well as to make them perceive that their responses to the survey potentially influence the final outcome(s). According to Carson, Groves and Machina (1999) the surveys that meet these two conditions are labelled as 'consequential survey questions'.

2.2.1.3 Survey elicitation question

Once the respondent has been given the description of the environmental change(s) and the contingent market involving such a provision, he/she is asked to report monetary valuation. This involves the choice of informational support through which the respondent is able to report valuation responses, that is, the choice of the elicitation question format. We review five elicitation formats, in more or less a chronological order, and discuss the various pros and cons associated with each of these methods (see Table 2.1).

Bidding game

One the earliest elicitation formats was developed by Davis (1963) and is called the bidding game. The bidding game format was also applied by CV studies in the 1970s (Randall *et al.* 1974; Brookshire *et al.* 1976; Rowe *et al.* 1980). The assumption is that the individual's WTP will be obtained after a series of questions has been asked, that is, letting the interviewer iteratively raise, or lower, the proposed bid until the respondent alters his/her yes or no answer. A fine tuning of the bidding game format may be achieved by raising, or lowering, the bids in the reverse direction after a change in the yes/no answers by smaller amounts. An advantage of the bidding game is that respondents get some assistance in arriving at a WTP value; moreover, the choice process of the respondent is simplified, so that the number of non-responses may be reduced. These desirable features are, however, obtained at high costs. The principal disadvantage is the phenomenon of 'anchoring' or 'starting-point bias' (Mitchell and Carson 1989). This occurs when the respondent sees the initial bid as a clue, or reference point, for his/her final valuation. Thus the respondents who start with a lower initial bid will end up, *ceteris paribus,* with a lower WTP than the ones who start with a higher bid. To make matters worse, the bidding game format is highly vulnerable to a 'yea-saying': respondents tend to agree with increasing bids regardless of their true valuations (Kanninen 1993). Consequently, the bidding game may be expected to result in an overestimation of the environmental change. Finally, the respondents become bored during the bidding game, especially if the iterative process is particularly long, resulting in a decline in their motivation, so that the respective answers will be less accurate.

Open-ended

The open-ended WTP elicitation question format, also know in the literature as direct questioning, consists of one single question which straightforwardly asks for the maximum amount that the respondent is willing to pay for the described environmental change: 'what is the maximum amount of money that you are willing to pay'. The main advantage of this format is that it immediately gives the information that the researcher is looking for. However, this method opens up the possibility of some form of strategic behaviour: many respondents may immediately state zero WTP although the amenity has value for them, simply because they may attempt to misreport their preferences by bidding untruthfully and thus affecting the outcome (Hoehn and Randall 1987). That is to say, there is a possibility that the respondents will reveal a WTP that is biased downward in the hope of getting 'something for nothing'. The

Table 2.1: A review of the five elicitation formats

	Advantages	Disadvantages
Bidding game	• simple and assisted iterative process • high participation rate	• anchoring • yea-saying • boring
Open ended	• displays the WTP information in the format that the research is looking for • higher accuracy of the relevant statistics	• low participation rates • vulnerable to strategic behavior • no valuation 'assistance' • procedure not familiar in market related behavior
Payment card	• no anchoring • displays the WTP information in the format that the research is looking for	• the limited range of the cards • vulnerable to strategic behavior
Dichotomous choice (random bids)	• simple and assisted iterative process • high participation rate • no anchoring • incentive compatible • procedure familiar in market related behavior	• yea-saying • too expensive • lower accuracy of the relevant statistics
Dichotomous choice with one follow-up (random bids)	• simple and assisted iterative process • high participation rate • no anchoring • incentive compatible • procedure familiar in market related behavior	• yea-saying • too expensive • higher accuracy of the relevant statistics • complexity of the involved estimation procedures

reluctance of individuals to contribute to the support of public goods is a well-known phenomenon in the literature and is referred to as the free-rider problem (Stiglitz 1988). Furthermore, the open-ended question may be very difficult for the individual to answer because most of the time the described environmental change is not particularly familiar to them (Cummings *et al.* 1986; Hoevenagel 1994). In this context, Mitchell and Carson (1989) argue that 'respondents often find it difficult to pick up a value out of the air, as it were, without some form of assistance' (page 97). Finally, individual consumers are not used to this procedure in normal market behaviour; generally speaking, consumers make choices about buying (or not) a given good at fixed market prices.

Payment card

This elicitation question format was developed as a response to the large proportions of non-responses and protest 'zeros' which were obtained in the CV applications with open-ended formats (Mitchell and Carson 1989). The payment card format means that the respondents are offered a card that contains a list of bid amounts. Then the respondents are asked to indicate which amount of money on the card they are willing to pay for the described environmental change. According to Mitchell and Carson the payment card would give the respondents some assistance in searching for their valuation. Furthermore, it would avoid the phenomenon of start bid 'anchoring', as described in the bidding game, and still maintain the positive feature of the open-ended format, that is, measure the respondent's WTP by mean of a single question. However, the validity of the stated WTP amounts may be questioned because the range of the payment card, especially the maximum bid amount, may influence the final WTP answers of the respondents (Hoevenagel 1994). From an economic point of view, the range of the payment card should be irrelevant: the different maximum amounts on the payment card do not reduce the set of choices of the respondents because each card contains the category 'other, namely: (…)'.

Dichotomous choice

The dichotomous choice referendum format, also known as the take-it-or-leave-it (TIOLI) approach, asks the respondents how would they vote (for or against) upon a described programme, and respective environmental benefits, upon the payment of an individual cost which is specified in the question format (for example, 'is your household willing to pay $ xx?'). The main reason for the dichotomous choice is that such a TIOLI valuation question is more likely to reflect real world market decisions which individuals are confronted with, rather than, for example, when respondents are facing an open-ended question. Technically speaking, the dichotomous choice elicitation format is simply the first round of the bidding game: the respondents are asked to accept or reject a specific bid amount in return for an environmental change. Therefore, one of the properties of the bidding game is kept: it burdens the respondent less than the open-ended question formats. This elicitation format also avoids most of the disadvantages of the bidding game. Firstly, the dichotomous choice elicitation uses various bid amounts and randomly assigns them to the respondents thus minimizing the 'starting-point' phenomenon. Second, this elicitation format has the characteristic of being incentive compatible, that is, truth telling is the individually optimal strategy (Hoehn and Randall 1987).[11] Nevertheless, when compared to the elicitation question formats mentioned above, the dichotomous choice format involves a stronger financial effort in interviewing since it requires substantially larger samples to obtain the same degree of accuracy of the relevant statistics and thus the same level of value estimation precision. This format may also encourage the yea saying phenomenon where the posted bid is accepted as a hint of what is a reasonable payment (Kanninen 1995).

Dichotomous choice with one follow-up

The dichotomous choice with one follow-up elicitation format, also called the double-bounded dichotomous choice, was first proposed in 1986 (Carson et al. 1986) and is an extension of the (single-bounded) dichotomous choice format. This elicitation format involves the simple addition of one extra dichotomous choice question, containing a proposal for a bid that is dependent on the first bid. So, if the respondent answers yes (no) to the initial bid, then the bid amount proposed in the second question is increased (decreased). As in the single-bounded dichotomous choice, a nice property of this elicitation format is that the empirical survival function can be estimated from which the mean and median can be assessed (Cameron 1988;

---

[11] We return to this point in 2.2.2.1 where we discuss the characteristics of the dichotomous choice format and its links to strategic bidding behaviour.

Kriström 1990; Cameron and Quiggin 1994). It has also been proved that the follow-up greatly improves the statistical efficiency of the dichotomous choice format (Hanemann *et al.* 1991). This means that for each observation, that is for each respondent, the CV researcher has more information about the 'location' of the respondent's WTP. In econometric terms, this additional information is reflected (1) in a higher precision in the estimation of the truncated intervals of the c.d.f. and (2) more robust valuation estimates. In other words, this means that it is possible to get more precise WTP value estimates with the same sample dimension and thus without incurring additional interviewing costs.

2.2.2 Strategic behaviour in the WTP responses

The presence of strategic behaviour in CV surveys is closely linked to the possibility of strategic misrepresentation of preferences. As Samuelson (1954) argued 'It is in the selfish interest of each person to give false signals to pretend to have less interest in a given collective activity than she really has' (p. 388). He made specific reference to the possibility of strategic behaviour with respect to the use of surveys. Samuelson's point, repeated in many textbook discussions of public goods, had a strong effect on how economists view the survey questions. The wrong inference made by many CV critics is to equate strategic behaviour with lying. As the term is used in the modern mechanism design literature in economics, 'strategic behavior is merely synonymous with a rational agent maximising (broadly defined) self-interest' (Carson *et al.* 1999, p. 3). Mechanism design theory has shown that the optimal strategic behaviour for the individual consumers in many instances is to reveal their preferences truthfully. Whether this is the case or not depends upon the particular format of the survey elicitation question and other aspects of the scenario, including the payment vehicle and the level of information. These issues are discussed in the following sub-sections.

2.2.2.1 Strategic behaviour vs. the choice of the question elicitation format

Much of the attention focused on the binary choice question elicitation format in recent years is due to the NOAA Panel on contingent valuation's recommendation for its use (NOAA 1993). One of the reasons underlying the Panel's recommendation is related with the fact that the dichotomous (binary) choice format is 'an appropriate elicitation mechanism for estimating the demand for public goods' because of its (defensive) properties with respect to strategic bidding behavior. Indeed, one of the core results in mechanism design theory as derived by Gibbard and Satterthwaite (Gibbard 1973; Satterthwaite 1975) is that the binary choice question is the only response format that is *potentially* incentive compatible in the sense that truthful preference revelation represents an optimal (and the dominant) strategy for the respondent. It has long been known that in some settings the binary choice question format is incentive compatible (Farquaharson 1969). The best known examples are political races with only two candidates and binding (approve/disapprove) referendums with plurality (usually majority approval) vote requirement. The discussion of whether the binary choice question meets the incentive compatible property raises two questions.

The first question is whether it is the binding nature of the referendum that makes it incentive compatible: it creates no incentive for respondents to reveal their preferences untruthfully. In this respect, Carson *et al.* (1999) argue if such an elicitation format can be considered 'an advisory referendum vote', that is a situation where respondents interpret government more likely to undertake the survey described action the larger in the percentage in favour, the proposed voting rule is incentive compatible. The second question is whether substituting 'an advisory survey' for 'an advisory referendum' alters the incentive properties of the mechanism. Green and Laffont (1978) have shown that the economic mechanism geared by the binary choice question can be implemented using a sampling approach rather than complete information. In other words 'It is possible to replace the binding nature of an incentive compatible referendum with the more general assumption that the government is more likely to undertake the action the higher the percentage in favour. It is also possible to substitute a survey of the public good for a vote of the public on the issue. Neither of these changes, alone or together alter the original incentive structure of the binding referendum' (Ibid., p. 11).

In a much-cited paper Hoehn and Randall (1987) illustrated the case for truth telling as the individually optimal strategy 'in a policy referendum model with individual parametric costs' and concluded that the 'values elicited with parametric cost referendum format weakly dominate the valuations obtained with a [open ended] willingness to pay format' (p. 237 and 239). The authors consider the simple case of an environmental improvement, $z_1 > z_0$ with b_j representing the maximum willingness to pay for the environmental change, that is

$$v\left(p, M_j - b_j, z_1\right) = v\left(p, M_j, z_0\right)$$

and c_j the cost written in the survey instrument as presented to the j respondent. When choosing within the dichotomous choice referendum, the respondent is informed that (a) the proposed policy is implemented if the majority of the respondents approve it, and that (b) for each respondent approval is conditional on an individual cost as stated in the survey instrument. Since the respondent is uncertain about how others will vote, and (a) holds, then (s)he faces an incentive for participation. Therefore, the respondent considers his/her vote as decisive to approve (or reject) the environmental improvement. If $c_j < b_j$, the respondent attains a welfare gain if the project is approved, and thus it is optimal to report approval. Conversely, for $c_j > b_j$ the respondent suffers a welfare loss if the project is approved and it is optimal to report disapproval. If $c_j = b_j$ then the respondent perceives no welfare loss (or gain) from how the preference survey is answered. It is important to remark, however, that it is not casting the preference question as a referendum that provides its desirable incentive properties. It is the cast of the preference question is terms of being able to influence a government decision with a binary agree/not agree format.

On the contrary, when choosing an open-ended elicitation question format, the respondent is informed that (a) the proposed policy is implemented if the sum of the reported aggregated benefits exceed the costs and that (b) each respondent pays in proportion to the sample mean bid. This setting may lead respondents to misrepresent preferences and to state a monetary value that is not their true willingness to pay but an amount sufficiently small to manipulate the sample mean bid in the hope of getting 'something for nothing' (Bohm 1972, p. 113). In other words, the respondent may attempt to give 'false signals' and wait to see if the good is provided without his/her contribution. The empirical evidence shows that, on average, the open-ended estimation results are, on average, lower when compared to the dichotomous choice referendum estimates.[12] This empirical finding suggests that understating may be the overwhelming bidding force in the open-ended elicitation question format and this is interpreted as free-riding to the supposed lower overall mean.

---

[12] For this reason, the open-ended elicitation question format is also known as the 'conservative' elicitation model formulation.

2.2.2.2 Strategic behaviour and the choice of the payment vehicle

A key assumption is being made in the preceding discussion of the binary choice question as an incentive compatible mechanism. The assumption is that the government can compel payment for a good if provided. The ability coercively to collect payment for the provision of the public good is the property that causes the agent to try to influence the government's decision in the desired direction *taking into account* both the costs and the benefits of the action to the respondent. Relaxing such an assumption will destroy the incentive properties of the 'referendum advisory survey' (see Table 2.2).

Table 2.2: Incentive properties of binary discrete choice questions

Type of good and nature of the payment obligation	Incentive property
New public good with coercive payment	Incentive compatible
New public good with voluntary payment	Not Incentive compatible

Adapted from Carson *et al.* (1999, p. 17)

To illustrate Table 2.2, let us consider the case where a (charitable) organization wants to provide an increase in the environmental quality (for example, creation of a forest recreation area) via voluntary contributions. A yes to the question of the form 'is your household willing to pay $xx to purchase the specified good if we started the fund' will support the fund-raising effort and thus encourage the organization to undertake the proposed creation of a forest recreation area. Given the public nature of the environmental quality – once the natural reserve is implemented there is no way that any individual could be excluded from its benefits[13] – the optimal strategy of an agent who wants to visit the forest is to contribute less than his/her true willingness to pay and, in many instances sit back and wait to see if the forest recreation area is provided without any contribution.

The CV researchers, borrowing from Samuelson's notion of 'false signals' maintain *a priori* that different payment schemes provide different incentives for engaging in strategic behaviour and thus influencing the expected valuation results. A significant number of CV applications use the referendum tax formulation or the voluntary contribution as payment schemes and investigate the empirical significance of free riding.[14] Swedish economist Peter Bohm presented one of the first CV studies focusing on strategic bidding behaviour. Bohm (1972) conducted a CV experiment with the objective of selecting an appropriate method for estimating the demand for public goods. The valuation experiment is based on the WTP assessment of a popular Swedish television show:

'We would like for you to try to estimate in money terms and in advance how much you think it would be worth to you to watch this programme. That is to say, we ask you to state the

---

[13] In some cases, exclusion would be possible but very costly. For example, it would be costly to exclude individuals from recreational areas in natural parks; to do so would require a fence to be constructed around the park (which might interfere with its visual enjoyment) and there would have to be someone always on duty to check permits or to collect entrance fees.

[14] Higher prices or additional gas tax are also present in some CV applications as the selected payment vehicle. The empirical evidence shows, however, that such payment vehicles are associated with a low degree of acceptance as a fair method of paying for the environmental change: an increase in the gasoline tax, for example, may fail to meet general acceptance as a fair payment instrument since it would not be relevant to households without a car. Extensive pre-testing of the payment vehicle to be used in the CV survey contributes to achieving a payment instrument that is fair in the respondent's eyes.

highest 'admission fee', so to speak that you would be willing to pay to watch the programme' (Ibid., p. 127)

The respondents are also informed that if the sum of the stated amounts of all participants covers the costs (Kr. 500) of showing the programme, it will be shown and the respondent will have to pay: (sample 1) the amount the respondent has stated; (sample 2) some percentage – as explained – of the amount that the respondent has stated; (sample 3) either the amount the respondent has stated or a percentage – as explained – of this amount or Kr. 5 or nothing, to be determined later by a lottery that the respondent can witness; (sample 4) Kr. 5; (sample 5) nothing: in this case the respondents were informed that the costs were to be paid by the Swedish National broadcasting company, that is, by the taxpayers in general. A final group, sample 6, who received instructions which differed from the instructions of the first five groups, were simply asked how much they found the programme to be worth at a maximum.

The hypothesis to be tested is to check whether policy decision rules 1 to 5 would yield identical estimates. In other words, the objective is to test whether value estimates are sensitive to the alternative configurations of the payment rules. If the empirical results turned out to give significantly different expected values, then the question would be: which one gives the best estimate of the true demand? In order to answer that question, Bohm added sample 6 to the test with the (optimistic) assumption that it could reveal the actual level of aggregate demand, or more exactly, an interval containing the true aggregate demand.[15] The final estimation results revealed that no significant differences can be found between any pair of 1 to 5 samples, that is, the reactions received from the different groups were compatible with the possibility of getting 'identical' responses. With such results the proposed role of sample 6 was redundant. According to author Bohm, a possible explanation for this result is that 'people do not use available 'cheating strategies' even when made explicit' (Ibid., p. 124). Naturally, Bohm's results do not rule out the hypothesis that different policy decision rules engage different strategic behaviour incentives, but the empirical evidence makes it unlikely that these differences are 'very large' – and this result is of considerable practical importance.

More recently, Champ, Bishop, Brown and McCollum (1997) set up a experiment involving contingent donations and actual donations (that is, coercive payment) for an environmental project along the North Rim of the Grand Canyon. The project involved old, unpaved roads that must be removed before it can be officially designated as a *Wilderness Area*. The experiment was characterized by the use of two survey versions: one posed a dichotomous choice question which gave the opportunity to actually donate a specific amount for road removal, whereas the second asked a parallel contingent donation question. The estimations results showed that '23% of the contingent donation respondents were inconsistent in the sense that they said yes to the dichotomous choice contingent donation question but our model predicts that they not actually donate if they had been in the dichotomous choice actual donation treatment' (Champ *et al.* 1997, p. 159).[16]

2.2.2.3 Strategic behaviour and the level of information in the survey

Some studies have directly manipulated the strategic incentives for preference revelation. An early example of a CV that did this was Rowe, d'Arge and Brookshire, who looked at the

---

[15] The author also assumes that the approach embedded in sample 6 would give 'a slightly overestimate of this [true] demand, since it involved no payment obligations (nor did it involve any output decisions)' (Bohm 1972, p. 120).

[16] Other empirical surveys confirm the predicted divergence between survey based predictions and actual contributions (see section 2.2.3).

WTP for air visibility. The authors designed the interview process such that after the description of the contingent market, and before bidding, a first group of respondents is given information concerning the mean bid of the other (supposed) respondents. In a second variant of the interview, the respondents do not receive any information before bidding. However, once the respondents state their bid amount, they are informed about the mean bid value with respect to the other respondents and asked whether they would revise their initial bid. In both scenarios, the respondent is told that he/she will have to 'pay' the average bid and not her own. The authors operationalized the test for strategic bidding behaviour by querying all respondents about their environmental stance after bidding and assessed whether 'environmentalists, when given mean bid information, increase their bid and developers decrease their bid in order to impose their preference by altering the overall mean' (Rowe *et al.* 1980, p. 15). In other words, they tested whether developers (environmentalists) attempt to bias the mean bid and revise their initial bid downward (upward) if their initial stated bid is below (above) the mean bid of the other (supposed) respondents. The results yielded no significant strategic bias. As a matter of fact, of the 40 respondents who received information after bidding, only one revised the stated initial bid and that was to free-ride the supposed lower overall mean.

Weak empirical evidence for Samuelson's strategic behaviour hypothesis has also been found in more recent laboratory experiments (Pearce and Markandya 1989; Mitchell and Carson 1989). On the contrary, Cronin (1982) in a CV study looking at the WTP for improving water quality on the Potomac River found that the WTP from the sub-sample of respondents given a statement to the effect that the federal government was likely to pay for most of the cost of the project was substantially higher than the sub-sample not given this statement on possible cost sharing. Lunander (1998) provides a recent example of directly manipulating the strategic incentives for preference revelation, again with the result that the incentives work in the expected direction. Still, and according to Mitchell and Carson (1989), the strategic bias is, on balance, of minor importance in well-designed CV studies.

2.2.3 Hypothetical bias

Hypothetical bias is defined as the systematic difference between the stated payments response in a hypothetical market and the actual payments when individuals are presented with the opportunity in reality. Hypothetical bias may occur in the CV responses because respondents may not be able to visualize the described scenario situation, or it may not seem realistic enough to spend time thinking it through. Respondents may also not believe that their answers will have any effect on the policy. More recently, the divergence between actual and survey behaviour may also be interpreted (and expected) as additional empirical evidence of strategic behaviour in CV surveys. To see this, let us return to the case where the government wants to provide a forest recreation area. The incentive structure is illustrated in Table 2.3. If one takes a compulsory tax as the payment vehicle, the government can compel payment for the public good if the majority of the electors vote for the provision of the forest recreation area. Therefore, the agent perceives that he/she is able to influence a government decision and his/her optimal strategy is to state her true valuation of the public good. On the contrary, if we consider that a (charitable) organization wants to provide the forest recreation area via voluntary contributions, the optimal strategy of agents who want to visit the forest is to contribute less than their maximum willingness to pay for the good and, in many instances to contribute nothing. This is the classic free-riding incentive behaviour − see arrow (a) in Table 2.3. However, Carson *et al.* (1999) argue that 'the same incentive structure which should cause free riding with respect to the actual contributions should induce respondents in a survey

Table 2.3: Strategic behaviour, payment vehicles, and payment settings

Actual payment setting (with cash transaction)		Hypothetical payment setting
Compulsory tax	Voluntary contributions	Survey based contributions
• ability to coercively collect payment for the provision of the public good • agent is able to influence a government decision	• agent sits back and waits to see if the good is provided without contribution • agent contributes less than own WTP ◀━▶ (a)	• agent over-pledges (Carson *et al.* 99) • agent contributes more than her WTP ◀━▶ (b)
⇒ incentive compatible	⇒ not incentive compatible	⇒ not incentive compatible

to over pledge because doing so helps to obtain the latter opportunity to free ride' (p. 12). Therefore, according to these authors, the survey-based predictions of contributions, when compared to the actual contributions, are influenced by an over-pledge incentive – see arrow (b) in Table 2.3. The hypothetical bias is difficult to test, except by comparison with real payments. But clearly, if it were possible to obtain real cash payments for the good in question, the CV method would not be necessary. In fact, there are few CV experiments that combine the use of the hypothetical market value elicitation with actual payments. Furthermore, empirical evidence has not always supported Carson *et al.* 'over pledge' argument. On one hand, CV experiments conducted by Bohm (1972) and Bishop and Heberlein (1979) show that the correspondence between the hypothetical market and the simulated market is quite strong for goods which are well understood and familiar to the respondents, that is a television show and hunting permits, respectively. On the other hand, when the CV study is focused on the value assessment of public goods, such as environmental protection, the empirical evidence has presented mixed results.

In one CV experiment, Seip and Strand (1992) asked a sample of 101 persons about their WTP for membership in the Norwegian Association for the Protection of Nature (NNV). The respondents were asked to contribute an annual amount to the NNV, equivalent to the proposed membership for 1990, of 200 Norwegian kroner (NOK): 62 persons indicated that they were willing to do this. The same individuals later received a membership application form with a letter asking them to join the NNV. However, no reference was made to the previous CV survey. Only 10 %, that is six respondents, joined the association and paid the membership fee. A similar CV study was conducted by Stale Navrud concerning the valuation of the world's endangered species (Navrud 1992). The experiment consists of three steps. First, the Worldwide Fund for Nature (WWF) published four one-page, colour advertisements in one of Norway's largest newspapers, informing people and asking for their *support* to preserve the world's endangered species by becoming a WWF member. Despite the fact that no membership fee was mentioned in the newspaper ad, still 1349 persons responded that they were willing to support the Fund to preserve the world's endangered species by becoming a WWF member. In a second stage, all the 1349 persons later received a membership application form with a letter asking them to join the WWF. Enclosed was also a post money order saying 'yes, I will support WWF with an annual contribution', with the possibility of ticking off amounts ranging from 75 to 1000 NOK. From the 1349 persons who answered the ad 423 persons, that is 31 % of the respondents, actually paid. This share is three times higher than Seip and Strand had found (1992). In the third and last step, a random telephone survey was conducted among those who actually paid the membership fee (labelled as 'members') and among those that did not pay (labelled as 'non-members') with the objective of identifying the reasons for the observed discrepancy between intended and actual behavior. The telephone survey revealed that, on one hand, '67% of the members had responded to the ad expressing monetary support to WWF', but on the other hand only '26–51 % of the non-members had responded to the ad expressing monetary support to WWF' (Navrud 1992, p. 245). Moreover, Navrud also finds that 'assuming that all members and the 26–51 % share of the non-members who perceive the ad as a WTP question, the correspondence between intended and actual payment improves from [the initial] 31 % to 47–64 %." (Ibid., p. 245).

Naturally these empirical results brought about the discussion of a number of possible interpretations. One of the possible reasons for the discrepancy between intended and actual behaviour is that an individual may judge consumption of a public good (for example, preserve global biological diversity) as something quite different from consuming the same good as a private one (for example WWF membership fee). Hence, 'the transformation of a public good into a private good may be considered highly inefficient'. Another possible reason explaining the difference between hypothetical and actual behaviour is the respondent's lack of foreknowledge of an obligation to pay in accordance with one's verbal statements. According to Navrud, 'a carefully constructed CV survey should contain an explicit payment obligation' (Navrud 1992, p. 245).

In contrast, other studies provide considerable evidence that hypothetical bias may not be a problem. Sinden (1988) conducted 17 experiments comparing the hypothetical and actual money donations to a fund for soil conservation and a eucalyptus planting programme. He found that there was no statistical difference between the two markets in any of the experiments. Finally, some studies found that hypothetical estimates may even be slightly smaller than actual payments. Bateman *et al.* (1993) cite experiments that 'clearly show that stated willingness to pay in a hypothetical market may be below the willingness to pay in a real market' (p. 39). Furthermore, Randall, Hoehn and Brookshire (1983) obtained lower willingness to pay responses from hypothetical markets. A possible reason for this situation is that in the 'real market', the version of the good as a 'private' (excludable and rival) good, introduces elements of competition, exclusivity and 'auction fever' completely absent from the good conceived as a 'public good'.

None the less, the only problem with such cases, from the perspective of economic theory, is not whether there should be a divergence between actual behaviour and the survey estimate, but rather whether the magnitude of the divergence empirically observed should be even larger, that is, to assess whether 'the incentive in a survey to over-pledge' is indeed a statistically significant driving force of the stated WTP responses. Arrow *et al.* (NOAA 1993) suggest that the response to the issue of the hypothetical nature of the CV method is to make both the hypothetical market and the payment vehicle as credible and realistic as possible. Moreover, the members of the NOAA Panel also recommend that a CV survey should contain, together with the explicit payment obligation, the use of budget constraint reminders and substitute reminders before eliciting the WTP question.

2.2.4 Other potential biases

The early CV literature was mainly concerned with 'hypothetical bias' and 'strategic bias' issues. The valuation process of the respondents was assumed to concern only the value of the question, with all other elements of the hypothetical market being neutral (Hoevenagel 1994). However, it is now recognized that there are many other factors related to the execution of the questionnaire that also affect the responses obtained by contingent valuation surveys. Some of these factors are endemic to social survey research in general; interviewer bias, sampling bias, non-response bias and question mode bias are examples that are very well covered in the literature in this field (Groves 1989). For example, the CV researcher has to make a choice over the data collection instrument, that is, choose the question mode. The survey instrument can be executed either by face-to-face interviewing, telephone interviewing or mail. Telephone interviews are frequently used. However, to convey information about the environmental commodity may be difficult over the phone, partly due to the limited time span of the call. Furthermore, telephone interviews are not compatible with the use of visual schemes, an important communication aid in conveying the information described verbally by the interviewer. Mail surveys are the least preferred method since this method suffers from potential non-response bias and low response rates.[17] Moreover, the double-bounded dichotomous choice, an important elicitation question format, cannot be used in mail surveys. Face-to-face interviewing with well-trained interviewers offers the most scope for detailed questions and answers, allows the introduction of important visual aids and fits the double-bounded dichotomous choice like a glove. Nevertheless, when facing a interviewer, the respondent may be more vulnerable to interviewer 'pressure' (for example, choosing socially desirable answers).

2.3 Hausman critique: valuation embedding phenomenon

Well-known scholars such as Jerry Hausman, Peter Diamond, William Desvousges and Paul Milgrom express their doubts with respect to the suitability of CV results for inclusion in benefit-cost analyses (Hausman 1993; Diamond *et al.* 1993; Desvousges *et al.* 1993; Milgrom 1993). The scepticism is particularly strong when the CV application is addressed to measure non-use values and Hausman raises the question: 'is some number better than no number?' (Hausman 1994). Most of the critiques have their origin in the so called 'embedding' valuation effect. The term 'embedding' was first put forth by Kahneman after he conducted a CV experiment which focused on the assessment of the WTP of Toronto residents to preserve fish stock in lakes. The empirical results showed that the willingness to pay to prevent the drop in fish populations in all Ontario lakes was only slightly higher than the willingness to pay for the fish stocks in only a small area of the province (Kahneman 1986).

Since Kahneman's CV experiment in the Ontario lakes, additional CV studies focused their research work on the identification of the embedding and discussed possible explanations. As a matter of fact, today embedding is an issue in the CV literature which receives a large amount of attention. Nevertheless, the term 'embedding' has been used to describe different effects and has created some confusion over the extent and occurrence of the phenomenon. Hanemann (1994), and more recently Carson and Mitchell (1995), have substantially clarified and redefined the terminology and concepts related to 'embedding'. According to Hanemann, the term 'embedding' 'combines three distinct notions: the scope effect, the sequence effect and the sub-additivity effect' (Hanemann 1994, p. 34). These notions are discussed in the following sections.

---

[17] For a detailed account of data collection procedures, see Mitchell and Carson (1989).

2.3.1 Scope effect

The *scope effect* exists when the respondents do not distinguish differences in the quantity or scope of the public good (Hanemann 1994). In a well-known CV application, Desvousges, Johnson, Dunford, Boyle, Hudson and Wilson tested whether the *scope bias* is present in the CV estimation results (Desvousges *et al.* 1993a). The CV application used brief shopping mall interviews to elicit the WTP for preventing the deaths of migratory waterfowl from exposure to waste-oil holding ponds. In order to test the scope effect hypothesis, three separate survey versions were designed. The three survey versions said, respectively, that 2000, 20 000 and 200 000 out of 85 million migratory waterfowl could be saved under the adoption of the described protection programme. The statistical results in the three independent experiments indicate that the 'the WTP do not increase when the level of the services increases: the WTP estimates for protecting 2 000 birds are not statistically different than the WTP estimates for protecting 100 times as many birds' (Desvousges *et al.* 1993a, p. 113). If the value of a given public good is much larger when it is evaluated on its own than when it is valued as a part of a more inclusive package of public goods, which measure is the correct one? According to Desvousges, no measurement can be taken seriously if its permitted range of applications yields drastically different measures of the same object.

The interpretation of Desvousges's estimation results were heavily criticized in terms of CV design and execution. First, the use of shopping mall interviews encompasses major risks in terms of CV information error because: (1) there is a high probability that the respondent allocates the minimum time to answer the CV questions,[18] and (2) the motivation and concentration usually required of the CV respondents may be difficult to obtain in the environment of a mall. The information error argument becomes stronger if we believe that the scope effect phenomenon is closely related to issues concerning the misperception of the scenario elements, particularly due to symbolic bias and part–whole bias,[19] because respondents most of the time are 'unfamiliar with valuing environmental goods directly and consequently do not have a valuation frame of reference to rely on' (Hoevenagel 1994, p. 110). Second, one can maintain that the CV application results are jeopardized since the survey instrument fails to describe the valuation scenario: there is no clear mention of reference and target levels for the environmental quality changes. Therefore, if we believe that the respondents perceived the described bird protection programmes in terms of their relative magnitude – contributing towards the protection of 0.0024 per cent, 0.024 per cent and 0.24 per cent, respectively, of the total waterfowl population – then, it is to be expected that the CV estimates across the three experiments are about the same: effectively the difference involved in the protection programmes is less than 0.5 per cent.

Contrary to Desvousges's findings, other CV applications, also focused upon testing the scope effect, show that empirical evidence rejects the hypothesis that WTP does not vary significantly with scope.[20] For example, Carson, Wilks and Imber (1994a) designed two CV experiments to assess the WTP to prevent mining near a national park in Australia. The two experiments involved the design of two distinct survey formats: the description of two

---

[18] One can easily see that the reason for visiting a shopping mall is not to answer surveys, but rather to (window)shop.

[19] Symbolic bias refers to the situation where respondents answer to a perceived symbolic meaning of the environmental good instead of the good as defined in the survey instrument. Conversely, part–whole bias refers to the situation where respondents answer to a larger environmental good (for example, geographic location, range of benefits) rather than the policy package as defined in the survey instrument (Boyle *et al.* 1994).

[20] Carson (1997) reviews over 30 studies that used split-sample tests, all of which clearly rejected the hypothesis that respondents are insensitive to the scope of the good being valued.

protection programmes, to prevent respectively 'major' and 'minor' impacts – as clearly described in the survey instrument – of mining. The empirical results show that the WTP for the prevention of the 'major' impact mining scenario is different (larger) than the WTP for the prevention of the 'minor' impact mining scenario.

Therefore, empirical results show mixed evidence with respect to the rejection of the underlying null hypothesis that indicates the presence of scope effect in CV estimates. Nevertheless, and according to Carson and Mitchell (1993a), all precautionary measures should be taken into account during the survey design and execution. The main strategy recommended to minimize the likelihood of scope effects is to design the scenario in such a way that the attention of the respondents is focused on the good which is of interest, with clear instructions (with the use of maps and diagrams, for example) so as not to confuse the good with the general class of which the good is a component. Moreover, and following the NOAA Panel, shopping mall interviews are not among the recommendations for the selection of the question mode.

2.3.2 Sequence effect

The *sequence effect* exists when the respondents value a given public good differently if it is placed early in the list of public goods to be valued than if it is placed near the end (Hanemann 1994). The potential biases associated with valuation sequencing are discussed in a CV experiment conducted by Samples and Hollyer (1990). The test was developed in the context of a cost–benefit study of marine mammal preservation in Hawaii. The CV experiment involved the valuation of two marine mammals, both with federal endangered status, the humpback whale (W) and the Hawaiian monk seal (S). Two versions of a standard survey instrument were designed. The surveys identify the order in which the mammals are valued: in the Seal–Whale (S–W) survey version, with the seals valued first and the whales valued second; in the Whale–Seal (W–S) version, where the sequential order is reversed and whales are valued first. Respondents were asked to imagine a situation in which a rare disease had killed two seals and two whales. Furthermore, the respondents were told that the disease would rapidly destroy the entire mammal populations unless expensive medical attention was provided. Moreover, the survey instrument clearly stated that all contributions made to save the second resource would be 'in addition' to all the contributions made for the first resource. Respondents were not allowed to revise their initial valuation response. The results show that, for seals, expected WTP was directly related to the order in which the resource was valued. Expected WTP dropped from $103 to $62, a reduction of 39 per cent, when seals were valued second rather than first in the sequence. In the case of the whales, the effects of valuation sequence were less pronounced compared with seals and worked in the opposite direction. The estimated WTP rose $125 to $142, an increase of 14 per cent, when the whales were valued second in the sequence.

One explanation for the observed reduction in the WTP for seal preservation may have been the public's lack of familiarity with monk seals and low awareness of seals' endangered status. Contrary to the whales, where 'media attention has given considerable publicity to the humpback whales and their plight for survival … during their five month visit to Hawaiian waters, a small fleet of whale-watching vessels provides excursions for both residents and tourists" (Ibid., p. 182), the monk seals' natural habitat is on the remote, and human inhabited, islands of Hawaii where 'except for a handful of military personnel and naturalists, few humans have had the opportunity to see a live seal monk in the wild' (Ibid., p. 182). Another possible explanation suggests that when respondents are initially confronted with the whales' valuation, and if they perceive whales as substitutes for seals, this could explain why seals have a lower value than when valued second in the sequence. It is curious, however, that the WTP for the whales' preservation increases, when the whales are valued second in the sequence. It could be argued that respondents somehow view whale preservation as being complementary to seal preservation. This would explain why whales have a greater worth when valued in the presence of seals (S–W) than when valued in the absence of seals (W–S). However, this explanation is fallacious because whales and seals cannot be both complements to and substitutes for one another at the same time. A final alternative explanation was offered based on the interviewer's debriefing. Apparently, when respondents valued seals first, they used their behaviour in this market situation to guide their responses to whale valuation questions. Since whales are more popular than seals, respondents were reluctant to behave more benevolently towards seals compared with the whales. Alternatively, respondents may have perceived the described whales' protection programme to have a greater meaning than intended, that is, respondents may have been valuing 'a symbolic mean', which usually is associated with the preservation of whales. Consequently, the value of the whales' protection programme was inflated in the S–W questionnaire version to maintain a relatively higher value to the humpbacks. This 'behavioural anchoring effect' did not exist in the W–S version, where the whales were valued first.

2.3.3 Sub-additivity effect

The *sub-additivity effect* (also called in the literature the *adding-up hypothesis* or the *value aggregation issue*) exists when the respondents value differently a given set of public goods when valued individually than when valued aggregately (Hanemann 1994). In a well-known paper, Diamond, Hausman, Leonard and Denning (1993) explored the adding-up hypothesis using a CV application that focused on the WTP assessment for the protection of wilderness areas in the United States. The test is based on the premise that 'the same economic preferences can be measured in two different ways' (Ibid., p. 47). One way to measure this is directly: simply ask people to value the wilderness areas jointly. The second way is to ask people to value individually each wilderness area. In other words: (a) let the value of the wilderness area X, given the presence of Y at current prices and quantities, be called WTP $(X|Y)$; (b) let the value of the wilderness area Y, given the presence of X at current prices and quantities, be called WTP $(Y|X)$; (c) let the value of the joint wilderness areas X and Y be called WTP $(X \& Y)$.

The test for the adding-up hypothesis compares WTP $(X \& Y)$ with the sum of the values attached to the areas individually, X and Y. According to Diamond *et al.*, the premise is that WTP $(X \& Y)$ equals WTP $(X|Y)$ + WTP $(Y|X)$, i.e., the adding-up property holds, 'if the WTP answers reflect economic preferences'.[21]

The survey questionnaire begins by describing the existence of the 57 wilderness areas and then describes a proposal to reduce the federal budget deficit by having the federal government lease some wilderness areas – a number described in the survey instrument – for commercial development. The stated alternative is to raise money through a federal income tax surcharge designated for wilderness preservation. The respondents are asked about their WTP to protect an additional wilderness area also being considered for commercial development. The study

---

[21] According to the authors, 'the adding-up property should hold whether the areas are viewed as the same or different' and exemplify 'consider asking one group how much they are willing to pay for a cup of coffee. Ask a second group how much they are willing to pay for a doughnut if they already had been given a cup of coffee. Ask a third group how much they are willing to pay for a cup of coffee and a doughnut. The value obtained from the third group should equal the sum of the values obtained from the first two groups if the answers people give reflect underlying economic preferences' (Diamond *et al.* 1993, p. 48).

considered three wilderness areas: the Selway Bitterroot Wilderness (SBW) in northern Idaho, the Washakie Wilderness (WW) in western Wyoming and the Bob Marshall Wilderness (BMW) in Montana. The final WTP mean estimates, across the different survey versions, are presented in Table 2.4. The adding-up tests were operationalized as follows:

(a) stated WTP for Selway plus stated WTP for Washakie equals stated WTP for Selway and Washakie jointly;
(b) stated WTP for Selway plus stated WTP for Washakie plus stated WTP for Bob Marshall equals stated WTP for Selway, Washakie and Bob Marshall jointly;
(c) stated WTP for Selway and Washakie jointly plus stated WTP for Bob Marshall equals stated WTP for Selway, Washakie and Bob Marshall jointly.

Table 2.4: Comparison of mean estimates

Survey	WTP question	Number of observations	Parametric mean ($)
1	SBW	174	51.6
2	WW	171	39.7
3	BMW	174	28.9
4	SBW and WW	169	46.3
5	SBW, WW and BMW	168	47.2

Adapted from Diamond *et al.* (1993, p. 53)

All hypotheses can be restated in terms of the parametric means of the stated WTP distributions. Hypothesis (a) asserts that the mean of the distribution of the stated WTP underlying Survey 4 should equal the sum of the means of the stated WTP underlying Surveys 1 and 2. Likewise, hypothesis (b) asserts that the mean of the distribution of the stated WTP underlying Survey 5 should equal the sum of the means of the stated WTP underlying Surveys 1, 2, and 3. Finally, hypothesis (c) asserts that the mean of the distribution of the stated WTP underlying Survey 5 should equal the sum of the means of the stated WTP underlying Surveys 3 and 4. From Table 2.4, the sum of the parametric mean estimates from Surveys 1 and 2 is about $91, whereas the sample mean from Survey 4 is about $46. Thus, in contradiction to hypothesis (a), the sum of the stated WTP for SBW and WW does appear to be much larger than the stated WTP for the two areas jointly. A formal statistical test, rejects hypothesis (a) with a *P*-value of 2 per cent. For testing hypothesis (b), Table 2.4 indicates that the sum of parametric mean estimates in Surveys 1, 2 and 3 is about $120, whereas the parametric mean estimate from Survey 5 (all three areas jointly) is $47. According to the authors, 'if the answers were to reflect economic preferences, we should get two numbers which are approximately the same. Instead, we get a number, $120, about two and half-times the other number, $47' (Ibid., p. 54). The formal test statistic strongly rejects hypothesis (b), with a *P*-value of 0.03 per cent. To test hypothesis (c), the sum of the parametric mean WTP estimates for Surveys 3 and 4 compare to the parametric mean WTP estimate of Survey 5. Again, the two WTP figures are found to be far apart, respectively $75 and $47, when they should be approximately the same if the WTP answers 'reflect economic preferences'.

If people give answers that do not 'reflect economic preferences', what might they be doing when answering WTP questions?

A possible explanation could be that 'WTP answers may also reflect the desire on the part of people to state their support for environmental issues' (Ibid., p. 48). This idea is referred in the literature as a 'warmglow' explanation and is similar to the argument modelled by James Andreoni. The argument posed by Andreoni concerns whether donations (or private efforts to supply some public goods) lead to two types of contributions to an individual's utility (Andreoni 1988, 1989, 1990). One of them is associated with the amount personally given, and the second with the overall provision level of the public good across all people involved, including the individual's contribution. The analysis of the warmglow valuation effect in the WTP responses motivated further CV research work, namely testing whether the individual's different use – and non-use – related motives affect the stated WTP. In this research line, Kahneman and Knetsch (1992) tested the hypothesis that the WTP for public goods is also an expression of WTP to acquire 'moral satisfaction'. The purchase of the moral satisfaction argument and its linkage to the interpretation of CV responses, as suggested by Kahneman and Knetsch, is discussed in the following section.

2.4 The Kahneman and Knetsch theory for CV embedding: the purchase of 'moral satisfaction'

Kahneman's embedding argument, as described in the CV experiment in the Ontario Lakes in 1986, received considerable attention in CV research. However, CV researchers initially attributed the possible insensitivity of CV estimates to survey and sampling design methodology (for example, the failure to describe the valuation scenario with clear mention of reference and target levels for the environmental quality changes). On the contrary, Kahneman and Knetsch offered an alternative hypothesis to embedding. According to them, embedding could be explained in terms of an impure altruistic motivation of the individual consumer, originally not considered in the valuation framework. In other words, they proposed an explanation that maintains that the WTP for public goods is also an expression of WTP to acquire 'a sense of moral satisfaction (also known as warmglow of giving)' (Kahneman and Knetsch 1992, p. 64). If the 'warmglow' explanation holds, then the sum of the WTP answers for public goods, when measured individually, may be larger than the WTP answer for the group of the public goods because each answer will contain a 'warmglow' component.

Consider the question of the preservation of two natural areas: area 1 and area 2. Suppose that the WTP for the two areas jointly is $(X + C)$, where X is the economic value of preserving the areas and C is the value attached to the warmglow of giving. Now suppose the answer to the question for area 1 individually is $(Y + C)$ and the answer to the question for area 2 individually is $(Z + C)$, where $X = Y + Z$. Then, the sum of the answers for the areas individually will be $(X + 2C)$, which is greater by the amount C than the answer for the two areas jointly.

In order to explore the analysis of the warmglow in the WTP responses, Kahneman and Knetsch conducted three telephone surveys with adult residents in Vancouver and investigated (a) the presence of an embedding valuation effect for a wide array of public goods and (b) the effect of the individual motivations on the reported WTP responses (Kahneman and Knetsch 1992). Respondents in one sample, were initially asked to state their WTP for 'a special fund to improve environment services', described in the survey instrument as 'preserving the wilderness areas, protecting wildlife, providing parks, preparing for disasters, controlling air pollution, insuring water quality, and routine treatment and disposal of industrial wastes' (Ibid., p. 60). In a second question, the respondents were asked to focus their attention on 'preparedness for disasters' and were asked to state 'what part of the total amount you allocated to improving environmental services do you think should go specifically to improve preparedness for disasters with the contributions to go to a special fund to improve

Table 2.5: Kahneman and Knetsch valuation results

Public Good	Group 1 (N=66) ($)	Group 2 (N=78) ($)	Group 3 (N=74) ($)
Environmental Services	50,0		
Improved disaster preparedness	10,0	50,0	
Improve rescue equipment and personal	1,5	16,0	25,0

Adapted from Kahneman and Knetsch, page 61

preparedness for disasters' (Ibid., p. 60). A third question was asked after some aspects of preparedness for disasters were listed 'emergency services in hospitals, maintenance of large stocks of medical supplies and communication equipment, ensuring the availability of equipment and trained personnel for rescue operations, and preparing for cleanup for oil, toxic chemicals or radioactive materials' and the respondents were asked to state 'what part of the total amount you allocated to improving preparedness for disasters do you think should go specifically to improve the availability of equipment and trained personnel for rescue operations with the contributions to go to a special fund to improve availability of equipment and trained personnel for rescue operations' (Ibid., p. 61). The same elicitation was followed by the second group, except that the initial question to be answered referred to 'a special fund to improve preparedness for disasters' with a subsequent allocation to go to 'a special fund to improve availability of equipment and trained personnel for rescue operations'. Respondents in the third sample were told to focus on preparedness for disasters and asked to state their WTP for 'a special fund to improve availability of equipment and trained personnel for rescue operations'. Table 2.5 presents the final median of the WTP responses to each of the questions across the three surveys.

According to the authors, the bottom rows of Table 2.5 'display the embedding effect on stated WTP for "equipment and trained personnel". The median amounts allocated to "equipment and trained personnel" vary from $25 when the goods is valued on its own to $1.5 when the initial question concerns the WTP for "environmental services"'. In other words, the value of a particular good is much larger when it is valued on its own that when it is evaluated as part of a more inclusive package of public goods.

The embedding effect, as presented in Kahneman and Knetsch's CV experiment, is difficult to reconcile with the standard value theory and interpretation of CV results. That is, it is difficult to reconcile with the interpretation that the WTP for a public good is a measure of the economic value associated with that good, which is fully comparable to values derived from market exchanges and on the basis of which allocative efficiency judgements can be made.[22]

If the value of a given public good is much larger when it is evaluated on its own than when it is valued as part of a more inclusive package of public goods, which measure is the correct one? Which public good's valuation is fully comparable to values derived from market exchanges? Which measure, on the basis of which allocative efficiency judgements, can be made? To better clarify the difficulty of reconciling the embedding effect with the standard interpretation of the CV results, the authors explored the conditions under which assessments of the private goods would exhibit these embedding effects. First, embedding could be

---

[22] However, Kahneman and Knetsch's results have been heavily criticized for many aspects of survey design, implementation and data analysis, which casts doubt on the empirical evidence of the 'observed' embedding (Smith 1992).

expected in 'goods for which people are willing to pay a large part of their wealth'. However, this explanation, that is, the argument that embedding effects are produced by limited wealth, is troublesome because WTP estimates in CV studies commonly fall in the range of $5–150 (Desvousges et al. 1996), magnitudes far too small to be severely restrained by wealth. Second, embedding could also be expected when 'the goods are perfect substitutes for one another and for which satiation is attained by the consumption of one unit'. For example, one could expect that 'most adults have a zero WTP for a second large ice cream cone offered immediately after the consumption of the first one … under these circumstances the value of an ice cream cone also exhibits an embedding effect: WTP for 100 ice cream cones will not be higher than the WTP for 1' (Kahneman and Knetsch 1992, p. 59). However, even if this explanation applies, i.e., the argument of substitution and satiation applies to some environmental resources, it does not readily extend to existence values for natural sites or endangered species. If it is found that the WTP to save all threatened species in a region is not much higher than the WTP to save all the threatened species in a single site, this can hardly be plausible because each individual site provides as much utility as the entire collection of sites in the region. Indeed, as discussed by Krutilla (1967), the uniqueness of the valued good is the essence of the existence value.

But, according to Kahneman and Knetsch, embedding is not in conflict with the standard value theory; according to Kahneman and Knetsch embedding can be explained in terms of an impure altruistic motivation of the individual consumer, and that aspect of consumer behavior was not considered in the standard valuation framework. In other words, Kahneman and Knetsch proposed an explanation that maintains that the WTP for public goods is also an expression of WTP to acquire moral satisfaction:

'respondents express a willingness to contribute for the acquisition of many public goods, and there is no reason to doubt their sincerity or seriousness … what is the good that respondents are willing to acquire in CV surveys? We offer the general hypothesis that responses to CV questions express a willingness to acquire a sense of moral satisfaction, (also known as warmglow of giving).' (Kahneman and Knetsch 1992, p. 62 and 64).

Moreover, the moral satisfaction valuation transmission effect can be 'read' along the general model formulation for private donations developed by James Andreoni (1988, 1989, 1990). According to Andreoni the individual consumer contributes to the provision of a particular public good for two reasons. First, because he/she simply wants more of it and, second, because he/she derives some private benefit from giving to the good – an impure altruistic behavioural argument. Therefore, the individual's financial contribution to the public good enters into his/her utility function twice: once as a private good and once as a contribution to a public good. By inference, it seems plausible that the act of participating in a CV market so as to assist in the supply of an environmental good could provide a mixture of private, warmglow benefits and public services from the increased supply of the good.

2.5 Conclusions

Despite the fact that CV survey design has been a target of extensive methodological research and quality improvements, this valuation method is today an object of diverse critiques. The embedding effect is a major critique of the CV method. Embedding is attributed to the possibility that CV is insensitive to the scope of the public policy formulated in the instrument survey. The argument for criticizing the CV method goes as follows: how can cost–benefit analysis and damage cost assessment rely on a valuation tool that discloses, for the same public good, different value estimates, whether the public good is valued alone or included in a wider policy programme? Kahneman and Knetsch offered an explanation for embedding that has its roots in the individual consumer behaviour. According to these authors there is no reason to doubt the seriousness of the respondents' answers: the CV insensitivity may be present because the CV responses also reflect 'a purchase of moral satisfaction', that is, a feeling of well-being associated with the act of contributing to good causes. Moreover, we propose the study of the *moral satisfaction* valuation transmission in the light of the general model formulation for private donations as initially developed by Andreoni. According to Andreoni, the individual consumer contributes to the provision of a particular public good for two reasons. First, because he/she simply wants more of it and, second, because he/she derives some private benefit from giving to the good. Therefore, his/her financial contribution to the public good enters into the utility function twice: once as a private good and once as a contribution to a public good. By inference, it seems plausible that the act of participating in a CV market so as to assist in the supply of an environmental good could provide a mixture of private, warmglow benefits and public services from the increased supply of the good.

In the present work, we carry out an extensive CV survey design research, following the state-of-art guidelines, so as to ensure the validity of the proposed survey as a measurement instrument. In the valuation exercise, we are particularly interested in the study of the warmglow effect and explore its 'linkage' to standard microeconomic consumer theory. Furthermore, we propose an operationalization of the warmglow and test the empirical validity of the warmglow valuation transmission mechanism, that is, examine whether the warmglow effect is present in valuing the use and non-use values. Finally, we propose to predict a WTP measure 'free' from warmglow and run formal hypothesis tests so as to better understand the nature of the WTP responses.

Chapter

3

MODELLING CONSUMER PREFERENCES

3.1 Introduction

The present chapter addresses the study of the structure of preferences of individual consumers so that we can better understand consumers' contribution behaviour in the provision of a public good. Therefore, we propose the development of an analytical setting whereby we can analyse and interpret the theoretical basis that underpins individual contribution behaviour for the provision of a public good. We focus our attention on the joint characteristic product model, as presented by Cornes and Sandler (1984, 1986, 1994), and provide an intuitive interpretation of the initial formulation. In this context, we explore the concept of consumer motivations, originally introduced by (Becker 1965, 1976; Stigler and Becker 1977), which we postulate as (a) responsible for setting the relationship between the goods and characteristic space dimensions and which we (b) interpret as forming the cornerstone of individual consumer choice behaviour (Lancaster 1966, 1971; Rosen 1974). An environment protection programme, such as the protection of Natural Areas, is assumed to jointly generate a flow of public characteristics: the use and non-use characteristics. The use characteristic refers to the set of recreational possibilities that the individual consumer is able to enjoy whenever visiting the Natural Area. The non-use characteristic is associated with the Natural Area function of wildlife diversity protection and respective guarantee of non-extinction of some species. Moreover, in addition to the gain in utility associated with the recreational consumption and protection of wildlife diversity, the individual consumer may also be willing to contribute for the protection of the Natural Area due to the feeling of well-being associated with the act of contributing to good causes. This valuation transmission mechanism was originally modelled by Andreoni who developed a model formulation for private donations (Andreoni 1988, 1989, 1990). According to Andreoni, individual consumers contribute to the provision of a particular public good for two reasons. First, because they contribute due to the fact that they simply want more of it and, second, because they derive some private benefit from giving to the good, the 'warmglow' effect. By inference, it seems plausible that the act of participating in a CV market so as to assist in the supply of an environmental good could provide a mixture of private, warmglow benefits and public services from the increased supply of the environmental good. Consequently, the stated CV contribution for the preservation of the

Natural Area may be interpreted in terms of the gain in utility reflecting the increase of the use and non-use services flows provided by the Natural Area, as well as by the warmglow associated with the act of giving.

This chapter is divided into three sections. In section 3.2, we present the concept of consumer motivation functions and describe their role in translating information with respect to consumer preferences. Then, we explore the analysis of Cornes and Sandler's joint characteristic product model. We pay particular attention to the analytical formulation of consumer motivation functions, here interpreted as the cornerstone of individual consumer choice behavior. In section 3.3, we proceed with the study of the joint characteristic product model and investigate the different strategic effects involving individual participation in provision of the public good. In particular, we focus attention on the analysis of the 'referendum tax' and the 'voluntary contribution' payment schemes. Finally, in section 3.4, we explore the comparative static properties of the consumer's contribution responses. Since consumer preferences are originally mapped in the characteristics space, the derivation of comparative static results is done by exploring the concept of virtual prices and income.

3.2 The multiattribute model formulation

3.2.1 The introduction of consumer motivation functions

We postulate that the structure of the individual consumer preferences is characterized by the presence of use, non-use and warmglow motivations.[23] The use motivation captures the individual consumer's recreation motives and general attitudes of the consumer as a (outdoor) recreationist. The consumer non-use motivation profile refers to the consumer's moral or ethical motives with respect to the protection of Nature, most of the time not directly connected to its human use.[24] Finally, warmglow motivation translates the consumer's well-being generated, *per se*, by the act of giving to good causes. This latter motivation function is modelled so as to capture the effect identified in the literature as the consumer's 'purchase of moral satisfaction'. Therefore, we may interpret the individual consumer's motivational profile in terms of the individual consumer psychological characteristics. Formally we can express individual consumer's motivational structure as follows:

$$
\begin{aligned}
m_u^j &= f_u\left(\mathbf{d}^j\right) \\
m_{nu}^j &= f_{nu}\left(\mathbf{d}^j\right) \\
m_{wg}^j &= f_{wg}\left(\mathbf{d}^j\right)
\end{aligned}
\tag{3.1}
$$

where m_u, m_{nu}, and m_{wg} represent, respectively, the consumer ratings associated to the use, f_u,

---

[23] Motivations and their relation to sources of utility have been discussed by Weisbrod (1964), Schokkaert (1980), and Schokkaert and Van Ootegem (1990) and, more recently, by Milgrom (1993), Kahneman and Knetsch (1992) and Schkade and Payne (1993, 1994).

[24] We refer to motives as the consumer Q-altruism, a motivation argument that claims that, apart from any source of direct use, the Natural Area has a right to exist. Closely related to the Q-altruism is the consumer's sympathy belief for other living organisms incapable of protecting themselves against human actions. Both are responsible for giving rise to the existence value (Norton 1982, 1988; Sagoff 1980; Van der Veer and Pierce 1986).

non-use, f_{nu}, and warmglow, f_{wg}, motivation functions.[25] $\mathbf{d}^j$ is the vector of psychological characteristics of the consumer and j indexes the individual consumers. For example, we may expect individual consumers who identify themselves as 'environmentalists' to have strong ethical concerns towards the protection of nature and thus be associated with higher ratings in the non-use motivation function.

The individual motivational ratings are pooled across the sample and used to explain the level of financial contribution stated by the j individual consumer in the instrument survey:

$$q^j = q\left(m_u^j, m_{nu}^j, m_{wg}^j, \mathbf{h}^j\right)$$

(3.2)

where q^j defines the vector of the individual's contributions and $\mathbf{h}$ the vector of socio-economic characteristics of the respondents. Therefore, differences in the CV stated financial contributions may be interpreted not only in terms of a household's socio-economic characteristics (for example, income, age, education), but also in term of the household's motivation profile (for example respondent's recreational motivation, respondent's ethical beliefs towards protection of Nature, respondent's attitude with respect to charity giving) – see Figure 3.1. In the next sub-section we propose to develop Cornes and Sandler's analytical framework, whereby we can study the individual consumer's decisions, i.e., analyse the underlying financial contribution's driving factors, namely m_u, m_{nu}, and m_{wg}.

3.2.2 Integration of concepts: the valuation model

We use the joint characteristic product model developed by Cornes and Sandler (1984, 1986, 1994) to analyse the properties of the individual consumer with respect to the level of financial contributions for the introduction of an environmental protection programme. Furthermore, we extend the initial Cornes and Sandler's analytical formulation and provide an intuitive interpretation of the joint characteristic product model, i.e., of the relationship that makes the connection between the goods space, where consumer decisions are observed, and characteristics space, where the consumer's preferences are originally mapped.

We define an economy with J consumers where each consumer is given exogenous income, M^j. The individual consumer is able to purchase the quantity of tradable private goods Y^j and q^j. Y is a standard numeraire private good, the price of which is set at unity throughout. One can think of each unit as generating a unit of private characteristic, which is also denoted by Y. q is the level of financial contributions for the environmental protection plan. A unit of q is subjectively understood by each individual consumer to jointly generate θ units of warmglow characteristic (a private characteristic), together with ρ units of use and τ units of non-use characteristics (both public characteristics).[26] Therefore, the importance of ρ, τ, and θ is twofold: first, because they are assumed to be the cornerstone variables in defining the relationship between goods and characteristics space dimensions, and second, because they

---

[25] Since we postulate that warmglow comes, in part, from the social esteem generated by being a generous contributor, this motivation may be fed by actions that make act of giving more evident, e.g., we may expect that an individual who often participates as a donor to charitable organisations is associated to higher m_{wg} values (to higher warmglow motivational rating) than an individual who does not participate. Conversely, the stronger the individual consumer recreational profile, *ceteris paribus*, the higher the m_u value.

[26] The private tradable good, Y, is assumed to be responsible only for the generation of one attribute. Moreover, we shall assume that each unit of the good equally generates one attribute; here one may think about its use component.

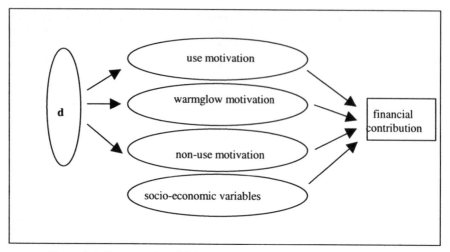

Figure 3.1: Conceptual model depicting the consumer financial contribution

are interpreted as disclosing information aboutthe consumer's preferences with respect to his/her use, non-use and warmglow motivations or attitudes.

Given the public nature of the use and non-use attributes generated by the contribution to the environmental protection plan, consumers may consume units of such characteristics even if they do not contribute (they would then be free-riding on a level of provision generated by the contributions of others). On the contrary, the consumption of the warmglow characteristic is exclusively dependent upon their own level of financial contribution. Formally, the individual consumer's problem is defined as follows:

$$\text{Max} \quad U = U\left(Y^j, B_u^{\ j}, B_{nu}^{\ j}, B_{wg}^{\ j}\right) \tag{3.3}$$

$$\left\{Y^j, q^j\right\}$$

s.t.

$$Y^j + pq^j = M^j \tag{3.4}$$

$$B_u^j = \rho^j Q \tag{3.5}$$

$$B_{nu}^{\ j} = \tau^j Q \tag{3.6}$$

$$B_{wg}^{\ j} = \theta^j q^j \tag{3.7}$$

$$\text{and } Q = \sum_{j=1}^{J} q^j \tag{3.8}$$

where the consumer preference's mapping is defined over a set of four characteristics (3.3), and $U(.)$ is assumed to be a strictly quasi-concave utility function. Equation (3.4) depicts the individual's consumer's budget constraint in the goods space. p is here interpreted as a fiscal term: when negative it is interpreted as a subsidy to the financial contribution and thus reducing the opportunity cost in terms of forgone consumption of the tradable private good; on the contrary when p is positive it is interpreted as a tax on the financial contribution. Equations (3.5)–(3.7) translate the consumer motivational constructs and define the relationship between the goods and characteristics dimensions, and j indexes individual numerical ratings. Finally, (3.8) describes the public good's quantity provision rule (where Q defines the environment protection plan for the Natural Area). Using equations (3.5)–(3.7), that relate goods to characteristics, we can write:

$$ U\left(Y_c^{\ j}, B_u^{\ j}, B_{nu}^{\ j}, B_{wg}^{\ j}\right) = U\left(Y^j, \rho^j Q, \tau^j Q, \theta^j q^j\right) = U^+\left(Y, Q, q; \rho^j, \tau^j, \theta^j, \bar{q}\right) \qquad (3.9) $$

Given particular values of $\bar{q}$ [27] and of the parameters ρ, τ, and θ the individual consumer confronts a standard problem:[28]

$$ \underset{Y,q}{\text{Max}}\left\{U^+\left(Y, Q, q\ ; \rho, \tau, \theta, \bar{q}\right)\middle| Y + pq = M\right\} \qquad (3.10) $$

where $U^+(.)$ has the usual properties of any utility function. This formulation in terms of induced preferences indicates that, for a given value of $\bar{q}$, the individual's choice of Y and q can be modelled using either uncompensated or compensated demand functions that possess all the standard properties of demand functions.

There are, however, questions that this good space formulation is less suited for analysis. For example, what are the comparative static responses of the financial contribution with respect to changes in the consumer motivational profile, e.g. changes in ρ, τ, and θ? Such changes shift the preference map defined over Y and q in ways that are not always evident. Moreover, suppose that the three characteristics are normal characteristics, in the sense that Engel income curves in the characteristics space are upward sloping; does this guarantee that an increase in income will also stimulate the amount of financial contributions? Or, in other words, does it guarantee that q is a normal good? If not, what kind of preferences imply that q is inferior in the sense that $\partial q(.)/\partial M$ is negative? To give answers to such questions, we need to work explicitly in the characteristics space, since this is where the consumer's preferences are originally mapped – see section 3.4. We start, however, with a description of a model formulation that is able to capture different strategic incentives involving individual participation in the provision of the public good.

---

[27] The term $\bar{q}$ represents the sum of contributions from all other consumers, i.e., $\displaystyle\sum_{\substack{i=1 \\ i \neq j}}^{J} q^i$

[28] To avoid notational overload, we omit the subscript and treat ρ, τ, and θ as one element of the respective vectors, that is, the element that is applicable to the individual.

3.3 Modelling individual consumer strategic behaviour

The objective of this section is to present a model that is able to capture different strategic incentives involving individual participation in the provision of the public good. In particular, we focus attention on the analysis of two alternative payment mechanisms. We refer to the 'referendum tax' and 'voluntary contribution' schemes. First, we investigate the voluntary contribution equilibrium solution, as described by equations (3.3)–(3.8) in the previous section, also known in the literature as the Nash–Cournot equilibrium. Second, we explore an alternative formulation to model the 'referendum tax' payment scenario. Finally, we compare the equilibrium solutions under the two payment mechanisms.

3.3.1 A simple representation of voluntary contribution behaviour

Consider an economy consisting of two consumers,[29] each of whom behaves as described by equations (3.3)–(3.8). Thus, each consumer has the problem:

$$\text{Max} \quad U = U\left(Y^j, B_u^{\ j}, B_{nu}^{\ j}, B_{wg}^{\ j}\right) \tag{3.11}$$

$$\left\{Y^j, q^j\right\}$$

s.t.

$$Y^j + pq^j = M^j \tag{3.12}$$

$$B_u^j = \rho^j Q \tag{3.13}$$

$$B_{nu}^{\ j} = \tau^j Q \tag{3.14}$$

$$B_{wg}^{\ j} = \theta^j q^j \tag{3.15}$$

$$\text{and } Q = q^j + q^i, \qquad i, j = 1,2; \ i \neq j \tag{3.16}$$

The resulting solution derives from solving simultaneously the first-order conditions:

$$\frac{\rho^j \dfrac{\partial U}{\partial B_u^j} + \tau^j \dfrac{\partial U}{\partial B_{nu}^j} + \theta^j \dfrac{\partial U}{\partial B_{wg}^j}}{\dfrac{\partial U}{\partial Y^j}} = p. \quad i, j = 1,2; \ i \neq j \tag{3.17}$$

which states that the marginal rate of substitution between the contribution and the numeraire private good equals the price ratio. Equation (3.17) may be rewritten as follows:

$$\rho^1 \tilde{p}_u^1 + \tau^1 \tilde{p}_{nu}^1 + \theta^1 \tilde{p}_{wg}^1 = p, \text{ and}$$
$$\rho^2 \tilde{p}_u^2 + \tau^2 \tilde{p}_{nu}^2 + \theta^2 \tilde{p}_{wg}^2 = p \tag{3.18}$$

---

[29] For clarity's sake, we concentrate the analysis on a two consumer set-up.

with the individual specific variables $\tilde{p}_u^j$, $\tilde{p}_{nu}^j$ and $\tilde{p}_{wg}^j$ representing, respectively $U_{B_u^j}/U_{Y^j}$,

$U_{B_{nu}^j}/U_{Y^j}$ and $U_{B_{wg}^j}/U_{Y^j}$.

According to equation (3.18), each individual consumer adjusts the level of contributions to the point at which his/her private marginal cost, the right hand side of the equation, equals the private marginal valuation of the contributions, the left-hand side. The intuition goes as follows: an increment of the contribution yields a marginal benefit to the individual, of $\rho^j \tilde{p}_u^j + \tau^j \tilde{p}_{nu}^j$ (due to increased consumption of the public characteristics) plus $\theta^j \tilde{p}_{wg}^j$ (due to the increased consumption of the warmglow characteristic). The marginal cost is the quantity of the numeraire good that has to be sacrificed. The utility cost of this sacrifice, measured in monetary terms, is p. This optimality condition provides, however, no information with respect to the levels of individuals' contributions. Furthermore, equation (3.18) neither confirms (nor rejects) the usual claim that the higher the expected contribution by the rest of the community, the lower the individual's own contribution will be. In other words, equation (3.18) provides no information concerning the slope of the individual Nash–Cournot reaction curves.

In a two-agent setting, the rest of the community's contribution is simply the other individual's provision, q_2. We denote consumer 1's own contribution as q_1. The confirmation (or rejection) of the usual claim that the higher the expected contribution by the rest of the community, the lower the individual's own contribution is easily explored with the help of some duality theory. Consumer 1's optimal choice can be thought of as minimizing the level of e:

$$e(Q, q_1, U_1^+) = \underset{e}{\text{Min}}\{e \mid U_1^+(Y, Q, q_1) = \overline{U}_1^+\}^{30} \tag{3.19}$$

where Y is a standard numeraire private good and $\overline{U}_1^+$ the maximum utility level that consumer 1 may achieve given the rest of the community's contribution, q_2^*. We assume that $e(.)$ is everywhere twice continuously differentiable. Point Z in Figure 3.2 depicts the solution to this problem. It is clear that the response $\partial Y/\partial q_1$ is simply the slope of the indifference curve at the equilibrium, i.e., it is minus the marginal rate of substitution:

$$\frac{\partial Y}{\partial q_1} = -\text{MRS} = -\pi(Q, q_1, U) \tag{3.20}$$

---

[30] Since $U(Y, B_u, B_{nu}, B_{wg}) = U(Y, \rho Q, \tau Q, \theta q_1) = U^+(Y, Q, q_1; \rho, \tau, \theta) = U^+(Y, q_1 + q_2, q_1; \rho, \tau, \theta)$.

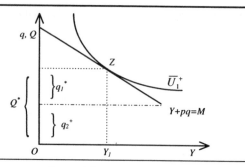

Figure 3.2: Indifference map

where $\pi(.)$ is the ratio defining the marginal rate of substitution (MRS) of good Y for good q, that is, the rate at which the consumer is willing to substitute a little less consumption of good Y for a little more consumption of good q. Since good Y represents the consumption of 'all other goods', and is measured in dollars that the consumer can spend on other goods, then the MRS measures the marginal willingness to pay for good q. The MRS is interpreted as 'how many dollars the consumer would just be willing to give up spending on other goods [good 2] in order to consume a little more of good 1' (Varian 1990, p. 51).

Combining equations (3.18)–(3.20) we can link individual virtual prices, $\tilde{p}_u^j$, $\tilde{p}_{nu}^j$ and $\tilde{p}_{wg}^j$, and the marginal willingness to pay, $\pi(.)$, as follows:

$$\pi\left(Q, q_1, U\right) = \rho^1 \tilde{p}_u^1 + \tau^1 \tilde{p}_{nu}^1 + \theta^1 \tilde{p}_{wg}^1 \qquad (3.21)$$

that is, the marginal willingness to pay for the environmental protection plan is defined according to the individual marginal benefit associated with the contribution. The marginal benefit is, in turn, defined in terms of the well-being increase associated with the additional consumption of the use, non-use and warmglow characteristics, respectively, captured by the individual virtual prices $\tilde{p}_u^j$, $\tilde{p}_{nu}^j$ and $\tilde{p}_{wg}^j$. Moreover, combining (3.21) with (3.18) we can characterize the points on the Nash–Cournot reaction as follows:

$$p = \pi\left(Q, q_1, U\right) \equiv \pi\left(q_1 + q_2, q_1, U\right) \qquad (3.22)$$

Letting q_1 and q_2 vary, while holding p constant, yields:

$$0 = \pi_Q dq_1 + \pi_Q dq_2 + \pi_{q_1} dq_1 + \pi_U dU \qquad (3.23)$$

from which individual 1's response to a change in q_2 is easily derived:

$$\frac{dq_1}{dq_2} = -\frac{\pi_Q}{\pi_Q + \pi_{q_1}} - \frac{\pi_U}{\pi_Q + \pi_{q_1}}\left(\frac{dU}{dq_2}\right)$$

$$= -\frac{1}{\pi_Q + \pi_{q_1}}\left[\pi_Q + \pi_U\left(\frac{dU}{dq_2}\right)\right]$$

(3.24)

Equation (3.24) defines individual 1's Nash–Cournot reaction curve. According to equation (3.24) the total response of individual 1's contribution to a change in the community's provision is broken down into two parts: the pure compensated substitution effect and the real income effect.

The pure compensated substitution effect is captured by the term $-\pi_Q / (\pi_Q + \pi_{q1})$. The denominator reflects the fact the demand for the public good is characterized by two driving forces; on the one hand, the individual consumer's well-being derived from the provision of the public good and, in the other hand, the individual consumer's well-being related to the participation in the provision of the public good. If we admitted that no well-being is related to the participation in the provision of the public good we would have $\pi_{q1} = 0$. In such a case the pure compensated substitution response would be equal to -1, that is, the individual consumer would be substituting Q and q at a one-to-one rate. In other words, Q and q would be perfect substitutes.

The second term captures the real income effect. Since we admit that Q is a 'good', then dU / dq_2 is positive. Therefore, the overall income effect depends on whether $-\pi_U / (\pi_Q + \pi_{q1})$ is positive or negative; a positive value indicates that Q is a normal good. Therefore, the sign of the response of individual 1's contribution to a change in the community's provision, the sign of the whole expression (3.24), will depend on the magnitude of the substitution and the real income effects.[31] Moreover, equation (3.24) demonstrates the possibility that if Q is a normal good and the income effect is sufficiently strong, the Nash–Cournot reaction curve may have a positive slope – see Table 3.1.

Table 3.1: Expected sign of dq_1/dq_2

Income response (IR)	Substitution response (SR)	Slope of the Nash-Cournot reaction curve sign of equation (3.24)	
Positive	Negative	Ambiguous	Positive (+) if $|IR| > |SR|$
(+)	(−)	(+/−)	Negative (−) if $|IR| < |SR|$
Negative	Negative	Negative	
(−)	(−)	(−)	

Let us use a graphical representation to help better understand the Nash–Cournot reaction curves. Measuring individual 2's contribution along the vertical axis, we obtain 1's reaction curve, that is, the set of best responses of individual 1 with respect to the action of consumer 2. The same holds for individual 2. The intersection of their reaction curves – the point E^{NC} in Figure 3.3, where each individual is choosing his/her optimal q given the other's current

---

[31] The assessment of the sign of dq_1/dq_2 implies the study of the consumer preferences in the characteristics space, since this is the space where the consumer's preferences are originally mapped (see section 3.4.1.5).

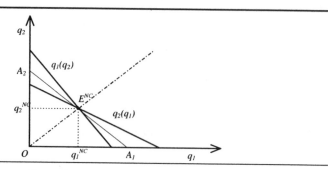

Figure 3.3: Nash-Cournot equilibrium

contribution[32] – is called a Nash–Cournot, or simply a Nash, equilibrium. The plotted equilibrium refers to an economy consisting of two identical consumers: $\rho^1 = \rho^2$, $\tau^1 = \tau^2$, $\theta^1 = \theta^2$ and $M^1 = M^2$. Thus, the reactions curves are reflections of one another about the 45° ray through the origin, OE. The aggregate provision of the public good, Q, may be read by drawing a line through E^{NC} of slope –1 and measuring the distance between its intersection with either axis and the origin, for example OA_1.

3.3.2 A simple representation of referendum tax behaviour

In the national tax referendum setting, the individual consumer is informed that the aggregate provision of the public good equals the sum of the individual's contributions and that individual contribution is set at the same amount for everyone. Thus, consumer 1 has the problem:[33]

$$\text{Max} \quad U = U\left(Y_u^{\,1}, B_u^{\,1}, B_{nu}^{\,1}, B_{wg}^{\,1}\right) \tag{3.25}$$

$$\left\{Y^1, q^1\right\}$$

s.t.

$$Y^1 + pq^1 = M^1 \tag{3.26}$$

$$B_u^1 = \rho^1 Q = 2\rho^1 q^1 \tag{3.27}$$

$$B_{nu}^{\ 1} = \tau^1 Q = 2\tau^1 q^1 \tag{3.28}$$

$$B_{wg}^{\ 1} = \theta^1 q^1 \tag{3.29}$$

$$\text{and } Q = q^1 + q^2, \qquad \text{with } q^1 = q^2 \equiv q \tag{3.30}$$

---

[32] In Figure 3.3 it is assumed that Nash–Cournot reaction curves are linear with negative slope.

[33] Again, for clarity's sake, we concentrate the analysis on a two consumer set-up.

Note that in the impure altruism setting, we also conceive the possibility that tax payments generate warmglow (see equation 3.29), one may think of q as the individual contribution to a specific national tax, a tax for Nature conservation. The resulting solution comes from solving simultaneously the first-order conditions:

$$\frac{2\rho^1 \dfrac{\partial U}{\partial B_u^1} + 2\tau^1 \dfrac{\partial U}{\partial B_{nu}^1} + \theta^1 \dfrac{\partial U}{\partial B_{wg}^1}}{\dfrac{\partial U}{\partial Y^1}} = p \qquad (3.31)$$

If we consider two identical individuals, we may rewrite equation (3.31) as follows:

$$\frac{\rho^1 \dfrac{\partial U}{\partial B_u^1} + \tau^1 \dfrac{\partial U}{\partial B_{nu}^1} + \theta^1 \dfrac{\partial U}{\partial B_{wg}^1}}{\dfrac{\partial U}{\partial Y^1}} = p - \frac{\rho^2 \dfrac{\partial U}{\partial B_u^2} + \tau^2 \dfrac{\partial U}{\partial B_{nu}^2}}{\dfrac{\partial U}{\partial Y^2}} \qquad (3.32)$$

or, rearranging the terms in the same way as we did in equation (3.18):

$$\rho^1 \tilde{p}_u^1 + \tau^1 \tilde{p}_{nu}^j + \theta^1 \tilde{p}_{wg}^1 = p' \qquad (3.33)$$

with $p' \equiv p - \left(\rho^2 \dfrac{\partial U}{\partial B_u^2} + \tau^2 \dfrac{\partial U}{\partial B_{nu}^2} \right) \Big/ \dfrac{\partial U}{\partial Y^2} < p$.

Each individual consumer adjusts the level of contributions to the point at which the private marginal cost, the right-hand side of the equation, equals the private marginal valuation of the contributions, the left-hand side. As before, an increment in the contribution yields a marginal benefit to the individual, of $\rho^j \tilde{p}_u^j + \tau^j \tilde{p}_{nu}^j$ (due to increased consumption of the public characteristics) plus $\theta^j \tilde{p}_{wg}^j$ (due to the increased consumption of the warmglow characteristic). The marginal cost is the quantity of the numeraire good that has been sacrificed. The utility cost of this sacrifice, measured in monetary terms, is now p'. Comparison with equation (3.18) provides direct information with respect to the Nash–Cournot equilibrium. In equation (3.33) we can see that $p' < p$, which means that at the 'referendum tax' equilibrium the consumer faces, at the margin, a lower cost, in terms of forgone consumption of the numeraire, which is associated with an increment in the financial contribution. The reason behind this is that consumer 1 knows that the amount of contribution of individual 2 is set at the same level as his/her own. Therefore, consumer 1 understands that each 1euro of his/her own contribution means 2 euro for the provision of the public good. So, when compared to the Nash-Cournot situation, consumer 1 has adjusted (that is, increased) the level of contribution, until the point where his/her marginal rate of substitution equals marginal cost, i.e., p'. The same holds for consumer 2. Together, they contribute to a larger provision of Q.

Point E^{TAX} in Figure 3.4 depicts a possible solution to this equilibrium. How do we characterize such an equilibrium? From equation (3.32) we know that the FOC for individual 1 is described as follows:

$$\left(\rho^1 \frac{\partial U}{\partial B_u^1} + \tau^1 \frac{\partial U}{\partial B_{nu}^1} + \theta^1 \frac{\partial U}{\partial B_{wg}^1} \right) \bigg/ \frac{\partial U}{\partial Y^1} = p - \left(\rho^2 \frac{\partial U}{\partial B_u^2} + \tau^2 \frac{\partial U}{\partial B_{nu}^2} \right) \bigg/ \frac{\partial U}{\partial Y^2} \qquad (3.34)$$

or alternatively:

$$MRS_{q,Y}^1 = p - \left(\rho^2 \frac{\partial U}{\partial B_u^2} + \tau^2 \frac{\partial U}{\partial B_{nu}^2} \right) \bigg/ \frac{\partial U}{\partial Y^2} \qquad (3.35)$$

Conversely, for individual 2 the FOC would be:

$$MRS_{q,Y}^2 = p - \left(\rho^1 \frac{\partial U}{\partial B_u^1} + \tau^1 \frac{\partial U}{\partial B_{nu}^1} \right) \bigg/ \frac{\partial U}{\partial Y^1} \qquad (3.36)$$

If we consider identical consumers, we have:

$$\left(\rho^1 \frac{\partial U}{\partial B_u^1} + \tau^1 \frac{\partial U}{\partial B_{nu}^1} \right) \bigg/ \frac{\partial U}{\partial Y^1} = \left(\rho^2 \frac{\partial U}{\partial B_u^2} + \tau^2 \frac{\partial U}{\partial B_{nu}^2} \right) \bigg/ \frac{\partial U}{\partial Y^2} = \left(\rho \frac{\partial U}{\partial B_u} + \tau \frac{\partial U}{\partial B_{nu}} \right) \bigg/ \frac{\partial U}{\partial Y} \qquad (3.37)$$

So, we may rewrite the FOC as follows:

$$MRS_{q,Y}^1 = p - \left(\rho \frac{\partial U}{\partial B_u} + \tau \frac{\partial U}{\partial B_{nu}} \right) \bigg/ \frac{\partial U}{\partial Y} \qquad (3.38)$$

$$MRS_{q,Y}^2 = p - \left(\rho \frac{\partial U}{\partial B_u} + \tau \frac{\partial U}{\partial B_{nu}} \right) \bigg/ \frac{\partial U}{\partial Y}$$

respectively for individual 1 and individual 2. Combining the FOCs, we get:

$$MRS_{q,Y}^2 = MRS_{q,Y}^1 = p' \qquad (3.39)$$

with $p' \equiv p - \left(\rho \frac{\partial U}{\partial B_u} + \tau \frac{\partial U}{\partial B_{nu}} \right) \bigg/ \frac{\partial U}{\partial Y}$, which is precisely the condition describing point E^{TAX} in Figure 3.4. In other words, at E^{TAX} the marginal rate of substitution between the contribution and the private numeraire for individual 1 and 2 (measured by the tangency of the utility function at E') is equal to the price ratio, p'. Furthermore, at E^{TAX}, the amount of contribution

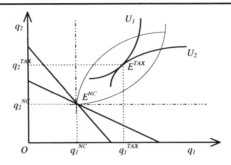

Figure 3.4: Voluntary contribution equilibrium vs. referendum tax equilibrium

of the individual 1 is q_1^{TAX} (higher than q_1^{NC}), and the amount of contribution of the individual 2 is q_2^{TAX} (higher than q_2^{NC}). Together, they contribute to a provision of $\qquad Q = q_1^{TAX} + q_2^{TAX} > Q^{NC}$.

3.4 Exploring the properties of the voluntary contributions

To better understand the properties of the individual financial contribution to the environmental protection plan, we need to work within the characteristics space since it is in this space that the preferences are originally mapped. In this context, eliminating the contribution variable, q, provides us the means to reformulate (3.3)–(3.8) problem as,[34]

$$\text{Max} \qquad U\left(Y_c, B_u, B_{nu}, B_{wg}\right) \qquad\qquad (3.40)$$

$$\left(Y_c, B_u, B_{nu}, B_{wg}\right)$$

s.t.

$$Y_c + p\frac{B_{wg}}{\theta} = M \qquad\qquad (3.41)$$

$$B_u = \rho\left(\frac{B_{wg}}{\theta}\right) + \rho\,\bar{q} \qquad\qquad (3.42)$$

$$B_{nu} = \tau\left(\frac{B_{wg}}{\theta}\right) + \tau\,\bar{q} \qquad\qquad (3.43)$$

---

[34] The comparative static effects are derived for the general model formulation, as described by the (3.3)–(3.8) problem. However, the comparative static results are the same for both approaches – the voluntary contribution formulation, as described by (3.11)–(3.16), and the referendum tax formulation, as described by (3.25) – (3.30) – as presented in the last section. Once again, to avoid notation overloading, we drop the j superscript.

The solution to this problem determines the consumption bundle allocation:

$$B_u = \hat{B}_u\left(\rho,\tau,\theta,M;\overline{q}\right)$$
$$B_{nu} = \hat{B}_{nu}\left(\rho,\tau,\theta,M;\overline{q}\right) \qquad (3.44)$$
$$B_{wg} = \hat{B}_{wg}\left(\rho,\tau,\theta,M;\overline{q}\right)$$

where $\hat{B}_u(.)$, $\hat{B}_{nu}(.)$ and $\hat{B}_{wg}(.)$ represent, respectively, the use, non-use and warmglow restricted demand functions. There is, however, an equivalent way of formulating the present consumer's choice problem (Cornes and Sandler 1994). Cornes and Sandler's approach is characterized by defining a virtual income $\tilde{M}$ as well as a set of virtual prices of characteristics $\tilde{p}_{Y_c}(=1)$, $\tilde{p}_u$, $\tilde{p}_{nu}$ and $\tilde{p}_{wg}$.[35] These magnitudes are defined such that, if the individual consumer could act as a price taker in the characteristics space, and subject to the budget constraint $Y_c + \tilde{p}_u B_u + \tilde{p}_{nu} B_{nu} + \tilde{p}_{wg} B_{wg} = \tilde{M}$, he/she would choose the same resource allocation as described by (3.44). Formally, the consumer would face the following problem:

$$\text{Max} \qquad U\left(Y_c , B_u , B_{nu} , B_{wg}\right) \qquad (3.45)$$
$$\left(Y_c , B_u , B_{nu} , B_{wg}\right)$$

s.t.

$$Y_c + \tilde{p}_u B_u + \tilde{p}_{nu} B_{nu} + \tilde{p}_{wg} B_{wg} = \tilde{M} \qquad (3.46)$$

The solution of this problem, the unrestricted demand functions, is defined as:

$$B_u^j = \tilde{B}_u\left(\tilde{p}_u,\tilde{p}_{nu},\tilde{p}_{wg},\tilde{M}\right)$$
$$B_{nu}^j = \tilde{B}_{nu}\left(\tilde{p}_u,\tilde{p}_{nu},\tilde{p}_{wg},\tilde{M}\right) \qquad (3.47)$$
$$B_{wg}^j = \tilde{B}_{wg}\left(\tilde{p}_u,\tilde{p}_{nu},\tilde{p}_{wg},\tilde{M}\right)$$

whose arguments are the virtual prices, $\tilde{p}_u$, $\tilde{p}_{nu}$ and $\tilde{p}_{wg}$, and virtual income, $\tilde{M}$. The virtual magnitudes clearly depend on the location of the consumption allocation as defined in equation (3.44), which itself depends on the five parameters that describe the constraint set. Therefore, the virtual magnitudes can be thought of as functions of the five parameters that describe the constraint set, that is:

---

[35] Virtual because they refer to instrumental, non-observable parameters. However, they are crucial to explaining individual consumer choice behaviour with respect to the allocation of financial contributions. We explicitly omit the superscript j indexing the individual to avoid notational overloading.

$$\tilde{p}_u = \tilde{p}_u(\rho,\tau,\theta,M;\overline{q})$$
$$\tilde{p}_{nu} = \tilde{p}_{nu}(\rho,\tau,\theta,M;\overline{q})$$
$$\tilde{p}_{wg} = \tilde{p}_{wg}(\rho,\tau,\theta,M;\overline{q}) \qquad (3.48)$$
$$\tilde{M} = \tilde{M}(\rho,\tau,\theta,M;\overline{q})$$

Furthermore, we know that at the consumption allocation defined by (3.44) the price of a unit of voluntary contribution, q, equals its demand price. Since the individual consumer only contributes to the protection of the Natural Area on account of the attributes that it generates, this demand price must be equal to the sum of demand prices for the attributes generated by a unit of q – see equation (3.18). Therefore at equilibrium we have:

$$p = \rho\tilde{p}_u + \tau\tilde{p}_{nu} + \theta\tilde{p}_{wg} \qquad (3.49)$$

Moreover, taking into account the characteristics joint production formulation, as defined by equations (3.41)–(3.43), the virtual magnitudes, $\tilde{p}_u$, $\tilde{p}_{nu}$, $\tilde{p}_{wg}$, and $\tilde{M}$ must be such that:

$$\theta\tilde{B}_u(\tilde{p}_u,\tilde{p}_{nu},\tilde{p}_{wg},\tilde{M}) = \rho\left[\tilde{B}_{wg}(\tilde{p}_u,\tilde{p}_{nu},\tilde{p}_{wg},\tilde{M}) + \theta\rho\overline{q}\right] \qquad (3.50)$$

$$\theta\tilde{B}_{nu}(\tilde{p}_u,\tilde{p}_{nu},\tilde{p}_{wg},\tilde{M}) = \tau\left[\tilde{B}_{wg}(\tilde{p}_u,\tilde{p}_{nu},\tilde{p}_{wg},\tilde{M}) + \theta\tau\overline{q}\right] \qquad (3.51)$$

$$\tilde{M} = Y_c + \tilde{p}_u\left[\rho\left(B_{wg}/\theta\right) + \rho\overline{q}\right] + \tilde{p}_{nu}\left[\tau\left(B_{wg}/\theta\right) + \tau\overline{q}\right] + \tilde{p}_{wg}B_{wg}$$

Since $p = \rho\tilde{p}_u + \tau\tilde{p}_{nu} + \theta\tilde{p}_{wg}$ and $B_{wg} = \theta q$ we may rewrite the last equation as follows:

$$\tilde{M} = Y_c + pq + \rho\,\tilde{p}_u\,\overline{q} + \tau\,\tilde{p}_{nu}\,\overline{q} = M + \rho\,\tilde{p}_u\,\overline{q} + \tau\,\tilde{p}_{nu}\,\overline{q} \qquad (3.52)^{36}$$

Equations (3.49)–(3.52) implicitly determine the virtual price magnitudes, $\tilde{p}_u$, $\tilde{p}_{nu}$ and $\tilde{p}_{wg}$, and virtual income, $\tilde{M}$, and, as we shall see in the following sections, play a crucial role in assessing the comparative static responses of consumer restricted demand functions and, in this way, help us to better understand the properties of the consumer's financial contributions for the provision of the environmental protection plan.

3.4.1 Some comparative static results: the general approach

Up to now, we have explicitly assumed fixed values for ρ, τ, θ, M and $\overline{q}$. It is of interest to consider the consequences of changes in these parameters. First, we are able to explore the

---

[36] Equation (3.52) corresponds to the concept of 'full income' as initially introduced by Bergstrom et al. (1986) and Cornes and Sandler (1984). However, in the present formulation, the contributions of the others are valued at the individual virtual prices, $\tilde{p}_u$ and $\tilde{p}_{nu}$.

comparative static responses of the individual's own contribution, bearing in mind the substitutability/complementary consumption pattern across the different characteristics. Second, we are able to confront the comparative static results, as expected by the present analytical model formulation, with the econometric results obtained from the empirical CV analysis of the respondents' answers.

All the comparative static exercises start from the observation that restricted and unrestricted demand functions, being simply alternative ways of defining the same magnitudes, must be equal at any consumer optimum both before and after a change in any of the parameters, that is:

$$\hat{B}_u\left(\rho, \tau, \theta, M; \overline{q}\right) = \tilde{B}_u\left(\tilde{p}_u, \tilde{p}_{nu}, \tilde{p}_{wg}, \tilde{M}\right)$$

$$\hat{B}_{nu}\left(\rho, \tau, \theta, M; \overline{q}\right) = \tilde{B}_{nu}\left(\tilde{p}_u, \tilde{p}_{nu}, \tilde{p}_{wg}, \tilde{M}\right) \qquad (3.53)$$

$$\hat{B}_{wg}\left(\rho, \tau, \theta, M; \overline{q}\right) = \tilde{B}_{wg}\left(\tilde{p}_u, \tilde{p}_{nu}, \tilde{p}_{wg}, \tilde{M}\right)$$

Furthermore, the virtual magnitudes, $\tilde{p}_u$, $\tilde{p}_{nu}$, $\tilde{p}_{wg}$ and $\tilde{M}$ are taken as functions of the five parameters, ρ, τ, θ, M and $\overline{q}$ – see equation (3.48). Therefore, by differentiating (3.53), the response to a change in any of the parameters can be expressed as:

$$\frac{\partial \hat{B}_k}{\partial \varphi} = \frac{\partial \tilde{B}_k}{\partial \tilde{p}_u}\frac{\partial \tilde{p}_u}{\partial \varphi} + \frac{\partial \tilde{B}_k}{\partial \tilde{p}_{nu}}\frac{\partial \tilde{p}_{nu}}{\partial \varphi} + \frac{\partial \tilde{B}_k}{\partial \tilde{p}_{wg}}\frac{\partial \tilde{p}_{wg}}{\partial \varphi} + \frac{\partial \tilde{B}_k}{\partial \tilde{M}}\frac{\partial \tilde{M}}{\partial \varphi}, \quad \forall B_k \qquad (3.54)$$

with k indexing the *use, non-use* and *warmglow* characteristics and φ denoting any element of the vector of 'shift variables' $\Phi \equiv \{\rho, \tau, \theta, M, \overline{q}\}$. As we can observe in equation (3.54), the demand responses can be split into two components. To understand the underlying driving forces, we remember that (1) the virtual magnitudes depend on the location of the allocation as defined by (3.44), and (2) the allocation itself depends on the vector of 'shift variables'. So a change in one of the 'shift variables' causes a change in the location of the consumption allocation and, therefore, a change in the virtual magnitudes. This is captured by the terms $\partial \tilde{p}_u / \partial \varphi$, $\partial \tilde{p}_{nu} / \partial \varphi$, $\partial \tilde{p}_{wg} / \partial \varphi$ and $\partial \tilde{M} / \partial \varphi$ of equation (3.44). This component of the demand response can be assessed by differentiating equations (3.49)–(3.52). The second component, captured by the terms $\partial \tilde{B}_k / \partial \tilde{p}_u$, $\partial \tilde{B}_k / \partial \tilde{p}_{nu}$, $\partial \tilde{B}_k / \partial \tilde{p}_{wg}$ and $\partial \tilde{B}_k / \partial \tilde{M}$, measures uncompensated price and income responses. This component can be assessed with the use of the Slutsky decomposition and can be broken down into compensated price and income responses, that is, $\partial \tilde{B}_i / \partial \tilde{p}_k = C_{i,k} + \tilde{B}_k \partial \tilde{B}_i / \partial \tilde{M}$. Finally, we assume:

H.1) symmetrical cross compensated price effects, i.e.,

$$C_{wg,u} = C_{u,wg} \quad \text{and} \quad C_{nu,wg} = C_{wg,nu} \quad \text{and} \quad C_{u,nu} = C_{nu,u};$$

which comes directly from the symmetric Slutsky matrix obtained by totally differentiating the first-order equilibrium conditions; and

H.2) weak cross compensated price effects involving the non-use characteristics,

$$C_{u,nu} \cong 0 \quad \text{and} \quad C_{wg,nu} \cong 0$$

which comes from admitting only a weak complementary-substitution between the non-use and each of the other characteristics.

The combination of equations (3.49)–(3.54), hand-in-hand with hypotheses H.1–H.2, and the Slutsky decomposition will allow the derivation of the comparative static responses of the restricted demand functions of characteristics and thus will infer the properties of the consumer's financial contributions for the provision of the environmental protection plan. A detailed mathematical analysis of the comparative static responses is presented in Appendix A.

3.4.1.1 A change in *M*

Consider a change in income, with all the other parameters held constant. Differentiating (3.49)–(3.52), holding constant all parameters except *M*, we get:

$$0 = \rho \frac{\partial \tilde{p}_u}{\partial M} + \tau \frac{\partial \tilde{p}_{nu}}{\partial M} + \theta \frac{\partial \tilde{p}_{wg}}{\partial M} \qquad (3.55)$$

$$\theta \left(\frac{\partial \tilde{B}_u}{\partial \tilde{p}_u} \frac{\partial \tilde{p}_u}{\partial M} + \frac{\partial \tilde{B}_u}{\partial \tilde{p}_{nu}} \frac{\partial \tilde{p}_{nu}}{\partial M} + \frac{\partial \tilde{B}_u}{\partial \tilde{p}_{wg}} \frac{\partial \tilde{p}_{wg}}{\partial M} + \frac{\partial \tilde{B}_u}{\partial \tilde{M}} \frac{\partial \tilde{M}}{\partial M} \right) = \rho \left(\frac{\partial \tilde{B}_{wg}}{\partial \tilde{p}_u} \frac{\partial \tilde{p}_u}{\partial M} + \frac{\partial \tilde{B}_{wg}}{\partial \tilde{p}_{nu}} \frac{\partial \tilde{p}_{nu}}{\partial M} + \frac{\partial \tilde{B}_{wg}}{\partial \tilde{p}_{wg}} \frac{\partial \tilde{p}_{wg}}{\partial M} + \frac{\partial \tilde{B}_{wg}}{\partial \tilde{M}} \frac{\partial \tilde{M}}{\partial M} \right) \qquad (3.56)$$

$$\theta \left(\frac{\partial \tilde{B}_u}{\partial \tilde{p}_u} \frac{\partial \tilde{p}_u}{\partial M} + \frac{\partial \tilde{B}_u}{\partial \tilde{p}_{nu}} \frac{\partial \tilde{p}_{nu}}{\partial M} + \frac{\partial \tilde{B}_u}{\partial \tilde{p}_{wg}} \frac{\partial \tilde{p}_{wg}}{\partial M} + \frac{\partial \tilde{B}_u}{\partial \tilde{M}} \frac{\partial \tilde{M}}{\partial M} \right) = \tau \left(\frac{\partial \tilde{B}_{wg}}{\partial \tilde{p}_u} \frac{\partial \tilde{p}_u}{\partial M} + \frac{\partial \tilde{B}_{wg}}{\partial \tilde{p}_{nu}} \frac{\partial \tilde{p}_{nu}}{\partial M} + \frac{\partial \tilde{B}_{wg}}{\partial \tilde{p}_{wg}} \frac{\partial \tilde{p}_{wg}}{\partial M} + \frac{\partial \tilde{B}_{wg}}{\partial \tilde{M}} \frac{\partial \tilde{M}}{\partial M} \right) \qquad (3.57)$$

$$\frac{\partial \tilde{M}}{\partial M} = 1 + \rho \bar{q} \frac{\partial \tilde{p}_u}{\partial M} + \tau \bar{q} \frac{\partial \tilde{p}_{nu}}{\partial M} \qquad (3.58)$$

With the help of *Mathematica,* and the use of the Slutsky decomposition, we can solve the system of (3.55)–(3.58) equations for $\partial \tilde{p}_u / \partial M$, $\partial \tilde{p}_{nu} / \partial M$, $\partial \tilde{p}_{wg} / \partial M$ and $\partial \tilde{M} / \partial M$. Finally, to make these expressions neater, we fix the parameters ρ, τ and θ at unity throughout.[37] The solutions for the virtual magnitudes are,

$$\frac{\partial \tilde{M}}{\partial M} = 1 + \left\{ \bar{q} \left[\left(-C_{nu,nu} - C_{u,wg} \right) \frac{\partial \tilde{B}_u}{\partial \tilde{M}} + \left(-C_{u,u} + C_{u,wg} \right) \frac{\partial \tilde{B}_{nu}}{\partial \tilde{M}} + \left(C_{nu,nu} + C_{u,u} \right) \frac{\partial \tilde{B}_{wg}}{\partial \tilde{M}} \right] \right\} / D \qquad (3.59)$$

$$\frac{\partial \tilde{p}_{wg}}{\partial M} = \left[\left(C_{nu,nu} + C_{u,wg} \right) \frac{\partial \tilde{B}_u}{\partial \tilde{M}} + \left(C_{u,u} - C_{u,wg} \right) \frac{\partial \tilde{B}_{nu}}{\partial \tilde{M}} + \left(-C_{nu,nu} - C_{u,u} \right) \frac{\partial \tilde{B}_{wg}}{\partial \tilde{M}} \right] / D \qquad (3.60)$$

$$\frac{\partial \tilde{p}_u}{\partial M} = \left[\left(-C_{nu,nu} - C_{wg,wg} \right) \frac{\partial \tilde{B}_u}{\partial \tilde{M}} + \left(C_{wg,wg} - C_{u,wg} \right) \frac{\partial \tilde{B}_{nu}}{\partial \tilde{M}} + \left(C_{nu,nu} + C_{u,wg} \right) \frac{\partial \tilde{B}_{wg}}{\partial \tilde{M}} \right] / D \qquad (3.61)$$

---

[37] A similar normalization is presented by Cornes and Sandler (1994) with the same goal: to make the expressions simpler.

$$\frac{\partial \tilde{p}_{nu}}{\partial M} = -\left[\left(C_{u,wg} - C_{wg,wg}\right)\frac{\partial \tilde{B}_{u}}{\partial \tilde{M}} + \left(C_{u,u} - 2C_{u,wg} + C_{wg,wg}\right)\frac{\partial \tilde{B}_{nu}}{\partial \tilde{M}} + \left(C_{u,wg} - C_{u,u}\right)\frac{\partial \tilde{B}_{wg}}{\partial \tilde{M}}\right]\bigg/ D \quad (3.62)$$

where D is defined as $D \equiv C_{nu,nu}C_{u,u} - 2C_{nu,nu}C_{u,wg} - C_{u,wg}{}^{2} + C_{nu,nu}C_{wg,wg} + C_{u,u}C_{wg,wg}$ and $C_{i,j} = \partial\tilde{B}_{i}/\partial\tilde{p}_{j} + \tilde{B}_{j}\partial\tilde{B}_{i}/\partial\tilde{M}$. We shall assume that $D > 0$.[38] We now substitute the (3.59)–(3.62) expressions into (3.54). Having done this, the Slutsky decomposition, $\partial\tilde{B}_{i}/\partial\tilde{p}_{k} = C_{i,k} - \tilde{B}_{k}\partial\tilde{B}_{i}/\partial\tilde{M}$, is again used to break up price responses. This leads to the cancelling out of a number of terms, ultimately yielding:

$$\frac{\partial \hat{B}_{wg}}{\partial M} = \frac{\partial \hat{B}_{u}}{\partial M} = \frac{\partial \hat{B}_{nu}}{\partial M} = \left[C_{nu,nu}\left(C_{wg,wg} - C_{u,wg}\right)\frac{\partial \tilde{B}_{u}}{\partial \tilde{M}} + \left(C_{u,u}C_{wg,wg} - C_{u,wg}{}^{2}\right)\frac{\partial \tilde{B}_{nu}}{\partial \tilde{M}} + \right.$$
$$\left. + C_{nu,nu}\left(C_{u,u} - C_{u,wg}\right)\frac{\partial \tilde{B}_{wg}}{\partial \tilde{M}}\right]\bigg/ D \quad (3.63)$$

Finally, and in order to give the expression for the comparative statics of the consumer's own contribution, we return to equation (3.7), which relates one's own contribution to characteristics. If we proceed to the total differentiation of equation (3.7) we get:

$$\frac{\partial B_{wg}}{\partial \varphi}d\varphi = \theta\,\frac{\partial q}{\partial \varphi}d\varphi \quad\quad (3.64)$$

Thus, we assign the effect of changes in the consumer's own contribution as income changes with the same sign as the final effect of changes in the restricted demand for warmglow – see results in Table 3.2. Even if the attributes are normal, so that $\partial\tilde{B}_{u}/\partial\tilde{M}$, $\partial\tilde{B}_{nu}/\partial\tilde{M}$ and $\partial\tilde{B}_{wg}/\partial\tilde{M}$ are positive, we are able to verify that there is no direct mechanism that implies the same nature on the restricted demand responses. Furthermore, we can observe that the sign of the contribution responses is not always predeterminate on analytical grounds. For example, if we admit that use and the warmglow are Hicksian complements, we can observe that (a) consumption of the public use and non-use characteristics; (b) the consumer's own contribution, together with his/her consumption of the (c) private warmglow characteristic may either fall or rise in response to an increase in income. Moreover, we are able to verify that, even if the attributes are normal, there is no direct mechanism that implies the same nature of his/her own contribution response. So under which conditions can we guarantee that q is also a normal good? What kind of preferences imply that q is a normal good? According to Table 3.2, we can reasonably expect that such a consumption behavioural pattern is more likely to happen, *ceteris paribus,* when use and warmglow characteristics are Hicksian substitutes or weak Hicksian complements.

---

[38] Further analysis is presented in Appendix A.

Table 3.2: Income effect

	$C_{u,wg} > 0$	$C_{u,wg} < 0$		
		$C_{wg,wg} < C_{u,wg} \wedge C_{u,u} < C_{u,wg}$	$C_{wg,wg} < C_{u,wg} < C_{u,u}$	$C_{u,u} < C_{u,wg} < C_{wg,wg}$
$\hat{B}_{u,M}, \hat{B}_{nu,M}, \hat{B}_{wg,M}$	+	+	+/–	+/–
q_M	+	+	+/–	+/–

Note: with $\hat{B}_{i,M} \equiv \partial \hat{B}_k / \partial M$ and $q_M \equiv \partial q / \partial M$.

If, however, we admit that the preferences are quasi-linear (qL), the utility function takes the form:

$$U\left(Y_c, B_u, B_{nu}, B_{wg}\right) = Y_c + G\left(B_u, B_{nu}, B_{wg}\right)$$

and the marginal rates of substitution between Y_c on the one hand and B_u, B_{nu} and B_{wg} on the other are independent of the value Y_c. Any increase in $\tilde{M}$, virtual income, would be spent entirely on Y_c, so that $\partial \tilde{Y}_c / \partial \tilde{M} = 1$ and $\partial \tilde{B}_u / \partial \tilde{M} = \partial \tilde{B}_{nu} / \partial \tilde{M} = \partial \tilde{B}_{wg} / \partial \tilde{M} = 0$. Such an assumption, while certainly extreme, is a commonly exploited device for removing income effects. In this case, it is clear from equation (3.63) that $\partial \hat{B}_{wg} / \partial M = \partial \hat{B}_u / \partial M = \partial \hat{B}_{nu} / \partial M = 0$ and $\partial q / \partial M = 0$.

3.4.1.2 A change in the ρ coefficient

Consider a change in the consumer use motivation, ρ. With the help of *Mathematica*, we are able to differentiate equations (3.49)–(3.52), break up the price responses into compensated and real income effects, solve the system of equations for changes in the quantities demanded and plug in the respective solutions in (3.54). This finally yields:[39]

$$\frac{\partial \hat{B}_u}{\partial \rho} = \left\{ -\bar{q}\left(C_{nu,nu}C_{u,wg} - C_{u,u}C_{wg,wg} + C_{u,wg}^2 - C_{nu,nu}C_{u,u}\right) + \tilde{p}_u\left(C_{nu,nu}\left(C_{u,wg}^2 - C_{u,u}C_{wg,wg}\right)\right) + \right.$$

$$+ Q_{wg}\left(C_{nu,nu}C_{u,u} - C_{nu,nu}C_{u,wg} - C_{u,wg}^2 + C_{u,u}C_{wg,wg}\right) + \left[\left(C_{nu,nu}C_{u,wg} + C_{nu,nu}C_{wg,wg}\right)\frac{\partial \tilde{B}_u}{\partial \tilde{M}} + \quad (3.65)\right.$$

$$+ \left(C_{u,u}C_{wg,wg} - C_{u,wg}^2\right)\frac{\partial \tilde{B}_{nu}}{\partial \tilde{M}} + \left(C_{nu,nu}C_{u,u} - C_{nu,nu}C_{u,wg}\right)\frac{\partial \tilde{B}_{wg}}{\partial \tilde{M}}\right](\bar{q} + B_{wg})\right\} / D$$

---

[39] A detailed mathematical analysis is presented in Appendix A.

$$\frac{\partial \hat{B}_{nu}}{\partial \rho} = \frac{\partial \hat{B}_{wg}}{\partial \rho} = \left\{ 2\bar{q}\left(C_{nu,nu}C_{u,wg} - C_{nu,nu}C_{wg,wg}\right) - Q_{wg}\left(C_{nu,nu}C_{wg,wg} - C_{nu,nu}C_{u,wg}\right) + \right.$$

$$+ \tilde{p}_u\left(C_{nu,nu}\left(C_{u,wg}{}^2 - C_{u,u}C_{wg,wg}\right)\right) + \left[\left(C_{nu,nu}C_{u,wg} + C_{nu,nu}C_{wg,wg}\right)\frac{\partial \tilde{B}_u}{\partial \tilde{M}} + \right. \tag{3.66}$$

$$\left.\left. + \left(C_{u,u}C_{wg,wg} - C_{u,wg}{}^2\right)\frac{\partial \tilde{B}_{nu}}{\partial \tilde{M}} + \left(C_{nu,nu}C_{u,u} - C_{nu,nu}C_{u,u}\right)\frac{\partial \tilde{B}_{wg}}{\partial \tilde{M}}\right]\left(\bar{q} + B_{wg}\right)\right\} \middle/ D$$

If preferences are qL, the income terms disappear, and thus the expressions simplify in a way that greatly helps to better understand the various forces at work. In that case, the comparative static expressions become:

$$\frac{\partial \hat{B}_u}{\partial \rho} = \left\{\left(\bar{q} + Q_{wg}\right)\left(C_{u,u}C_{wg,wg} - C_{nu,nu}C_{u,wg} - C_{u,wg}{}^2 + C_{nu,nu}C_{u,u}\right) + \right.$$

$$\left. + \tilde{p}_u\left(C_{nu,nu}\left(C_{u,wg}{}^2 - C_{u,u}C_{wg,wg}\right)\right)\right\} \middle/ D \tag{3.65-qL}$$

$$\frac{\partial \hat{B}_{nu}}{\partial \rho} = \frac{\partial \hat{B}_{wg}}{\partial \rho} = \left\{\left(2\bar{q} - Q_{wg}\right)\left(C_{nu,nu}C_{u,wg} - C_{nu,nu}C_{wg,wg}\right) + \right.$$

$$\left. + \tilde{p}_u\left(C_{nu,nu}\left(C_{u,wg}{}^2 - C_{u,u}C_{wg,wg}\right)\right)\right\} \middle/ D \tag{3.66-qL}$$

The question is now: What can we infer from equations (3.65-qL) and (3.66-qL) in terms of comparative statics of the consumer's own contribution? Can we guarantee an unequivocal sign of the change of ρ upon the level of financial contributions? Or, conversely, is the sign not defined? In order to give the expression for the comparative statics of the consumer's own contribution, we need to return to equation (3.7), which relates one's own contribution to characteristics. The final effects of changes in ρ on the consumption of the characteristics may be of either sign – see Table 3.3. However, and as we would expect, we can observe that the derivation of the ρ comparative static responses is less clear when examining the consumption of non-use benefits than when examining the consumption of the recreation benefits. According to Table 3.3, an increase in ρ always rises B_u with the exception of the situation where $C_{wg,wg} < C_{u,wg} < C_{u,u}$. In this case the sign is not determinate. Furthermore, the final effects of changes in ρ on the consumer's own contribution is also of either sign. As we can observe, the sign of the comparative static responses depends upon the complementary-substitution relationships across the different characteristics. But if use and the warmglow are Hicksian complements and $C_{u,u}$ is numerically large, then an increase in ρ raises q. This situation becomes of particular interest if we believe not only that the consumption of warmglow goes 'hand-in-hand' with the consumption of the use/recreational attributes of the Natural Park (that is warmglow and use characteristics are Hicksian complements), but also if we assume that the consumption of the use/recreational attributes is exceptionally sensitive to its own price.

Table 3.3: ρ coefficient (quasilinear preferences)

	$C_{u,wg} > 0$	$C_{u,wg} < 0$		
		$C_{wg.wg} < C_{u.wg} \wedge C_{u.u} < C_{u.wg}$	$C_{wg.wg} < C_{u.wg} < C_{u.u}$	$C_{u.u} < C_{u.wg} < C_{wg.wg}$
$\hat{B}_{u,\rho}$	+	+	+/−	+
$\hat{B}_{nu,\rho},\ \hat{B}_{wg,\rho}$	+/−	+/−	+/−	+
q_ρ	+/−	+/−	+/−	+

3.4.1.3 A change in the τ coefficient

Holding constant all parameters but τ, and solving for the changes in the virtual magnitudes with respect to τ, we finally get:

$$\frac{\partial \hat{B}_u}{\partial \tau} = \frac{\partial \hat{B}_{wg}}{\partial \tau} = \Big\{ 2\bar{q}\big(C_{u.wg}{}^2 - C_{u.u}C_{wg.wg}\big) + \tilde{p}_{nu}\big(C_{nu.nu}\big(C_{u.wg}{}^2 - C_{u.u}C_{wg.wg}\big)\big) +$$
$$+ B_{wg}\big(C_{u.wg}{}^2 - C_{u.u}C_{wg.wg}\big) + \Big[\big(C_{nu.nu}C_{u.wg} + C_{nu.nu}C_{wg.wg}\big)\frac{\partial \tilde{B}_u}{\partial \tilde{M}} +$$
$$+ \big(C_{u.u}C_{wg.wg} - C_{u.wg}{}^2\big)\frac{\partial \tilde{B}_{nu}}{\partial \tilde{M}} + \big(C_{nu.nu}C_{u.u} - C_{nu.nu}C_{u.wg}\big)\frac{\partial \tilde{B}_{wg}}{\partial \tilde{M}}\Big]\big(\bar{q} + B_{wg}\big)\Big\}\Big/ D \tag{3.67}$$

$$\frac{\partial \hat{B}_{nu}}{\partial \tau} = \Big\{ \bar{q}\big(2C_{nu.nu}C_{u.u} + 2C_{nu.nu}C_{wg.wg} - 4C_{nu.nu}C_{u.wg}\big) + \tilde{p}_{nu}\big(C_{nu.nu}\big(C_{u.wg}{}^2 - C_{u.u}C_{wg.wg}\big)\big) +$$
$$+ B_{wg}\big(C_{nu.nu}C_{u.u} + C_{nu.nu}C_{wg.wg} - 2C_{nu.nu}C_{u.wg}\big) + \Big[\big(C_{nu.nu}C_{u.wg} + C_{nu.nu}C_{wg.wg}\big)\frac{\partial \tilde{B}_u}{\partial \tilde{M}} +$$
$$+ \big(C_{u.u}C_{wg.wg} - C_{u.wg}{}^2\big)\frac{\partial \tilde{B}_{nu}}{\partial \tilde{M}} + \big(C_{nu.nu}C_{u.u} - C_{nu.nu}C_{u.wg}\big)\frac{\partial \tilde{B}_{wg}}{\partial \tilde{M}}\Big]\big(\bar{q} + B_{wg}\big)\Big\}\Big/ D \tag{3.68}$$

If preferences are quasilinear (qL), these expressions (3.67)–(3.68) simplify, and we can write:

$$\frac{\partial \hat{B}_u}{\partial \tau} = \frac{\partial \hat{B}_{wg}}{\partial \tau} = \Big\{ \big(2\bar{q} + B_{wg}\big)\big(C_{u.wg}{}^2 - C_{u.u}C_{wg.wg}\big) + \tilde{p}_{nu}\big(C_{nu.nu}\big(C_{u.wg}{}^2 - C_{u.u}C_{wg.wg}\big)\big)\Big\}\Big/ D \tag{3.67-qL}$$

$$\frac{\partial \hat{B}_{nu}}{\partial \tau} = \Big\{ \big(4\bar{q} + B_{wg}\big)\big(C_{nu.nu}C_{u.u} + C_{nu.nu}C_{wg.wg} - 2C_{nu.nu}C_{u.wg}\big) +$$
$$+ \tilde{p}_{nu}\big(C_{nu.nu}\big(C_{u.wg}{}^2 - C_{u.u}C_{wg.wg}\big)\big)\Big\}\Big/ D \tag{3.68-qL}$$

Table 3.4: τ coefficient (quasilinear preferences)

	$C_{u,wg} > 0$	$C_{u,wg} < 0$		
		$C_{wg,wg} < C_{u,wg} \wedge C_{u,u} < C_{u,wg}$	$C_{wg,wg} < C_{u,wg} < C_{u,u}$	$C_{u,u} < C_{u,wg} < C_{wg,wg}$
$\hat{B}_{nu,\tau}$	+	+	+/−	+/−
$\hat{B}_{u,\tau}$, $\hat{B}_{wg,\tau}$	+/−	+/−	+/−	+/−
q_{τ}	+/−	+/−	+/−	+/−

The final sign of the individual's consumption of attributes is not always determined. It depends upon the complementary-substitution relationships across the different characteristics – see results in Table 3.4. However, and reiterating once again what one could initially expect, we see that the derivation of the τ comparative static responses are clearer when examining the consumption of the non-use benefits than when examining the consumption of the other characteristics. As a matter of fact, little can be said about the direction of the comparative static properties of B_u, B_{wg} and B_{nu}. Yet, when use and the warmglow are Hicksian substitutes (or weak complements), an increase of τ unambiguously raises the consumption of the non-use characteristic. Not much can be said about the direction of q_{τ}, that is, the individual's own contribution may either fall or raise in response to an increase in τ.

3.4.1.4 A change in the θ coefficient

Running the same computational exercise as described in the previous sections, but now holding constant all parameters except θ, we finally get:

$$
\frac{\partial \hat{B}_u}{\partial \theta} = \frac{\partial \hat{B}_{nu}}{\partial \theta} = \left\{ B_{wg} \left(C_{nu,nu} C_{u,wg} - C_{nu,nu} C_{u,u} \right) + \tilde{p}_{wg} \left\{ C_{nu,nu} \left(C_{u,wg}^2 - C_{u,u} C_{wg,wg} \right) + \right. \right.
$$
$$
\left. + \left[\left(C_{nu,nu} C_{u,wg} + C_{nu,nu} C_{wg,wg} \right) \frac{\partial \tilde{B}_u}{\partial \tilde{M}} + \right. \right.
$$
$$
\left. \left. + \left(C_{u,u} C_{wg,wg} - C_{u,wg}^2 \right) \frac{\partial \tilde{B}_{nu}}{\partial \tilde{M}} + \left(C_{nu,nu} C_{u,u} - C_{nu,nu} C_{u,wg} \right) \frac{\partial \tilde{B}_{wg}}{\partial \tilde{M}} \right] B_{wg} \right\} \right\} \Big/ D
$$

(3.69)

$$
\frac{\partial \hat{B}_{wg}}{\partial \theta} = \left\{ B_{wg} \left(C_{nu,nu} C_{wg,wg} - C_{nu,nu} C_{u,wg} - C_{u,wg}^2 + C_{u,u} C_{wg,wg} \right) + \right.
$$
$$
+ \tilde{p}_{wg} \left\{ C_{nu,nu} \left(C_{u,wg}^2 - C_{u,u} C_{wg,wg} \right) + \left[\left(C_{nu,nu} C_{u,wg} + C_{nu,nu} C_{wg,wg} \right) \frac{\partial \tilde{B}_u}{\partial \tilde{M}} + \right. \right.
$$
$$
\left. \left. + \left(C_{u,u} C_{wg,wg} - C_{u,wg}^2 \right) \frac{\partial \tilde{B}_{nu}}{\partial \tilde{M}} + \left(C_{nu,nu} C_{u,u} - C_{nu,nu} C_{u,wg} \right) \frac{\partial \tilde{B}_{wg}}{\partial \tilde{M}} \right] B_{wg} \right\} \right\} \Big/ D
$$

(3.70)

If preferences are quasilinear (qL), these expressions simplify, and we rewrite (3.69)–(3.70) as follows:

$$\frac{\partial \hat{B}_u}{\partial \theta} = \frac{\partial \hat{B}_{nu}}{\partial \theta} = \left\{ Q_{wg}\left(C_{nu.nu}C_{u.wg} - C_{nu.nu}C_{u.u}\right) + \tilde{p}_{wg}\left(C_{nu.nu}\left(C_{u.wg}^{\;2} - C_{u.u}C_{wg.wg}\right)\right) \right\}/D \qquad \text{(3.69-qL)}$$

$$\frac{\partial \hat{B}_{wg}}{\partial \theta} = \left\{ B_{wg}\left(C_{nu.nu}C_{wg.wg} - C_{nu.nu}C_{u.wg} - C_{u.wg}^{\;2} + C_{u.u}C_{wg.wg}\right) + \right. \qquad \text{(3.70-qL)}$$
$$\left. + \tilde{p}_{wg}\left(C_{nu.nu}\left(C_{u.wg}^{\;2} - C_{u.u}C_{wg.wg}\right)\right) \right\}/D$$

Once more, we can see that (a) the final signs are not always determined; they depend upon the complementary-substitution relationships across the different characteristics, and (b) the derivation of the θ comparative static responses is much clearer when examining the consumption of the warmglow characteristics than when examining the consumption of the public characteristics – see results in Table 3.5. How about the comparative static properties of the consumer's own contribution: will an individual who shows a higher propensity to contribute to good causes, *ceteris paribus*, always be willing to contribute more to the provision of the public good? As before, when totally differentiating (3.7), we get:

$$\frac{\partial B_{wg}}{\partial \theta} d\theta = \theta \, \frac{\partial q}{\partial \theta} d\theta + q d\theta \qquad \text{(3.71)}$$

Since θ changes, it is no longer true that the sign of the effects of changes in the consumer's own contribution as the warmglow motivation changes is unambiguously given by the sign of the comparative static responses of the private characteristic. This means that we can not assign the direction of q_θ with the direction of $\hat{B}_{wg,\theta}$. Therefore, the final assessment of the direction of q_θ will depend of the magnitudes of the underlying driving forces, and not much can be said about them as we bear in mind the assumed hypothesis concerning the complementary-substitution relationships across the characteristics.

Table 3.5: θ coefficient (quasilinear preferences)

	$C_{u,wg} > 0$	$C_{u,wg} < 0$		
		$C_{wg.wg} < C_{u.wg} \wedge C_{u.u} < C_{u.wg}$	$C_{wg.wg} < C_{u.wg} < C_{u.u} < 0$	$C_{u.u} < C_{u.wg} < C_{wg.wg}$
$\hat{B}_{u,\theta}, \hat{B}_{nu,\theta}$	+/–	+/–	+	+/–
$\hat{B}_{wg,\theta}$	+	+/–	+	+/–
q_θ	+/–	+/–	+/–	+/–

3.4.1.5 A change in $\bar{q}$

Holding constant all parameters but $\bar{q}$, and solving for the changes in the virtual magnitudes with respect to $\bar{q}$, we finally get,

$$\frac{\partial \hat{B}_u}{\partial \bar{q}} = \frac{\partial \hat{B}_{nu}}{\partial \bar{q}} = \left\{ \left(\tilde{p}_u + \tilde{p}_{nu} \right) \left[C_{nu,nu} \left(C_{wg,wg} - C_{u,wg} \right) \frac{\partial \tilde{B}_u}{\partial \tilde{M}} + \left(C_{u,u} C_{wg,wg} - C_{u,wg}{}^2 \right) \frac{\partial \tilde{B}_{nu}}{\partial \tilde{M}} + \right. \right.$$
$$\left. \left. + C_{nu,nu} \left(C_{u,u} - C_{u,wg} \right) \frac{\partial \tilde{B}_{wg}}{\partial \tilde{M}} \right] + \left(C_{nu,nu} C_{u,u} - C_{nu,nu} C_{u,wg} \right) \right\} \Big/ D \tag{3.72}$$

$$\frac{\partial \hat{B}_{wg}}{\partial \bar{q}} = \left\{ \left(\tilde{p}_u + \tilde{p}_{nu} \right) \left[C_{nu,nu} \left(C_{wg,wg} - C_{u,wg} \right) \frac{\partial \tilde{B}_u}{\partial \tilde{M}} + \left(C_{u,u} C_{wg,wg} - C_{u,wg}{}^2 \right) \frac{\partial \tilde{B}_{nu}}{\partial \tilde{M}} + \right. \right.$$
$$\left. \left. + C_{nu,nu} \left(C_{u,u} - C_{u,wg} \right) \frac{\partial \tilde{B}_{wg}}{\partial \tilde{M}} \right] + \left(C_{nu,nu} C_{u,wg} + C_{u,wg}{}^2 - C_{nu,nu} C_{wg,wg} - C_{u,u} C_{wg,wg} \right) \right\} \Big/ D \tag{3.73}$$

The question is then: how can equations (3.72)–(3.73) help us to derive the comparative static responses? Since the individual consumer only contributes to the protection of the Natural Area on account of the attributes that it generates, we can use these expressions to infer the effect of $\bar{q}$ on the level of the individual's own contribution. It is clear that (the numerators of) (3.72)– (3.73) reiterate the presence – as suggested before by equation (3.24) – of two major driving forces underlying the final comparative static responses: (a) the income effect, captured by the first three terms associated to $\partial \tilde{B}_u / \partial \tilde{M}$, $\partial \tilde{B}_{nu} / \partial \tilde{M}$ and $\partial \tilde{B}_{wg} / \partial \tilde{M}$, and (b) the compensated price responses, captured by the last terms of the numerator of (3.72) and (3.73). If preferences are qL, the income terms disappear, and expressions (3.72)–(3.73) simplify to:

$$\frac{\partial \hat{B}_u}{\partial \bar{q}} = \frac{\partial \hat{B}_{nu}}{\partial \bar{q}} = \left(\tilde{p}_u + \tilde{p}_{nu} \right) \left(C_{nu,nu} C_{u,u} - C_{nu,nu} C_{u,wg} \right) \Big/ D \tag{3.72-qL}$$

$$\frac{\partial \hat{B}_{wg}}{\partial \bar{q}} = \left(\tilde{p}_u + \tilde{p}_{nu} \right) \left(C_{nu,nu} C_{u,wg} + C_{u,wg}{}^2 - C_{nu,nu} C_{wg,wg} - C_{u,u} C_{wg,wg} \right) \Big/ D \tag{3.73-qL}$$

Moreover, we totally differentiate equation (3.7), holding constant all parameters except $\bar{q}$, and get:

$$\frac{\partial B_{wg}}{\partial \bar{q}} d\bar{q} = \theta \, \frac{\partial q}{\partial \bar{q}} d\bar{q} \tag{3.74}$$

Table 3.6: $\bar{q}$ effect (quasilinear preferences)

	$C_{u,wg} > 0$	$C_{u,wg} < 0$		
		$C_{wg,wg} < C_{u,wg} \wedge C_{u,u} < C_{u,wg}$	$C_{wg,wg} < C_{u,wg} < C_{u,u}$	$C_{u,u} < C_{u,wg} < C_{wg,wg}$
$\hat{B}_{u,q^{-j}}$, $\hat{B}_{nu,q^{-j}}$	+	+	−	+
$\hat{B}_{wg,q^{-j}}$	−	−	−	−
$q_{q^{-j}}$	−	−	−	−

thus assigning the effect of changes in consumer's own contribution as $\bar{q}$ changes with the same sign as the final effect of changes in the restricted demand for warmglow – see results in Table 3.6.

We can observe that the change in $\bar{q}$ reveals two interesting response patterns. On the one hand, we can observe that an increase of the other individuals' contributions increases with the consumption of use and non-use characteristics. This situation reflects the public good nature of the use and non-use characteristics: an increase of the other individuals' contributions will, *ceteris paribus*, increase the provision of the public good, Q. Therefore, even without any contribution from oneself, the consumer can consume units of the public characteristics generated by activities of others.[40] On the other hand, we can observe that not only the individual's consumption of the private characteristic, but also his/her own contribution will fall as the rest of the community's contribution rises. How can we interpret this situation? This situation is precisely the case in which the reaction curve, $q(\bar{q})$, is negatively sloped. This result allows us to sign the whole expression (3.24) as negative and assert negative Nash-Cournot reaction curves.[41] Finally, we would like make explicit that the comparative static results with respect to $\bar{q}$ do not crucially depend on the assumed payment vehicle.

3.4.2 Comparative static results: a bridge with the empirical results

A formal analysis of the consumer motivations coefficients, and their relationship with the consumer characteristics, is presented in Chapter 10. In Chapter 11 we confront the results of the present theoretic/mathematical section with the econometric results obtained from the empirical analysis of survey answers. Therefore, Chapter 11 is important in shedding some light upon the nature of the comparative static results and thus giving a more precise answer upon the direction, and magnitude, of the effect of respective consumer motivation coefficients.

---

[40] The only situation where we can have a negative direction is when the warmglow and use characteristics are Hicksian complements and $C_{u,wg} < C_{u,u}$. The situation will no longer obtain if we consider $C_{u,wg} \cong 0$.

[41] We should emphasize that this result is inherently due to price compensated substitution responses, since conventional income effects are absent by virtue of the quasi-linearity assumption.

3.5 Conclusions

In this chapter we explored an analytical setting where we could interpret the consumer's contributions to an environmental project, as stated in the instrument survey. We modelled the public good in terms of its provision of use and non-use service flows plus the warmglow associated with the act of giving *per se*. Furthermore, we developed the concept of consumer motivation functions to structure consumer preferences. The underlying premise is that one can draw a portrait of the structure of consumer preferences in terms of the consumer's motivational profile. We characterize consumer preferences in terms of the consumer recreation, ethical and warmglow motivation profiles. In this context, individual consumer contributions to the protection of the Natural Area are interpreted in terms of the characteristics that they generate. The stated amount depends upon consumer recreation, ethical and warmglow motivation profiles. Two payment mechanisms were studied: voluntary contributions and a tax referendum. We also explored the comparative static properties of the consumer's own contribution level and assessed how the differences in the consumer preference structure are reflected in the contribution's level. Since we admit that the consumer's preferences were originally mapped in the characteristics space, we derived the comparative static responses by exploring the concept of virtual prices and income. The sign of the expressions for the comparative statics of the consumer's own contribution were, most of the time, ambiguous. This means that we cannot assign the direction of the changes. Strong simplifications – namely on the choice of a specific utility function and functional form for the consumer motivation functions – are necessary to understand the various forces at work. According to the comparative static results it was clear that the final assessment of the direction depends on the Hicksian complementary-substitution magnitudes assumed across the different characteristics.

PART II
Survey Design and Implementation

Chapter
4
PRELIMINARY DESIGN RESEARCH

4.1 Introduction

In this chapter we focus on the construction of the survey as a measurement instrument for assessing the individual's valuation of the Alentejo Natural Park. The development of the survey instrument took about 10 months, starting in early November 1996 and finishing in September 1997, the period in which the final survey was used in the field. The fieldwork was conducted by the Survey Research Department of the Portuguese Catholic University that contributed professional interviewers, provided field supervision and exercised quality control over the sample.[42] The central part of the survey instrument establishes a hypothetical market for eliciting the respondent's willingness to pay for the prevention of tourism/commercial development plans at the Alentejo Natural Park. Other questions, preceding and following the scenario description, ask for the respondent's attitudes and beliefs regarding the protection of the environment, the respondent's motivation structure and socio-economic characteristics.

This chapter is divided into three sections corresponding, respectively, to three stages of the survey instrument's development. In section 4.2 we focus on the formulation of the policy scenarios and present the protection plans as described in the survey. In section 4.3 we review the choices concerning the design of a CV questionnaire, namely the choice of the payment vehicle. Finally, in section 4.4 we describe preliminary survey design research work. This stage, which involved working with focus groups and the execution of pilot studies, was crucial for the success of the CV application.

4.2 Scenario formulation

The present scenario formulations deal with the economic valuation of the use and non-use protection benefits of the *Área Natural do Sudoeste Alentejano e Costa Vicentina*, one of the

---

[42] The survey research project was developed in co-operation with the Portuguese Institute for Conservation of the Nature *(Instituto de Conservação da Natureza – ICN)*. The Survey Research Department of the Portuguese Catholic University *(Centro de Sondagens de Opinião Pública da Universidade Católica Portuguesa – CESOP)* was responsible for carrying out the survey.

least urbanized littoral areas of Portugal – see Figure 4.1. As in many other countries, Portugal has seen an intensification of the conflicts and disputes over the alternative use possibilities of natural sites (MARN 1995). On one hand we find the Portuguese Governmental Agency for Nature Protection (*Instituto Conservação da Natureza – ICN*) that advocates the preservation of the natural envioronment. Recently, more specifically in 1995, ICN established the *Parque Natural do Sudoeste Alentejano e Costa Vicentina*[43] (MARN 1995a). The Alentejo Natural Park is a protected area where roads, commercial and tourism development, mechanical equipment and other improvements are prohibited (MARN 1995b). On the other hand we see the tourism industry, together with the local municipalities, lobbying in favour of the development of the tourism potential of the Natural Park and the creation of employment in the area.

The issue we wish to address is the determination of the value that Portuguese households place on keeping the area free from the various tourism development plans recently proposed by the tourism industry. Since the major values in dispute are typically referred to as non-use or existence values,[44] we selected the contingent valuation method as the measurement approach since it is the valuation technique capable of including the non-use value component when measuring the total value of the natural resource. Following the NOAA panel (1993) and survey research guidelines (Mitchell and Carson 1989; Groves 1989; Friedman and Sunder 1994), the description of the policy scenario plans was extensively analysed and pilots were organized to assess the overall quality of the questionnaire. The objective is to ensure a good formulation of the policy scenarios and thus guarantee the comprehension of the valuation exercise in the respondent's eyes.[45]

4.2.1 Description of the protection scenarios: research goals

When formulating the protection plans, we sought to fulfil the following goals:

1. scenario accuracy;
2. scenario comprehensibility;
3. scenario plausibility; and
4. an overall perception by the respondents of time balance and neutrality of wording.

The first goal requires a careful description of the environmental quality changes involved in the various environmental protection programmes. The description was based on multidisciplinary work that was undertaken with biologists with solid experience in the field, making use of all available scientific information.[46]

---

[43] Shortly, the Alentejo Natural Park (ANP).

[44] The measurement of the non-use or existence values plays an important role in the proposed valuation exercise because the Portuguese may be willing to pay to continue to keep the Alentejo Natural Park free from any tourism development independently of any recreational use.

[45] One of the difficulties in designing a constructed market was reaching a balance with respect to the level of information provided to the respondent: too much information may drive the respondent's attention away, but, on the other hand, 'what is out of sight, is out of mind' (Tversky and Kahneman 1973; Woo 1996).

[46] The scientific facts were provided in discussions with Dr Pedro Beja, head of the Department for Nature Conservation at the Alentejo Natural Park.

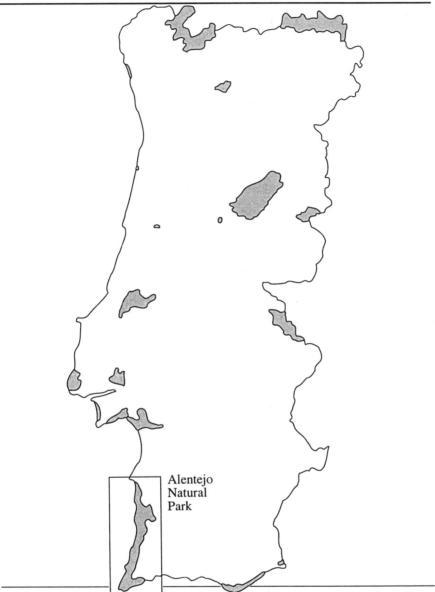

Figure 4.1: Alentejo Natural Park lies in the south-west of Portugal

So as to ensure as far as possible that respondents understood the issue correctly, we used visual material to enhance the information conveyed by the narrative description. This included diagrams, photos and manipulated photography. The latter required the help of an expert in image editing and manipulation techniques.

The second goal is a core issue in survey design research: respondents from all educational levels and with varied life experiences should be able to understand the valuation exercise. Language, wording and visual material is pre-tested in focus groups. Given (a) the relatively high Portuguese illiteracy rate and (b) the low degree of familiarity of Portuguese households with the CV surveys, in the survey pre-testing we focused on population samples which we would expect to have more difficulties in understanding the scenario's description and the valuation exercise. Therefore, during the pre-tests we targeted samples relatively advanced in age and with relatively low education. This work was revealed to be crucial for reaching a comprehensive scenario description.

The third goal implies that respondents find the protection scenarios and payment vehicles convincing and therefore take the elicitation question seriously. To this end, we adopted the referendum format which asks each respondent to make a judgement as to whether they would vote for or against the described programme which, when adopted, would cost their household a certain amount of money.

The fourth goal refers to the achievement of a time balance in the execution of the questionnaire and neutrality in the wording of the survey narrative. On one hand the questionnaire format should not be too extensive. If the interview were too long the interviewers would have serious difficulties in keeping the interest of the respondents and this would drive away respondents who face stronger time constraints. On the other hand, the information and wording in the instrument should not be perceived by respondents as promoting the interests of any particular party. Furthermore, interviewers were told, during the training sessions, that they could not say to the respondents that the Portuguese Ministry of Environment was sponsoring the survey.

4.2.2 The Alentejo Natural Park: wilderness areas, recreational areas, and tourism development

Early in the survey design we engaged in interdisciplinary co-operation with the Park's Management Agency staff. This first stage revealed itself to be crucial for the development of the survey instrument, namely in getting at an accurate, balanced and plausible scenario description. Careful wording and meaningful language was provided without making the questionnaire so complex that its understanding was beyond the ability or interest of many respondents. We were able to reduce the complex information provided by the legislation (MARN 1995a) concerning the zoning of the Park and to characterize the Natural Park in terms of two major zones (or attributes): the Wilderness Areas (WA) and the Recreational Areas (RA) – see Table 4.1.

Table 4.1: Identification of Alentejo Natural Park's value component

---

WA: Wilderness Areas (non-use value component)

RA: Recreational Areas (use value component)

The first zone refers to the geographical area of the Park that is allocated to the protection of the local biodiversity: the visitors' access is here restricted. Roads, commercial development, mechanical equipment and other improvements are prohibited – the Park's non-use value component (see Figure 4.2). The second category refers to the geographical area of

Figure 4.2: Wilderness Area (integral reserve at the Ribeira de Ceixe)

the Park that is allocated for human use: it is open to all visitors and here able they are to enjoy a set of recreational activities in a natural environment – the Park's use value component (see Figure 4.3). The next step consisted of the identification of the major development threat(s) to the preservation of the Alentejo Natural Park. This task played a crucial role in the formulation of a plausible scenario description.

Figure 4.3: Recreational Area (beach near Porto Corvo)

The geographical position of the Alentejo Natural Park, on the south-west coastline, which is one of the least urbanized littoral areas of Portugal, and its proximity to the Algarve, a region responsible for a major income source in the tourism sector of Portugal, make this natural site a highly valuable asset for the tourism industry. Therefore, important tourism lobbies, together with the support of the local municipalities, have requested the introduction of urbanization plans for the commercial and tourism development of the Natural Park and the creation of employment in the area. This is well-known among the Portuguese population since the media, for one reason or another, often publicize this issue. In this context, we decided to mark commercial and tourism development as the alternative use to the current protection of the Alentejo Natural Park.

The introduction of the commercial development plans in the Alentejo Natural Park will involve describing both WA and RA zones in two different states, respectively 'policy on' and 'policy – see Table 4.2.

Table 4.2: Identification of the two alternative allocations of the Alentejo Natural Park

---

'Policy on': continue with the protection of the Alentejo Natural Park
'Policy off': tourism development in the Alentejo Natural Park

---

The state identified as *policy on* describes the situation of the WA and RA in a scenario characterized by the prevention of commercial development plans in ANP as described in the survey instrument. On the contrary, the state *policy off* describes the two attributes, the WA and RA, in a scenario characterized by the introduction of commercial development plans.

In order to make the commercial development scenario as real as possible, we transformed Figure 4.2 and Figure 4.3, respectively a photo from a Wilderness and a Recreational Area, with the use of computer manipulation techniques so as to help visualize the infrastructural changes involved with commercial development (see Figures 4.4 and 4.5).

Figure 4.4: Tourism development of a Wilderness Area

Figure 4.5: Tourism development of a Recreational Area

Given the present zoning we were able to design three survey versions corresponding to three protection policy options. First, we have the WA tourism development scenario; then we have the RA tourism development scenario; finally, we consider a scenario version which is characterized by the tourism development of both WA and RA, that is, a total opening up of the Natural Park area to tourism and the real estate industry (see Table 4.3).

Table 4.3: Identification of the protection scenarios

Version 1: Preventing tourism development in WA	
Policy on:	Policy off:
WA: protected	WA: developed
RA: protected	RA: protected

Version 2: Preventing tourism development in RA	
Policy om:	Policy off:
WA: protected	WA: protected
RA: protected	RA: developed

Version 3: Preventing tourism development in WA and RA	
Policy on:	Policy off:
WA: protected	WA: developed
RA: protected	RA: developed

4.3 Key design issues

The survey instrument's goal is to assess the economic value of the preservation of the Alentejo Natural Park by estimating the monetized gain in utility experienced by each respondent as a result of preventing the introduction of tourism development plans as described in the questionnaire. Successfully describing the protection plans is only half the problem. Decisions must also be taken concerning the choice of the welfare measurement measure, the elicitation method, the nature of the payment vehicle, the market conditions as well as the agents involved in the transaction.

4.3.1 Welfare measure

As far as the welfare measure is concerned, we followed closely the NOAA panel's suggestions and adopted willingness to pay (WTP) to prevent the introduction of the commercial development plans. The WTP is characterized as being a conservative choice and, in this way, increases the reliability of the stated responses (NOAA 1993). Furthermore, when subscribing to the WTP, we compel individuals to look forward, not backward: paying to prevent future damage in the Natural Park thus confronts them with a situation that closely mimics a market situation.[47] Moreover, the WTP contains the presumption that the individual has an obligation to accept the introduction of the commercial development plans in the Natural Park and must make a payment if the new (and lower) environmental quality level is not to be pursued. That is to say, there is not an implied property right in the status quo but rather an implied property right in the change. This distribution of property rights depicts the situation well: most of the geographical area of the Alentejo Natural Park is private property (owned by a handful of real estate developers).

The willingness to accept (WTA) would be an alternative welfare measure. In this situation the property right of the ANP would be spread across Portuguese families[48] and therefore the respondents would require a compensation if the new (and lower) environmental quality level is to be attained. When the WTA is adopted the respondents are asked to state a monetary amount that would make them 'accept' the introduction of the commercial development plans in the Alentejo Natural Park. However, this implicit property rights distribution does not correspond to reality: the ANP is not state owned but rather privately owned, and the (handful of) owners want to develop it: they are the major lobbying group for the tourism industry in the area.

4.3.2 Elicitation question format

We adopted a referendum elicitation question format (NOAA 1993). When applying the referendum format the respondent is faced with a specific cost and asked whether s/he is willing to pay that amount, a yes or no response, to prevent the development plan (Cameron and James 1987; Cameron 1988; and Cameron 1991). In the present study, we used the double-bounded dichotomous choice question (Cameron and Quiggin 1994): each respondent is asked to give a yes or no response to a second pre-specified bid amount which is higher (lower) if the initial bid was accepted (rejected). In using both answers to infer the respondent's maximum WTP we increase the statistical efficiency of the estimates; it

---

[47] In daily market situations the respondents are used to facing a market price for a given commodity and their decision is either to buy or not to buy.

[48] This is the same as saying that the ANP would be state owned.

produces, when compared with the single-bounded dichotomous choice question, a tighter confidence interval for the WTP estimates for any fixed sample size (Hanemann *et al.* 1991).

4.3.3 Design of the bid vector

The use of referendum questions involves the design of a range of bids, that is, the development of a scheme that specifies, for each respondent, the initial bid and the respective follow-ups. Thus, we have to decide how many bids to use, the lowest and the highest bid, how the bids should be spaced and what proportion of respondents should be offered each bid. The empirical evidence has shown that the number, range and intervals of bids offered in the discrete choice survey can affect the estimates of the value of the good (Cooper 1993). Formal methods of finding an optimal range and intervals of bids also contribute to improve bid design, for example in Duffield and Patterson (1991), Kanninen (1993a, 1993b) and Alberini (1995). Given that the heavy statistical procedures involved with optimal bid design methods are not always associated with satisfactory results, in the present study the bid amounts are initially chosen in a *ad hoc* way and submitted to rigorous statistical analysis during the pilots executed during the pre-testing (Cooper and Loomis 1992; Carson *et al.* 1992; Kriström 1995).

We rely on pre-testing in order to establish a reasonable range setting of bids, that is, in order to cover most of the values respondents are likely to hold. In the pilots, open-ended questions are designed in order to obtain a sharper idea of the respondent's WTP distribution.[49] This information is taken into account when designing the interval of the bids offered in the final survey instrument. Most of the studies use 10 to 15 bid amounts, although some use up to 20. We applied 12 bid amounts in the final questionnaire – see Table 4.4.

Table 4.4: Bid amounts used in the survey instruments (in PTE)

Bid Cards	P-9: Initial Bid	P-10: Increased Bid	P-11: Decreased Bid
Card 1	1 200	3 600	600
Card 2	2 400	4 800	1 200
Card 3	4 800	9 600	2 400
Card 4	9 600	24 000	4 800

In each of the four bid cards, the increased (decreased) bid is the double of (half) the initial bid. The exceptions are the lower and the upper bid cards, which received special attention. We designed the highest bid such that no more than 10 per cent of the respondents answer yes. Boman and Bostedt (1995) in a CV application in Sweden suggest, as 'rule of the thumb', that if less than 10 per cent of the respondents answer yes to the highest bid, then the bid vector has captured the range of the WTP distribution well. As far as the lower bid range is concerned, we designed the upper bid as the triple, and not the double, of the initial bid. This is because during the first pilots we found that almost all respondents who answered yes to the initial bid of the first card also answered yes to the second bid (initially set at double). This situation created estimation problems since these answers provided little information with respect to the localization of the true WTP of the respondents. Therefore, we increased the second upper bid and, as we would expect, we found more reverse answering patterns, that is, yes followed by a no, than before.

---

[49] This information is for respondents who answer yes to both questions.

4.3.4 Payment vehicle

With respect to the choice of a payment vehicle, the crucial point is to find a scheme that best fits the environmental change in a way that: first, creates a situation which convinces the respondents to accept the payment vehicle as a likely way to pay for the described programme;[50] second, is associated with a fair method of paying for the programme: all respondents, independently of their socio-economic characteristics, life experiences or place of residence, would be equally compelled to pay;[51] and third, is viewed as appropriate for the good being valued and not subject to waste and fraud. Therefore, and following preliminary research hints, we adopted a national tax and a voluntary contribution as payment vehicles and rejected other choices such as higher gasoline prices or higher prices on a basket of goods. The reason why the present study works with two payment vehicles is explained by the fact that we are interested in exploring CVM methodological issues, namely the internal validity of the WTP estimates by testing the eventual presence of a payment vehicle bias (Rowe *et al.* 1980; Greenley *et al.* 1981).[52]

4.3.5 Market conditions and agents involved

Finally, we had to decide upon the market conditions as well as upon the agents involved in the transaction. All markets and all monetary transactions occur in a social context. Since this market is rather unfamiliar to the respondents, its conditions have to be carefully described. First, the questionnaire makes it clear that the money raised will be managed by the Institute for Nature Conservation, the Portuguese national governmental institution responsible for the management of the Portuguese protected areas, and exclusively allocated to the protection of the Alentejo Natural Park, respecting the protection programme as described in the survey instrument. Second, the respondents are informed that the current budget allocated by the Portuguese government is not sufficient and without any further funds it is no longer possible to continue to guarantee to all Portuguese that ANP will be free from any tourism development. Third, in the questionnaire it is also made clear that the protection of the Alentejo Natural Park is a national interest issue and that all Portuguese households will be asked to pay to avoid the introduction of the commercial development plan as described in the survey instrument. Finally, we chose the number of years over which payments would be collected. We did not work with a multiyear payment mechanism since it is very difficult to guarantee the respondent's 'commitment' toward the last stream of payments.[53] Therefore we adopted a one-year payment plan. Nevertheless, periodic monthly payments will be explicitly mentioned in the questionnaire so as to make the budget constraint less tight, specially among poor households.

---

[50] Plausibility is one of NOAA's pillar recommendations. This issue is closely related with the hypothetical situation bias. This bias refers to the possibility that the description of the hypothetical situation differs systematically from the actual situation, and that these differences would result in systematic errors. One of the differences could be perceived as the certainty of paying.

[51] For exapmle, a gas tax will not be relevant to households without a car.

[52] Chapter 8 describes the testing procedures developed to investigate the effect of the payment vehicle on the WTP answers.

[53] This way we also eliminate the need to determine what rate ought to be applied to discount the future payments.

4.4 Preliminary survey design research

4.4.1 Focus groups

At this stage of the instrument's development we conducted two series of focus groups: group discussions, centred around ten elements, where a moderator introduces topics for discussion. This qualitative research is used because it is an efficient way to explore people's beliefs, attitudes and knowledge about the subject matter, obtaining from their reactions a basis for language formulation and scenario description for use on a first draft of the questionnaire. The series took place in Lisbon, at the Social Communications Department of the Portuguese Catholic University, on 6 and 14 February 1997. Each session lasted about two and half hours. All participants were 18 years and older and were recruited by the Survey Research Department of the Portuguese Catholic University (CESOP).

First session

In the first focus group session, general topics concerning major social and economic problems were discussed. We explored the participants' opinion with respect to a wide range of governmental policy actions. We continued the discussion by introducing environmental protection policy issues and by focusing the participants' attention on issues concerning the conservation of natural areas in Portugal. Here the discussions explored the participants' knowledge of the Portuguese National System of Protected Areas and their beliefs regarding how the 'success' of Alentejo Natural Park helps to prevent tourism development in such an area of Portugal.

Second session

In the second focus group we conducted more detailed discussions. We introduced some material that we were thinking of including in the questionnaire draft, and registered the group feedback. We focused special attention on the formulations of the different protection plans. We registered how participants perceived the damage involved. This allowed us to explore the conceptualization of the environmental protection programme in the participants' eyes and in this way we formed an initial idea about the plausibility of the described scenarios. Visual material was also submitted here for the participants' consideration. Finally, we explored their reactions to possible CV elements, namely the payment vehicle (higher prices, higher taxes, or higher specific prices such as higher oil prices), the payment schedule format (one or more years) and the institutions involved.

4.4.2 Formal field testing

A first draft of the questionnaire was written and used for pilot interviews. The interviews were conducted face to face at the respondent's home by trained interviewers. The pre-testing stage took place from February to May 1997, in the period on which the CESOP interviewers conducted three sequential pilots. Since the pilots constitute the first contact of the survey instrument with the general public we preferred to consider people from diverse sites in the country, with different range of ages and educational attainments. The location, date and sample size (n) of the pilot surveys are given in Table 4.5.

The pilots were selected to represent different demographic groups of interest. The sample size reflected the relative size of the different demographic groups in the Portuguese national context. Each pilot survey was followed by an interval long enough to allow the respondents' answers to be analysed. In addition to the quantitative data set based on the respondent's

Table 4.5: Pilot surveys	
Pilot I	Lisbon's metropolitan area, February 1997, n=59
Pilot II	Pousos parish, Leiria, March 1997, n=25
Pilot III	Ajuda parish, Lisbon, May 1997, n=52

answers to the questionnaire, each pilot produced two types of qualitative information: the interviewers' comments and suggestions and the results of the follow-up questions at the end of the questionnaire. Previously, interviewers had been told to write a short note describing the major problems they faced in the execution of the interview. Furthermore, after each pilot a debriefing session was organized, gathering together the interviewers involved. The debriefings were designed to discover any problems they had noticed with the instrument's wording, question sequence and visual aids. Finally, we proceeded to the analysis of all information provided by each pilot and revised the initial questionnaire for the following pilot. This iterative process is responsible for the fine-tuning of the survey instrument.

Pilot I – Lisbon's metropolitan area

This pilot was the first formal test of the questionnaire. The interviews for the first pilot were conducted in five parishes located in Lisbon's metropolitan area: Benfica, Laranjeiras, Carnaxide, Campolide and Estoril. These areas were chosen because they gave the opportunity of interviewing relatively young households living in an urban environment, characterized by higher education and income levels: we selected a socio-demographic group that was likely to understand the questionnaire even in its early stage of development. The overall feeling of the 11 interviewers involved in the pilot was that the instrument worked well despite the unusually lengthy text to be read when compared to other questionnaires with which they were familiar. Nevertheless, in many places they recommended wording changes to make the questionnaire clearer for the respondents.

This pilot was used with respect to the consideration of the national tax and the voluntary contribution as payment vehicles for the proposed protection plans. As expected, a number of respondents reacted negatively to the national tax as proposed payment vehicle. They argued that they 'already pay too many taxes'. Therefore, we paid particular attention to the study of the respondents who refused to contribute any escudo amount and assessed the reasons why they have such an answer pattern; these respondents are identified in the CV literature as no–no respondents, that is, respondents who say no to both dichotomous elicitation questions. During the briefing, the interviewers also reported that some respondents had difficulty in understanding the elicitation question. The section on the attitudes toward the willingness to pay for the protection of the Alentejo Natural Park turned out to be too long. As far as the visual material was concerned, the interviewers said that it was seen with interest by the respondents and helped in communicating the material expressed in the text. Some interviewers thought that some maps were redundant and recommended their removal. Moreover, the interviewers suggested making the questionnaire shorter since during the final questions the respondents were much less concentrated and somewhat more impatient. Having introduced wording changes, shortened the elicitation questions and revised the visual material, the instrument was ready for the next pilot study.

Pilot II – Rural parish of Pousos, Leiria

In the second pilot the interviews were conducted in one rural parish in the middle of Portugal: Pousos – see Figure 4.1 to find its location. This parish was selected in the expectation that its lower socio-economic status,[54] rural natural and geographical distance from the Alentejo Natural Park would help us assess whether the extra improvements in wording and visual material would be needed to communicate the scenario to this type demographic group. According to the results of the interviewer evaluation questions,[55] in Pilot II, the language used in the narrative is seen by the interviewers as 'very helpful' in explaining the scenario description than in the Pilot I – see Table 4.6. On the other hand, maps and photos were considered less important in explaining the scenario description in Pilot II than in Pilot I – see Table 4.7.

Table 4.6: How helpful was the language in explaining the scenario description?

	Frequency (%)		Cumulative (%)	
	Pilot I	Pilot II	Pilot I	Pilot II
Very helpful	69.5	83.3	69.5	83.3
Of some help	28.8	16.7	98.3	100.0
Not helpful	1.7	0.0	100.0	100.0

Table 4.7: How helpful were the maps and photos in explaining the scenario description?

	Frequency (%)		Cumulative (%)	
	Pilot I	Pilot II	Pilot I	Pilot II
Very helpful	27.1	12.5	27.1	12.5
Of some help	61.0	58.3	88.1	70.8
Not helpful	11.9	29.2	100.0	100.0

These results may be interpreted as a sign of a successful revision in wording and language used in the instrument survey: the improvements made the narrative clearer to the respondents, with the visual material seen to convey complementary information. These survey design improvements make the questionnaire easier to understand. This is confirmed by our Comprehension Index[56], which remained approximately the same across the two pilots, despite the lower educational attainment levels of the respondents in the Pilot II sample. Nevertheless, the national tax scheme still raised some problems. The interviewers still reported doubts among some respondents concerning the nature of the taxation. We agreed that, at the beginning of the elicitation question, the tax would be referred to as an additional one-year payment introduced as a rubric in the household annual income IRS tax letter.

---

[54] The Pousos sample was characterized by relatively old households who had much lower educational and income levels than Lisbon's metropolitan sample.

[55] These questions constitute the final section of the survey instrument, the follow-up section. All the questions in this section were answered by the interviewers after they had left the presence of the respondent.

[56] See Appendix B.

Pilot III – Parish of Ajuda, Lisbon

The questionnaire and visual aid used in this survey instrument incorporated revisions identified in the two preceding pilots. The site for this pilot was chosen to represent a balanced sample, both economically and educationally. The interviewers were very positive in the debriefing. They mentioned that this pilot was now easier to administer and that the reading of valuation questions went more smoothly. This perception is confirmed by the analysis of the responses to the follow-up question concerning the ability to understand the elicitation question – see Figure 4.6. According to the interviewers, half of the respondents in Pilot III 'well understood' the elicitation question, while for more than 30% of the sample the interviewers thought that the respondents 'understood very well'. These results are very promising when compared to the results of Pilot I, the sample with relatively high education and income, which is assumed to target the group of respondents most likely to understand the questionnaire. Nevertheless, we still have around 14% of the respondents who 'poorly understood' the willingness-to-pay question.[57] The interviewers also stated that the fine-tuning of the text and the revisions introduced to the visual aids were responsible for making the interview substantially shorter to administrate. Bearing in mind these results, we concluded that the survey instrument was ready for the national survey.

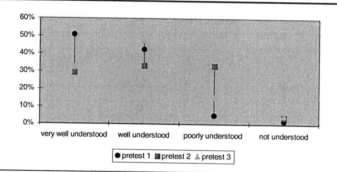

Figure 4.6: How well did the respondent understand the elicitation question?

4.5 Conclusions

The survey design work played a crucial role in framing the CV questionnaire as a valid measurement instrument. First, we explored the various survey design tools so as to formulate the valuation questions in a plausible and understanding way. In addition, we made extensive use of focus groups and pilots. These enabled us to check for the clarity of the payment vehicles and improve the language in the narrative; calibrate the bid vector; adjust the initial visual aids package; and adjust the size of the original survey since it proved to be too long. At the last debriefing, interviewers reported that the survey was now easier to administer.

---

[57] Before the execution of the main survey, we still carried out a number of wording changes intended to make the elicitation question more understandable to the less educated respondents. This revealed itself to be not an easy task since Portugal has a relatively high illiteracy rate, around 12% (INE 1991).

Chapter
5
STRUCTURE OF THE FINAL SURVEY INSTRUMENT

5.1 Introduction

This chapter presents a description of the final structure of the survey instrument used in the national CV application. Although the questionnaire was revised many times during the pilot stage, the basic structure of the survey instrument used in the last pilot proved to work well and was used in the national survey. The structure of the final survey used for the study of the Alentejo Natural Park is characterized by four sections. An original survey is provided in Appendix C.

The first section begins with a set of questions to assess the respondent's opinion with respect to the protection of the environment in general, and the conservation of the natural areas, in particular. The survey questions get more and more concrete, to obtain information useful to the valuation study. Therefore, in the second section, the interviewer focuses strictly on the Alentejo Natural Park. He begins by presenting to the respondent a sequence of visual material concerning the description of the two management options: the protection plan and the tourism development plan for the Park. The third section contains the valuation questions. In each questionnaire a bid card is randomly assigned across the respondents. The respondent is asked if s/he is willing to contribute to the protection of the ANP if that protection costs him/her a certain amount. If the answer is yes then the bid amount is increased and the respondent is asked if she is still willing to pay for the protection. If the initial answer from the respondent is no, then the bid amount is decreased. In the fourth section we sought to measure the respondent's motivations, attitudes and socio-economic characteristics. This information helps us to understand, and predict, the stated willingness-to-pay responses. The fifth and final section of the survey instrument contains the interviewer's evaluation questions.

5.2 Section A

The first part of the survey instrument consists of questions regarding a broad range of socio-economic issues. Afterwards, the interviewer focuses the respondent's attention solely on environmental issues. Section A ends by questioning the respondent's background knowledge on Natural Protected Areas. But first, and given the relatively high degree of illiteracy in the country, the interviewers were given strict instructions to inform the respondents that the survey is addressed to all Portuguese families without any discrimination:

> Most of the questions ask about attitudes and opinions of Portuguese families. There are no right or wrong answers. The survey completion does not require any special education or skills: all material is read and carefully explained.

5.2.1 General issues

The questionnaire starts by encouraging the respondent to think about five social problems: health care and social security; environmental protection; public security; unemployment; and quality of the public education system. These problems were previously discussed at the focus group sessions. They are also often identified in other surveys as objects of concern to the general public.[58] The interviewers asked the respondents to evaluate their importance in terms of governmental action:

> **P-1.** The Portuguese have been expressing different opinions about the seriousness of various social and economic problems in Portugal. According to you, how important are each of the following areas of governmental action in terms of their degree of priority?

Four of the problems are not environmentally related. The respondents' answers will provide us information by which we can rank the major areas of governmental intervention and infer the relative degree of importance of the government's environmental protection action. Following the standard practice to minimize order effects, the items were read in a random order (Boyle *et al.* 1993).

5.2.2 Environmental issues

In the second question we focus the respondents' attention on the domain of *environmental protection*. The goal here is to assess the respondent's opinion about the different areas of environmental intervention such as air pollution, protection of the wildlife, dangerous chemical waste, water pollution and recycling:[59]

> **P-2.** Please state your opinion and indicate the degree of priority (extremely urgent, very urgent, somehow urgent, not very urgent) for each of the following areas in terms of public funding.

Again the respondents' answers will provide us with information with which we can rank the different areas of environmental protection. We are interested in assessing the relative weight of governmental areas of 'protection of the wildlife/conservation of the nature' in terms of their importance with respect to public funding.

---

[58] Namely in the survey *Europeans and the Environment*, published by the Commission of the European Communities (1992).

[59] The areas of governmental intervention taken into account in our survey constitute specific working vectors of the Portuguese Ministry of Environment as defined in the National Plan for Environmental Policy (Acções Programáticas Específicas do Ministério do Ambiente e Recursos Naturais), in Plano Nacional da Política de Ambiente (MARN 1995b).

5.2.3 Natural Protected Areas issues

The last part of Section A concentrates on the Natural Protected Areas issue. At this stage the goal is to measure the respondent's background knowledge on this topic:

> **P-3.** Prior to this survey, had you, or anybody in your family, heard or read anything about the Protected Areas in Portugal?
> **P-4.** Which Area(s) or Park(s)?
> **P-5.** Had you, or anybody in your family, visited a natural area in Portugal?
> **P-6.** Which one(s)?

Section A finishes by asking the respondents if the conservation of nature and the protection of natural areas is an urgent problem, or is a problem for the future generations or, on the contrary, is not a problem.

5.3 Section B

In the second section of the survey instrument, the interviewers present a sequence of materials concerning the description of the Alentejo Natural Area and two scenario formulations. The first describes the policy option characterized by the preservation of the Alentejo Natural Area (*policy on*); the second describes the introduction of a tourism development plan (*policy off*). During the descriptions, the respondents are shown a series of visual aids – maps, photos and diagrams. These materials were designed to help the respondents understand the information that is being read to them and to visualize the damage involved with each scenario. The interviewer training emphasised helping the interviewers to combine narrative and visual material in a way that would maintain respondent interest and enhance comprehension of the questionnaire.

5.3.1 Alentejo Natural Area

Section B begins by conveying information about the location of the Alentejo Natural Area. The respondents are shown two maps: one that describes the Alentejo Natural Area and a second in which we plot the perimeter of the area within the entire geographic area of continental Portugal. The interviewers continued the characterization of the Alentejo Natural Area with a narrative description of the recreational possibilities, historical patrimony and the wildlife present in this natural area. The respondents are informed that some animal species are seriously threatened in Portugal, namely the Iberian lynx whose total population in Portugal is estimated to be no more than four. This information goes hand in hand with a set of photos that are presented to the respondents.

5.3.2 Protection scenario

In the second part of Section B, the interviewer identifies and describes the protection scenario – we labelled it *policy on*. This scenario corresponds to the current management policy of the Natural Area, that is, the existence of Alentejo Natural Park. The Park was created in 1995 by the Portuguese government as an effective instrument for the conservation of such a natural habitat, keeping the area free from urbanisation for tourism development. The Natural Park is characterized for the respondents in terms of two main areas: the Recreational Areas and Wilderness Areas. Then the interviewer asked:

> **P-8.** Have you, or anybody in your family, visited the Alentejo Natural Park?

The respondents who answered positively are asked to report the major reason why they visited the Park. At this stage we are interested in measuring the national visiting rate of the Natural Park as well as inferring the underlying visiting motives. The next section presents the narrative of the survey instrument, which describes the tourism development scenario.

5.3.3 Tourism development scenarios

In the third part of Section B, the interviewer presents and describes one, and only one, tourism commercial development plan – labelled *policy off*. The urbanization of the Alentejo Natural Park for tourism expansion is the most important development proposal and rather well known to Portuguese households. This plan is supported by the tourism industry and local municipalities that have been strongly lobbying the Portuguese government and conducting an active charm campaign in the media. They support the development of high-quality tourism and the creation of employment in an area that now has a very low population density.

Table 5.1: WA protection programme

Policy on – Photo 6	Policy off – Photo 6-1
WA: protected RA: protected	WA: allocated to tourism development RA: protected

With the commercial and tourism development of the WA, it is no longer possible to guarantee the preservation of local biodiversity: species such as the Iberian lynx, the bald eagle and the otter will disappear. This development proposal does not directly interfere with the RA: the government will continue to preserve the recreational areas where visitors will still be able to enjoy going to the beach in a relaxed environment.

Show Map 6-1

Combining the zoning of the Alentejo Natural Park with our research interests, we come up with three different tourism development plans. We refer to the plan describing the urbanization of the WA for tourism development; the plan characterized by the urbanization of the RA for tourism development; and, finally, the plan characterized by the urbanization of both WA and RA for tourism development – see Tables 5.1, 5.2 and 5.3. Each plan is associated with a different narrative description. So as to help the respondents to visualize the changes involved, the text is accompanied by a set of computer manipulated photos and

Table 5.2: RA protection programme

Policy on – Photo 6	*Policy off* – Photo 6-2
WA: protected	WA: protected
RA: protected	RA: allocated to tourism development

| With the commercial and tourism development of the RA and the privatisation of the sports and recreational activities, it is no longer possible to visit the Park's recreational perimeter and enjoy going to the beach in a relaxed environment.

This development proposal does not directly interfere with the WA: the government will continue the preservation of the wilderness areas and guarantee the preservation of the local wildlife diversity. |
|---|

Show Map 6-2

Table 5.3: (WA+RA) protection programme

Policy on – Photo 6	*Policy off* – Photo 6-3
WA: protected	WA: allocated to tourism development
RA: protected	RA: allocated to tourism development

| With the commercial and tourism development of the wa, it is no longer possible to guarantee the preservation of the local biodiversity: species such as the iberian lynx, the bald eagle and otter will disappear.

With the commercial and tourism development of the RA and the privatisation of the sports and recreational activities, it is no longer possible to visit the park's recreational perimeter and enjoy going to the beach in a relaxed environment. |
|---|

Show Map 6-3

maps.[60] In the next section of the survey instrument, the respondents are given the valuation questions, the core of the survey instrument.

5.4 Section C

This section consists of a sequence of questions that are used to infer the respondent's willingness to pay for preventing the introduction of the described development plans. At this stage we design four instrument versions. They reflect the use of different information levels and payment vehicles.

---

[60] The complete visual aid material is presented in Appendix C.

5.4.1 Information level

As far as the information level is concerned, we have, on the one hand, a survey instrument version in which the respondents are informed about the national government's financial effort in running the Alentejo Natural Park as a protected area:

> The Portuguese government invested in the last three years 560 million
> escudos[61] for running the Alentejo Natural Park as a protected area.

We labelled this scenario as 'information on'. On the other hand, we designed a survey version in which that paragraph is omitted: this scenario is labelled as 'information off'. Nevertheless, in both versions the narrative informed the respondents that the government does not have sufficient funds to keep the management of Alentejo Natural Area as a protected area, free from any tourism development:

> The [Portuguese government's] budget is not sufficient to continue
> guaranteeing to all Portuguese that there will not be any tourism
> development of the Park.

We introduced these two information levels because we are interested in investigating the presence of a valuation 'behavioural anchoring effect', that is, we are interested in assessing whether the respondents who are informed about the government's financial effort in running the Alentejo Natural Park answer differently from the respondents who are not so informed. For example, if we believe that the respondents have difficulties in transforming into monetary terms a good that is rather unfamiliar to them, then we could expect that the information about the government's financial effort could be used as a cue in the formulation of respondents' WTP answers. Alternatively, we could also think that the information about Government's financial effort in running the Alentejo Natural Park could be interpreted by the respondent as an important source for strategic behaviour: if his/her true WTP is below the (average) stated government expenditure, then these may be an incentive to understate his/her preferences, expecting that the overall financial effort made to run the Alentejo Natural Park will be reduced. Conversely, if the true WTP is above the (average) stated government expenditure, then s/he may have an incentive to overstate his/her preferences, expecting that the overall financial effort made to run the Alentejo Natural Park will be increased. A formal analysis of these two survey versions is presented in Chapter 8.

5.4.2 Payment vehicle

As far as the payment vehicle is concerned, we design a voluntary contribution (VC) and a national park tax (TAX). In both versions the respondent is guaranteed that the funds raised will be exclusively allocated to the protection of the Alentejo Natural Park – see Table 5.4. Before running the elicitation question, and following the NOAA guidelines and empirical findings (Hoehn and Loomis 1993; Kemp and Maxwell 1993; Hoevenagel and Linden 1993; Cummings et al. 1994; Loomis et al. 1994; Whitehead and Blomquist 1995), the interviewer calls the respondent's attention to his/her budget constraint and the existence of substitutes for the Alentejo Natural Park:

---

[61] Circa 2.8 million euro; 1 euro = 200 PTE and 1 euro   1,0479 US$ (June 1999).

Please think about:
- Your current household income
- Your current household expenses
- The existence of other Natural Areas

Table 5.4: Payment vehicles

VC	TAX
The government, together with other national organizations for environmental protection, launches a national money raising campaign in which funds will be exclusively applied to keep the Alentejo Natural Park free from any tourism development.	The government proposes a referendum regarding the introduction, only for a period of one year, of the National Park Tax. Its revenue will be exclusively applied to keep the Alentejo Natural Park free from any tourism development. All Portuguese households would have to pay the tax if the majority votes yes.

5.4.3 Valuation questions

To better simulate price taking in market behaviour, the respondents are asked whether they are willing to pay a given monetary amount in order to continue the protection of the Park. The monetary amount is stated in the instrument survey and varies randomly from respondent to respondent.[62] We used the same bid design across the three protection programmes. The bid ranges were carefully tested in the three pilots. For example, when the voluntary contribution is selected as the payment vehicle, the elicitation question goes as follows:

> **P-9.** Would your household contribute a donation of 1 200 escudos (or equivalently 100 escudos/month during one year) to protect WA and this way guarantee the non-extinction of local wildlife such as the Iberian Lynx and the Fishing Eagle?

If the respondent says yes, then the interviewer goes to a follow-up valuation question with a higher amount:

> **P-10.** And would your household still be willing to contribute with a donation of 3600 escudos (or equivalently 300 escudos/month during one year)?

On the contrary, if the respondent says no to P-9, then the interviewer goes to a follow-up valuation question with a lower amount:

> **P-11.** And would your household already be willing to contribute a donation of 600 escudos (or equivalently 50 escudos/month during one year)?

---

[62] The bid design used in the final questionnaire was reproduced is Table 4.4.

After answering both referendum questions, each respondent is asked to state, through an open-ended question (OE), his/her maximum willingness to pay – see Figure 5.1.

Combining the use of (a) the three protection programmes, (b) the two surveys' information levels concerning the government's financial effort in running the Alentejo Natural Park as a protected area, (c) the two payment vehicles and (d) the four bid cards used in the double-dichotomous willingness-to-pay questions, results with the final CV application are characterized by 28 versions of the survey instrument – see Table 5.5.

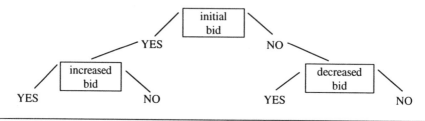

P-111. Could you please now state the maximum that your household is prepared to contribute?

Figure 5.1: Elicitation question format: double dichotomous with an open-ended follow-up

The last questions presented in section C are targeted for the analysis of the refusals, i.e., the respondents who answered "no" to both elicitation questions followed by a zero valuation of an open ended question.

5.4.4 Debriefing of the 'no–no' WTP responses

One of the crucial issues in the analysis of the stated willingness to pay answers is how to deal with those respondents who stated no–no to the elicitation question. To understand better such answering behaviour, the survey instrument includes a list of arguments that could possibly capture the underlying reason why the respondent answered in such a way. Without being too exhaustive, the list presented in the survey to the no–no respondents is described in Table 5.5. There is a general belief that the respondents may give a zero bid for strategic reasons, and not because the respondents have a zero valuation of the described environmental protection plan: this is the so-called *zero protest bids* (Mitchell and Carson 1989; Römer and Pommerehne 1992). The possible reasons for no–no refusals will help us to identify the most important reasons for such bidding, as well as to identify the *zero protest* arguments. In Chapter 8 we advance an extensive analysis of the *zero protest bids*.

5.5 Section D

This section consists of a sequence of questions that are used to retrieve various characteristics of the respondents (for example, age, household size, level of education and income) and which will help us to understand and predict the willingness-to-pay responses.

Table 5.5: Survey versions

Protection programme	WA		RA		(WA+RA)		
Level of information	ON	ON	ON	ON	OFF	OFF	ON
Payment vehicle	TAX	VC	TAX	VC	TAX	VC	VC
P-9	1 200	1 200	1 200	1 200	1 200	1 200	1 200
P-10	3 600	3 600	3 600	3 600	3 600	3 600	3 600
P-11	600	600	600	600	600	600	600
	A1	B1	C1	D1	E1	F1	G1
P-9	2 400	2 400	2 400	2 400	2 400	2 400	2 400
P-10	4 800	4 800	4 800	4 800	4 800	4 800	4 800
P-11	1 200	1 200	1 200	1 200	1 200	1 200	1 200
	A2	B2	C2	D2	E2	F2	G2
P-9	4 800	4 800	4 800	4 800	4 800	4 800	4 800
P-10	9 600	9 600	9 600	9 600	9 600	9 600	9 600
P-11	2 400	2 400	2 400	2 400	2 400	2 400	2 400
	A3	B3	C3	D3	E3	E3	G3
P-9	9 600	9 600	9 600	9 600	9 600	9 600	9 600
P-10	24 000	24 000	24 000	24 000	24 000	24 000	24 000
P-11	4 800	4 800	4 800	4 800	4 800	4 800	4 800
	A4	B4	C4	D4	E4	F4	G4

However, first the survey instrument presents a set of motivational questions. The underlying idea is to use the respondent's answers to these questions to retrieve unobserved attitudinal or motivational factors. For the most part, these variables are suggested by the theory as mentioned in Chapters 2 and 3. In the following subsections we report how we construct the motivational factors and describe the questions addressed to measure the respondent's socio-economic characteristics.

5.5.1 Motivation factors

The motivation factors are obtained by means of a Likert technique (Likert 1967; Swanborn 1993; Wiestra 1996) from a list of items previously discussed during the focus group sessions and tested during the pilot sessions. The relevance of these variables is two-fold: first, we are able to test the empirical validity of the consumer preferences' structure as proposed in the model developed in Chapter 3; second, we are able to estimate the marginal magnitudes for each motivation function in the WTP function, paying particular attention to the warmglow valuation effect.

In Chapter 3 we postulate that the motivation functions influence the financial contribution to the protection of the Alentejo Natural Area. These functions are:

1. The degree to which the respondents feel that the protection of nature, in general, and the preservation of the Alentejo Natural Park, in particular, is important to their well-being since it provides tangible recreation services. Thus, the stated WTP for the Natural Park preservation may be explained in terms of recreation consumption accruing to the respondents or other individuals who visit such natural areas. This is the 'use' function.

2. The degree to which the respondents feel that the preservation of endangered species from extinction is important, independently of the fact that they may or may not observe such species in their natural habitat. For this motive respondents may be willing to pay for the conservation of the Alentejo Natural Park, even though they may never visit the Park. This is the 'existence' function.

3. The degree to which the respondents feel moral satisfaction with the act of giving. They may interpret the financial contribution as a 'good action' and therefore feel happier with themselves when contributing. This is the 'warmglow' function.

Table 5.6: List of reasons for a zero bid

i) I cannot afford to contribute so much money.

ii) I do not believe in the described tax scheme/national fund campaign.

iii) I prefer to spend that amount of money elsewhere.

iv) The proposed protection plan is not worth so much money.

v) I do not agree with this type of question.

vi) The proposed protection plan is a break in the development of the region.

vii) I believe that this questionnaire is not the best approach to the topic.

viii) The protection of nature does not have a price.

ix) I do not accept any increase in the taxes/I do not accept participating in funding this campaign.

The 26 items (translated from Portuguese) of the questionnaire that served to determine the motivational factors are given below:

I1. My family and I would have great pleasure in knowing that the SIC, RTP and TVI together have agreed to introduce in their TV schedules more documentary films about wildlife and its natural habitats. ('use')

I2. My family and I think that the preservation of the Alentejo coastline is important because this is a place which all of us can visit and see very beautiful natural landscapes. ('use')

I3. My family and I like to see the Portuguese government giving more support to the national organisations which are promoting work in the field of environment conservation. ('warmglow')

I4. My family and I think that the preservation of the Parks is important because these are privileged places where everybody may enjoy a walk or a picnic in a relaxed environment. ('use')

I5. My family and I take great satisfaction in knowing that it is today guaranteed that our children, and future generations, will continue to be able to observe wildlife in its natural habitat. ('use')

I6. Despite the fact that my family and I may never see an otter in its natural habitat, we will be very worried if the total population of otters in Portugal becomes extinct. ('existence')

I7. My family and I like to spend the weekends at home or going to the movies rather than going out for a walk in the countryside or by the beach. ('use')

I8. Our family admires the individuals who, on a voluntary basis, participate in collecting donations for national programmes for social aid and solidarity. ('warmglow')

I9. My family and I take great pleasure in knowing that we are still able to visit villages in Alentejo which keep their true identity and their typical houses, façades and streets. ('use')

I10. Despite the fact that my family and I may never see an Iberian lynx in its natural habitat, we are very happy to know that we have the guarantee that the lynx is kept safe from extinction in Portugal. ('existence')

I11. My family and I think that the preservation of the natural areas is important since they are privileged sites for recreational activities such as sightseeing or biking in a natural environment. ('use')

I12. There are some funding campaigns to which my family and I feel very close and therefore we would not hesitate to contribute a donation. ('warmglow')

I13. Despite the fact that my family and I may never visit a Natural Park, we are very happy to see these natural areas protected so that other Portuguese citizens may also be able to observe wildlife in its natural habitat. ('use')

I14. My family and I think that the preservation of the Alentejo coastline is important because this is a privileged place where all of us may enjoy going to the beach in a relaxed environment and being in contact with nature. ('use')

I15. It is difficult for me to decline my help to other individuals who, either in the streets or at my door, beg for charity. ('warmglow')

I16. Whenever I am approached by identified personnel, it is not hard to me to refuse to make a financial contribution to a national fund raising campaign. ('warmglow')

I17. The protection of the forests is very important because for Portugal they are a very important source of wealth. ('use')

I18. With the increasing use of the media in our elementary schools as well as an increasing number of school visits to the zoo, it will no longer be important to take the children on educational trips to the Natural Areas. ('use')

I19. Sometimes our help in national fund raising campaigns can be explained because we come under observation and feel 'socially-pressured' to contribute, and therefore we do not decline to make a contribution. ('warmglow')

I20. I am happy with myself whenever I give a financial contribution to national fund raising campaigns. ('warmglow')

I21. With Portuguese participation in the EU, the preservation of our national diversity is no longer so important since we are constructing a common and shared European culture. ('existence')

I22. Despite the fact that my family and I may never observe an eagle in nature, we take great pleasure in knowing that the eagles are kept safe from extinction. ('existence')

I23. My family and I like to contribute to good causes such as the protection of the environment, and whenever we can afford it we do not decline our help to such fund raising campaigns. (warmglow)

I24. Giving blood is giving life. ('warmglow')

I25. During the holidays, my family and I prefer to stay home or to go to the beach rather than travelling around Portugal visiting our traditional villages. ('use')

I26. My family and I think that the preservation of the Alentejo coast line is important because in this way we are protecting the typical lifestyle of the local inhabitants, which is a part of our national identity. ('use')

5.5.2 Socio-economic questions

These questions supplement the motivational information obtained from the answers of the respondent to the 26 statements. The first questions asked in this part of the survey are demographic questions. They measure the age, education level, gender, household dimension and professional activity of the respondent:

> The final questions concern the characterization of your household.
> P-14. Could you please tell me to which age you belong?
> P-15. Could you please tell me your education studies level?
> P-17. What is your current job?

Respondent who are unemployed will then be asked:

> P-18. Would you be interested in working in the tourism industry in the Alentejo Natural Area?

The last demographic question measures the respondents' household income. Interviewers use a card on which different income categories are listed. The respondents are asked to report their income category from such a list.

> P-19. This card shows amounts of monthly incomes. Could you please tell me to which net income your household belongs?

The remainder of the questions in Section D asks the respondents, or members of the household, if they have ever enrolled in recreational activities and if they have ever participated in donation schemes:

> P-20. In which of the following activities (going to the beach; surfing or sailing; biking; walking; camping; fishing or hunting) have you, or your family, participated?
> P-21. During the last year, have you, or anybody in your family, made a donation to a national fund raising campaign? P-22. How many times?
> P-23. During the last year, have you, or anybody in your family, contributed to charity?
> P-24. How many times?
> P-25. During the last year, had you, or anybody in your family, given blood?
> P-26. How many times?

The final two questions in this section were:

> P-27. Counting yourself, how many people live in your household?
> P-28. Are you, or anyone in your family, a member of the following organizations (National Geographic Society, Greenpeace, World

> Wildlife Fund, Scouts, Quercus, Liga para a Protecção da Natureza,
> Fundo de Protecção para os Animais Selvagens (FAPAS), Grupo de
> Estudo de Organização do Território e Ambiente (GEOTA))

At this stage interviewers inform the respondents that the questionnaire is finished, and before leaving thanks the respondents for their co-operation.

5.6 Section E: follow-up questions

Unlike earlier questions, these questions are addressed to the interviewers. The objective is to assess opinions with respect to the degree of comprehension of the interview by the respondent. For this reason this section is also known in the literature as interviewer evaluation questions; it comprises two questions. Both were answered by the interviewers after they left the presence of the respondent. The first question seeks to capture the respondent's degree of understanding of the valuation question:

> **FU 1.** In your opinion, would you say that the respondent understood
> very well, understood, poorly understood or did not understand at all the
> valuation question?

In the last question, interviewers are asked for their opinion with respect to the role of the language and visual material in explaining the scenario description to the respondent:

> **FU 2.** In your opinion what was the role (very important, important,
> somewhat important or of little importance) of the survey language and
> visual aids in the respondent's ability to comprehend the description of
> the protection programme?

These questions provided useful information that is analysed as an indicator of the overall comprehensibility of the survey instrument to the respondents.

5.7 Conclusions

This chapter presented the structure of the survey instrument that was used in the national interviews. Following NOAA guidelines, we choose to work with face-to-face interviews. To better simulate price taking consumer market behaviour, the double dichotomous choice model has been the selected format for the elicitation question. The survey instrument involved the elaboration of different policy options, different payment vehicles and different survey information levels concerning the government financial effort in running the Alentejo Natural Park as a protected area. As far as the policy options are concerned, we designed three protection programmes: (a) protection recreational areas of the Alentejo Natural Park from tourism development; (b) protection wilderness areas of the Alentejo Natural Park from tourism development, and (c) protection of both the wilderness areas and recreational areas of the Alentejo Natural Park from tourism development. This will allow us to develop formal test procedures and test whether the valuation results violate the adding-up property, that is, whether valuing two programmes individually and adding up the respective WTP estimates gives the same result as valuing the two programmes jointly. The design of the survey instrument takes also into account two payment vehicles, respectively, the national tax scheme and the voluntary payment scheme. This will allow us to develop formal test procedures and test whether free-riding was present in the estimation results. Finally, we take into account two survey information levels: in one survey version before framing the elicitation question the respondent is informed about the current governmental financial effort in running the Alentejo Natural Park as a protected area while in the second version s/he is not. This will make it possible to test whether starting point bias was present in the double dichotomous valuation model.

Chapter
6
SURVEY EXECUTION

6.1 Introduction

The administration of the national survey took place during two week-ends, 13–14 and 20–21 September 1997. Before the execution of the national in-person survey, a sampling procedure needed to be selected. An essential requirement for any probability sample mechanism is the construction of a sampling frame. Given that one of the objectives of the present CV application is to provide a national valuation of the Alentejo Natural Park, we defined the sampling frame as the residents in continental Portugal. The household is taken as the unit of analysis. The definition of the sample population was conducted according to a multistage probability rule constructed by the statistics office of the CESOP. The final goal was to achieve a sample representative of the Portuguese household population.

Together with the selection of the sampling mechanism, we follow closely the set of working proceedures as defined in the *Exxon Valdez* CV study (Carson *et al.* 1992). Therefore, the execution of the national in-person survey was preceded by interviewer training, accompanied by a field interviewer's supervision and followed by the validation of the completed interviews. Finally, the responses were coded and entered into ASCII data set sheets.

This chapter contains three sections. In section 6.2 the selected sampling procedure is presented and characterized. Sections 6.3 and 6.4 discuss, respectively, the training and field supervision tasks involved in the administration of the questionnaire.

6.2 The sampling design

A complete enumeration of all the households in the population of continental Portugal is not feasible as a sampling selection mechanism because this way of collecting the data would generate unbearable costs. Therefore, we looked for a sampling method that guarantees the quality of the collected data and is still compatible with the research budget. In this context, we followed a two-stage area probability sample.[63] As the name suggests, this sampling mechanism is characterized by two stages or steps of selection (Kalton 1983; Thompson

---

[63] Non-probability sampling procedures were rejected, for example, volunteers or 'representative' samples chosen by an expert, since they are based on subjective premises (Kalton 1983).

1992). In the first stage, a set of Primary Sampling Units (PSUs) are drawn. This corresponds to the selection of a sample of parishes across Portugal. In the second stage, a set of Residential Dwelling Units (RDUs) were drawn from the selected PSUs. This corresponds to the housing units which will be later visited by the interviewer.

The execution of the first task, that is, the selection of a sample of parishes across Portugal, involves the construction of a sampling frame. According to CESOP's Master Sampling Plan, the sampling frame is defined by the total population of Residential Dwelling Units registered in the 3898 parishes across the five geographical blocks: north; centre; Lisbon and Tagus valey; Alentejo; and Algarve. Bearing in mind the distribution of parishes across the five geographical blocks, we are able to select the PSUs that will constitute the survey sample. The sample selection mechanism of the PSUs is done with specific sample design software developed by the CESOP. Generally speaking, the programme selects the parishes by performing repeated independent drawings with probabilities defined as proportionate to their population counts. The size is given by the number of occupied housing units in the parish as registered in the 1991 Decennial Census (INE 1992). At the end of this stage, 37 parishes were drawn (see the complete list in Table 6.1).

In the second stage of sampling, we proceed to the selection of RDUs within the selected parishes. In each parish, the interviewers followed a random walk path where the pace, that is, the number of skipped household residential units between two consecutive interviews, is defined by the ratio between the total number of residential units and the number of sampled residential units within the selected parish. This process yields a wide geographical coverage of the parish. The interviewer teams paid visits to 3597 households but 21% of them could not be interviewed since the residents were not at home. From the households that were successfully contacted, we received a total of 1678 completed interviews, corresponding to a non-participation response of approximately 40%.[64] This relatively high figure, in the overall context of CV surveys, is not atypical in the context of Portugal; indeed the Portuguese are not particularly engaged in co-operating in household surveys.

6.3 Interviewer training

All of the 64 interviewers involved in the administration of this questionnaire attended one of the three training sessions held during the month of September of 1997. The reason why we used so many interviewers was due to the short time period over which the national survey was conducted, two weekends, and we did not want to allocate too much working effort per interviewer. In order to minimize measurement errors due to interviewer bias, they all received the same training. However, and due to the lack of identification of the interviewer in each survey, we were not able to test interviewer bias.

The training sessions took place in the Lisbon, Porto and Viseu departments of the CESOP. The sessions were conducted by the project co-ordinator and the CESOP's field director. The training sessions were a mix of lectures, group discussions and interview simulation exercises. Nevertheless, and in order to achieve training homogeneity across sessions, we followed a training plan prepared in advance. The plan is characterized by three major points: a brief overview of the survey; a complete demonstration of the main interview; and, finally, the execution of a simulation interview. The sessions started with an overview of

---

[64] The CV in-person interviews are characterized by higher overall response rates than, for example, mail surveys. The latter typically range between 20% and 60% (Whitehead et al. 1993a). However, survey researchers have been facing an increasing trend in non-cooperation over time, especially in developing countries (see Deaton 1997).

Table 6.1: CESOP's national sample plan

Geographical block	PSUs Parish (municipality)	Total RDUs	Sampled RDUs
	Santa Marinha (Vila Nova de Gaia)	10.198	78
	Perozinho (Vila Nova De Gaia)	1.503	52
	Mafamude (Vila Nova de Gaia)	10.891	74
	Oliveira do Douro (Vila Nova de Gaia)	6.090	52
North	Valbom (Gondomar)	4.085	52
	Ermesinde (Valongo)	10.543	78
	Anta (Espinho)	2.785	52
	Maceira (Lousada)	1.507	34
	São Vitor (Braga)	5.530	52
	Santo António dos Olivais (Coimbra)	12.633	100
	Albergaria-a-Velha (Albergaria -a-Velha)	1.939	52
	Maceira (Fornos de Algodres)	3.146	52
Centre	Nossa Senhora de Fátima (Ourem)	565	28
	Oliveira do Conde (Carregal do Sal)	1.182	28
	Marinha Grande (Marinha Grande)	8.728	52
	Setubal -N. Senhora da Anunciada (Setúbal)	5.779	52
	Setubal -S. Sebastião (Setúbal)	15.029	80
	Encarnação (Lisboa)	1.294	28
	Lumiar (Lisboa)	11.499	52
Lisbon	Portela (Lisboa)	4821	32
and Tagus valley	Marateca (Palmela)	1195	28
	Sesimbra-Castelo (Sesimbra)	3919	48
	Alpiarça (Alpiarça)	2767	32
	Caparica (Almada)	5099	48
	São Martinho do Porto (Alcobaça)	804	28
	Vale de Amoreira (Moita)	3658	28
	Verderena (Barreiro)	4707	28
	Santo António da Charneca (Barreiro)	3248	28
	Alto do Seixalinho (Barreiro)	7953	48
	Rio de Mouro (Sintra)	9656	52
	Sta Maria do Castelo (Alcacer do Sal)	1602	28
	Santiago do Cacém (Santiago do Cacém)	2155	28
Alentejo	Estremoz -Sta Maria (Estremoz)	1652	28
	Évora -Sé (Évora)	11859	36
Algarve	Santa Maria (Lagos)	1534	28
	Portimão (Portimão)	10657	30

the questionnaire and research objectives. Various aspects of the questionnaire were also here discussed. The attention of the interviewers was drawn to the use of 28 versions of the questionnaire. Interviewers were prepared to work with a rather intensive questionnaire in terms of its narrative descriptions in order to keep the respondents attentive throughout the reading. The interviewers were also instructed on how combine the narrative and visual support.

The overall objective was to give interviewers a sense of the way in which the questionnaire was to be administered. The key features of the interview were then highlighted, paying special attention to the use of visual aids in interaction with the reading of the survey material. The training session ended by conducting a complete interview simulation exercise among the group of the trainees. It was followed by a debriefing. This allowed everyone to hear the feedback given after the role-playing. The interviewers were also asked to complete an interview in their household before beginning their actual assignments. If the interviewers still found difficulties in running the interview exercise at home, then the CESOP's field director, who also followed the training, had instructions to organise a second section focusing on the particular situations described by the interviewers.

6.4 Field supervision and data validation

In the field work, the interviewers are divided into 16 teams; each is composed of four interviewers and one supervisor. The supervisors were responsible for following *in loco* the interviewers' work progress, guaranteeing the control of the sample walk and checking the validity of the responses. Supervisors validated at least 10 per cent of the sample of each interviewer's assignment. Most validations were done by telephone; thosedone without a telephone were done later by mail. According to CESOP supervisors, all the cases checked were successfully validated. At the end of the day, the supervisors were asked to telephone the field director and report on the work in progress.

At the same time, and as the questionnaires were returned from the field, responses were coded and registered by the CESOP's data entry teams. When the data entry was completed, CESOP created an EXCEL® dataset.

6.5 Conclusions

This chapter describes the administration of the CV application. We followed closely the set of proceedings defined in the *Exxon Valdez* CVM study. In this context, we provided formal training to the interviewers and proceeded to quality check control of the interviewer's field work. The underlying objective was to guarantee the quality of the questionnaire responses. According to a two-stage area probability sampling procedure defined by the CESOP, the interviewers visited 37 parishes in Portugal and received 1678 completed interviews.

PART III
Analysis of the Survey Results

Chapter

7

DESCRIPTIVE ANALYSIS OF THE SURVEY RESPONSES

7.1 Introduction

In this chapter the responses of the national sample to the final survey instrument are analysed. The goal is, first, to obtain information about the knowledge and opinion of the respondents with respect to the conservation of the environment, in general, and protection of nature, in particular. Second, we want to present the information with respect to the socio-economic and demographic characteristics of the respondents. This information will describe the main features of the sample population and will be used to better understand the respondents' stated WTP responses (Nunes 1997).

This chapter contains five sections. In section 7.2, we analyse the responses with respect to the conservation of the environment, the protection of the natural areas and, in particular, the protection of the Alentejo Natural Park. In section 7.3, the responses to the willingness to pay are presented. In section 7.4, the socio-economic and demographic responses are examined. Finally, in section 7.5, the interviewer assessment responses are presented.

7.2 Opinion with respect to governmental policy action and nature conservation issues

The initial question asks the respondents' opinion about their priority for governmental policy actions. Despite the fact that 70% of the respondents consider *environmental protection* as a 'very important' policy area, we can verify that *unemployment, medical assistance* and *social security* constitute the most important priorities.[65] With the second question we begin the process of narrowing the scope of the interview to its primary focus. The respondents were asked to state their opinion about the different priorities in public spending on the environment. We were able to conclude that the *nature and wildlife conservation* is not the leading priority for Portuguese households in terms of environmental policy action; as a matter

---

[65] See Appendix D. For more detailed information concerning the Portuguese households' opinion about their priority for governmental policy action see and Nunes (1998a).

of fact, *water pollution* was considered 'very important' by more than 70% of the respondents and thus assumed the top priority for public funding.

The third question assessed the knowledge of the respondents with respect to Protected Areas. Then an open-ended question asked the respondents to mention which area they were referring to. The Peneda Gerês, the only Portuguese National Park, constitutes, without any doubt, the best-known Natural Area among Portuguese families – see results in Table 7.1.

Table 7.1: Heard or read issues concerning protected areas (%)

Yes	No	Don't know	No answer
64.9	31.6	2.9	0.6

Areas mentioned (%)

Peneda Gerês	Arrábida	S. Estrela	Costa Alentejana	Montesinho	Sintra-Cascais	Sado Estuary
38.5	18.3	8.1	6.1	5.6	4.5	3.5

The next question asked the respondents for their opinion with respect to the conservation of the Natural Areas. The great majority of the respondents, around 82%, stated that conservation is 'an urgent problem' – see Table 7.2. This represented a shift of 9% when compared to the 1992 Eurobarometer survey results (Commission of the European Communities 1992).

Table 7.2: Conservation of the Natural Areas (%)

An urgent problem	A problem for the future generation	Not a problem
82.1	12.9	0

Finally, the survey presents the Alentejo Natural Park. At the end of the narrative, respondent are asked whether they, or any member of the household, have ever visited this Natural Area. The respondents who answered positively were asked to state the most important reason for the visit. The results are presented in Table 7.3.

If we compare the results as described in Table 7.1 with the number of visits to the Alentejo Natural Park, we are forced to believe that either (a) the Costa Alentejana is not vivid in the respondents' memory, and thus it was not spontaneously reported by respondents, or, if we still admit that the Costa Alentejana is known among the respondents, (b) the respondents have in their mind other areas which are far and away more popular than the Alentejo Natural Park.[66] Finally, we may also believe that respondents, when visiting the Costa Alentejana area, were not aware (or did not perceive) that they were visiting the Parque Natural do Sudoeste

---

[66] The Peneda Gerês was the first natural area in continental Portugal to received the status of Protected Area – in early 1970s. Moreover, the Peneda Gerês is the only National Park that exists in Portugal in contrast to the Alentejo Natural Park that is a Regional Park, which was created in mid 1990s.

Alentejano e Costa Vicentina.[67] We would like remind readers that the ANP begins at the South of Sines, on the west coast, and ends near Lagos, in the Algarve, involving more than 100 km of coastal area.

The major motives underlying the visit of the ANP are intrinsically related to its characteristics: a coastal area practically in its natural state. Infrastructure, and other tourism-related equipment, hardly exists when compared, for example, to the Algarve's coast, a few kilometres away. More than half of the reported visits consisted of walking and trekking recreation activities – see Table 7.3. On the contrary, 'fun holidays', here characterized by a high frequency of visits to pubs and discos, are, unlike in the Algarve, not important for visits to the Alentejo coastal area.

Table 7.3: Number of reported visits to the ANP

Yes	No	Don't Know	No Answer
33.4	62.7	1.4	1.3

Reasons Mentioned (%)

Walking and trekking	going to the beach	visiting the local villages	fishing and hunting	fun holidays: bars and discos
52.9	21.8	8.5	0.9	0.2

The questionnaire continues with the description of the protection programmes and the questions assessing the respondent's willingness to pay. These questions will be taken up in the next section.

7.3 WTP responses

The survey instrument used a double-bounded dichotomous choice question elicitation framework (Hanemann *et al.* 1991; Cameron and Quiggin 1994) to obtain information about the respondent's maximum willingness to pay to continue the protection of the Park. The three protection programmes used the same bid card design. In Table 7.4 we recall the bid design used in the survey instruments.

Table 7.4: Bid design used in the survey instruments (in PTE)

Bid cards	P-9: Initial bid	P-10: Increased bid	P-11: Decreased bid
Card 1	1 200	3 600	600
Card 2	2 400	4 800	1 200
Card 3	4 800	9 600	2 400
Card 4	9 600	24 000	4 800

---

[67] As a matter of fact, the recreational areas of the Alentejo Natural Park have relatively few panel information boards. In contrast, the Meerdal-Heverlee Forest (a Natural Area nearby Leuven, Belgium) is characterized by abundant boards; the visitor simply cannot miss them.

A 'yes–no' response, that is, a 'yes' to the initial bid amount and a 'no' to increased bid amount, indicates that the respondent's maximum willingness to pay lies between the initial bid amount and the increased bid amount. According to respondents' answers, 34 % of the respondents' WTP for the (WA + RA) protection programme lies between 1 200 and 3 600 escudos – see Table 7.5.

Table 7.5: Sample frequencies of the responses to the P-9, P-10 and P-11 questions (%)

Bid card	Protection programme											
	WA: Wilderness Area				RA: Recreational Area				(WA + RA)			
	NN	NY	YN	YY	NN	NY	YN	YY	NN	NY	YN	YY
1	32.7	8.8	32.7	25.7	31.3	2.7	43.7	22.3	40.2	4.4	34.0	21.2
2	43.4	7.1	23.0	25.7	48.7	5.1	24.7	21.4	43.3	5.5	30.5	20.5
3	46.0	4.4	35.4	8.8	42.9	37	37.3	15.9	56.4	5.0	23.7	14.6
4	51.3	9.7	31.9	6.2	62.8	1.8	30.0	5.3	56.7	6.9	30.6	5.7

On the other hand, a 'no–yes' response indicates that the respondent's maximum WTP lies between the amount asked in the P-11 question and the amount asked in P-9 (e.g. around 7 % of the respondents' WTP for the (WA + RA) protection programme lies between 4 800 and 9 600 escudos).

The 'yes–yes' responses capture the upper range of the willingness to pay distribution of the population sample. As we would expect, the 'yes-yes' responses fall as the amount the respondent is asked to pay increases. For example, in a WA survey, around 26 % of the respondents are willing to pay more than 3 600 escudos for the WA protection programme, while only 6 % are willing to pay more than 24 000 escudos it. In all three protection programmes, fewer than 10 % of the respondents answered 'yes' to the highest bid. According to Boman and Bostedt (1995) this can be interpreted as a signal that the bid card is well-designed; the range of the bid card's distribution has captured well the range of willingness to pay.

As far as the 'no–no' responses are concerned, we expect them to increase as we increase the amount on the WTP question (for example, in RA protection programme we have, at bid card 1, 31.3 % of 'no–no' responses and about 63 % at the bid card 4). It should be noted, though, that this group of respondents is also likely to include some who may be considered as zero-protests.[68]

7.4 Demographic and socio-economic responses

The sample demographics and socio-economic characteristics collected in Section D of the instrument survey are discussed here. The median respondent is between 40–49 years old, with a household is constituted by two other persons, and s/he has completed the lower level of secondary education – see Tables 7.6, 7.7 and 7.8. We also verified that the majority of the respondents were women, corresponding to 56.2 % of the sample.[69]

---

[68] An extensive analysis of the zero-protests is provided in the following chapter.

[69] According to INE, the female population over 12 years old represents 52.3% of the Portuguese population.

Table 7.6: Age (%)

20–29 years	30–39 years	40–49 years	50–59 years	60–69 years	+ 69 years
19.5	19.7	21.8	17.0	14.2	7.7

Table 7.7: Household size (%)

One	Two	Three	Four	Five	Six or more
7.5	21.8	26.9	29.1	14.0	0.0

Table 7.8: Education level (%)

Primary education		Secondary education			University education
Lower level	Higher level	Lower level	Medium level	Higher level	
Less than 4 years of school	5–6 years of school	7–9 years of school	10–11 years of school	12 years of school	More than 12 year of school
10.9	39.2	20.5	10.3	11.0	8.2

We confronted the data of our survey with demographic statistics available from the last Census[70] (INE 1992) - see Table 7.9. When comparing the Census figures with the survey's response answers, we did not find many surprises; in general terms it is valid to say that the different demographic clusters of the Portuguese population were well covered in the national CV application.

Table 7.9: Census 91 demographic data

Age					
20-29 years	30-39 years	40-49 years	50-59 years	60-69 years	+69 years
21.2	19.2	17.1	14.3	15.9	12.4

Household dimension					
One	Two	Three	Four	Five	Six or more
13.8	25.3	23.8	21.7	8.8	6.6

Education				
less than primary	primary	secondary lower	secondary higher	university
10.4	47.4	14.7	21.4	7.0

Adapted from Censos 1991, *Instituto Nacional de Estatística (INE)*, pages 16, 106 and 414)

---

[70] We did not, however, run a formal statistical test to assess the representativeness of the demographic data of the sample.

As far as the respondent's occupation is concerned, the survey answers were coded according to the National Classification of Occupations (MESS 1994). CESOP added three occupation categories: (1) the housewives (or househusbands), that is, people who decide to stay at home and care for the house and family rather than to work; (2) the retired; and (3) the working students. The results are presented in Table 7.10. According to the survey results, 99 respondents, corresponding to 5.9% of the sample, declared themselves to be unemployed.[71] Among the unemployed respondents, more than two-thirds answered negatively when asked if they would be interested in working in the tourism industry at the Alentejo Natural Park. On the other hand, the remaining respondents expressed interest in moving to the area so as to get a job in the tourism industry. According to these figures, tourism development of the ANP, and the associated local employment promotion, are not really seen as constituting attractive job opportunities among the unemployed respondents.

Table 7.10: Respondents' occupation (%)

Executive civil servants, industrial directors and executives	3.9
Intellectuals and scientists	9.4
Middle management and technicians	9.8
Administrative and related workers	8.6
Service and sales workers	8.5
Farmers and skilled agricultural and fisheries workers	0.8
Skilled workers, craftsmen and similar	12.6
Machine operators and assembly workers	3.0
Unskilled workers	2.8
Housewives	13.1
Retired	17.8
Working students	3.0
Unemployed	5.9

To further determine the sample's socio-economic characterization, the respondents were asked to report their net household income, P-19. We got an overall response rate of approximately 83 %. The median household income was in the 150,000–299,000 escudos category. Nevertheless, around 20 % of the sample reported a household income lower than 75,000 escudos per month – see results in Table 7.11.

Table 7.11: Monthly household net income (%)

<75,000 escudos	>75,000 <149,000	>150,000 <299,000	>300,000 <450,000	>451,000 <599,000	>600,000 <799,000	>800,000 <1200,000	>1200,000 escudos
19.9	29.4	20.6	8.3	2.5	1.3	0.8	0.8

The next block of questions, P-20 to P-26, asked the respondents whether they had participated in outdoor recreation activities, fund raising campaigns and charity – see Tables 7.12 and 7.13. Finally, the respondents were asked whether they were members of any environment-friend organization: 20 % of the respondents answered positively. About 42 % of the 'yes' responses corresponded to members of local Scouting organisations and 46 %

---

[71] According to INE figures, the unemployment rate in 1997 was about 6.1%.

Table 7.12: Recreation activities (%)

Walking or trekking	Going to the beach	Biking	Camping	Surf, boating or sailing	Fishing or hunting
96.1	93.7	75.0	49.0	48.9	40.7

Table 7.13: Past gift behaviour (%)

Funds Donations				Charity Contributions				Blood Giving			
82.8				84.5				25.9			
Frequency				Frequency				Frequency			
# 1	# 2	# 3	# 4	# 1	# 2	# 3	# 4	# 1	# 2	# 3	# 4
23.9	18.8	15.4	30.3	11.7	8.5	8.9	56.4	38.7	26.7	15.7	13.1

corresponded to memberships of one of the various national organizations as reported in the questionnaire – see Table 7.14.

Table 7.14: Organizations (%)

National organizations	Scouts	International organizations
46.0	41.3	12.6

7.5 Interviewer assessment responses

According to the interviewers, 31 % of the respondents have 'very well understood", 50 % 'understood', 15 % 'understood poorly' and 3 % 'not understood'. Furthermore, the interviewers perceived that 39 % of the respondents had seen the narrative as 'very helpful' and another 44 % as 'helpful' in making the scenario description comprehensible. According to the interviewers, the maps and photos were seen by a great majority of the respondents as 'helpful' and thus confirmed our initial objective of using it as support information to the narrative description conveyed by the interviewer.

Finally the interviewers were asked to describe the nature of the residential area of the respondent and the type of house. The results are presented in Tables 7.15 and 7.16.

Table 7.15: CESOP's house classification

Hut or degraded place	Low rank accommodation	Medium rank accommodation	High rank accommodation	Luxurious flat or palatial house
4.8	29.6	53.3	10.7	1.5

Table 7.16: Residential area (%)

Rural	Rural/Urban	Urban
10.7	53.9	35.5

7.6 Conclusions

This chapter provided a descriptive statistical analysis of the survey responses. We verified that the CV application covered rather well the different demographic clusters of the Portuguese population. Therefore, we conclude that the sample is representative. Finally, and according to the interviewer assessment responses, we can also conclude that the great majority of the respondents understood the survey narrative and the elicitation question.

Chapter

8

NON-PARAMETRIC TESTING PROCEDURES OF THE STATED WTP RESPONSES

8.1 Introduction

In this chapter we test the methodological validity of the CV survey instrument as a technique for the value measurement of the recreation and non-use benefits provided by the Alentejo Natural Park (Nunes 1998a). In this context, we designed different survey formats. These reflect the use of different survey information levels and different payment vehicles.

The chapter is organized as follows. In section 8.2 we describe the different survey versions and respective sample dimensions. Then, we focus on the 'no–no' answers and identify the possible arguments underlying such response behaviour. In section 8.3 we proceed to the study of the WTP responses and explore formal testing procedures so as to assess the validity of the CV as a measurement instrument. First, we focus on the different levels of survey information concerning the government's finance effort in running the Alentejo Natural Park and test whether the different levels influence the stated willingness to pay responses. Second, we test whether different payment vehicles influence the stated willingness to pay responses. Given the nature of the elicitation question, we perform formal testing under the single and double bounded responses model. In all the test specifications we do not assume any particular underlying distribution prior, that is to say, this chapter explores non-parametric testing procedures of the stated willingness to pay responses.

8.2 The survey formats

Given the present zoning of the Alentejo Natural Park, we are able to characterize the Park in terms of two major zones: the Wilderness Areas and the Recreational Areas. The first refers to the geographical area of the Park that is allocated to the protection of local biodiversity. The second category refers to the geographical area of the Park that is allocated to recreational use. Given that, we design three survey versions corresponding to three protection policy options – see Table 8.1.

Table 8.1: Protection policy options

Version 1: Preventing tourism development in WA
Version 2: Preventing tourism development in RA
Version 3: Preventing tourism development in both WA and RA

Combining the three protection policy options with the use of the 'TAX' and 'VC' payment vehicles as well as with the 'ON' and 'OFF' information levels, we come up with a set of seven survey formats – see Table 8.2.

Table 8.2: Survey formats

	WA Protection programme		RA Protection programme		(WA + RA) Protection programme		
Information	ON	ON	ON	ON	OFF	OFF	ON
Payment vehicle	TAX	VC	TAX	VC	TAX	VC	VC
Survey formats	A	B	C	D	E	F	G
N	230	241	220	242	173	194	378

As far as the level of information is concerned we distinguish two survey formats: in one the respondent, just before the elicitation question, is explicitly informed about the government costs in keeping the Natural Park as a protected area (ON); in the other one the respondent is not provided with such information (OFF). As for the payment vehicle, we also design two survey variants. We refer to the national tax (TAX) and the voluntary contribution (VC) schemes. In all survey versions it is clear to the respondents that the current government expenditures allocated to the Alentejo Natural Park are insufficient to continue guaranteeing to all Portuguese that there will not be any tourism development in the Park. The respective testing procedures are discussed in the following section.

8.3 Stated WTP responses: testing procedures

The first step in testing the validity of the WTP responses consisted in the analysis of the no–no' responses. This is because such an answering pattern usually accounts for a substantial proportion of the total responses[72] and there is a general belief that some respondents, despite the fact that they may have a positive value for the good in question, will give a 'no–no' for strategic reasons (Römer and Pommerehne 1992). These respondents are described in the literature as zero-response protests, or simply protests. So as to identify zero-response protests, the 'no–no' respondents are asked to state their motive for bidding zero.

8.3.1 'No–no' responses

In this study, we found that the overall sample 'no–no' response rate remains approximately the same across the three survey versions ranging from 39% to 49% – see results in Table 8.3.

---

[72] Some studies report significant zero bids, including Kirkland (1988) with 73% and, more recently, Johansson, Kriström and Nyquist (1994) with 78%.

Table 8.3: The 'no–no' response distribution

	WA protection programme			RA Protection programme			(WA + RA) protection programme			
	TAX	VC	Pool	TAX	VC	Pool	TAX	VC(a)	VC(b)	Pool
Total responses	230	241	471	220	242	462	175	194	378	745
% of 'no–no' responses	39.6	43.6	41.7	37.2	52.4	45.2	39.3	47.9	49.5	46.7
Test statistic χ^2		0.77			10.7*					5.0

(a) Information OFF
(b) Information ON;
* Significant at 5% confidence level

Other CV studies find similar response proportions: 42% in a CV mail survey in Australia that focused on the flora and fauna (Jakobsson and Dragun 1996); 40% in a personal interview survey focused on the *Exxon Valdez* oil spill (Carson *et al.* 1992). To understand better such a response pattern we propose to investigate the 'no–no' answering behaviour. Therefore, we propose to test:

Hypothesis 1: the 'no–no' response distribution across the TAX and VC survey formats is the same for the identified protection programmes.

and compare the overall 'no–no' response sample proportion across the payment vehicles, expecting that the underlying response distribution will remain unchanged (Kriström 1990). We test the hypotheses in a non-parametric way and use the standard Pearson chi-square test.[73] The results are reported in Table 8.3. The computed test statistics are χ^2 distributed with 1, 2 and 1 degrees of freedom, respectively for the WA, (WA + RA) and RA protection programmes, with an associated critical value of 5.02 and 7.38 at the 5% confidence level.

We can observe that, for each survey version, the 'no–no' response rate is systematically higher in the VC format than in the TAX format. These results suggest the eventual presence of free-riding behaviour. As we have shown in our theoretical analysis in Chapter 3, unlike the TAX survey format, the respondents in the VC survey format are not informed that this contribution has to be an obligation for everyone. Therefore, the respondents in the VC scheme have a stronger incentive to understate their true preferences, expecting the others to come up with the payment for the provision of the described protection plan. Furthermore, the incentive to 'over pledge', as referred by Carson *et al.* (1999) in the hypothetical voluntary contribution setting, seems here not to receive much support from empirical evidence.

Nevertheless, with the exception of the RA protection programme, all the χ^2 values are insignificant. This indicates that there is no statistical difference in the 'no–no' distribution across the two payment formats. As far as the RA programme is concerned, the 'no–no' response sample proportion in the VC is statistically different (higher) from the 'no–no' response proportion in the TAX format. To understand better such 'no–no' answering behaviour we include a section in the survey instrument containing a list of arguments that could possibly justify such answering behaviour. The complete list presented in the instrument

---

[73] We use Monte Carlo algorithms provided by the StaXact3 to calculate the χ^2 test statistics.

survey is given in Table 8.4. Without having the ambition of being exhaustive, the list tries to capture the possible reasons for 'no–no' refusals.

	Table 8.4: Reasons for not being willing to pay for the protection programme (%)	
i)	I can not afford to contribute so much money	45.2
ii)	I do not believe in the described tax scheme	11.0
	I do not believe in the national fund campaign	
iii)	I prefer to spend that amount of money elsewhere	2.7
iv)	The proposed protection plan is not worth so much money	2.8
v)	I do not agree with this type of question	4.3
vi)	The proposed protection plan is a break in the development of the region	4.5
vii)	I believe that this questionnaire is not the best way to approach the topic	2.6
viii)	The protection of nature does not have a price	4.9
ix)	I do not accept any increase in the taxes	22.0
	I do not accept participation in a funding campaign	

From this list, respondents are asked to choose the most important motive that them think is responsible for being unwilling to pay any positive amount of money. A major share of the respondents were unwilling to contribute with the stated bids, arguing that they could not afford it. As a matter of fact, reason i) constitutes the major factor for the 'no–no' answering behaviour, accounting for about 46 %. This can be interpreted as an indicator that the transaction is taken seriously, meaning that the respondent considers a 'yes' answer to imply the payment of the stated bid. The response associated with the argument that protection programmes are not worth the stated monetary amount was given by fewer than 3 % of the respondents. Around the same number of respondents argued that they would prefer to spend the money on other things rather than contribute to the protection of the Park. Surprisingly, fewer than 5 % of the respondents did not accept putting any monetary amount into the protection programmes (reason viii).[74] Suggestions about the lack of seriousness of the payment vehicles were frequently made, reason ii), counting for 11 % of the 'no–no' responses. The respondent's reluctance to accept the questionnaire to deal with the topic, reasons v) and vii), account for 7 %. Such magnitudes may be associated with the fact that the Portuguese respondents are rather unfamiliar with this kind of survey approach and thus may be reluctant to accept CV as a possible valuation tool.

The explicit objection to the payment mechanism is 22 %, by far the strongest factor manifesting the respondent's zero protest response. Unlike the other reasons, ii), v), vii) and ix) are zero bids given for other reasons than a zero value being placed on the resource in question. Actually, they reflect a set of the respondent's objections concerning the lack of seriousness of the proposed payment mechanism – reason ii); or the respondent's disapproval towards the payment mechanism – reason ix) – or even the respondent's reluctance to accept the questionnaire as an approach to deal with the topic – reasons v) and vii). For these motives

---

[74] Some authors interpret this answer's motive as an indicator of the presence of lexicographic preferences towards environmental commodities (Ehrenfield 1988; Norton 1988; Hanley and Spash 1993; Hanley and Milne 1996).

we interpret these respondents as *zero protesters*. [75] These observations are removed from the tests as described in the present chapter.

8.3.2 Testing for the presence of valuation 'anchoring'

The present study distinguishes two survey formats corresponding to two different levels of the information. In one survey format, the respondent is explicitly given an indication as to how much money is currently being spent by the government in keeping the Natural Park as a protected area (ON); in the other one the respondent is not provided with such information (OFF). Both survey formats are applied to scenario version three, which focuses on preventing the tourism development in both WA and RA of the Alentejo Natural Park. Moreover, in ON and OFF survey formats, all respondents face the voluntary contribution scheme as a payment vehicle.

Some authors suggest that respondents do not have a well-defined valuation for environmental goods because they are not familiar with the CV valuation exercise. In this context, the indication in the survey as to how much money is spent on protection is interpreted by those authors as the major determinant of the respondent's final valuation (Bergstrom *et al.* 1989; Desvousges *et al.* 1993). In the presence of such 'anchoring' phenomena, we may expect a WTP_{ON} distribution with a fatter (thinner) tail than the WTP_{OFF} distribution, since informing respondents about the large government financial effort spent on the protection of the Park might be used by them as a signal about the Park monetary valuation and, in this way, might influence upwards (downwards) their stated WTP response (Herriges and Shogren 1996). Therefore, we wish to test the following proposition:

Hypothesis 2: the WTP distribution in the survey format OFF and ON is the same.

If we expect to support the internal validity of our contingent valuation experiment, we believe that CV responses reflect respondents' unobserved WTP and thus are robust as to whether respondents are given an initial financial indication. That is, we expect not to reject Hypothesis 2. The elicitation format used in the survey allows us to perform two types of non-parametric tests. The first deals with the stated WTP answers to the first question of the referendum, that is, the single bounded response model; the second approach deals with the stated WTP answers to both the first question and the follow-up question of the referendum, that is, the double bounded response model.

Single bounded response model

We test Hypothesis 2 in a non-parametric fashion by calculating the 'no' response rate at each initial bid for both survey types. The proportion of respondents rejecting the identified bids in the survey type OFF is then compared with the observed proportion of rejections in the survey type ON, expecting that the underlying distribution remains unchanged (Kriström 1990). Table 8.5 gives the response results for both survey types. For testing the null hypothesis the standard Pearson chi-square test is used. [76] The computed test statistics have one degree of freedom with a critical value of 5.02 at the 5% confidence level. The empirical evidence fails to reject the hypothesis that the underlying response distribution is the same across the two information types (all the χ^2 values are clearly insignificant).

---

[75] These respondents are often not taken into account in the estimation analysis (see Halstead *et al.* 1992).

[76] We use Monte Carlo algorithms provided by the StaXact3 *for* Windows® to calculate the exact test statistics.

Table 8.5: Response distributions to the initial WTP question

Bid card		Survey format		Statistic χ^2
		Information ON	Information OFF	
1 200	Total responses	78	40	
	Percentage of 'yes'	60.26	65.00	0.25
2 400	Total responses	81	41	
	Percentage of 'yes'	49.38	65.85	2.98
4 800	Total responses	86	41	
	Percentage of 'yes'	38.37	36.59	0.03
9 600	Total responses	77	39	
	Percentage of 'yes'	40.24	35.88	0.20

Double bounded response model

We use the Turnbull (1976) likelihood estimation approach[77] to estimate the cumulative density of the WTP in the intervals defined by the monetary thresholds used in the different bid designs. So as to exclude the effect of potential outliers, and thus improve the statistical power of the non-parametric tests, we truncate the right-hand side of the tail of the distribution. In this context, we construct a sub-sample of the WTP distribution in which we exclude all the stated WTP answers that are more than 5% of the reported income of the respondent (Diamond *et al.* 1993; Ready and Hu 1995). For both samples the stated WTP data is brought in one single 'sample', which is captured by the *pool* column – see Table 8.6. According to the pooled data set, we verify that the median estimate lies in the 2400 – 3600 escudos interval.

Table 8.6: Response distributions to the double WTP question

Bid intervals		Change in the cumulative density function					
		All sample			5% trimmed		
Lower bound	Upper bound	Format ON	Format OFF	Pool	Format ON	Format OFF	Pool
0	600	0.39	0.31	0.36	0.44	0.37	0.41
6 00	1 200	0.39	0.37	0.38	0.44	0.43	0.43
1 200	2 400	0.48	0.45	0.47	0.54	0.52	0.53
2 400	3 600	0.66	0.67	0.67	0.73	0.65	0.73
3 600	4 800	0.66	0.67	0.67	0.73	0.65	0.73
4 800	9 600	0.81	0.78	0.80	0.85	0.74	0.84
9 600	24 000	0.99	0.99	0.99	0.99	0.99	0.99
	N	322	161	483	287	138	425
	Ln N	–392.55	–198.50	–594.14	–327.04	–153.54	–484.59
	LR			6.18			8.02

---

[77] The Turnbull estimation procedure is a non-parametric estimation approach, that is, no assumption is made about the shape of the underlying WTP distribution.

The maximum logarithm likelihood statistic is estimated for each type of data. We test if the estimated cumulative distributions of the WTP are the same across the survey formats and run the likelihood ratio test (LR). The computed test statistics are χ^2 distributed with ten degrees of freedom with a critical value of 20.48 for the overall sample, and eight degrees of freedom with a critical value of 17.53 for the trimmed subsample.[78] Both tests clearly fail to reject the hypotheses of equal distributions for the two types of surveys, that is, the empirical evidence rejects the 'anchor' valuation phenomenon, thus the indication in the questionnaire of how much money is spent in the protection does not have an effect in the respondents' final valuation. Therefore, we pool the data across the two survey formats, ON and OFF, and work with a single *pooled* data set.[79]

8.3.3 Testing for the presence of free riding

In this section we focus on the effects of the payment vehicle upon the stated WTP answers. We propose the empirical investigation of the National Park tax (TAX) and voluntary contribution (VC) effects on the stated WTP as modelled in Chapter 3. As we have seen, these two payment vehicles disclose different strategic behaviour. When compared to the TAX referendum rule, the VC payment vehicle does not imply an obligation to pay on everyone and so each respondent has a stronger incentive to free ride on another's contributions. Therefore, we may expect that the WTP_{TAX} distribution has a fatter right-hand side tail than the WTP_{VC} distribution or, in other words, a lower overall 'no-no' response sample proportion. Thus we test the following proposition:

Hypothesis 3: the WTP distribution in the survey format TAX and VC is the same.[80]

Once more, the elicitation format used in the national survey allows us to perform two non-parametric testing procedures: the first deals with the single bounded response model; the second approach deals with the double bounded response model.

Single bounded response model

We test Hypothesis 3 by calculating the 'no' response rate to the initial question contained in each bid card. The proportion of respondents rejecting the identified bids in the survey type TAX is then compared with the observed proportion of rejections in the survey type VC, expecting that the underlying distribution would remain unchanged. Again, the standard Pearson chi-square test and the respective test statistic is used. For the great majority of the bid amounts, across the three protection programmes, we can verify that the percentage of individuals saying 'yes' to the initial question is higher in the TAX survey format than in the

---

[78] The test statistic is computed by the formula $-2\ln\Lambda$ with Λ defined as the ratio between the maximum likelihood under H_0 and the maximum likelihood under H_1, with H_0: restricted model is true, and H_1: unrestricted model is not true. Finally, v denotes the degrees of freedom of the test statistic and is defined as $2*(d_{f1} - d_{f2})$, with d_{f1} = degrees of freedom of the unrestricted model and d_{f2} = degrees of freedom of the pooled (or restricted) model.

[79] Since the chi-square test statistics are referred to relatively small samples, we also test the impact of information in a parametric fashion. Therefore, we suggest assuming the 'information context' to be an explanatory variable of the stated WTP responses, together with other variables such as the respondent's income and attitudes towards conservation. The estimation results confirm the chi-square test results. See Appendix E, which comprehension is much easier after having read Chapters 10 and 11.

[80] In other words, Hypothesis 1 (in a indirect way) and Hypothesis 3 (in a direct way) test whether free-riding behaviour is present.

Table 8.7: Response distributions to the initial WTP question

Bid	Responses	Environmental protection plan								
		WA			RA			(WA + RA)		
		VC	TAX	χ^2	VC	TAX	χ^2	VC	TAX	χ^2
1 200	total	53	46		49	49		40	39	
	% of yes	60.4	73.9	2.03	71.4	71.4	1.00	65.0	58.9	0.02
2 400	total	55	44		53	41		41	31	
	% of yes	47.3	65.9	3.44	49.1	70.7	4.74	65.8	80.6	0.30
4 800	total	51	48		55	43		41	34	
	% of yes	45.1	56.2	1.23	43.6	72.0	7.94*	36.7	52.9	1.92
9 600	total	56	38		52	41		39	31	
	% of yes	44.6	47.3	0.07	26.7	20.8	10.9*	35.8	58.0	2.02

* = indicates significantly different at 5% level.

VC format. Table 8.7 gives the response results for the three environmental protection plans. These empirical findings confirm our theoretical analysis of the individual's own contributions as presented in Chapter 3, i.e., the TAX payment vehicle, when compared to the VC scheme, presents a weaker incentive for free riding. However, the statistical magnitude of free riding behavior is not particularly strong in the sample. As a matter of fact, most of the test statistics results lead us not to reject Hypothesis 3 (with the exception of the last two bid values at the RA programme, all the χ^2 values are insignificant). This means that, despite the fact that the empirical evidence cannot deny the presence of free riding behavior in the sample, the respective statistical magnitude is not sufficiently strong to lead us to say that WTP_{TAX} and WTP_{VC} follow different underlying distributions.

Finally, and to conclude, a possible interpretation of the higher (and statistically significant) percentage of 'yes' in the VC scheme for RA – see the last bid value for the protection of the Recreation Area – could be the point of Carson *et al.* (1999), that is, that voluntary contributions can exceed tax payments when the payment vehicle is hypothetical. However, the support for such an argument seems to us here rather weak: if we agree that this result is an outcome of over pledging, how can we explain that the VC 'yes' percentage is smaller for the other protection programmes? According to us, such a contingent result is more easily interpreted by the hypothesis that the respondents are signalling a strong aversion to pay relatively high tax amounts for recreational protection of the Alentejo Natural Park.

Double bounded response Model

We proceed to the study of the payment vehicle impact in the stated WTP responses and examine the respondent answering behaviour in the follow-up question. We use the Turnbull likelihood estimation approach for estimating the cumulative density of the WTP in the intervals defined by the monetary thresholds used in the different bid cards. The estimated non-parametric distributions for the two types of payment vehicles across the different protection plans are reported in Table 8.8. Included in the table is a single distribution that is constructed by pooling the data across the national tax and the voluntary contribution.

For each protection plan, we test if the estimated cumulative distributions of the WTP are the same across the TAX and VC survey formats by calculating the LR test. These test statistics are χ^2 distributed with 10, 12 and 10 degrees of freedom, respectively, for the RA, WA and (WA + RA) protection programmes. In all bid intervals the cumulative density of

Table 8.8: Response distributions to the double WTP question – full sample

Bid intervals		Environmental protection plan								
		WA			RA			(WA + RA)		
Lower bound	Upper bound	TAX	CV	Pool	TAX	CV	Pool	TAX	CV	Pool
0	600	0.18	0.40	0.30	0.16	0.40	0.27	0.23	0.31	0.28
600	1 200	0.24	0.40	0.33	0.20	0.40	0.30	0.23	0.36	0.30
1 200	2 400	0.36	0.47	0.42	0.29	0.52	0.41	0.32	0.44	0.38
2 400	3 600	0.59	0.62	0.60	0.49	0.70	0.60	0.59	0.66	0.63
3 600	4 800	0.59	0.63	0.60	0.49	0.70	0.60	0.59	0.66	0.63
4 800	9 600	0.79	0.79	0.78	0.69	0.83	0.76	0.75	0.78	0.76
9 600	24 000	0.99	0.99	0.99	0.98	0.97	0.98	0.96	0.99	0.97
	N	176	215	391	174	209	383	135	161	296
	Ln N	−232.2	−278.5	−518.9	−232.8	−238.3	−485.2	−190.9	−198.5	−393.6
	LR			16.48			28.10[*]			8.54

*= indicates significantly different at 5% level

distribution is systematically higher for the TAX format. However, such differences are not statistically significant for both WA and (WA + RA) protection programmes. As in the single response model setting, we are not able to reject Hypothesis 3 in the WA and (WA + RA) protection programmes. However, the hypothesis of equal distributions for the two payment vehicles continues to be rejected at the 5% level for the RA protection programme: the value of LR=28.10 is still significant at the 1% significance level. We can verify that in the RA subsample the estimated cumulative WTP_{TAX} distribution presents a rather fatter tail: at 9 600 escudos there is about 69% of accumulated density - much less than in other sub-samples, which are all above 75%.

How can we interpret this result? Would not it seem more reasonable to expect to find stronger free riding in the WA protection programme whose characteristics are closer to the pure public good? Well, one possible way of looking at the present results is to admit that the RA protection programme, when compared to the remaining protection plans, is seen and understood by the respondents as the least hypothetical development scenario, thus making the financial transaction more likely to occur. In this context, together with the understanding of the impossibility of excluding anyone from visiting the Park, the VC payment vehicle, when compared to the TAX scheme, presents particularly strong incentives to free ride. We repeat the same test exercise but now truncate the right-hand tail of the distribution so that we can exclude potential outliers, that is, respondents who stated a high WTP response. The sample trimming criterion is characterized by excluding the respondents who stated high WTP responses. In this context, we construct a sub-sample of the WTP distribution in which we exclude all the stated WTP answers that are more than 5% of the reported income of the respondent. The respective estimates of the distributions across the two types of payment vehicles for the three protection plans are reported in Table 8.9. The computed χ^2 test statistics have 10, 10 and 8 degrees of freedom, respectively for the WA, RA and (WA + RA) protection programmes. As far as the RA protection programme is concerned, the test statistic is slightly below the critical value 20.48, and thus leads us to say that free riding is no longer statistically significant. As far as the WA and (WA + RA) protection programmes are concerned, the tests results continue to fail to reject Hypothesis 3. A possible interpretation for such a finding is admitting that, by trimming the respondents who report a relative high WTP

Table 8.9: Response distributions to the double WTP question – 5% trimmed

Bid intervals		Environmental protection plan								
		WA			RA			WA+RA		
Lower bound	Upper bound	TAX	CV	Pool	TAX	CV	Pool	TAX	CV	Pool
0	600	0.21	0.49	0.36	0.21	0.47	0.34	0.29	0.36	0.34
600	1 200	0.28	0.49	0.40	0.27	0.47	0.38	0.29	0.43	0.37
1 200	2 400	0.43	0.58	0.52	0.40	0.62	0.52	0.40	0.52	0.47
2 400	3 600	0.67	0.73	0.70	0.65	0.80	0.73	0.69	0.75	0.73
3 600	4 800	0.67	0.73	0.70	0.65	0.80	0.73	0.69	0.75	0.73
4 800	9 600	0.87	0.88	0.87	0.83	0.89	0.86	0.87	0.84	0.85
9 600	24 000	0.98	0.99	0.98	0.98	0.98	0.98	0.97	0.99	0.97
	N	146	175	321	129	178	307	109	138	247
	Ln N	−179.3	−207.3	−395.8	−168.1	−176.0	−353.6	−146.2	−153.5	−305.7
	LR			18.4			18.9			11.9

when compared to their income, we are excluding respondents who reveal a stronger desire for the good in question and thus less inclined to free ride. In further statistical analysis, the data are pooled across the two survey formats and we work with a single data set. But since the empirical evidence cannot reject the presence of free riding (surely not always statistically significant), special attention is given to the payment vehicle. Therefore, we suggest assuming the payment vehicle as an explanatory variable of the stated WTP responses, together with other variables such as the respondent's income and attitudes towards conservation.

8.4 Conclusions

The present CV application makes use of different information levels and payment vehicles. As far as the information level is concerned, we designed two survey versions: in one the respondent is informed about government expenditures in keeping the Natural Park free from any commercial development, in the other s/he is not informed. As far as the payment vehicle is concerned, we also designed two survey versions: in one survey version a national tax scheme is selected as the payment vehicle; in the second survey version a voluntary contribution to a national fund is selected as the payment vehicle. We explored non-parametric formal test procedures and investigated whether the stated WTP are affected by the proposed payment vehicle and level of survey information. The test results suggested that the stated WTP distribution in the scenario where the respondent is informed about the government expenditures in keeping the Natural Park free from any commercial development is not statistically different from the WTP distribution in the scenario where the respondent is not provided with such information. This test result can be interpreted as a rejection of the starting point bias hypothesis. That is, the hypothesis that states that the indication in the survey of how much money is spent on the Alentejo Natural Park is used by the respondent as a 'clue' about the Park's valuation is rejected. The test results also confirmed that in the national tax scheme free-riding behaviour is less strong when compared to the voluntary contribution – though the respective magnitudes are hardly statistically significant. These results were interpreted as important indicators in confirming the validity of the proposed questionnaire as a value measurement instrument.

Chapter
9

A UNIVARIATE ESTIMATION OF THE STATED WTP RESPONSES

9.1 Introduction

In this chapter we assume that the stated willingness to pay (WTP) responses follow a particular distribution family and compute WTP estimates for each of the described protection programmes. The proposed estimation approach is anchored in the double dichotomous choice elicitation format (Nunes 1998b). The underlying idea is that the respondents evaluate their utility in two stages, with and without protection plan, and if they think that their willingness to pay for the described scenario exceeds the stated bid, then they would agree to pay, or else refuse it. Consequently we use a limited dependent variable choice model and explore the variation of the bid values across the sample to assess the underlying valuation (Maddala 1983; Judge *et al.* 1985; Agresti 1990). Moreover, we use the predicted values to investigate the respondent's structure of preferences. In this context, we tested the degree of sensitivity of the WTP estimate with respect to the described protection programmes and check whether an embedding is present in the stated WTP responses.

The chapter is divided into three sections. In the first section, we present the limited dependent variable choice model and proceed to the choice of the distribution that best fits the data. In the second section, having adopted the distributional prior, we compute univariate WTP estimates for the WA, RA and (WA + RA) protections programmes. Finally, in the third section, we explore inference analysis so as to investigate the sensitivity of the computed estimates across the different protection programmes.

9.2 The model

We use the observed respondent's decision upon the two bid amounts offered to him/her in sequence as a proxy variable for the unobserved $WTP(t_{WTP})$. Therefore, for each respondent we face four possible response outcomes: 'yes–yes', 'no–no', 'yes–no' and 'no–yes'. The probability of a 'yes–yes' outcome is given by:

$$\pi_{YY}(b_i, b_h) = P(b_h \leq t_{WTP}) = 1 - F(b_h; \theta) \tag{9.1}$$

The probability of a 'no–no' outcome is given by:

$$\pi_{NN}(b_i, b_l) = P(b_l > t_{WTP}) = F(b_l; \theta) \tag{9.2}$$

The probability of a 'yes–no' outcome is given by:

$$\pi_{YN}(b_i, b_h) = P(b_i \leq t_{WTP} \wedge b_h > t_{WTP})$$
$$= F(b_h; \theta) - F(b_i; \theta) \tag{9.3}$$

and finally the probability of a 'no–yes' outcome is given by:

$$\pi_{NY}(b_i, b_l) = P(b_l \leq t_{WTP} \wedge b_i > t_{WTP})$$
$$= F(b_i; \theta) - F(b_l; \theta) \tag{9.4}$$

where b_i, b_h and b_l are, respectively, the initial, lower and higher bids used for the respondent[81] and $F(b; \theta, x)$ is some statistical distribution function with parameter vector θ. F is here interpreted as the cumulative distribution function (cdf) of the respondent's WTP. The underlying distribution is characterized by vector a θ, which is constituted by two elements, respectively the location and scale parameters. Finally, x represents the vector of explanatory variables of the WTP (for example, the individual's motivation functions and socio-demographic characteristics). The contribution to the likelihood function from one observation is then:

$$r_{nn}{}^i \ln F(b_l) + r_{ny}{}^i \ln[F(b_i) - F(b_l)] + r_{yn}{}^i \ln[F(b_h) - F(b_i)] + r_{yy}{}^i \ln[1 - F(b_h)] \tag{9.5}$$

with $r_{nn}{}^i$, $r_{ny}{}^i$, $r_{yn}{}^i$ and $r_{yy}{}^i$ denoting binary indicators variables, for example, a 'no–no' response corresponds to a $r_{nn}{}^i = 1$ and $r_{ny}{}^i = r_{yn}{}^i = r_{yy}{}^i = 0$. The sum of these contributions to the likelihood function over the sample is maximized assuming a parametric form for the distribution function F. So, we fit several distributions to the double bounded data. We use the Weibull distribution, the log-normal distribution, the exponential distribution and the log-logistic. Moreover, these distributions have been used by practitioners of CV.[82] The task is to choose the distribution that best fits the data. For that we compute the log-likelihood statistic for each of the distributions across the different survey versions – see Table 9.1.

---

[81] To avoid over-notation we suppressed the ith respondent superscripts.

[82] An example of use of the Weibull distribution is Imber, Stevenson, and Wilks (1991). Mitchell and Carson (1989) assert that stated WTP often appears to be log-normally distributed. Rowe et al. (1991), among others, use log-normal assumption in their analysis.

Table 9.1: Log likelihood statistics across different distributions for all survey versions

Survey version	Log-normal	Weibull	Exponential	Log-logistic
WA	–515.25	–504.14	–522.81	–517.09
RA	–488.62	–479.78	–500.28	–491.13
(WA + RA)	–807.78	–796.72	–841.17	–810.67

The analysis of the Weibull vs. Exponential distribution is straightforward because these are nested distributions. Using the restricted and unrestricted log-likelihood, we are able to reject the exponential distribution in favour of the Weibull.[83] This test cannot be extended to the log-normal and log-logistic because these distributions are nested neither with the Weibull nor with the Exponential. For the Weibull, log-normal and log-logistic distribution families, we choose to run the analysis of the goodness of fit on the basis of the Akaike information criteria (AIC). The AIC is a method for deciding which type of parametric assumption provides a better fit to the data (Akaike 1973). According to this method, the distribution family that presents the best fit is characterized by the lowest AIC value. Table 9.2 reports the AIC values for each distribution family across the three protection programmes.

Table 9.2: AIC values

Protection programme	Log-normal	Weibull	Log-logistic
WA	1035	1012	1038
RA	835	828	837
(WA + RA)	1620	1597	1625

The Weibull provides the best fit according to AIC; the AIC value is the lowest with the Weibull. We can also observe that the respective AIC's are not a lot smaller when compared with the log-normal, which presents the second best fit. Furthermore, the log-normal presents an heavier tail than the Weibull distribution (see Figure 9.1). Since we believe in the presence of a heavy tail on the true WTP underlying distribution,[84] we choose to run our parametric estimations assuming a log-normal distribution. Finally, when assuming the log-normal we benefit from a lower complexity in the involved estimation procedures.

9.3 Estimated WTP

Maximizing the likelihood function for the double-bounded WTP data allows us to estimate the location and scale parameters of a parametric distribution, $\hat{\beta}$ and $\hat{\sigma}$, and in this way allows us to compute the mean of the population distribution for the WA, RA and (WA + RA) protection programmes (Carson *et al.* 1992; Diamond *et al.* 1993). We applied the parametric

---

[83] The Weibull distribution (unrestricted model) collapses to the exponential distribution (restricted model) when the scale parameter is 1. The likelihood test statistics equal 37.34, 34.32 and 88.9 respectively for the WA, RA and (WA + RA) protection programmes. The tests clearly exceed 3.84, the critical value at the 95 % reference level, dictating the rejection of the exponential distribution.

[84] The right-hand side tail corresponds to respondents with a very high WTP (Nunes 1998b).

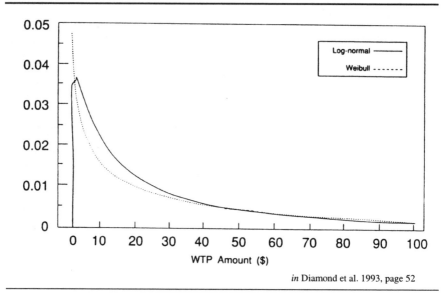

in Diamond et al. 1993, page 52

Figure 9.1: Probability density functions

approach to the full samples and the subsamples excluding the zero-protest-response (see estimates in Table 9.3).

As far as the full sample is concerned, we get WTP mean estimates of about 9600, 7200 and 9100 escudos, respectively for the WA, RA and (WA + RA) protection programmes.[85] After cleaning for strategic zero-protest-response, we get, as expected, higher WTP mean estimates. In the sample free from zero-protest-response the WTP mean estimates range from 9800 escudos, for the WA protection programme, to 7600 for the RA protection programme. The mean estimate for the (WA + RA) protection programme is 9300 escudos. The β and σ standard errors indicate that the parameters are estimated precisely. This precision is reflected in the 90 % confidence intervals. We can also observe that, for each protection programme, the median estimates are significantly smaller than the mean estimates.[86] This result reflects the asymmetric shape of the log-normal probability distribution. This means that the mean estimates are particularly sensitive to the right-hand side of the distribution, and thus to the respondents who say 'yes–yes' to the higher stated bid amounts, Conversely, the median estimates are particularly sensible to the left-hand side of the distribution, and thus the respondents who say 'no–no' to the stated bids. Since a great deal of respondents say 'no' to both WTP questions, this drags down substantially the median estimates (when compared to the mean values) and we get median estimates that vary from 2200 escudos, for the RA protection programme, to 2700 escudos for the WA protection programme - in the sample free from zero-protest-responses.

---

[85] Which corresponds, respectively, to 48, 36 and 45 euro.

[86] For a parametric model with a log-normal distribution, the mean WTP is given by $WTP = e^{\hat{\beta}+\frac{1}{2}\hat{\sigma}^2}$ where β and σ denote the location and scale parameters of the distribution. The median for the log-normal distribution is given by $WTP = e^{\hat{\beta}}$ (see Johnson and Kotz 1970). Calculations are performed using $SAS^{\circledR}$ programming.

If we compare the valuations results to other valuation studies we do not find any major surprise: (a) the mean WTP for the protection of the Wilderness Area is similar to the results obtained by Diamond *et al.* 1991; (b) the mean WTP for the protection of the Recreational Area is similar to the results obtained by Boyle 1990 – see results in Table 9.4.

We analyse the dichotomous-choice (DC) estimation results and contrast them with the estimation results obtained with the respondents' answers to the open-ended (OE) questions.[87] The OE results are reported in Table 9.5 and plotted against the DC estimates in Figure 9.2. In Figure 9.2 we can observe three important results concerning the population mean.

First, the point estimate of the mean associated with the OE elicitation question is, for all the survey versions, lower than the point mean estimate resulting from the DC. This is in accordance with the CV state-of-the-art literature which considers the OE as a conservative elicitation question format when compared to the WTP estimates calculated with the dichotomous choice question format.[88] Second, the width of the mean estimate confidence interval is, for all survey versions, wider in the DC format than in the OE format. This reflects the statistical inefficiency of the DC format that requires substantially larger samples for the same level of precision. In this context, and for the same sample dimension, the DC format provides a lower level of estimation precision when compared to the OE elicitation format. Finally, we observe that, for each protection programme, there are overlapping confidence intervals for the estimated parametric mean across the two elicitation question formats, that is, the DC and OE. These suggest that significant differences do not exist between such estimates.

As far as the population median is concerned, the difference in the open-ended and dichotomous predicted WTP estimates are of opposite sign, that is, the DC median estimates present more conservative values than the OE estimates. Again, this fact reiterates the asymmetric shape of the log-normal probability distribution function, where the highest share of the probability distribution function is concentrated in the left-hand tail of the distribution, and confirms the high proportion of 'no–no' responses in the DC elicitation format. Finally, we can verify that the log-normal median WTP estimates are consistent with the median confidence intervals as estimated by the non-parametric approach presented in the previous chapter. This fact constitutes an additional reason supporting the choice of working with the log-normal distribution so as to compute parametric WTP estimates.

---

[87] The open-ended (OE) estimates were also calculated with the help of SAS assuming that the WTP are drawn from a log-normal distribution.

[88] The DC format encourages the 'yea saying' where the posted bid is accepted as a hint of what is a reasonable payment (Arndt and Crane 1975; Kanninen 1993; Holmes and Kramer 1995).

Table 9.3: Mean and median log-normal estimates

Double-bounded dichotomous choice estimation models (DC)

ALL SAMPLE

Parameter estimates	WA protection programme		RA protection programme		(WA + RA) protection programme	
	Estimate	Standard error	Estimate	Standard error	Estimate	Standard error
Location (β)	7.642	0.099	7.491	0.099	7.553	0.082
Scale (σ)	1.751	0.109	1.679	0.106	1.774	0.090
Log-likelihood	–565.32		–527.74		–860.60	
Mean	9 600	[6 300–15 000]*	7 200	[4 800–11 100]*	9 100	[6 200–13 700]*
Median	2 100	[1 800–2 400]*	1 800	[1 500–2 100]*	1 900	[1 700–2 200]*

PROTEST-RESPONSES ELIMINATED SAMPLE

Parameter estimates	WA protection programme		RA protection programme		(WA + RA) protection programme	
	Estimate	Estimate	Estimate	Standard error	Estimate	Standard Error
Location (β)	7.918	0.092	7.710	0.094	7.751	0.077
Scale (σ)	1.598	0.096	1.577	0.100	1.662	0.084
Log-likelihood	–515.25		–488.62		–807.72	
Mean	9 800	[6 700–14 600]*	7 600	[5 200–11 700]*	9 300	[6 600–13 300]*
Median	2 700	[2 400–3 200]*	2 200	[1 900–2 600]*	2 300	[2 100–2 600]*

Note: * 90% confidence interval.

Table 9.4: Use and non-use values: some recent empirical studies

Study	Natural resource	Value measured	Survey and year	Sample size	Question format	Payment vehicle	Range of estimates
Nunes (1999)	Wilderness Areas and Recreational Areas of the Alentejo Natural Park, south-western Portugal	Total Value	Personal interview; 1997	1876	Dichotomous question	National fund and national tax	WA programme: $51 RA programme: $40 (WA + RA) programme: $49
Diamond et al. (1993)	Protection of wilderness areas in Colorado, Idaho, Montana, and Wyoming from timber harvesting	Total value (substantial portion is non-use)	Telephone survey; 1991	1400	Direct question	Federal income tax surcharge each year	Mean: $29–$66 Median: $2–$10
Boyle (1990)	Preservation of the Illinois Beach State Nature Preserve	Total value (for both users and nonusers)	Mail survey; 1985	378	Dichotomous question	Contribution to a nonprofit foundation	Mean: $37–$41
Walsh et al. (1984)	Wilderness areas in Colorado	Total value	Mail survey; 1980	218	Direct question	Annual fee to be placed in special fund	Mean: $32
Bennett (1984)	Nadgee Nature Reserve, Southeastern Australia	Existence value	Personal interview; 1979	544	Direct question	One-time lump-sum payment	Mean: $27 Median: $5
Carson et al. (1994)	Kakadu Conservation Zone and National Park, Northern Territory, Australia	Total value	Personal interview; 1990	2561	Dichotomous question	Tax and contribution to a park fund.	Major impact scenario: $123–$143 Minor impact scenario: $52–$80

Source: adapted from Desvousges et al. 1996, p. 120–134.

Table 9.5: Estimated mean and median across the protection programmes

Open-ended estimation models (OE)

Survey version	Mean	90% confidence interval	Median	90% confidence interval	Log likelihood
WA	6100	[5200–7200]	3900	[3500–4300]	–306,48
RA	7100	[6100–8400]	4700	[4300–5300]	–249,15
(WA + RA)	6400	[5700–7300]	4200	[3800–4500]	–470,71

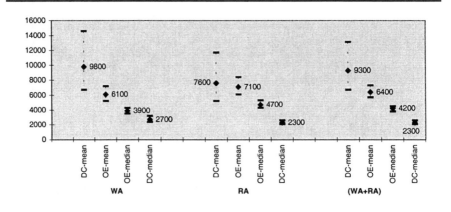

Figure 9.2: WTP parametric estimates

9.4 Sensitivity analysis of the WTP estimates

In a first stage, we check whether the RA and the WA are viewed by the respondents in the same or in different ways, that is, whether the respondents value the recreation and the non-use function of the Alentejo Natural Park equally. Formally we test the following hypothesis:

Hypothesis 4: $E(\text{WTP}_{\text{WA}}) = E(\text{WTP}_{\text{RA}})$,

or in other words, the mean WTP estimates for the recreation and for the wilderness area of the Alentejo Natural Park are the same where WTP_{WA} and WTP_{RA} are defined, respectively, as the solution for each individual to:

$$u\left(p, M, z_{\text{WA}}^{1}\right) = u\left(p, M - \text{WTP}_{\text{WA}}, z^{0}\right)$$

and

$$u\left(p, M, z_{RA}^{1}\right) = u\left(p, M - WTP_{RA}, z^{0}\right)$$

where z represents the environmental quality level. The superscript when equal to 0 denotes the original environmental quality level, that is, the natural park's services flows in the scenario where tourism development is avoided and, when equal to 1 denotes the natural park's services flows in the scenario where tourism development is introduced. Therefore, WTP_{WA} represents the maximum amount that the individual is willing to pay to avoid changes in the environmental quality, that is, to avoid the tourism development of the WA.

If we admit that the RA and WA reflect two different value components of the Alentejo Natural Park, respectively the recreation and the non-use value components, Hypothesis 4 assesses whether the respondents value such components differently or, on the contrary, are willing to pay about the same for both. The log-normal model is fitted to the double referendum responses with the protest responses eliminated. The resulting maximum likelihood estimates for the location parameter and scale parameter are reported in Table 9.6. Included in the table is also the estimated standard error of the parameters, between parentheses, and the likelihood ratio (LR) value for pooling the different programmes into one single model. These statistics are chi-square distributed with two degrees of freedom. Since the LR test statistic is below the critical value, 7.38 at 5%, we conclude that the empirical evidence does not reject the hypothesis that WTP for the WA is about the same as the WTP for the RA.

A further step in the sensitivity analysis of the WTP estimates consists of investigating

Table 9.6: WTP estimates for the RA and WA protection programmes (in PTE)

	Protection programme WA	Protection programme RA	Pooled
$\hat{\beta}$	7.918	7.710	7.814
	(0.092)	(0.094)	(0.066)
$\hat{\sigma}$	1.598	1.577	1.589
	(0.096)	(0.100)	(0.070)
WTP	9800	7600	8600
lnL	−515.25	−488.62	−1005.35
N	380	375	755
LR			2.96

whether the add-up hypothesis holds, that is, whether the sum of the WTP estimate for the WA and for the RA, when measured individually, is larger than the WTP estimate for the two programmes, when measured jointly. One way of proceeding is to investigate whether:

Hypothesis 5: $E\left(WTP_{WA}\right) = E\left(WTP_{(WA+RA)}\right)$,

or in other words, the mean WTP estimate for the wilderness area is the same as the WTP estimate for both wilderness and recreation areas, and,

Hypothesis 6: $E\left(WTP_{RA}\right) = E\left(WTP_{(WA+RA)}\right)$, or in other words, the mean WTP estimate for the recreation area is the same as the WTP estimate for both wilderness and recreation areas where $\mathrm{WTP}_{(WA + RA)}$ is defined according to:

$$u\left(p, M, z^1_{(WA+RA)}\right) = u\left(p, M - \mathrm{WTP}_{(WA+RA)}, z^0\right)$$

As before, $\mathrm{WTP}_{(WA + RA)}$ represents the maximum amount that the individual is willing to pay to avoid changes in the environmental quality, i.e., to avoid the tourism development of the (WA + RA) of the Alentejo Natural Park.

As in the previous test, these statistics are chi-square distributed with two degrees of freedom. When testing Hypothesis 5 the LR test statistic is below the critical value, 5.02 at 5%. Therefore, we conclude that the empirical evidence does not reject the hypothesis that WTP for the WA is about the same as the WTP for the (WA + RA). The same holds for the test of the Hypothesis 6 test; the LR test statistic is also not significant. This means that the WTP estimates for the RA and for the (WA+RA) protection programmes are approximately the same – test results are reported in Tables 9.7 and 9.8.

Table 9.7: WTP estimates for the WA and (WA + RA) protection programmes (in PTE)

	Protection programme WA	Protection programme (WA+RA)	Pooled
$\hat{\beta}$	7.918 (0.092)	7.751 (0.077)	7.824 (0.059)
$\hat{\sigma}$	1.598 (0.096)	1.662 (0.084)	1.638 (0.064)
WTP	9800	9300	9400
lnL	−515.25	−807.72	−1324.27
N	380	608	988
LR			2.66

Table 9.8: WTP estimates for the RA and (WA + RA) protection programmes (in PTE)

	Protection programme RA	Protection programme (WA + RA)	Pooled
$\hat{\beta}$	7.710 (0.094)	7.751 (0.077)	7.743 (0.601)
$\hat{\sigma}$	1.577 (0.100)	1.662 (0.084)	1.629 (0.064)
WTP	7600	9300	8500
lnL	−488.62	−807.72	−1297.80
N	375	608	983
LR			2.92

Bearing in mind the test results as presented in Tables 9.6, 9.7, and 9.8, together with the valuation of the WA and RA protection programmes, as presented in Table 9.3, we are able to conclude that the adding-up hypothesis does not hold, that is, the WTP estimates clearly indicate that $E(\text{WTP}_{WA}) + E(\text{WTP}_{RA}) > E(\text{WTP}_{(WA+RA)})$. How can we interpret these results? What are the respective implications in terms of policy action?

First, according to the WTP estimates across the different protection programmes, as described in Table 9.3, we can observe that:

a) the welfare loss for the Portuguese households associated with the commercial development of the RA of the ANP is estimated to be approximately 114 (68) million euro;[89]

b) the welfare loss for the Portuguese households associated with the commercial development of the WA of the ANP is estimated to be approximately 148 (89) million euro;

c) the welfare loss for the Portuguese households associated with the total commercial development of the ANP is estimated to be approximately 140 (84) million euro.

Therefore we can conclude that the policy action characterized by the partial commercial development of the Alentejo Natural Park is not always preferred to a policy option strategy characterized by the total commercial development of the ANP – the strategy characterized by commercial development of the wilderness areas is the protection programme associated with the highest welfare loss. Furthermore, and if we admit that the final strategy is characterized by the partial commercial development of the ANP,[90] then the Portuguese households clearly prefer to keep the WA of the ANP always protected and introduce the commercial development in the RA.

Second, from the sensitivity analysis of the mean WTP estimates, as described in Table 9.6, 9.7 and 9.8, we can observe that:

d) the WTP for the WA is approximately the same as the WTP for the RA;

e) the WTP for the WA is approximately the same as the WTP for the (WA + RA); and finally

f) the WTP for the RA is approximately the same as the WTP for the (WA + RA).

We can interpret these valuation results in two possible ways. One possible explanation is characterised by admitting that the different service flows provided by the Alentejo Natural Park, respectively the recreational use characteristics and the nonuse characteristics, are pure substitutes. If we admit that the WA and the RA are perfect substitutes then the WTP for the WA is the same as the WTP for the (WA + RA), and the WTP for the RA is the same as the WTP for the (WA + RA). Another possible interpretation is characterized by admitting an eventual presence of embedding in the stated WTP responses, that is, if we admit that the financial contribution, by itself, provides warmglow and thus constitutes also a source of well-being to the individual. Clearly, additional investigation of the structure of the consumer preferences, taking into account the different respondents' characteristics and motivations, will shed light on the interpretation of the WTP estimation results. We will proceed to such an analysis in the following chapter.

---

[89] This number is obtained by multiplying the mean WTP estimate of 7200 PTE, equivalent to 36 euro, by the number of Portuguese households, 3 016 303. The value between brackets gives us a lower bound of the programme valuation, if we assume that the percentage of the households that did not respond have zero WTP.

[90] For example, if the political authority searches for a compromise solution together with the 'developers' and gives land to the lobbying tourism industries.

9.5 Conclusions

Bearing in mind the estimation exercises results we were able to verify that (a) the WTP associated with the policy option characterized by preventing the wilderness area from commercial development has the highest valuation, circa 148 million euro; (b) the valuation of the protection of the RA from commercial development is estimated to be 114 million euro; and, (c) the WTP to prevent the introduction of commercial development in both recreational and wilderness areas is estimated to be 140 million euro – approximately 0.012% of the Portuguese GDP. These valuation results of the protection programmes have important implications in terms of policy action. First, we can conclude that the policy action characterized by the partial commercial development of the Alentejo Natural Park is not always preferred to a policy option strategy characterized by the total commercial development of the Alentejo Natural Park. Second, if we admit that the government intends to pursue a policy action characterized by the partial commercial development of the Alentejo Natural Park, then the valuation results clearly indicate that Portuguese households prefer to keep the wilderness areas of the Alentejo Natural Park always protected and to introduce the commercial development in the recreational areas. This is a very important result since it reiterates the importance of the non-use value component of the Alentejo Natural Park, which can only be assessed with the use of the contingent valuation technique. Furthermore, according to the sensitivity analysis of the mean WTP estimates the valuation of (d) the protection of the wilderness areas from commercial development is approximately the same as the valuation of the protection of both wilderness areas and recreational areas from commercial development. The same holds for the valuation of the recreational areas, that is, (e) the WTP for the recreational areas is about the same as the WTP for both wilderness areas and recreational areas of the Alentejo Natural Park. These results can be interpreted in two possible ways. One explanation is characterized by admitting that the different service flows provided by the Alentejo Natural Park, respectively the recreational use characteristics and the non-use characteristics, are pure substitutes. Another possible interpretation is characterized by admitting an eventual presence of embedding in the stated WTP responses, that is, if we admit that the financial contribution, by itself, provides warmglow and thus constitutes also a source of well-being to the individual. Clearly, additional empirical investigation concerning the structure of the consumer preferences, and thus respondents' motivations, may shed some light on the interpretation of the WTP results. Special attention needs to be focused on the empirical measurement of the warmglow motivation. We will focus on these issues in the following chapters.

Chapter

10

OPERATIONALIZATION OF CONSUMER MOTIVATIONS[*]

10.1 Introduction

In this chapter we analyse the construction of motivational factors. These latent variables, together with the respondents' socio-economic characteristics, will help us to understand and predict the willingness-to-pay responses. The motivational factors are obtained by means of factor analysis.

In the present research we present a list of 26 attitudinal items. Each item is represented by a sentence as presented in Section D of the instrument survey. The respondents express their opinion by classifying each sentence using a five point semantic differential or Likert scale (Likert 1967): 'I completely agree', 'I agree', 'Sometimes I agree, sometimes I disagree', 'I disagree' and 'I completely disagree'. Bearing in mind the value of the scores on the underlying items, we use factor analysis to investigate the nature of the individual consumer preference structure. The relevance of these variables is twofold. First, we are able to test the validity of the proposed valuation model by checking whether the postulated motivational structure holds. Second, we are able to compute the motivation factor scores and introduce them, together with the respondents' socio-economic characteristics, in a multivariate regression of the stated WTP and check there for the statistical robustness of the respective parameter estimates.

This chapter is divided into three sections. In the first section we explore factor analysis as a data reduction technique. This procedure will help us to assess the reliability of the proposed three-factor motivation model, that is, test the validity of the proposed motivational structure. In the second section we present the underlying estimation method and discuss the assumptions made. In the final section we compute the factor scores and discuss the respective estimation results.

---

[*] Reprinted from the *European Journal of Operational Research*, 2002, Nunes: 'Using Factor Analysis to Identify Consumer Preferences for the Protection of a Natural Area in Portugal' with kind permission from Elsevier Science.

10.2 Factor analysis

Factor analysis is a data reduction technique often used in the empirical research in social sciences (Harman 1976; Kim and Mueller 1990; Hatcher 1994; Rencher 1995). Political scientists, when comparing the attributes of nations in terms of a variety of political and socio-economic variables, have applied factor analysis in an attempt to determine which characteristics are the most important in classifying nations (Rummel 1979); sociologists have determined 'friendship groups' by examining which people associate most frequently with each other (Asher 1976); psychologists have used this statistical technique in order to study individuals' intelligence dimensions (Thomson 1951), to assess how people perceive different stimuli and categorize them into different response sets (Stukat 1958); economists have used factor analysis in the study of consumer behaviour, namely in assessing individual consumer living standards (Schokkaert and Ootegem 1990) and in studying individual consumer charity behavior (Ootegem 1994).

In the present research, we have included in the instrument survey a list of 26 attitudinal items in order to disclose the respondents' structure of preferences. However, before running the factor analysis exercise, we assume that we are able to characterize the respondents' motivational structure in terms of following latent constructs:

- the **use motive** $\left(f_{u,j}\right)$: captures the j-respondent's well being derived from the tangible use of the Alentejo Natural Park, that is, respondents may feel better-off because they, or their children, are able to visit the area and enjoy there the consumption of a set of recreational activities;

- the **non-use motive** $\left(f_{nu,j}\right)$: captures the j-respondent's well being derived from the knowledge that the Alentejo Natural Park guarantees the preservation of wildlife, and respective habitats, independently of any human recreation use;

- the **warmglow motive** $\left(f_{wg,j}\right)$: captures the j-respondent's feeling that the contribution for the protection of Alentejo Natural Park, like the participation in donations funds, is, *per se*, a source of well being.

Therefore, we use factor analysis not only as a data reduction technique but also as a important procedure to test the validity of the proposed consumer motivation structure as described in Chapter 3. Practically, we wish to assess the empirical validity of the following motivation factor model:

$$av_{m,j} - \overline{av}_{m,j} = \lambda_{m,u} f_{u,j} + \lambda_{m,nu} f_{nu,j} + \lambda_{m,wg} f_{wg,j} + \phi_{m,j} \qquad (10.1)$$

Where:

$m = 1,..., M$ representative attitudinal items,

$j = 1,..., J$ survey respondents,

with:

$av_{m,j}$ response of the j respondent to the m item (observable variable),

$\overline{av}_{m,j}$ sample response average to the m item,

$f_{u,j}, f_{nu,j}, f_{wg,j}$ respondent's motivational factor scores (unobservable variable),

$\lambda_{m,u}, \lambda_{m,nu}, \lambda_{m,wg}$ loading coefficients associated with the m item,

$\phi_{m,j}$ error term.

In a matrix notation, and for all individuals, we may rewrite equation (10.1) as:

$$\mathbf{av} = \Lambda\mathbf{f} + \Xi \tag{10.2}$$

where **av** captures the matrix giving the answers of the sample respondents on the 26 attitudinal items as presented in the instrument survey; **f** captures the matrix of factor scores giving the position of the sample respondents on the three retained motivations; Λ captures the matrix of factor loadings showing the correlations between the answers on the 26 items and the respondents' factor scores; and Ξ captures the matrix of the residual terms. It is assumed that the structure of the latent factor scores is characterized by:

$$E(\mathbf{f}) = \mathbf{0} \tag{A1}$$

$$\mathrm{cov}(\mathbf{f}) = \mathbf{I} \tag{A2}$$

$$E(\Xi) = \mathbf{0} \tag{A3}$$

$$\mathrm{cov}(\Xi) = \Omega = \begin{bmatrix} \omega_1 & 0 & \cdots & 0 \\ 0 & \omega_2 & \cdots & 0 \\ \vdots & \vdots & & \vdots \\ 0 & 0 & \cdots & \omega_{26} \end{bmatrix} \tag{A4}$$

$$\mathrm{cov}(\mathbf{f}, \Xi) = \mathbf{0} \tag{A5}$$

Assumptions A1 and A2 state that the underlying consumer factors scores are normalized or standardized variables, therefore they have mean zero and variances one. Moreover, A2 declares that the consumer motivation factors scores are uncorrelated with each other – as such the consumer motivations do not overlap. Assumptions A3 and A4 assert that the residual part is assumed to have zero mean and have specific variance – given by the main diagonal of Ω. Assumption A4 also declares that the residual parts are uncorrelated with each other. These assumptions imply that the motivation factors account for all the correlations among the observable variables. Finally, A5 assigns that the residual component and the constructed motivation factors scores are uncorrelated with each other. Bearing in mind such premises, we obtain a simple expression for the covariance matrix of the observed attitudinal items:

$$\mathrm{cov}(\mathbf{av}) = \Lambda\Lambda' + \Omega \tag{10.3}$$

This way we are able to model the covariance of the attitudinal items in term of the loading coefficients, for example,

$$\mathrm{var}(av_m) = \lambda_{m,u}^{\ 2} + \lambda_{m,nu}^{\ 2} + \lambda_{m,wg}^{\ 2} + \omega_m \tag{10.4}$$

where the variance of the m item variable is broken down into a two components: (a) a common component, called the *communality* $h_m^2 = (\lambda_{m,u}^2 + \lambda_{m,nu}^2 + \lambda_{m,wg}^2)$, and (b) a component unique to the m item, called the *specific variance, ω_m*.

With equation (10.4) we can describe the proportion of variance in the observed variables that is determined by the consumer motivation factors by analysing the communalities scores, h_m^2. The communalities are, however, not known, since they are the elements of information based on the unobserved factor loadings. Therefore, the main objective is to estimate the communalities such that the underlying motivational structure is able to reproduce these correlations as well as possible. The first step consists of attempting to find an estimator $\hat{\Lambda}$ that will approximate the fundamental expression (10.3) with $\mathbf{S}$, the sample correlation matrix,[91] in place of $cov(\mathbf{av})$, that is:

$$\mathbf{S} \cong \hat{\Lambda}\hat{\Lambda}' + \hat{\Omega} \qquad (10.5)$$

We propose to estimate the communalities using the squared multiple correlation (SMC). This way we are able to neglect $\hat{\Omega}$ and factor $\mathbf{S}$ into $\mathbf{S} = \hat{\Lambda}\hat{\Lambda}'$. Finally, and in order to find a frame of reference where the three retained factors are more interpretable, the estimated matrix $\hat{\Lambda}$ will be submitted to a rotation and $\hat{\Lambda}^* = \hat{\Lambda}\mathbf{T}$ (where $\mathbf{T}$ is orthogonal) will be obtained. We propose the varimax method as the selected orthogonal rotation procedure because this method is characterized by seeking rotated loadings that maximize the variance of the squared loadings in each column of $\hat{\Lambda}^*$. Therefore it attempts to make the loadings either large (in absolute value close to one) or small (close to zero) so as to help the interpretation of the motivational structure.[92] The empirical results are presented in the next section.

10.3 Empirical results

In this section we present the results associated with the described sequence of steps made while applying an exploratory factor analysis. The first step involves the initial extraction of the factors. At this stage we do not specify the number of factors to be retained and rotated. We proceed to the determination of the factors that are meaningful and worthy of being retained for rotation and interpretation. In the second step we perform a confirmatory analysis of the proposed latent structure: we test whether the three-factor structure is supported by the data and explore the interpretation of each common factor. Finally, we provide an estimation, and respective interpretation, of the respondent's actual standing on the retained three common factors.

10.3.1 Initial extraction of factors

In the first step of the exploratory analysis we proceed to the extraction (or identification) of the factors without specifying the number of factors to be retained. Because 26 variables are

---

[91] Since the objective of the factor analysis is the reproduction of the covariances and correlations rather than variances, we will take the sample correlation matrix of the observed variables as the primary data to be used in our analysis. In practice the sample correlation matrix is more often used in empirical work than the sample covariance matrix and is the default matrix in most software packages, namely *SAS®*.

[92] See Appendix F for further details.

being analysed, 26 factors will be initially extracted. However, at this initial stage four factors are retained. This decision was based on the visual inspection of the scree graph, that is, the plot of the eigenvalues of S; after the fourth factor, the plot of the eigenvalues is characterized by a straight line. The matrix of factor loadings is presented in Table 10.1.

Table 10.1: Principal factor analysis (F=4)

	Factor 1	Factor 2	Factor 3	Factor 4
M14	70 *	19	10	−9
M2	68 *	17	7	−9
M4	66 *	13	7	−2
M11	64 *	14	22	−9
M13	64 *	18	19	−6
M9	60 *	16	19	−13
M26	58 *	17	14	−15
M5	57 *	3	13	−11
M3	52 *	16	12	−8
M1	50 *	12	14	−1
M24	25	9	7	−8
M17	23	17	8	17
M12	19	60 *	10	−6
M23	27	58 *	7	−1
M20	17	57 *	1	4
M8	12	55 *	4	12
M15	10	46 *	3	14
M10	43	7	67 *	−8
M22	42	15	61 *	−7
M6	34	9	58 *	−8
M18	−9	−3	−6	53 *
M21	−4	7	0	50 *
M25	−18	1	−13	47 *
M19	−2	18	−3	47 *
M7	−15	−3	−21	41
M16	−1	2	14	24

Printed results are multiplied by 100 and rounded to the nearest integer. The values of above 0.45 are flagged with an asterisk.[93] The factor pattern shows that the attitudinal questions M24, M17, M16 and M7 do not score above 0.45 and do not belong to any of the underlying latent factor construct. Therefore we interpret the M24, M17, M16 and M7 items as not being "pure" measures of any of the latent variables. For this reason we drop them from any further analysis.

We continue the exploratory factor analysis exercise so as to get a matrix of significant factor loadings, that is, a final estimated factor pattern where all the items belong to an

---

[93] The matrix of the factor loadings represent the product-moment correlation between the observable variable and the underlying factor. The factor loadings are analogous to the standardized regression coefficients as obtained in regression analysis. In other words, dropping attitudinal items which do not score above 0.45 – here assumed as the minimum correlation bound – means that we follow an exploratory rule based on the magnitude of the estimated regression coefficients, which is characterized by rejecting all the items that indicate low correlations with the common factors.

underlying factor construct. We selected the varimax method as the selected rotation procedure. The results after rotation are presented in Table 10.2. As we can observe, the factor model specification is characterized by four latent factor constructs: Factor 1, Factor 2, Factor 3 and Factor 4. A closer inspection to the attitudinal items that load on the fourth construct reveals that the underlying observable attitudinal items polled under the Factor 4 do not share any common conceptual meaning but rather is to be interpreted as a statistical 'junk' factor: first, M21 focuses on the preservation of the Portuguese heritage diversity and its importance within a constructed common European culture; second, M18 focuses on the educational role of natural protected areas as a substitute for the zoos, and finally, M19 seeks to identify the importance of 'social pressure' in the agent's contribution behaviour. Moreover, the rotated factor pattern shows that these attitudinal questions have very low scores next to the remaining latent factor constructs. Therefore, we interpret M18, M19 and M21 as not being 'pure' measures underpinning such latent factor constructs, and proceeded to the analysis by testing whether the tree-factor model is an adequate representation of these data.

Table 10.2: Rotated factor pattern (F=4)

	Factor 1	Factor 2	Factor 3	Factor 4
M14	69 *	20	14	-7
M2	67 *	18	11	-8
M4	65 *	13	10	2
M11	64 *	15	24	-6
M13	63 *	18	22	-3
M9	59 *	17	22	-10
M5	58 *	3	16	-7
M26	57 *	18	17	-15
M3	51 *	17	15	-8
M1	49 *	12	16	1
M12	18	60 *	11	-7
M23	27	58 *	9	0
M20	16	55 *	2	3
M8	10	55 *	6	12
M15	9	45 *	5	17
M10	40	8	69 *	-6
M22	38	15	63 *	-7
M6	31	9	60 *	-7
M21	-5	6	-2	53 *
M18	-11	-2	-5	50 *
M19	-3	17	-4	48 *

10.3.2 Confirmatory factor analysis

The second step in the empirical analysis consists of the confirmatory factor analysis. This is characterized by testing whether a latent motivation construct with three factors is confirmed by the sample, that is:

Hypothesis 7: $H_0 : \sum \Lambda\Lambda'+\Omega$,

where Λ is *(3xM)*; or equivalently,

H_0 : three factors are sufficient;

H_a : more factors are needed.

We used the maximum likelihood technique to test Hypothesis 7 and run the Kaiser test (1960). The rationale for the Kaiser test is as follows. Each observed variable contributes one unit of variance to the total variance in the data set. Thus, any component that displays an eigenvalue greater than one accounts for a greater amount of variance than had been contributed by one variable. On the other hand, a component that displays an eigenvalue less than one accounts for less variance than had been contributed by one variable. Since the purpose of the factor analysis is to assess a number of reduced components (or factors), this cannot be effectively achieved if one retains factors that account for less variance than had been contributed by individual variables. According to the ML estimation results, it is sufficient to retain three factors since $\Delta_3 = 1.57$ and $\Delta_4 = 0.88 < 1$ – see results in Table 10.3. Therefore, we do not reject the null hypothesis, that is, it is sufficient to retain three factors.

Table 10.3: Kaiser test

Eigenvalues			
Factor 1	Factor 2	Factor 3	Factor 4
4.23	1.84	1.57	0.88

The pattern of loadings of the retained three-factor model reflects a common conceptual meaning – see and Tables 10.4 and 10.5. Therefore we have:

Factor 1 collects a number of items related to the general attitude of the respondent with respect to the direct consumption of natural areas for recreational use. Therefore we label this latent construct as the 'use/recreation motivation'. A higher score on this factor indicates a strong propensity for recreation.

Factor 2 collects a number of items that are related with the general feeling of well-being or satisfaction generated by the act of giving. We label this latent factor as the 'warmglow motivation'. A high score on this factor reveals that the respondent experiences warmglow when contributing, that is, contributing makes him/her feel good.

Factor 3 collects a number of items indicating the respondent's ethical belief or moral consideration with respect to the preservation of wildlife, independent of its human use. For this reason we labelled this factor as the 'non-use motivation'. Highly scoring respondents are concerned with the existence of wildlife and its preservation.

We postulate that these motivations, the 'use/recreation', 'warmglow' and 'non-use/existence' motivation, play, together with the respondent's socio-economic characteristics, an important role in helping us to understand the stated WTP responses – see Figure 10.1. Therefore we are interested in measuring individual respondent's scores for each of the

Table 10.4: Rotated factor pattern

	Factor 1	Factor 2	Factor 3
M14	70 *	21	18
M2	67 *	19	15
M4	63 *	16	14
M11	63 *	16	27
M13	61 *	19	25
M9	58 *	17	26
M26	58 *	17	20
M5	56 *	4	19
M1	47 *	13	19
M12	18	60 *	13
M23	25	58 *	10
M20	14	57 *	3
M8	8	56 *	6
M15	6	47 *	4
M10	36	8	71 *
M22	35	15	66 *
M6	29	9	62 *

Table 10.5: Latent factor constructs

Factors	Statements	Motivations
Factor 1	M1, M2, M4, M5, M9, M11, M13, M14, M26	'use/recreation'
Factor 2	M8, M12, M15, M20, M23	'warmglow'
Factor 3	M6, M10, M22	'non-use/existence'

motivation factors. Moreover, we are particularly interested in estimating the respondent's 'warmglow' factor score since we want to test whether the respective magnitude plays (or not) a role in explaining the WTP estimates, that is, we are interested in assessing whether the warmglow effect is present in the stated WTP responses.

10.3.3 Estimation of the consumer motivation factor scores

At this stage we are sure that the empirical evidence does not reject the three-factor model. Moreover, we identified a common conceptual meaning for each latent factor. The third, and last step, of factor analysis consists of obtaining factor scores, which are defined as estimates of the underlying factor values for each observation - that is, estimate matrix $\mathbf{f}$ as defined by (10.2). According to the fundamental centered regression model equation we have:

$$\mathbf{av} = \Lambda \mathbf{f} + \Xi \qquad (10.2)$$

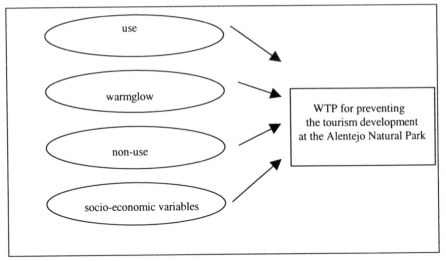

Figure 10.1: Conceptual model depicting the household WTP

Since **f** is not observed, we must estimate them as functions of the observed *avs*. The most popular approach to estimating the factors is based on regression (Thomson 1951). Taking into account the computed factor loadings for the three motivation factors and the respondents' answers to the motivation items, we can estimate their motivation scores using a least squares technique:[94]

$$\hat{\mathbf{f}} = \left(\hat{\Lambda}^{*\prime}\hat{\Lambda}^{*}\right)^{-1}\hat{\Lambda}^{*\prime}\mathbf{av} \tag{10.6}$$

where $\hat{\Lambda}^* = \hat{\Lambda}\mathbf{T}$ (**T** is orthogonal) and $\hat{\Lambda}$ the matrix of factor loadings showing the correlations between the answers on the 26 items and the position of the respondents on the three motivations. In order to understand better each individual motivation score, that is, with what respondent's characteristics each motivation is associated, we propose to run the following linear regression model:

$$\hat{f}_{use,j} = a_{0_{use}} + \sum_k a_{k_{use}} x_{k,j} + u_{use,j}$$

$$\hat{f}_{warmglow,j} = a_{0_{warmglow}} + \sum_k a_{k_{warmglow}} x_{k,j} + u_{warmglow,j} \quad \text{for all } j \tag{10.7}$$

$$\hat{f}_{nonuse,j} = a_{0_{nonuse}} + \sum_k a_{k_{nonuse}} x_{k,j} + u_{nonuse,j}$$

---

[94] The complete matrix **f** is immediately given by the PROC FACTOR in the SAS® package.

where $\hat{f}_l$ is the vector with all the individual observations for the level of motivation l, x_k is a vector with the observations of all individuals for the socio-economic characteristic k, u_l is a vector with disturbance terms and the a's are coefficients to be estimated.

The following characteristics of the respondents were included as explanatory variables: (a) age; (b) education level; (c) gender; (d) the number of individuals in the household; (e) the number of visits to the Alentejo Natural Park; (f) respondents' background information concerning the protection of natural areas; (g) his/her opinion with respect to the conservation of nature; (h) whether the respondent is a member of an 'environmental friendly' organization; (i) whether s/he has ever participated in a fund raising campaigns; (j) whether s/he has ever contributed to charity; (l) whether s/he has ever given blood. In additon, we include respondents' recreational characteristics: (m) whether the respondent has ever gone to the beach; (n) whether the respondent has ever participated in water recreation activities; (o) whether the respondent has ever biked; (p) whether the respondent has ever walked or trekked; (q) whether the respondent has ever camped, and finally (r) whether the respondent has ever gone hunting.

For each motivation factor we fit two equations. Model 1 corresponds to a broader model specification. Since many of the variables may be expected to be largely overlapping, specially among the different variables regarding the respondent's recreational profile, we proceed to the analysis of the goodness of fit of Model 1. Model 2 corresponds to a restrictive model specification based on the significant coefficients of Model 1.[95] The results of the regressions are presented in Table 10.6. We can observe that for all broad model specifications only a small part of the variance of the realized motivation factors can be explained by these characteristics – the respective R^2 is about 8–9 percent.[96] Nevertheless, we feel that the model regression's results contain some interesting and appealing information.

First, we verified that 'age' and 'gender' are not particularly important predictors in explaining the respondents' computed motivation scores. An exception lies in the 'warmglow' motivation, where the feeling of satisfaction provided by the act of giving revealed itself to be stronger among young women. Second, respondents with higher education levels are associated with higher 'use' and 'existence' motivation scores. On the contrary, the level of education had a negative impact on the 'warmglow' score, suggesting that the feeling of satisfaction provided by the act of giving is lower among the respondents with higher education. Third, the variables concerning the respondent's recreational characteristics, 'beach', 'water sports', 'biking', 'trekking' and 'camping' play, as one might initially expect, an important role in explaining the respondent's 'use' motivation factor score. The relationship is particularly strong among the respondents who go to the beach, engage in sporting activities and go camping. Furthermore, ethical beliefs with respect to the preservation of wildlife, independent of its human use, are stronger among respondents who reported having background information concerning the protection of natural areas and who had a clear opinion that the conservation of nature is *'an urgent issue'*. Therefore, these respondents were associated with high 'non-use/existence' scores.

---

[95] Model selection was done with the use of the STEPWISE procedure in *SAS®*. Variables are included in the equation if the probability associated with the F test for the hypothesis that the coefficient of the entered variable is statistically significant at 5%.

[96] Such a low R^2 is good news; such an apparent paradoxical result indicates that the factor scores, when contrasted to the individual characteristics, contain additional information for the characterization of the individual consumer profile, namely her stated WTP answers. In contrast, a high R^2 would say that most of the individual characteristics influence the individual motivation factor, thus indicating the individual motivation factor *per se* would convey redundant information.

Table 10.6: Functionings and social characteristics

Variable	Motivations					
	Use/recreation		Warmglow		Non-se/existence	
	Model 1	Model 2	Model 1	Model 2	Model 1	Model 2
Intercept	−1.055	−1.000	−0.269	−0.141	−0.616	−0.759
	(0.00)		(0.17)		(0.00)	
Age	−0.020	-	−0.025	−0.029	−0.010	-
	(0.21)		(0.11)		(0.52)	
Education level	0.061	0.072	−0.069	−0.068	−0.066	0.073
	(0.00)		(0.00)		(0.00)	
Sex	−0.006	-	−0.147	−0.128	0.071	-
	(0.87)		(0.00)		(0.09)	
# household	−0.014	-	−0.037	−0.034	0.031	0.042
	(0.47)		(0.05)		(0.09)	
Visit	0.087	0.095	0.009	–	0.113	0.114
	(0.07)		(0.83)		(0.01)	
Heard or read	0.038	-	0.003	-	0.089	0.093
	(0.44)		(0.93)		(0.05)	
Opinion	0.234	0.245	−0.075	-	0.108	0.095
	(0.00)		(0.22)		(0.07)	
Membership	−0.005	-	−0.051	-	−0.045	-
	(0.91)		(0.21)		(0.38)	
Donation	0.081	-	0.318	0.317	0.198	0.179
	(0.17)		(0.00)		(0.00)	
Charity	0.005	-	0.420	0.423	−0.099	-
	(0.92)		(0.00)		(0.08)	
Blood	0.030	-	0.007	-	0.033	-
	(0.54)		(0.86)		(0.47)	
Beach	0.405	0.448	0.036	-	−0.099	-
	(0.00)		(0.72)		(0.33)	
Water sports	0.098	0.107	0.004	-	0.073	0.086
	(0.03)		(0.92)		(0.09)	
Bike	0.044	-	0.062	-	0.087	0.110
	(0.42)		(0.25)		(0.10)	
Walk or trek	0.130	-	0.110	-	0.031	-
	(0.32)		(0.38)		(0.80)	
Camping	0.148	0.166	0.033	-	0.072	-
	(0.00)		(0.46)		(0.10)	
Hunt or fish	0.002	-	0.012	-	0.022	-
	(0.95)		(0.78)		(0.62)	
F value	8.51	22.98	8.22	22.29	7.59	14.55
R-square	0.096	0.091	0.093	0.089	0.087	0.078

Fourth, we observed that respondents who reported having participated in donation and charity schemes are strongly associated with higher 'warmglow' scores. This is not true for the respondents who said they had given blood. Finally, we observed that the respondents who visited the Alentejo Natural Area are associated with higher 'use' motivation scores. Since many reasons to visit the ANP, as reported in the survey, are related with recreation, then we can interpret this result by admitting recreationists are, on average, associated with higher 'use' motivation scores. In general, and to conclude, we can say that the estimation results presented in Table 10.6 allowed us to test (and support) the validity of the interpretation originally suggested from the factor scores.

10.4 Conclusions

In this chapter we used factor analysis to identify, measure and interpret motivation factors, a variable that we want to introduce, together with the socio-economic characteristics of the respondents, in the multivariate analysis of the WTP function. Therefore, we explored respondents' Likert responses to the 26 attitudinal items as presented in Section D of the instrument survey. The maximum likelihood motivation factor score estimates confirmed the three-factor factor model. As originally proposed by the analytical valuation framework, these were interpreted as the 'use/recreation', 'warmglow' and 'non-use/existence' factors. The 'use/recreation' factor was strongly associated with the motivational items that were related to the respondent's general attitude with respect to the consumption of recreation; a high score on this factor indicates a strong propensity for recreation. The 'warmglow' factor was strongly associated with the motivational items that were related to the respondent's general feeling of well-being or satisfaction generated by the act of giving; a high score on this factor reveals that the respondent is particular sensitive to warmglow. Finally, the 'non-use/existence' factor was strongly associated with the motivational items that were related to the respondent's ethical belief or moral consideration with respect to the preservation of wildlife. Furthermore, the regression estimation results showed that (a) respondents who are recreationally more active present a higher 'use' motivation score. Furthermore, (b) respondents who have visited the Alentejo Natural Park present as well higher 'use' motivation scores. As far as the 'warmglow' motivation is concerned, the estimation results show that (c) the general feeling of satisfaction generated by the act of giving is less strong among respondents with a higher education level and living in large families, and that (d) when compared to men, young women have a stronger feeling of warmglow. On the contrary, (e) the respondents who participated in donation and charity campaigns clearly reveal a higher 'warmglow' motivation score. Finally, the 'non-use' motivation estimation results showed that (f) the ethical beliefs regarding the preservation of wildlife independent of its human use is not dependent upon the respondent's gender and that it is particularly strong among the respondents with higher education.

Chapter

11

THE VALUATION FUNCTION[*]

11.1 Introduction

The present chapter focuses on the economic analysis of the protection programme's valuation. We integrate the socio-economic characteristics of the respondent, such as income and education, in the valuation function together with the respondent's motivational factor scores. We are particularly interested in the inference analysis concerning the warmglow motivation factor and assess whether the respective parameter estimates plays an important role in explaining the valuation functions. Bearing in mind the estimation results, we predict the mean WTP according to different motivation profiles of the respondents. Finally, we propose to purge the warmglow effect from giving and compute a *dry* WTP, that is, a WTP measure free from any embedding due to warmglow.

The chapter is divided into four sections. In section 11.2 we describe the empirical model specification that we chose to use for the multivariate analysis. In section 11.3 we present and interpret the regression estimation results. In section 11.4 we explore the sensitivity of the predicted mean WTP estimates according to different characteristics of the respondents. In section 11.5 we explore the warmglow valuation transmission mechanism, propose the prediction of a *dry* WTP measure and discuss the results obtained. Finally, in section 11.6 we discuss whether the original survey responses constitute correct information in order to estimate the demand for the public good or, on the contrary, whether the WTP estimates should be *dried out* before being used in cost benefit analysis.

11.2 Empirical model specification

For empirical model specification we assume the following structure for the WTP function:

$$WTP^j = e^{\beta + \alpha_{WA}^j WA^j + \alpha_{RA}^j RA^j + \varepsilon^j} \tag{11.1}$$

---

[*] Longer version of the manuscript 'Warmglow and Embedding in Contingent Valuation', Nunes and Schokkaert, 2002, printed at the *Journal of Environmental Economics and Management* with kind permission from Academic Press.

where WTP^j denote the unobserved individual willingness to pay (but known to lie within observed boundaries); WA^j and RA^j correspond to the non-use and recreation possibilities provided by the Alentejo Natural Park to the j individual consumer and denote, respectively, the Wilderness Areas and Recreational Areas (observed); β is the intercept and is the location parameter of a log-normal distribution function; α_{WA}^j and α_{RA}^j capture the individual marginal willingness to pay for the protection of the wilderness and recreation possibilities of the Alentejo Natural Park. The ε denotes the disturbance term.[97] The WA and RA are fixed by scenario description as presented in the survey instrument. Thus, in the empirical analysis we operationalize the WA and RA as a dummy variable – see Table 11.1.

Table 11.1: Operationalization of the WA and RA variables

$$\forall\ j',j'',WA^{j'} = WA^{j''}=d_{WA} = \begin{cases} 1, \text{ when the protection plan guarantees} \\ \text{the provision of the wilderness areas} \\ \\ 0, \text{ when the protection plan does not guarantee} \\ \text{the provision of the wilderness areas} \end{cases}$$

and

$$\forall\ j',j'',\ RA^{j'} = RA^{j''}=d_{RA} = \begin{cases} 1, \text{ when the protection plan guarantees} \\ \text{the provision of the recreational areas} \\ \\ 0, \text{ when the protection plan does not guarantee} \\ \text{the provision of the recreational areas} \end{cases}$$

Thus we may rewrite (11.1) as follows:

$$WTP^j = e^{\beta+\alpha_{WA}^j d_{WA} +\alpha_{RA}^j d_{RA} +\varepsilon^j} \tag{11.2}$$

We define the individual marginal WTP according to the following specifications:

$$\alpha_{WA}^j = \omega_0 +\omega_u \hat{m}_u^j +\omega_{nu} \hat{m}_{nu}^j +\omega_{wg} \hat{m}_{wg}^j +\omega_Y\, y^j +\sum_s \omega_s a_s^{\ j} \tag{11.3}$$

---

[97] Despite the fact that the individual respondent knows with certainty the choices that maximize his/her well-being, and therefore true willingness to contribute, for the CV researcher the individual respondent's WTP is not an observable variable. This is the reason why we add an error term in the empirical specification, ε. It is necessary to assume a distribution function for such a term. In the present study we assume that ε follows a standard normal distribution function.

$$\alpha_{RA}^j = \tau_0 + \tau_u \hat{m}_u^j + \tau_{nu} \hat{m}_{nu}^j + \tau_{wg} \hat{m}_{wg}^j + \tau_Y y^j + \sum_s \tau_s a_s^j \tag{11.4}$$

that is, for each household, the marginal magnitudes are defined as a linear combination of the individual characteristics including the household motivation factor scores, respectively $\hat{m}_u^j$, $\hat{m}_{nu}^j$ and $\hat{m}_{wg}^j$, the household income, denoted by y^j, and socio-economic information, denoted by a_s. We introduce expressions (11.3)–(11.4) in (11.2) to get:

$$WTP^j = \exp \left\{ \beta + \left[\left(\omega_0 + \omega_u \hat{m}_u^j + \omega_{nu} \hat{m}_{nu}^j + \omega_{wg} \hat{m}_{wg}^j + \omega_Y y^j + \sum_s \omega_s a_s^j \right) d_{WA} + \left(\tau_0 + \tau_u \hat{m}_u^j + \tau_{nu} \hat{m}_{nu}^j + \tau_{wg} \hat{m}_{wg}^j + \tau_Y y^j + \sum_s \tau_s a_s^j \right) d_{RA} \right] + \varepsilon^j \right\} \tag{11.5}$$

Rearranging expression (11.5), we get:

$$WTP^j = \exp \left\{ \beta + \left[\begin{array}{l} \left(\omega_0 d_{WA} + \tau_0 d_{RA} \right) + \left(\omega_u d_{WA} + \tau_u d_{RA} \right) \hat{m}_u^j + \\ \left(\omega_{nu} d_{WA} + \tau_{nu} d_{RA} \right) \hat{m}_{nu}^j + \left(\omega_{wg} d_{WA} + \tau_{wg} d_{RA} \right) \hat{m}_{wg}^j + \\ \left(\omega_Y d_{WA} + \tau_Y d_{RA} \right) y^j + \sum_s \left(\omega_s d_{WA} + \tau_s d_{RA} \right) a_s^j \end{array} \right] + \varepsilon^j \right\} \tag{11.6}$$

We can make expression (11.6) neater and rewrite it as follows,

$$WTP^j = e^{\delta_0 + \delta_u \hat{m}_u^j + \delta_{nu} \hat{m}_{nu}^j + \delta_{wg} \hat{m}_{wg}^j + \delta_Y y^j + \sum_s \delta_s a_s^j + \varepsilon^j} \tag{11.7}$$

that is, the respondent's WTP is defined in terms of the household motivation factors (data available indirectly via the estimation of the factor scores), together with income and socio-economic characteristics (data directly available from the national survey), with:

$$\delta_0 \equiv \beta + \omega_0 d_{WA} + \tau_0 d_{RA} \tag{11.8}$$

$$\delta_u \equiv \omega_u d_{WA} + \tau_u d_{RA} \tag{11.9}$$

$$\delta_{nu} \equiv \omega_{nu} d_{WA} + \tau_{nu} d_{RA} \tag{11.10}$$

$$\delta_{wg} \equiv \omega_{wg} d_{WA} + \tau_{wg} d_{RA} \tag{11.11}$$

$$\delta_Y \equiv \omega_Y d_{WA} + \tau_Y d_{RA} \tag{11.12}$$

$$\delta_s \equiv \omega_s \, d_{WA} + \tau_s \, d_{RA} \tag{11.13}$$

where the parameter estimates δ_{wg}, δ_u and δ_{nu} capture respectively the marginal impact of the warmglow, use and non-use household motivation functionings in the valuation function. These, together with δ_Y and δ_s, are coefficients to be estimated. We are particularly interested in the analysis concerning the warmglow motivation factor score. Formally, we want to test the respective statistical significance of the warmglow coefficient, that is, test:

Hypothesis 8:

$$H_0 : \delta_{wg} = 0$$

$$H_1 : \delta_{wg} \geq 0$$

The rejection of Hypothesis 8 would be then interpreted as the rejection of the warmglow valuation transmission mechanism.

11.3 Estimation of the valuation function

In this section we estimate a valuation function for the three protection programmes. As we have seen in the previous section, a large number of possible predictors are available to be integrated in the valuation function. The respondent motivation factor scores, as computed in the previous chapter, constitute an obvious choice. Other obvious choices are the respondent's income and level of education. Another candidate for predictor is the age and the professional situation of the respondents. The WTP expression used for the estimation is as follows:

$$e^{\delta_0 + \delta_u \hat{m}_u^j + \delta_{nu} \hat{m}_{nu}^j + \delta_{wg} \hat{m}_{wg}^j + \delta_{s_{a_i}} a_i^j + \delta_{s_{o_i}} o_i^j + \delta_{s_{e_i}} e_i^j + \delta_{pv} pv^j + \delta_Y y^j + \delta_N n^j + \delta_P p^j + \varepsilon^j} \tag{11.14}$$

where $\hat{m}_u^j$, $\hat{m}_{nu}^j$ and $\hat{m}_{wg}^j$ represent the individual (computed) motivation factor scores; a_i^j denotes a series of dummies and represents the individual respondent's age[98] (that is, $a_i^j = 20s$, 30s, 40s, 50s and 70s); o_i^j denotes a series of dummies and represents the individual respondent's occupation/job; e_i^j denotes a discrete variable and represents the individual respondent's education level; pv^j denotes a dummy variable and represents the payment vehicle as described in the survey instrument (with $pv = 1$ when voluntary contribution); y^j represents net income of the household, and n^j represents the number of individuals living at the respondent's household.

---

[98] Since the instrument survey contains categories (see survey question P-14), we operationalize age with dummy variables.

Table 11.2: Valuation function

Parameters	WA programme			RA programme			(WA + RA) programme		
	Est.	Sd. er.	p-val.	Est.	Sd. er.	p-val.	Est.	Sd. er.	p-val.
Factor scores									
Use/recreation	0.091	0.12	0.47	0.291*	0.13	0.02	0.165	0.11	0.13
Warmglow	0.536*	0.14	0.00	0.448*	0.12	0.00	0.238*	0.11	0.04
Non-use/existence	0.438*	0.12	0.00	0.254*	0.14	0.08	0.233*	0.11	0.03
Area									
Rural	0.390	0.33	0.23	−1.040*	0.37	0.00	0.019	0.29	0.94
Urban	0.148	0.23	0.53	0.336	0.21	0.12	0.094	0.18	0.60
Age									
20s	0.710	0.48	0.14	1.403*	0.50	0.00	0.774*	0.40	0.05
30s	0.956*	0.49	0.05	1.447*	0.46	0.00	0.655*	0.36	0.07
40s	0.279	0.48	0.56	0.885*	0.44	0.04	0.431	0.35	0.22
50s	0.242	0.41	0.56	0.954*	0.41	0.02	0.225	0.33	0.44
70s	−0.388	0.47	0.41	0.034	0.45	0.93	−0.598	0.42	0.15
Occupation									
Executives	0.891	0.68	0.19	−0.964	0.63	0.12	−0.565	0.53	0.29
Scientists	0.330	0.58	0.57	−0.341	0.59	0.56	−1.510*	0.54	0.00
Technicians	−0.006	0.50	0.98	−0.736	0.48	0.12	−0.121	0.42	0.77
Administrative	0.729	0.50	0.14	−0.751	0.46	0.10	−0.269	0.42	0.52
Sales services	−0.899*	0.51	0.08	−0.496	0.46	0.28	−1.040*	0.43	0.01
Farmers & fishers	0.242	0.72	0.73	−1.090	0.77	0.37	−2.680*	0.28	0.03
Craftsmen	0.295	0.47	0.54	−0.615	0.46	0.18	−0.170	0.39	0.66
Assembly workers	−1.045*	0.61	0.08	0.081	0.59	0.89	0.047	0.60	0.93
Unskilled workers	0.020	0.66	0.98	−0.723	0.61	0.24	−1.390*	0.58	0.01
Housekeepers	−0.295	0.45	0.51	−0.790*	0.45	0.07	−0.314	0.36	0.39
Working students	−1.683*	0.87	0.05	−0.305	0.77	0.69	−0.986	0.77	0.20
Education									
Primary (freq.)	0.057	0.62	0.92	0.201	0.60	0.73	−0.521	0.59	0.38
Primary	1.045*	0.52	0.04	0.318	0.47	0.50	−0.751	0.52	0.15
Secondary: low	1.262*	0.51	0.01	0.171	0.45	0.14	−0.770	0.49	0.11
Secondary: high	0.963*	0.53	0.07	−0.087	0.44	0.84	−0.258	0.50	0.61
University	1.000*	0.45	0.02	−0.000	0.54	0.99	0.871*	0.51	0.09
Payment vehicle	−0.094	0.20	0.64	−0.370*	0.19	0.05	−0.311	0.20	0.12
Net income	0.157*	0.09	0.09	0.291*	0.10	0.00	0.017	0.08	0.82
Household	−0.124	0.11	0.25	−0.082	0.09	0.38	0.099	0.08	0.22
Protest	−1.790*	0.31	0.00	−2.021*	0.32	0.00	−1.387*	0.27	0.00
Intercept *(β)*	6.589			6.899			8.243		
Scale *(σ)*	1.292			1.195			1.576		
Log-Likelihood	−305.06			−279.10			−573.12		

Notes: * significant at 10%. Reference group: respondent in her 60s who completed a medium level of secondary studies and is now retired

Finally p^j denotes a dummy variable and represents the protest bidders (that is, $p = 1$ means that the respondent is a protest bidder). The respective parameter estimations are presented in Table 11.2. The intercept, δ_0, is different from the univariate location parameter estimation results because now we are parameterizing the original intercept as a function of the various covariates included in the equation.

11.3.1 Interpretation of the estimation results

Motivation factor scores

The first three variables, 'use', 'warmglow' and 'existence', are factor scores indicating the position of the respondents on the three motivation functions. The estimated coefficients regarding the 'warmglow' motivation factor are statistically significant across all protection programmes. As we can observe from Table 11.2 all the p-values associated with the warmglow motivation's estimates are lower than 0.1. Therefore, we are able to reject Hypothesis 8, that is, the empirical evidence confirms the presence of a warmglow effect in the stated WTP responses. Furthermore, the warmglow parameter's estimates may suggest that the warmglow valuation transmission mechanism is not independent of the valuation object. Indeed, the warmglow marginal effect is revealed to be particularly strong in the valuation of the Wilderness Areas. However, formal testing leads us to reject the hypothesis that different protection programmes, or public goods in general, generate different amounts of warmglow. The respective test statistic is clearly below the 5% critical level of the chi-square distribution with two degrees of freedom – see Table 11.3. Thus, we are able to conclude that the individual respondents gets, at the margin, the same moral satisfaction from each escudo contribution independently of the public good that s/he is evaluating.[99]

Table 11.3:Warmglow motivation factor: formal hypothesis testing

Hypothesis 9:	
$H_0: \begin{cases} \delta_{WA_{wg}} = \delta_{RA_{wg}} \\ \delta_{WA_{wg}} = \delta_{(WA+RA)_{wg}} \end{cases}$	
Chi-test statistic	0.048

As far as the 'use' motivation factor is concerned, we are able to verify that it shows the greatest magnitude in the valuation of the recreation possibilities of the Alentejo Natural Park, that is, in the valuation of the RA. However, formal testing indicates that such a magnitude is equally strong when valuing the (WA + RA) protection programme – see in Table 11.4 that the respective t-test result is below the 10% critical level of the normal distribution.[100] On the contrary, the 'use' effect presents the lowest magnitude in the valuation of the WA. As a matter of fact, the estimation results show that the estimate is not statistically significant different from zero – see in Table 11.2 that the respective p-value is about 0.42. For us, these

---

[99] We also included the cross-effect warmglow-payment vehicle in the multivariate regression. The results do not involve much difference from the estimations as presented in Table 11.2. See Appendix G for more details.
[100] Which corresponds to 1.644 (for a two-tailed test).

Table 11.4: Use motivation factor: formal hypothesis testing

Hypothesis 10a:		Hypothesis 10b:	
$H_0 : \delta_{RA_u} = \delta_{WA_u}$		$H_0 : \delta_{RA_u} = \delta_{(WA+RA)_u}$	
$H_a : \delta_{RA_u} \neq \delta_{WA_u}$		$H_a : \delta_{RA_u} \neq \delta_{(WA+RA)_u}$	
t-test statistic	1.732	t-test statistic	0.455

are interesting results. On one hand, we see that respondents who present a stronger 'use' motivation profile are willing to pay more money for the RA protection programme than the average respondent. On the other hand, we find that when valuing the non-use possibilities of the Alentejo Natural Park, that is the services flows that involve no recreational consumption, the recreational profile of the respondent plays no important role.

As far as the 'existence' motivation factor is concerned, it presents the strongest effect in the valuation of the WA; respondents who think that the wildlife should be protected independently of human use are willing to pay much more for the WA than the average respondent. The same is true for the RA programme, but here it is associated with a lower magnitude. However, formal testing analysis indicates that such magnitudes are approximately the same – see test results in Table 11.5.

Table 11.5: Existence motivation factor: formal hypothesis testing

Hypothesis 11:	
$H_0 : \delta_{WA_{nu}} = \delta_{RA_{nu}}$	
$H_a : \delta_{WA_{nu}} \neq \delta_{RA_{nu}}$	
t-test statistic	0.998

Residential area

When including the residential area in the valuation function we try to assess whether the socio-demographic locality of the household has an impact on the stated WTP responses. The residential area is operationalized as a dummy variable indicating whether the respondent lives in a typical country-side or urban environment.[101] These variables are, respectively, labelled as 'rural' and 'urban'. According to the final estimation results, they do not play a particularly important role in explaining the valuation of the described protection programmes. An exception is made in the valuation of the RA protection programme. The valuation function of the RA shows that respondents who live in 'urban' ('rural') areas are willing to pay more (less) than the average respondent. These results may be interpreted as a signal of the scarcity of *green* sites in cities where individuals could enjoy the consumption of recreation activities. Conversely, the respondents living in 'rural' areas benefit from a local abundance of

---

[101] The reference point is the residential area category labelled by the CESOP as 'somewhat rural/somewhat urban'.

recreational *green* sites and thus are willing to pay relatively less for the protection of the RA.[102]

We also tried to assess the marginal effect of the 'distance' from the respondent to the site. However, we did not have an accurate measurement for such a variable - the survey did not provide such information. Nevertheless, we worked with a proxy variable, the geographical blocks of Continental Portugal, which could be retrieved directly from the questionnaire – see Table 6.1 in Chapter 6. The estimation results did not work out: most of the parameter estimates were not statistically significant. For this reason we dropped this variable from further analysis.

Age

Age is operationalized in the survey as a categorical variable. It is characterised by six age brackets. They refer to age ranges between 18 and 29 years (denoted by 20s), between 30 and 39 years (30s), and so on.[103] Since we believe that the marginal valuation magnitude is not the same across the different age categories, we respect the categorical nature of the variable and work with all its categories in the valuation exercise. Across the different valuation functions we can observe, in general terms, a negative relationship between the stated WTP responses and the age of the respondents. This relationship is particularly strong in the valuation of the RA; here not only the estimates have the largest magnitudes but also the majority of them are revealed to be statistically significant. Therefore, the nature related recreational possibilities provided by the Alentejo Natural Park are especially valued among young respondents.

Occupation

Occupation is the variable that denotes the job held by the respondent. This categorical variable was operationalized on the basis of the National Classification of Occupations[104] (MESS 1994).[105] In general, the final estimation results are hardly significant. Nevertheless, we can observe that white collar workers – particularly among the 'executives', the 'scientists' and the 'administrative' – present a higher propensity to pay for the protection of the WA than the average respondent. Conversely, working students and housewives together with salesmen are the occupation groups that are willing to pay the least for the protection of the WA. The relationship is reiterated in the valuation of the (WA + RA). However, the 'farmers' constitute the category which shows by far the lowest willingness to pay for the (WA + RA).

Education

Education captures the highest level of formal instruction attained by the respondent. At the lowest education category – denoted by 'primary (freq.)' - we can find the respondents who

---

[102] The urban/rural dichotomy is strongly present in Portugal.

[103] The reference point is the 60s age category.

[104] Together with the nine major groups that characterise NCO, CESOP added three additional groups: housekeepers, retired, and working students.

[105] The reference point is the occupation category labelled by the CESOP as 'Retired'.

report not having uderstaken any studies.[106] On the contrary, university studies correspond to the highest level of education. The estimation results show: (a) that with the exception of the WA protection programme, where education has more significant effects, the estimated magnitudes are hardly significant; and (b) that it is not always true that respondents with higher education studies are willing to pay more than the average respondent. In the valuation of the (WA + RA) and WA protection programmes we can verify that respondents with 'university' education are willing to pay more than the average respondent.

Payment vehicle

The payment vehicle captures the effect of the 'voluntary contribution' on the stated WTP responses. The results reiterate the presence of free-riding behaviour. As already discussed in Chapter 8, it is again confirmed that across all protection programme respondents who face the 'voluntary contribution' scheme are willing to pay less than the respondents who face the 'national tax'. Furthermore, the estimations results show also that, with the exception of the RA protection programme, the payment vehicle effects are hardly significant.

Net income

For all protection programmes, respondents with higher incomes are associated with higher WTP responses. The income relationship is stronger when the respondents are evaluating the RA protection programme than when evaluating the WA programme. As far as the valuation of the (WA + RA) protection programme, the income effect presents a lower magnitude; as a matter of fact it is not statistically different from zero.

Household dimension and protests

The covariates 'household dimension' and 'protest' represent, respectively, the number of individuals in the respondent's household and whether the respondent is a protester. According to the estimation results, in all protection programmes – with the exception of the (WA + RA) – respondents belonging to larger households are, on average, willing to pay less than respondents living in smaller households. However, all estimates are not statistically significant. Finally, the 'protest' parameter estimates have, as we would initially expect, a negative sign; the respondents identified with a 'protest' are, as naturally expected, willing to pay less than the average respondent.

11.4 Sensitivity analysis of the stated WTP responses with respect to the motivation factor scores

Depending on the respondent's characteristics, the mean willingness to pay for the protection programmes varies widely; the lowest WTP estimate in our sample is less than 200 Portuguese escudos and the highest is above 68000. In order to comprehend better the range of such magnitudes, we propose to predict some WTP values according to the different respondent's characteristics and assess how much they vary. We focus particular attention on the sensitivity analysis of the respondent's motivation factor scores – core of the proposed microeconomic model formulation – and investigate the respective magnitudes across the different protection

---

[106] In some statistical publications this category is referred to as the 'illiterate' category (see, for example, for *Main Economic Indicators* - OECD statistical publication). The respondents who completed a medium level of secondary studies are taken as the reference group.

Table 11.6: WA protection programme (in PTE)

Existence motivation factor	University				No University			
	HI		LOW		LOW		LOW-blue	
	20s	> 50s	20s	> 50s	20s	> 50s	20s	> 50s
(+)	30900	19500	22600	14400	10800	5200	2300	1100
(−)	3100	1900	2000	1400	800	500	300	200

programmes, that is, assess the empirical validity of the proposed valuation model specification.

11.4.1 Wilderness Areas protection programme

According to the final estimates, the estimates regarding the WA protection programme show that the 'existence' motivational factor, age, income, university educational level and the assembly workers – blue collar workers – are all significant predictors at 10 %. Bearing in mind the respective parameter magnitudes we are to predict WTP for different motivation *profiles*. The estimation results are presented in Table 11.6.

In the first column we read the position of the respondent with respect to the 'existence' motivation factor score.[107] The (+) indicates the class of respondents who present a *high* individual 'existence' motivation factor score, that is, respondents who reveal strong support for the protection of the wildlife independent of its human use. Conversely the (−) indicates the class of respondents who present a *low* individual 'existence' motivation factor score, that is, respondents who reveal weak ethical beliefs or moral considerations concerning the protection of the wildlife, independent of human use.[108] The first row considers two important levels of education: respondents with university studies and respondents without it. The second row indicates two distinct income levels.[109] Finally, we have a third column indicating two age classes: '20s' referring to the respondents 18 to 29 years old and '>50s' referring to respondents older than 50 years.

According to these results, a young respondent with a university degree, endowed with a high income and with strong ethical beliefs or moral considerations concerning the protection of the wildlife, is willing to pay about 30900 Portuguese escudos. This value drops to 22600 if we consider a respondent with low income level and is cut to a third, about 10800 escudos, if the respondent has no university diploma. Moreover, the estimations also make clear that the individual 'existence' factor score plays an important role in determining the mean WTP.

---

[107] As we have seen in the previous chapter, the individual motivation factor scores were computed bearing in mind (1) the respondent's answers to the motivation questions and the (2) estimated matrix of factor loadings - see expression (11.14).

[108] We fixed the (−) individual 'existence' motivation factor score at −4.8, which corresponds to the minimum individual 'existence' motivation score as registered in the sample. One the other hand, we fixed the (+) individual 'existence' motivation at 0.4.

[109] We fixed 'low' with the income category that indicates a net monthly household income lower than 150,000 escudos and 'high' with the 600,000–750,000 escudos income category. Furthermore, 'low-blue' indicates a net monthly household income lower than 150,000 escudos and for example a 'blue collar work', an *unskilled worker*.

11.4.2 Recreational Areas protection programme

According to the RA equation estimates, the 'use' factor, income, age and the geographical locality of the respondent's household are all statistically significant at 10 %. Taking into account the respective parameter magnitudes we are to predict WTP for the RA protection programme for different motivation *profiles*. The results are presented in Table 11.7.

In the first column we can read the position of the respondent with respect to the 'use' motivation profile. The (+) indicates the class of respondents who present a *high* individual 'use' motivation factor score, that is, respondents who reveal a strong propensity to engage in outdoor recreation. Conversely the (–) indicates the class of respondents who present a *low* individual 'use' motivation factor score, that is, respondents with weak propensity to consume recreational activities.[110] The first row indicates two distinct classes of respondents: on one hand we have the households who live in urban areas and, on the other hand, we have the households who live in rural areas. As before, we also distinguish two classes of income and age. According to the results, a young respondent living in the city, endowed with a high income and with a weak propensity to consume recreational activities is willing to pay about 6,200 Portuguese escudos for the protection of the RA. This value drops to 1600 if we admit that the respondent lives in a rural area, and is cut to 800 escudos if we admit that the respondent lives in a rural area and has a low income. Finally, we can also clearly see that the individual 'use' factor score plays an important role in determining the mean WTP. For example a young respondent living in a rural area, receiving a low income and with a low 'use' motivation is willing to pay about 800 Portuguese escudos; this rises to 3100 if we admit that the respondent reveals a high propensity to consume recreational activities – see results in Table 11.7.

Table 11.7: RA protection programme (in PTE)

Use	Urban				Rural			
motivation	HI		LOW		HI		LOW	
factor	20s	> 50s	20s	> 50s	20s	> 50s	20s	> 50s
(+)	26600	14600	12500	7800	5600	3600	3100	2000
(–)	6200	3900	3400	2200	1600	100	800	500

11.4.3 Wilderness and Recreational Areas protection programme

Finally we focus on the valuation function regarding the (WA + RA) protection programme. According to the estimation results we see that the 'existence' motivation factor, age and university education are significant covariates at the 10 % confidence level. Again we find out that the young respondents with university studies are the ones who present the highest WTP estimates. These can reach the value of 68000 escudos if such respondent shows strong ethical beliefs or moral considerations concerning the protection of the wildlife. This value is reduced to more than a half, about 28000 escudos, if we consider that the respondent has no university degree – see WTP estimates in Table 11.8.

---

[110] We fixed the (–) individual 'use' motivation factor score at –4, which corresponds to the minimum individual 'use' motivation score as registered in the sample. One the other hand, we fixed the (+) individual 'use' motivation at 0.4.

Table 11.8: (WA + RA) protection programme (in PTE)

Existence	University		No University	
motivation factor	20s	> 50s	20s	> 50s
(+)	68000	39000	28000	17600
(−)	22800	13000	9500	5500

According to estimation exercise, the 'warmglow' motivation factor score is revealed to be statistically significant at 10 % across all the described protection programmes. Therefore, we want to perform an extensive analysis of this explanatory variable. This is presented in the following section.

11.5 The warmglow valuation transmission effect

In this section we study the warmglow effect on the stated WTP values, that is, we investigate the warmglow valuation transmission mechanism. The goals are (a) to assess the magnitude of this valuation transmission mechanism with respect to the (univariate) estimations of the mean WTP, – as computed in Chapter 9 –, and (b) to disentangle the warmglow valuation effect from the original WTP values. The underlying idea is to use the individual information concerning the 'warmglow' motivation factor score and to simulate a WTP value in a scenario in which all the respondents are free from warmglow, that is, free from a general feeling of well-being or satisfaction generated by the act of giving. In other words, we propose to compute a *dry WTP*.

11.5.1 Predicting individual WTP responses

In this sub-section we explore a prediction exercise, that is, we explore the variation of the consumer characteristics and assess the respective impact on the mean WTP estimates. We follow an approach based on the multivariate regression results as described in Table 11.2. We predict the j-WTP responses to be as follows:

$$E\left(WTP^j\right) = \exp\left(\begin{array}{l} \hat{\beta} + \hat{\delta}_u\,\hat{m}_u^j + \hat{\delta}_{nu}\hat{m}_{nu}^j + \hat{\delta}_{wg}\hat{m}_{wg}^j + \hat{\delta}_{s_{a_i}}a_i^j + \hat{\delta}_{s_{o_i}}o_i^j + \\ \hat{\delta}_{se_i}e_i^j + \hat{\delta}_{pv}\,pv^j + \hat{\delta}_Y\,y^j + \hat{\delta}_N n^j + \hat{\delta}_P\,p^j + .5\sigma^2 \end{array}\right) \quad (11.15)$$

with the individual recreation, existence and warmglow motivation factor scores captured by $\hat{m}_u^j$, $\hat{m}_{nu}^j$ and $\hat{m}_{wg}^j$, respectively. All $\hat{\delta}s$ denote parameter estimates. In this context, $\hat{\delta}_u$, $\hat{\delta}_{nu}$, and $\hat{\delta}_{wg}$ denote the marginal estimates of the use, non-use and warmglow motivation functions. All these parameters are fixed according to the results obtained in the full model estimations, and illustrated in Table 11.12. This means that, for example, in the valuation of the WA protection programme $\hat{\delta}_u = 0.091$, $\hat{\delta}_{nu} = 0.438$, and $\hat{\delta}_{wg} = 0.536$. In order to calculate the population mean, we simply predict the individual predicted WTP using equation (11.15) and then average these across the sample, that is:

$$E\left(WTP_{\text{WA}}\right) = \frac{\sum\limits_{j}^{J} E\left(WTP^{j}\right)}{J} \qquad (11.16)$$

where J is the total respondents confronted with the valuation of the wilderness areas protection programme. We propose to explore the same model specification in order to predict the WTP assuming that the respondents do not show warmglow feelings. This is done is the next sub-section.

11.5.2 Predicting a *dry* WTP response

As we have seen in Chapter 10 respondents' 'warmglow' motivation factor score is computed regarding their answers – using a five point semantic differential scale 'I completely agree', 'I agree', 'Sometimes I agree, sometimes I disagree', 'I disagree' and 'I completely disagree' – to the motivational questions, as presented in Section D of the instrument survey – see Table 11.9. In such a context we simulate the presence of a respondent whose 'warmglow' motivation profile is characterised by answering 'I completely disagree' to the motivational items as described in Table 11.9. Bearing in mind such an answer pattern, we can compute the respective individual 'warmglow' motivation factor score. We interpret the respective magnitude as the 'warmglow' motivation factor score which would characterize a respondent whose motivation profile is free from any feeling of well-being or satisfaction generated by the act of giving, that is, a respondent who is not pursuing the mere purchase of moral satisfaction when contributing. We shall name this respondent *Mr Scrooge*. If we admit that all the respondents in the sample share *Mr Scrooge* warmglow motivation, we can predict a WTP measure free from any warmglow effect, that is, a *dry* WTP value, because it is free from any embedding due to warmglow feelings. In analytical terms we refer to the estimation of the following expression:

$$E\left(WTP_{\text{WA}}^{dry}\right) = \frac{\sum\limits_{j}^{J} E\left(WTP^{j,dry}\right)}{J} \qquad (11.17)$$

with

$$E\left(WTP^{j,dry}\right) = \exp\left(\begin{array}{l} \hat{\beta} + \hat{\delta}_{u}\,\hat{m}_{u}^{j} + \hat{\delta}_{nu}\hat{m}_{nu}^{j} + \hat{\delta}_{wg}\hat{m}_{wg}^{dry} + \hat{\delta}_{s_{ai}}\,a_{i}^{j} + \hat{\delta}_{s_{oi}}\,o_{i}^{j} + \\ \hat{\delta}_{se_{i}}\,e_{i}^{j} + \hat{\delta}_{pv}\,pv^{j} + \hat{\delta}_{Y}\,y^{j} + \hat{\delta}_{N}\,n^{j} + \hat{\delta}_{P}\,p^{j} + .5\sigma^{2} \end{array}\right) \qquad (11.18)$$

where $\hat{m}_{wg}^{dry}$ is fixed, for respondents, at *Mr Scrooge* level.

   Given the multiplicative nature of our empirical model specification, see equations (11.6), (11.15), and (11.16), an alternative approach to compute the *dry* WTP mean is to use the motivation factor variables, which have zero mean by construction. Therefore, we are able to compute the *dry* WTP mean with the information upon the construct factors together with the parameters that describe the log-normal distribution function. In other words, we are able to combine the individual motivation factor's information with the univariate location and scale

Table 11.9: Motivational items as presented in Section D of the survey instrument

M8.	'Our family admires the individuals who, on a voluntary basis, participate in collecting donations for national programmes for social aid and solidarity.'
M12.	'There are some funding campaigns to which my family and I feel very close and therefore we do not hesitate to contribute a donation.'
M15.	'It is difficult for me to decline my help to other individuals who, either in the streets or at my door, beg for charity.'
M20.	'I am happy with myself whenever I give a financial contribution to national fund raising campaigns.'
M23.	'My family and I like to contribute to good causes such as the protection of the environment, and whenever we can afford it, we do not decline our help to such fund raising campaigns.'

parameter estimates. This estimation approach shows an important advantage. Since we have observations of the motivation factors variables across all respondents, this estimation approach makes use of the totality of the data set. Therefore, the *dry* WTP mean is calculated as follows:

$$E\left(WTP^{j,dry}\right) = \exp\left(\hat{\beta}_{uni\,var\,ite} + \hat{\delta}_u\,\hat{m}_u^j + \hat{\delta}_{nu}\hat{m}_{nu}^j + \hat{\delta}_{wg}\hat{m}_{wg}^{dry} + .5\sigma_{uni\,var\,ite}^2\right) \qquad (11.19)$$

The *dry WTP* estimation results are presented in Table 11.10 and plotted against the original estimates in Figure 11.1. As we can observe by the simulation results, drying the stated WTP responses from warmglow does induce a significant reduction of the final mean estimates. The mean WTP estimate for the WA protection programme moves from 9600 Portuguese escudos to 2700 escudos – the WA protection programme presents the highest reduction in the WTP estimate. The RA valuation function is revealed to have a lower sensitivity to the warmglow effect – the mean estimate moves from 7200 escudos to 3500 escudos when the warmglow embedding is eliminated. Finally, we can observe that the mean *dry* WTP estimate for the (WA + RA) protection programme is about 6000 escudos. Therefore, we conclude that WTP mean estimates and *dry* WTP mean estimates constitute different welfare valuation magnitudes for the described protection programmes. In order to better understand the changes involved, we propose to explore the methodological properties of the *dry* WTP mean estimates and test the add-up valuation hypothesis. This is performed in the following section.

Table 11.10: Dry mean WTP estimates (in PTE)

	WA	RA	(WA + RA)
With equation (11.18)	2600	2800	5400
With equation (11.19)	2700	3500	6000

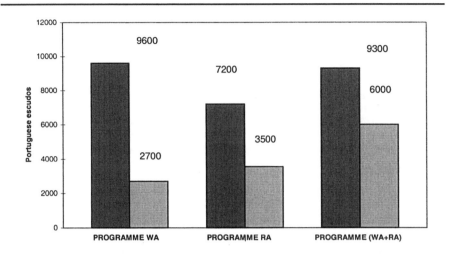

Figure 11.1: WTP vs dry WTP mean estimates

11.5.3 Analysis of the *dry* WTP: re-visiting the adding-up property

As the simulation results show, the 'warmglow' motivation factor score plays an important role in predicting the WTP responses, especially when assessing the WTP for the protection of the WA. At this moment we are interested in investigating the valuation properties of the *dry* WTP estimates. Once WTP has been *dried out*, do the valuation results reject the adding-up property? Does the *dry* WTP violate the adding-up property? To test the adding-up property, we sum the parametric mean estimates from the WA and RA protection programmes, when measured individually, and compare the result to the parametric mean estimate from survey (WA + RA). According to Hausman 'if the answers reflect economic preferences, we should get two numbers which are approximately the same'.[111] Therefore we propose to test:

Hypothesis 12: Stated *dry* WTP for WA plus stated *dry* WTP for RA equals stated *dry* WTP for WA and RA jointly

We used the Wilcoxon–Mann–Whitney test (1945). We use it assuming that the two distributions, the sum of the individual WTP measures and the joint WTP measure, have the same general shape, but that one of them is shifted relative to the other by a constant amount under the alternative hypothesis.[112] The P-value for the statistical test of Hypothesis 13 is 0.72, well above the 5% cutoff – see test results in Table 11.11. Therefore we do not reject Hypothesis 13, that is, the empirical evidence does not reject the adding-up property. Thus we get the same parametric WTP mean value attached to preserving the WA and RA jointly as we

---

[111] In Diamond *et al.* (1993, p. 52).

[112] For a detailed discussion of this test refer to Lehmann (1975).

Table 11.11: Adding-up hypothesis: P-value test result

Hypothesis 13:	$E\left(WTP_{\text{WA}}^{dry}\right) + E\left(WTP_{\text{RA}}^{dry}\right) = E\left(WTP_{(\text{WA}+\text{RA})}^{dry}\right)$	0.72

do when we sum the WTP values attached to preserving the two areas individually.[113] These results demonstrate our primary conclusion: the original WTP answers reflect a warmglow associated with a general feeling of well-being or satisfaction generated by the act of giving. Therefore we obtained test results such as described in Chapter 9. However, once we disentangle the warmglow from the original WTP estimates, that is, compute the *dry* WTP estimates, the adding-up hypothesis is no longer rejected.

11.6 What does the empirical evidence say about the structure of preferences?

Two questions about the adding-up test results arise at this point. First, do CV responses reflect, in some sense, the true WTP, or, alternatively, are they merely an artefact of the questionnaire method? Second, if CV responses are not merely an artefact, are WTP results consistent with economic theory? In other words, can we use the original WTP estimates in cost–benefit analysis? Or, on the contrary, should we correct the original estimates and use the *dry* measure?

11.6.1 Do CV responses reflect true preferences?

When CV data do not confirm the adding-up property, Diamond and Hausman – two strong critics of the CV – choose to reject the data and to hold to the assumption that WTP values based in 'true economic preferences' would not violate the adding-up property. Thus according to these economists the CV method is suspect and the respective valuation results should not be taken seriously. According to these authors CV estimates are simply an artefact of the questionnaire method: 'is some number better than no number?' However, the following question immediately arises: does economic theory *actually* make such a prediction? Should we, whenever the CV data do not confirm the adding-up property, automatically trust *the* theory and abandon the empirical evidence?

According to us there are many assertions about what *the* theory of economic preferences is. We firmly believe that it is possible to reconcile an economic formulation and the findings from CV surveys, even if the CV data reiterate the rejection of the adding-up hypothesis. In the present study, we raised an assertion regarding the presence of (impure) altruism motivations in the individual consumer's choice behaviour. In this context the rejection of the adding-up property can be interpreted as a sign that the WTP judgements are also expressions of attitudes about the moral satisfaction to be obtained from contributing. In the literature on contribution behaviour, Andreoni (1988, 1989, 1990) has extensively explored an analytical model formulation where valuing the provision of a public good takes into account impure altruist motives, that is, the warmglow provided by contributing is taken into account. There is no obvious reason to consider that a similar theoretical formulation is not relevant for

---

[113] The results were computed bearing in mind the estimation results provided by equation 11.9 that is the specification approach that makes use of the totality of the data set.

modelling how people answer CV surveys, and thus for interpreting the WTP responses. As a matter of fact, Schkade and Payne (1994) did find some respondents vocalising a parallel with charitable contributions when answering the WTP survey they used for their verbal protocol analysis. So, it does not seem inappropriate to explore the literature concerning the economic theory of contributions.

For these reasons we argue that the original WTP estimates are fully and directly comparable for cost–benefit exercises. This assertion is, however, not shared by all economists. Milgrom (1993) claims that the WTP values originating from an altruistic motive are incompatible with economic theory as he understands it. Therefore, for Milgrom WTP values estimates – as originally computed – should not be taken seriously and surely should not be used in policy decisions or cost–benefit analysis.

11.6.2 Should we not correct the original estimates and use the *dry* WTP measures in cost–benefit analysis?

There are several reasons to believe that the use of the *dry* WTP measures in cost-benefit analysis is not a compelling argument. The discussion may be raised at two levels. At a fundamental level, we find that some economists support the idea that (impure) altruism motives are incompatible with economic theory and thus should not be taken into account in cost–benefit analysis. Is this statement really accurate? At first glance, it seems hardly consistent with the notion of consumer sovereignty, a cornerstone in modern theory of social choice. It violates a long-standing tradition that one takes people's preferences as one finds them. Arrow (1951), who initiated the modern theory of social choice, emphasised from the outset that it was immaterial whether individual's preferences reflected selfish interest or moral judgement: 'The individual may order all social states by whatever standards he deems relevant'. In a similar vein, Becker (1993) said in his Nobel lecture that his work 'assumes that individual maximise welfare as they conceive it, whether they be selfish, altruistic, loyal, spiteful, or masochistic'.

Bearing such a premise in mind, can we both empirically measure and accurately interpret the demand for a public good in harmony with an analytical framework where warmglow is one of the structural motivations behind the utility function? The estimation results confirm that an individual's level of contribution is indeed an argument of his/her utility function, then – as Andreoni suggests – the estimation of the demand for the public good is characterized by two driving forces: (a) the increase in the individual consumer's well-being derived from the provision of the public good; and the (b) increase in the individual consumer's well-being related to the individual participation in the provision of the public good. Therefore, original WTP responses constitute correct information to be used in the estimation of the demand for the public good. In our opinion, if the estimated demand function for the public good disregards one of the underlying driving forces – such as the warmglow valuation component – the demand function is misspecified, and the respective value predictions not correct. Therefore, warmglow is a legitime valuation component and the original WTP estimates can (and should) be used in cost benefit–analysis. Moreover, we think that different public goods generate different amounts of warmglow, disregarding warmglow may even reverse the ranking of the programmes via cost benefit–analysis. In our study, initially the Wilderness Areas protection programme was ranked above the Recreation Areas, that is, $E(WTP_{WA}) > E(WTP_{RA})$, but once the warmglow is dried out from the original estimations the ranking of the projects is reversed. In other words, the use of a *dry* WTP measure in policy decisions or cost–benefit analysis would be associated with a misleading allocation of resources.

11.7 Conclusions

In this chapter we tested whether WTP estimates are consistent with the analytical framework where warmglow is one of the structural motivations behind the utility function. We proposed the estimation of a *dry* WTP estimate, that is, a WTP measure which is generated by the assumption that all respondents are free from a general feeling of well-being or satisfaction generated by the act of giving. We verified that the *dry* WTP was much lower than the original estimates. Moreover, formal testing demonstrated our primary conclusion: unlike the original estimates, the *dry* WTP estimates do not violate the adding-up property, that is, the $E\left(WTP_{WA}^{dry}\right) + E\left(WTP_{RA}^{dry}\right) = E\left(WTP_{(WA+RA)}^{dry}\right)$ proposition is no longer rejected.

In closing, we discussed whether to use (or not) *dry* or original WTP estimates in policy making and cost–benefit exercises. We stated that the survey responses are in harmony with the impure public good model formulation and, in this way, the original WTP responses constituted correct information to be used in the estimation of the demand for the public good. Therefore, the original WTP estimates can (and should) be used in cost–benefit analysis. In our opinion, there are several reasons to believe that use of the *dry* WTP measures in cost–benefit analysis does not constitute a compelling or convincing argument. First, it would mean a violation of a long-standing tradition that one takes people's preferences as one finds them 'whether they be selfish, altruistic, loyal, spiteful, or masochistic'. Second, we interpret the demand for the public good as characterized by two driving forces: on the one hand, the individual consumer's well-being derived from the provision of the public good, and on the other hand, the individual consumer's well-being related to participation in the provision of the public good. Therefore, if the estimated demand function for the public good disregards one of the underlying driving forces – such as the warmglow valuation component – the demand function is misspecified, and the respective value predictions not correct. In other words, the *dry* WTP estimate would be associated with a valuation bias when estimating the demand for the public good, and thus the use of such a WTP measure in policy decisions or cost–benefit analysis would be associated with a misleading allocation of resources.

Chapter
12
CONCLUSIONS

In this book we address the economic valuation of the protection of natural areas. More particularly, we analyse the warmglow or moral satisfaction effect that is associated with the act of contributing. In other words, we analyse the feeling of well-being associated with the act of contributing to the protection of natural areas. We build an analytical framework where warmglow is one of the structural motivations behind the utility function. This framework allows us to understand better the violation of the adding-up property as reported in many contingent valuation applications. This framework is empirically tested in a CV study of the protection of a natural Area in Portugal.

In Chapter 1 we identified the conservation benefits associated with the protection of a natural area like the Alentejo Natural Park. Generally speaking, the Alentejo Natural Park's benefits are classified in terms of the natural area's provision of use and non-use service flows. The use benefits, as the name suggests, refer to a set of recreational possibilities, for example, hiking or simply enjoying the aesthetic satisfaction of being in such a natural environment. The non-use benefits refer to the set of activities – not necessarily associated with any human use – that the natural area is also able to provide, e.g., areas closed to the general public and created to guarantee the protection of the local biodiversity in its natural habitat. In Chapter 1 we also discussed the different valuation instruments available to the researcher to assess the different conservation benefits associated with the protection of a natural area. Since stated preference techniques, and in particular the CV, are the only valuation techniques available to measure the non-use benefits – characterized by having no behavioral market trace – we decided to use the CV technique so as to measure the total value associated with the protection of the Alentejo Natural Park.

In Chapter 2 we focused our attention on the CV method, reviewed the state-of-art literature regarding survey design and discussed the respective methodological properties. Despite the fact that CV survey design has been a target of extensive methodological research and quality improvements, this valuation method is today an object of diverse critiques. We paid particular interest to the study of the embedding effect – an important critic of the CV – and proposed to explore Kahneman and Knetsch's 'purchase of moral satisfaction' argument as a possible driving force in valuation. Moreover, we proposed to investigate such a valuation transmission effect in the vein of the general model formulation for private donations as initially developed by Andreoni. Therefore, we interpreted the consumer's contributions, as stated in the survey instrument, as a result of two forces. First, a consumer's contributions could be interpreted as a valuation outcome because s/he simply wants more of the public good. Secondly, the consumer's contributions could also be interpreted as revealing an additional benefit that the individual consumer derives from contributing *per se* – this effect was identified by Andreoni as the warmglow benefit. By inference, it seems plausible that the act of participating in a CV market so as to assist in the supply of an environmental good could provide a mixture of private, warmglow benefits and public services from the increased supply of the good.

In Chapter 3 we explored an analytical setting in which we could interpret the consumer's contributions as stated in the instrument survey. We modelled the public good in terms of its provision of use and non-use service flows, plus the warmglow associated with the act of giving *per se*. Furthermore, we introduced the concept of consumer motivation functions so as to model the structure of the consumer preferences. The underlying premise is that one can draw a portrait of the structure of the consumer preferences in terms of the consumer's motivational profile. We characterize the consumer preferences in terms of the consumer recreation, ethical and warmglow motivation profiles. In this context, individual consumer contributions to the protection of the Natural Area were interpreted in terms of the characteristics that it generated. In order to better understand consumer behaviour and the respondents' WTP answers, we extended the original model formulation so that one could take into account the effect of the payment mechanism. Finally, we also explored the comparative static properties of the consumer's own contributions level, for example, we inferred the impact of the consumer's recreational motivation profile upon the contribution's level. The sign of the expressions for the comparative statics were, most of the time, ambiguous. This means that we could not assign the direction of the changes. Unless assuming major simplifications – namely the choice of a specific utility function and functional form for the consumer motivation functions – it would not have been possible to simplify the expressions and thus help us to better understand the various forces at work.

According to the comparative static results it was clear that:

- the sign of the effects of changes in the consumer's own contribution as the consumer's motivation profile changes was not unambiguously given. Therefore, the final assessment of the direction depends on the underlying Hicksian complementary substitution magnitudes assumed across the different characteristics.

In Chapter 4 we reviewed the research work involved with the design of the survey instrument. We made extensive use of focus groups and pilots and thus we were able to check for the comprehensibility of the payment vehicles and to improve the language in the narrative. Here, we were also able to frame the format of the elicitation questions, calibrate the bid vector and adjust the initial visual aids package and original size of the survey, since it proved to be too long. At the last pilot debriefing, interviewers reported that the survey was now easier to administer and that the valuation questions were better understood by the respondents.

In Chapter 5 we presented the structure of the survey instrument that was used in the national interviews. Following NOAA guidelines, face-to-face interviews had been chosen for data collection. To better simulate price-taking consumer market behaviour, the double dichotomous choice model was selected so as to estimate willingness to pay. The survey instrument involved the elaboration of different policy options, different payment vehicles and different survey information levels concerning the governmental financial effort in running the Alentejo Natural Park as a protected area. As far as the policy options are concerned, we designed three protection programmes: (RA) protection of recreational areas from tourism development; (WA) protection of wilderness areas from tourism development and (WA + RA) protection of both the Wilderness Areas and Recreational Areas of the Alentejo Natural Park from tourism development. This enabled us to develop formal test procedures and test whether the valuation results violated the adding-up hypothesis, that is, whether valuing two programmes individually and adding up the respective WTP estimates gives the same result as valuing the two programmes jointly. The survey instrument was also designed to take into account two payment vehicles, respectively, the national tax scheme and the voluntary payment scheme. This enabled us to develop formal test procedures and to test whether free-riding was present in the estimation results. Finally, we took into account two survey information levels: in one survey version respondents were informed about the current government financial effort in running the Alentejo Natural Park as a protected area, while in the second version, they were not. This enabled us to test whether a starting point bias was present in the double dichotomous valuation model.

In Chapter 6 we described the administration of the CV application. The national survey was executed by the Research Survey Department of the Portuguese Catholic University. We followed closely the set of procedures defined in the *Exxon Valdez* CVM study. In this context, particular attention was given to the formation of the interviewers and field quality control edits. The underlying objective was to guarantee the quality of the questionnaire responses.

In Chapter 7 we provided a general descriptive statistical analysis of the survey responses. Bearing in mind the survey information regarding the socio-economic characteristics of the respondents, on the one hand, and the national census information provided by Portuguese statistical authorities, on the other hand, we verified that the CV application covered rather well the different demographic clusters of the Portuguese population. Therefore, we conclude that the representativness of the sample had been successfully achieved.

In Chapter 8 we made use of non-parametric formal test procedures and investigated the stated WTP responses across the two payment vehicles and across the two survey information levels. The test results suggested that:

- the stated WTP distribution in the scenario where the respondent is informed about the governmental expenditures in keeping the Natural Park free from any commercial development is not statistically different from the WTP distribution in the scenario in which the respondent was not provided with such information. This test was interpreted as a clear rejection of the hypothesis of a starting point bias, that is, the hypothesis that the indication of how much money is spent may be used by the respondent as a 'clue' or 'anchor' in the valuation is rejected;
- in the national tax scheme, free-riding behaviour is less strong than in the voluntary contribution scheme, though the respective magnitudes are hardly statistically significant;
- The results of both non-parametric tests were interpreted as important indicators confirming the validity of our contingent valuation experiment and, this way, confirmed the quality of the proposed questionnaire as a value measurement instrument.

In Chapter 9 we computed univariate estimations for the described protection programmes. According to the estimation results we were able to verify that:

- the WTP of the policy option to prevent the wilderness area from commercial development has the highest valuation, approximately 148 million euro;
- the valuation of the protection of the RA from commercial development is estimated to be 114 million euro; and
- the WTP to prevent the introduction of commercial development in both recreational and wilderness areas is estimated to be 140 million euro.

The valuation results of the three protection programmes have important implications in terms of policy action:

- first, we can conclude that the policy action characterised by the partial commercial development of the Alentejo Natural Park is not always preferred to a policy option strategy characterized by the total commercial development of the Alentejo Natural Park;
- second, if we admit that the government intends to pursue a policy action which is characterized by the partial commercial development of the Alentejo Natural Park, then the valuation results clearly indicate that Portuguese households prefer to keep the wilderness areas of the Alentejo Natural Park always protected and to introduce the commercial development in the recreational areas.

This last point is a very important result since it reiterates the importance of the non-use value component of the Alentejo Natural Park, which it is only possible to assess with the use of the contingent valuation technique. Furthermore, the sensitivity analysis results indicated that:

- the valuation of the protection of the wilderness areas from commercial development is approximately the same as the valuation of the protection of both wilderness areas and recreational areas from commercial development.

The same holds for the valuation of the recreational areas, that is:

- the WTP for the recreational areas is about the same as the WTP for both wilderness areas and recreational areas of the Alentejo Natural Park.

We interpret the test results in two possible ways. One explanation is characterized by admitting that the different service flows provided by the Alentejo Natural Park, respectively the recreational use characteristics and the non-use characteristics, are pure substitutes. Another possible interpretation is characterized by the presence of embedding in the stated WTP responses, that is, if we admit that the financial contribution, by itself, provides warmglow and thus constitutes also a source of well-being to the individual respondent.

In Chapter 10 we used factor analysis to identify, measure and interpret motivation factors, a latent variable which we want to introduce – together with the socio-economic characteristics of the respondents – in the multivariate analysis of the WTP function. We explored the use of factor analysis upon the Likert responses of the respondents over the 26 attitudinal items as presented in Section D of the instrument survey. The maximum likelihood estimation results:

- confirmed the proposed motivation structure, that is, a three-factor model. These were interpreted as the 'use/recreation', 'warmglow' and 'non-use/existence' factors:
  - the 'use/recreation' factor was strongly associated to the motivational items which were related to the respondent's general attitude with respect to the direct consumption of natural areas for recreational use; a high score on this factor indicated a strong propensity for recreation;
  - the 'warmglow' factor was strongly associated with the motivational items, which were related to the respondent's general feeling of well-being or satisfaction generated by the act of giving; a high score on this factor reveals that the respondent was particularly sensible to warmglow;

- the 'non-use/existence' factor was strongly associated with the motivational items which were related to the respondent's ethical beliefs or moral considerations with respect to the preservation of wildlife; a high score on this factor revealed that the respondent had strong ethical beliefs or moral consideration toward the preservation of wildlife, independent of its human use.

The estimation results showed also that:

- respondents who go to the beach, practice sports and go camping present a higher 'use' motivation score. This is a reasonable result since such individuals are, on average, more recreationally active;
- respondents who visited the Alentejo Natural Park presented also higher 'use' motivation scores.

It was verified that,

- the general feeling of satisfaction generated by the act of giving revealed itself to be less strong among respondents with a higher education level and living in large families;
- young women have a stronger feeling of warmglow;
- respondents who participated in donation and charity campaigns clearly revealed a higher 'warmglow' motivation score;
- ethical beliefs with respect to the preservation of wildlife independently of its human use are stronger among the respondents with higher education and among those who reported having background information regarding environmental issues, but seem to be independent of the respondent's gender.

In Chapter 11 we performed an econometric analysis of valuation functions across the described protection programmes. Bearing in mind the regression estimation results, we were able to predict the WTP for different groups or types of respondents. We found out that:

- on average, respondents with university education, high income and ages lying between 18 and 39 years were willing to pay more than the average respondent.

Moreover, the RA valuation function showed that:

- the geographical locality of the respondent is an important predictor: respondents living in urban areas are willing to pay more than respondents who are living in rural areas.

We paid particular attention to the econometric analysis of the motivational factor scores and interpretation of the respective parameter estimates. We observed that:

- the warmglow motivation factor had an estimated coefficient statistically robust across all valuation functions;
- respondents with higher 'use' factor scores were willing to pay more for the protection of the RA than for any other protection programme - e.g., the 'use' factor was not statically significant in explaining the stated WTP for the WA;
- respondents with higher 'existence' scores were willing to pay more for the protection of the WA than the average respondent. However, the estimated magnitude of the 'existence' motivation factor was revealed to be independent of the protection programme.

Since the 'warmglow' factor score was statically significant across all valuation functions, we explored in detail the impact of the changes of the 'warmglow' factor score on the WTP estimates. Therefore we proposed the estimation of a *dry* WTP measure, that is, a WTP measure that was generated by a simulation exercise in which we admitted that all respondents were free from a general feeling of well-being or satisfaction generated by the act of giving. We verified that:

- the *dry* WTP were much lower than the original estimates. Moreover, formal hypothesis testing demonstrated our primary conclusion: unlike the original estimates, where the presence of a general feeling of well-being or satisfaction generated by the act of giving, the *dry* WTP estimates do not violate the adding-up hypothesis, that is, the $WTP_{WA}^{dry} + WTP_{RA}^{dry} = WTP_{(WA+RA)}^{dry}$ proposition cannot be rejected.

Finally, when discussing whether to use (or not) *dry* or original WTP estimates in policy making and cost–benefit exercises, we showed a strong conviction that the survey responses do reflect true WTP responses – the empirical results confirm the validity of the proposed impure public good model formulation – and, in this way, the original WTP responses constituted correct information to be used in the estimation of the demand for the public good. Therefore, warmglow is a legitimate valuation component and the original WTP estimates can (and should) be used in cost benefit analysis. In our opinion, there are several reasons to believe that the use of the *dry* WTP measures in cost–benefit analysis do not constitute a compelling argument. First, the statement that (impure) altruism motives are incompatible with economic theory is hardly consistent with the notion of consumer sovereignty, a cornerstone in modern theory of social choice. It violates a long-standing tradition that one takes people's preferences as one finds them. Modern theory of social choice has always emphasized that it was immaterial whether individual's preferences reflected selfish interest or moral judgement. According to Arrow 'the individual may order all social states by whatever standards he deems relevant'. In a similar vein, we can find the work of Becker, who always defended the premise that 'individuals maximise welfare as they conceive it, whether they be selfish, altruistic, loyal, spiteful, or masochistic'. Second, since the empirical evidence confirmed Andreoni's impure altruism model formulation, then we could interpret the demand for the public good as characterized by two driving forces; (a) the individual consumer's well-being derived from the provision of the public good; and (b) the individual consumer's well-being related to the individual personal participation in the provision of the public good. Therefore, if the estimated demand function for the public good disregards one of the underlying driving forces – such as the warmglow valuation component – the demand function is misspecified, and the respective value predictions not correct. In other words, the *dry* WTP estimate would be associated with a valuation bias when estimating the demand for the public good and thus the use of such a WTP measure in policy decisions or cost–benefit analysis would be associated with a misleading allocation of resources.

PART IV
Appendices and Bibliography

Appendix

A

DERIVATION OF COMPARATIVE STATIC RESULTS

A.1 The *D* expression

The D is defined as

$$D = C_{nu,nu}C_{u,u} - 2C_{nu,nu}C_{u,wg} - C_{u,wg}{}^2 + C_{nu,nu}C_{wg,wg} + C_{u,u}C_{wg,wg}$$

and represents the denominator of the comparative static exercise. Bearing in mind H.2), which states that $C_{u,wg} \cong 0$ and $C_{nu,wg} \cong 0$, we may rewrite D as follows:

$$D = C_{nu,nu}C_{u,u} + C_{nu,nu}C_{wg,wg} + C_{u,u}C_{wg,wg}$$

which is always positive.

Proof:

$$\underbrace{C_{nu,nu}C_{u,u}}_{+} + \underbrace{C_{nu,nu}C_{wg,wg}}_{+} + \underbrace{C_{u,u}C_{wg,wg}}_{+} > 0$$

A.2 General approach

All the subsequent comparative static exercises start from the observation that:

$$\frac{\partial \hat{B}_k}{\partial \varphi} = \frac{\partial \tilde{B}_k}{\partial \tilde{p}_u}\frac{\partial \tilde{p}_u}{\partial \varphi} + \frac{\partial \tilde{B}_k}{\partial \tilde{p}_{nu}}\frac{\partial \tilde{p}_{nu}}{\partial \varphi} + \frac{\partial \tilde{B}_k}{\partial \tilde{p}_{wg}}\frac{\partial \tilde{p}_{wg}}{\partial \varphi} + \frac{\partial \tilde{B}_k}{\partial \tilde{M}}\frac{\partial \tilde{M}}{\partial \varphi} \tag{A.1}$$

with

k indexing the *use, non-use* and *warmglow* characteristics

φ denoting any element of the vector $\Phi \equiv \left\{ \rho\ ,\tau\ ,\theta\ ,M\ ,\overline{q}^{-j} \right\}$

$$p = \rho\tilde{p}_u + \tau\tilde{p}_{nu} + \theta\tilde{p}_{wg} \qquad\qquad (A.2)$$

$$\theta\tilde{B}_u(\tilde{p}_u,\tilde{p}_{nu},\tilde{p}_{wg},\tilde{M}) = \rho\left[\tilde{B}_{wg}(\tilde{p}_u,\tilde{p}_{nu},\tilde{p}_{wg},\tilde{M}) + \theta\rho\overline{q}\right] \qquad\qquad (A.3)$$

$$\theta\tilde{B}_{nu}(\tilde{p}_u,\tilde{p}_{nu},\tilde{p}_{wg},\tilde{M}) = \tau\left[\tilde{B}_{wg}(\tilde{p}_u,\tilde{p}_{nu},\tilde{p}_{wg},\tilde{M}) + \theta\tau\overline{q}\right] \qquad\qquad (A.4)$$

$$\tilde{M} = M + \rho\,\tilde{p}_u\,\overline{q} + \tau\,\tilde{p}_{nu}\,\overline{q} \qquad\qquad (A.5)$$

A.2.1 A change in *M*

Differentiating (A.2)–(A-5), holding constant all parameters except M, we get:

$$0 = \frac{\partial\tilde{p}_u}{\partial M} + \frac{\partial\tilde{p}_{nu}}{\partial M} + \frac{\partial\tilde{p}_{wg}}{\partial M} \qquad\qquad (A.2\text{-}M)$$

$$\theta\left(\frac{\partial\tilde{B}_u}{\partial\tilde{p}_u}\frac{\partial\tilde{p}_u}{\partial M} + \frac{\partial\tilde{B}_u}{\partial\tilde{p}_{nu}}\frac{\partial\tilde{p}_{nu}}{\partial M} + \frac{\partial\tilde{B}_u}{\partial\tilde{p}_{wg}}\frac{\partial\tilde{p}_{wg}}{\partial M} + \frac{\partial\tilde{B}_u}{\partial\tilde{M}}\frac{\partial\tilde{M}}{\partial M}\right) = \rho\left(\frac{\partial\tilde{B}_{wg}}{\partial\tilde{p}_u}\frac{\partial\tilde{p}_u}{\partial M} + \frac{\partial\tilde{B}_{wg}}{\partial\tilde{p}_{nu}}\frac{\partial\tilde{p}_{nu}}{\partial M} + \frac{\partial\tilde{B}_{wg}}{\partial\tilde{p}_{wg}}\frac{\partial\tilde{p}_{wg}}{\partial M} + \frac{\partial\tilde{B}_{wg}}{\partial\tilde{M}}\frac{\partial\tilde{M}}{\partial M}\right) \;(A.3\text{-}M)$$

$$\theta\left(\frac{\partial\tilde{B}_u}{\partial\tilde{p}_u}\frac{\partial\tilde{p}_u}{\partial M} + \frac{\partial\tilde{B}_u}{\partial\tilde{p}_{nu}}\frac{\partial\tilde{p}_{nu}}{\partial M} + \frac{\partial\tilde{B}_u}{\partial\tilde{p}_{wg}}\frac{\partial\tilde{p}_{wg}}{\partial M} + \frac{\partial\tilde{B}_u}{\partial\tilde{M}}\frac{\partial\tilde{M}}{\partial M}\right) = \tau\left(\frac{\partial\tilde{B}_{wg}}{\partial\tilde{p}_u}\frac{\partial\tilde{p}_u}{\partial M} + \frac{\partial\tilde{B}_{wg}}{\partial\tilde{p}_{nu}}\frac{\partial\tilde{p}_{nu}}{\partial M} + \frac{\partial\tilde{B}_{wg}}{\partial\tilde{p}_{wg}}\frac{\partial\tilde{p}_{wg}}{\partial M} + \frac{\partial\tilde{B}_{wg}}{\partial\tilde{M}}\frac{\partial\tilde{M}}{\partial M}\right) \;(A.4\text{-}M)$$

$$\frac{\partial\tilde{M}}{\partial M} = 1 + \overline{q}\frac{\partial\tilde{p}_u}{\partial M} + \overline{q}\frac{\partial\tilde{p}_{nu}}{\partial M} \qquad\qquad (A.5\text{-}M)$$

With the help of *Mathematica*, and using the Slutsky decomposition, we can solve the above equations for $\partial\tilde{p}_{wg}/\partial M$, $\partial\tilde{p}_u/\partial M$, $\partial\tilde{p}_{nu}/\partial M$ and $\partial\tilde{M}/\partial M$. We get:[114]

$$\frac{\partial\tilde{M}}{\partial M} = 1 + \left\{\overline{q}\left[\left(-C_{nu,nu} - C_{u,wg}\right)\frac{\partial\tilde{B}_u}{\partial\tilde{M}} + \left(-C_{u,u} + C_{u,wg}\right)\frac{\partial\tilde{B}_{nu}}{\partial\tilde{M}} + \left(C_{nu,nu} + C_{u,u}\right)\frac{\partial\tilde{Q}_{wg}}{\partial\tilde{M}}\right]\right\}/D \qquad (A.6)$$

---

[114] We follow Cornes and Sandler's assumptions, as stated in their last paper, and normalized the motivation coefficients so as to make the expressions neater.

$$\frac{\partial \tilde{p}_{wg}}{\partial M} = \left[\left(C_{nu,nu} + C_{u,wg}\right)\frac{\partial \tilde{B}_u}{\partial \tilde{M}} + \left(C_{u,u} - C_{u,wg}\right)\frac{\partial \tilde{B}_{nu}}{\partial \tilde{M}} + \left(-C_{nu,nu} - C_{u,u}\right)\frac{\partial \tilde{B}_{wg}}{\partial \tilde{M}}\right]\Big/ D \qquad (A.7)$$

$$\frac{\partial \tilde{p}_u}{\partial M} = \left[\left(-C_{nu,nu} - C_{wg,wg}\right)\frac{\partial \tilde{B}_u}{\partial \tilde{M}} + \left(C_{wg,wg} - C_{u,wg}\right)\frac{\partial \tilde{B}_{nu}}{\partial \tilde{M}} + \left(C_{nu,nu} + C_{u,wg}\right)\frac{\partial \tilde{B}_{wg}}{\partial \tilde{M}}\right]\Big/ D \qquad (A.8)$$

$$\frac{\partial \tilde{p}_{nu}}{\partial M} = -\left[\left(C_{u,wg} - C_{wg,wg}\right)\frac{\partial \tilde{B}_u}{\partial \tilde{M}} + \left(C_{u,u} - 2C_{u,wg} + C_{wg,wg}\right)\frac{\partial \tilde{B}_{nu}}{\partial \tilde{M}} + \left(C_{u,wg} - C_{u,u}\right)\frac{\partial \tilde{B}_{wg}}{\partial \tilde{M}}\right]\Big/ D \qquad (A.9)$$

where D is defined as

$$D = C_{nu,nu}C_{u,u} - 2C_{nu,nu}C_{u,wg} - C_{u,wg}^{\;2} + C_{nu,nu}C_{wg,wg} + C_{u,u}C_{wg,wg} \qquad (A.10)$$

that we assumed to be positive. Plugging (A.6)-(A.10) in (A.1) and using again the Slutsky decomposition, we finally get:,

$$\frac{\partial \hat{B}_{wg}}{\partial M} = \left[C_{nu,nu}\left(C_{wg,wg} - C_{u,wg}\right)\frac{\partial \tilde{B}_u}{\partial \tilde{M}} + \left(C_{u,u}C_{wg,wg} - C_{u,wg}^{\;2}\right)\frac{\partial \tilde{B}_{nu}}{\partial \tilde{M}} + C_{nu,nu}\left(C_{u,u} - C_{u,wg}\right)\frac{\partial \tilde{B}_{wg}}{\partial \tilde{M}}\right]\Big/ D$$

$$\frac{\partial \hat{B}_u}{\partial M} = \left[C_{nu,nu}\left(C_{wg,wg} - C_{u,wg}\right)\frac{\partial \tilde{B}_u}{\partial \tilde{M}} + \left(C_{u,u}C_{wg,wg} - C_{u,wg}^{\;2}\right)\frac{\partial \tilde{B}_{nu}}{\partial \tilde{M}} + C_{nu,nu}\left(C_{u,u} - C_{u,wg}\right)\frac{\partial \tilde{B}_{wg}}{\partial \tilde{M}}\right]\Big/ D$$

$$\frac{\partial \hat{B}_{nu}}{\partial M} = \left[C_{nu,nu}\left(C_{wg,wg} - C_{u,wg}\right)\frac{\partial \tilde{B}_u}{\partial \tilde{M}} + \left(C_{u,u}C_{wg,wg} - C_{u,wg}^{\;2}\right)\frac{\partial \tilde{B}_{nu}}{\partial \tilde{M}} + C_{nu,nu}\left(C_{u,u} - C_{u,wg}\right)\frac{\partial \tilde{B}_{wg}}{\partial \tilde{M}}\right]\Big/ D$$

A.2.2 A change in the ρ coefficient

Differentiating (A.2)–(A.5), holding constant all parameters except ρ, we obtain:

$$0 = \tilde{p}_u + \frac{\partial \tilde{p}_u}{\partial \rho} + \frac{\partial \tilde{p}_{nu}}{\partial \rho} + \frac{\partial \tilde{p}_{wg}}{\partial \rho} \qquad (A.2\text{-}\rho)$$

$$\frac{\partial \tilde{B}_u}{\partial \tilde{p}_u}\frac{\partial \tilde{p}_u}{\partial \rho} + \frac{\partial \tilde{B}_u}{\partial \tilde{p}_{nu}}\frac{\partial \tilde{p}_{nu}}{\partial \rho} + \frac{\partial \tilde{B}_u}{\partial \tilde{p}_{wg}}\frac{\partial \tilde{p}_{wg}}{\partial \rho} + \frac{\partial \tilde{B}_u}{\partial \tilde{M}}\frac{\partial \tilde{M}}{\partial \rho} = \frac{\partial \tilde{B}_{wg}}{\partial \tilde{p}_u}\frac{\partial \tilde{p}_u}{\partial \rho} + \frac{\partial \tilde{B}_{wg}}{\partial \tilde{p}_{nu}}\frac{\partial \tilde{p}_{nu}}{\partial \rho} + \frac{\partial \tilde{B}_{wg}}{\partial \tilde{p}_{wg}}\frac{\partial \tilde{p}_{wg}}{\partial \rho} + \frac{\partial \tilde{B}_{wg}}{\partial \tilde{M}}\frac{\partial \tilde{M}}{\partial \rho} + 2\bar{q} + \tilde{B}_{wg} \qquad (A.3\text{-}\rho)$$

$$\frac{\partial \tilde{B}_{nu}}{\partial \tilde{P}_u}\frac{\partial \tilde{P}_u}{\partial \rho}+\frac{\partial \tilde{B}_{nu}}{\partial \tilde{P}_{nu}}\frac{\partial \tilde{P}_{nu}}{\partial \rho}+\frac{\partial \tilde{B}_{nu}}{\partial \tilde{P}_{wg}}\frac{\partial \tilde{P}_{wg}}{\partial \rho}+\frac{\partial \tilde{B}_{nu}}{\partial \tilde{M}}\frac{\partial \tilde{M}}{\partial \rho}=\frac{\partial \tilde{B}_{wg}}{\partial \tilde{P}_u}\frac{\partial \tilde{P}_u}{\partial \rho}+\frac{\partial \tilde{B}_{wg}}{\partial \tilde{P}_{nu}}\frac{\partial \tilde{P}_{nu}}{\partial \rho}+\frac{\partial \tilde{B}_{wg}}{\partial \tilde{P}_{wg}}\frac{\partial \tilde{P}_{wg}}{\partial \rho}+\frac{\partial \tilde{B}_{wg}}{\partial \tilde{M}}\frac{\partial \tilde{M}}{\partial \rho} \qquad (A.4\text{-}\rho)$$

$$\frac{\partial \tilde{M}}{\partial \rho}=\overline{q}\frac{\partial \tilde{p}_u}{\partial \rho}+\overline{q}\frac{\partial \tilde{p}_{nu}}{\partial \rho}+\overline{q}\tilde{p}_u \qquad (A.5\text{-}\rho)$$

Solving the system for the changes in the virtual magnitudes with respect to ρ we get the following solutions:

$$\frac{\partial \tilde{M}}{\partial \rho}=\overline{q}\Big\{2\overline{q}\big(C_{nu,nu}+C_{u,wg}\big)+B_{wg}\big(C_{nu,nu}+C_{u,wg}\big)+\tilde{p}_u\Big\{C_{nu,nu}\big(C_{u,u}-C_{u,wg}\big)+$$
$$+\Big[\big(-C_{nu,nu}-C_{u,wg}\big)\frac{\partial \tilde{B}_u}{\partial \tilde{M}}+\big(C_{u,wg}-C_{u,u}\big)\frac{\partial \tilde{B}_{nu}}{\partial \tilde{M}}+\big(C_{nu,nu}+C_{u,u}\big)\frac{\partial \tilde{B}_{wg}}{\partial \tilde{M}}\Big]\big(\overline{q}+B_{wg}\big)\Big\}\Big\}\Big/D \qquad (A.11)$$

$$\frac{\partial \tilde{p}_{wg}}{\partial \rho}=\Big\{-2\overline{q}\big(C_{nu,nu}+C_{u,wg}\big)-B_{wg}\big(C_{nu,nu}+C_{u,wg}\big)+\tilde{p}_u\Big\{C_{nu,nu}\big(C_{u,wg}-C_{u,u}\big)+$$
$$-\Big[\big(-C_{nu,nu}-C_{u,wg}\big)\frac{\partial \tilde{B}_u}{\partial \tilde{M}}+\big(C_{u,wg}-C_{u,u}\big)\frac{\partial \tilde{B}_{nu}}{\partial \tilde{M}}+\big(C_{nu,nu}+C_{u,u}\big)\frac{\partial \tilde{B}_{wg}}{\partial \tilde{M}}\Big]\big(\overline{q}+B_{wg}\big)\Big\}\Big\}\Big/D \qquad (A.12)$$

$$\frac{\partial \tilde{p}_{nu}}{\partial \rho}=\Big\{2\overline{q}\big(C_{u,wg}-C_{wg,wg}\big)+B_{wg}\big(C_{u,wg}-C_{wg,wg}\big)+\tilde{p}_u\Big\{C_{u,wg}\big(C_{u,wg}-C_{u,u}\big)+$$
$$+\Big[\big(C_{wg,wg}-C_{u,wg}\big)\frac{\partial \tilde{B}_u}{\partial \tilde{M}}+\big(2C_{u,wg}-C_{wg,wg}-C_{u,u}\big)\frac{\partial \tilde{B}_{nu}}{\partial \tilde{M}}+\big(C_{u,u}-C_{u,wg}\big)\frac{\partial \tilde{B}_{wg}}{\partial \tilde{M}}\Big]\big(\overline{q}+B_{wg}\big)\Big\}\Big\}\Big/D \qquad (A.13)$$

$$\frac{\partial \tilde{p}_u}{\partial \rho}=\Big\{2\overline{q}\big(C_{nu,nu}+C_{wg,wg}\big)+B_{wg}\big(C_{nu,nu}+C_{wg,wg}\big)+\tilde{p}_u\Big\{C_{nu,nu}\big(C_{u,wg}-C_{wg,wg}\big)+$$
$$+\Big[\big(-C_{nu,nu}-C_{wg,wg}\big)\frac{\partial \tilde{B}_u}{\partial \tilde{M}}+\big(C_{wg,wg}-C_{u,u}\big)\frac{\partial \tilde{B}_{nu}}{\partial \tilde{M}}+\big(C_{nu,nu}+C_{u,wg}\big)\frac{\partial \tilde{B}_{wg}}{\partial \tilde{M}}\Big]\big(\overline{q}+B_{wg}\big)\Big\}\Big\}\Big/D \qquad (A.14)$$

Plugging (A.11)–(A.14) in (A.1) and using again the Slutsky decomposition, we finally get:

$$\frac{\partial \hat{B}_u}{\partial \rho}=\Big\{-\overline{q}\big(C_{nu,nu}C_{u,wg}-C_{u,u}C_{wg,wg}+C_{u,wg}{}^2-C_{nu,nu}C_{u,u}\big)+\tilde{p}_u\big(C_{nu,nu}\big(C_{u,wg}{}^2-C_{u,u}C_{wg,wg}\big)\big)+$$
$$+B_{wg}\big(C_{nu,nu}C_{u,u}-C_{nu,nu}C_{u,wg}-C_{u,wg}{}^2+C_{u,u}C_{wg,wg}\big)+\Big[\big(C_{nu,nu}C_{u,wg}+C_{nu,nu}C_{wg,wg}\big)\frac{\partial \tilde{B}_u}{\partial \tilde{M}}+$$
$$+\big(C_{u,u}C_{wg,wg}-C_{u,wg}{}^2\big)\frac{\partial \tilde{B}_{nu}}{\partial \tilde{M}}+\big(C_{nu,nu}C_{u,u}-C_{nu,nu}C_{u,wg}\big)\frac{\partial \tilde{B}_{wg}}{\partial \tilde{M}}\Big]\big(\overline{q}+B_{wg}\big)\Big\}\Big/D \qquad (A.15)$$

$$
\frac{\partial \hat{B}_{nu}}{\partial \rho} = \left\{ 2\overline{q}\left(C_{nu,nu}C_{u,wg} - C_{nu,nu}C_{wg,wg}\right) - B_{wg}\left(C_{nu,nu}C_{wg,wg} - C_{nu,nu}C_{u,wg}\right) + \right.
$$

$$
+ \tilde{p}_u\left(C_{nu,nu}\left(C_{u,wg}^{\;2} - C_{u,u}C_{wg,wg}\right)\right) + \left[\left(C_{nu,nu}C_{u,wg} + C_{nu,nu}C_{wg,wg}\right)\frac{\partial \tilde{B}_u}{\partial \tilde{M}} + \right. \tag{A.16}
$$

$$
\left. \left. + \left(C_{u,u}C_{wg,wg} - C_{u,wg}^{\;2}\right)\frac{\partial \tilde{B}_{nu}}{\partial \tilde{M}} + \left(C_{nu,nu}C_{u,u} - C_{nu,nu}C_{u,wg}\right)\frac{\partial \tilde{B}_{wg}}{\partial \tilde{M}}\right]\left(\overline{q} + B_{wg}\right)\right\}\Big/D
$$

$$
\frac{\partial \hat{B}_{wg}}{\partial \rho} = \left\{ 2\overline{q}\left(C_{nu,nu}C_{u,wg} - C_{nu,nu}C_{wg,wg}\right) - B_{wg}\left(C_{nu,nu}C_{wg,wg} - C_{nu,nu}C_{u,wg}\right) + \right.
$$

$$
+ \tilde{p}_u\left(C_{nu,nu}\left(C_{u,wg}^{\;2} - C_{u,u}C_{wg,wg}\right)\right) + \left[\left(C_{nu,nu}C_{u,wg} + C_{nu,nu}C_{wg,wg}\right)\frac{\partial \tilde{B}_u}{\partial \tilde{M}} + \right. \tag{A.17}
$$

$$
\left. \left. + \left(C_{u,u}C_{wg,wg} - C_{u,wg}^{\;2}\right)\frac{\partial \tilde{B}_{nu}}{\partial \tilde{M}} + \left(C_{nu,nu}C_{u,u} - C_{nu,nu}C_{u,wg}\right)\frac{\partial \tilde{B}_{wg}}{\partial \tilde{M}}\right]\left(\overline{q} + B_{wg}\right)\right\}\Big/D
$$

If preferences are qL, the income terms disappear, and thus the expressions for responses of both virtual prices and quantities demanded simplify in a way that greatly help to better understand the various forces at work. Therefore the comparative static expressions become:

$$
\frac{\partial \hat{B}_u}{\partial \rho} = \left\{ \left(\overline{q} + B_{wg}\right)\left(C_{u,u}C_{wg,wg} - C_{nu,nu}C_{u,wg} - C_{u,wg}^{\;2} + C_{nu,nu}C_{u,u}\right) + \right.
$$

$$
\left. + \tilde{p}_u\left(C_{nu,nu}\left(C_{u,wg}^{\;2} - C_{u,u}C_{wg,wg}\right)\right)\right\}\Big/D \tag{A.15-qL}
$$

$$
\frac{\partial \hat{B}_{nu}}{\partial \rho} = \left\{ \left(2\overline{q} - B_{wg}\right)\left(C_{nu,nu}C_{u,wg} - C_{nu,nu}C_{wg,wg}\right) + \right.
$$

$$
\left. + \tilde{p}_u\left(C_{nu,nu}\left(C_{u,wg}^{\;2} - C_{u,u}C_{wg,wg}\right)\right)\right\}\Big/D \tag{A.16-qL}
$$

$$
\frac{\partial \tilde{B}_{wg}}{\partial \rho} = \left\{ \left(2\overline{q} - B_{wg}\right)\left(C_{nu,nu}C_{u,wg} - C_{nu,nu}C_{wg,wg}\right) + \right.
$$

$$
\left. + \tilde{p}_u\left(C_{nu,nu}\left(C_{u,wg}^{\;2} - C_{u,u}C_{wg,wg}\right)\right)\right\}\Big/D \tag{A.17-qL}
$$

A.2.3 A change in the r coefficient

Differentiating (A.2)–(A.5), holding constant all parameters except τ, we get

$$
0 = \tilde{p}_{nu} + \frac{\partial \tilde{p}_u}{\partial \tau} + \frac{\partial \tilde{p}_{nu}}{\partial \tau} + \frac{\partial \tilde{p}_{wg}}{\partial \tau} \tag{A.2-τ}
$$

$$\frac{\partial \tilde{B}_u}{\partial \tilde{p}_u}\frac{\partial \tilde{p}_u}{\partial \tau}+\frac{\partial \tilde{B}_u}{\partial \tilde{p}_{nu}}\frac{\partial \tilde{p}_{nu}}{\partial \tau}+\frac{\partial \tilde{B}_u}{\partial \tilde{p}_{wg}}\frac{\partial \tilde{p}_{wg}}{\partial \tau}+\frac{\partial \tilde{B}_u}{\partial \tilde{M}}\frac{\partial \tilde{M}}{\partial \tau}=\frac{\partial \tilde{B}_{wg}}{\partial \tilde{p}_u}\frac{\partial \tilde{p}_u}{\partial \tau}+\frac{\partial \tilde{B}_{wg}}{\partial \tilde{p}_{nu}}\frac{\partial \tilde{p}_{nu}}{\partial \tau}+\frac{\partial \tilde{B}_{wg}}{\partial \tilde{p}_{wg}}\frac{\partial \tilde{p}_{wg}}{\partial \tau}+\frac{\partial \tilde{B}_{wg}}{\partial \tilde{M}}\frac{\partial \tilde{M}}{\partial \tau} \qquad \text{(A.3-}\tau\text{)}$$

$$\frac{\partial \tilde{B}_{nu}}{\partial \tilde{p}_u}\frac{\partial \tilde{p}_u}{\partial \tau}+\frac{\partial \tilde{B}_{nu}}{\partial \tilde{p}_{nu}}\frac{\partial \tilde{p}_{nu}}{\partial \tau}+\frac{\partial \tilde{B}_{nu}}{\partial \tilde{p}_{wg}}\frac{\partial \tilde{p}_{wg}}{\partial \tau}+\frac{\partial \tilde{B}_{nu}}{\partial \tilde{M}}\frac{\partial \tilde{M}}{\partial \tau}=\frac{\partial \tilde{B}_{wg}}{\partial \tilde{p}_u}\frac{\partial \tilde{p}_u}{\partial \tau}+\frac{\partial \tilde{B}_{wg}}{\partial \tilde{p}_{nu}}\frac{\partial \tilde{p}_{nu}}{\partial \tau}+\frac{\partial \tilde{B}_{wg}}{\partial \tilde{p}_{wg}}\frac{\partial \tilde{p}_{wg}}{\partial \tau}+\frac{\partial \tilde{B}_{wg}}{\partial \tilde{M}}\frac{\partial \tilde{M}}{\partial \tau}+2\bar{q}+B_{wg} \qquad \text{(A.4-}\tau\text{)}$$

$$\frac{\partial \tilde{M}}{\partial \tau}=\bar{q}\frac{\partial \tilde{p}_u}{\partial \tau}+\bar{q}\frac{\partial \tilde{p}_{nu}}{\partial \tau}+\bar{q}\tilde{p}_{nu} \qquad \text{(A.5-}\tau\text{)}$$

Solving the system for the changes in the virtual magnitudes with respect to τ we get the following results:

$$\frac{\partial \tilde{M}}{\partial \tau}=\bar{q}\left\{2\bar{q}\left(C_{u,u}-C_{u,wg}\right)+B_{wg}\left(C_{u,u}-C_{u,wg}\right)+\tilde{p}_{nu}\left\{C_{nu,nu}\left(C_{u,u}-C_{u,wg}\right)+\right.\right.$$
$$\left.\left.+\left[\left(-C_{nu,nu}-C_{u,wg}\right)\frac{\partial \tilde{B}_u}{\partial \tilde{M}}+\left(C_{u,wg}-C_{u,u}\right)\frac{\partial \tilde{B}_{nu}}{\partial \tilde{M}}+\left(C_{nu,nu}+C_{u,u}\right)\frac{\partial \tilde{B}_{wg}}{\partial \tilde{M}}\right]\left(\bar{q}+B_{wg}\right)\right\}\right\}\bigg/D \qquad \text{(A.18)}$$

$$\frac{\partial \tilde{p}_{wg}}{\partial \tau}=\left\{-2\bar{q}\left(C_{u,u}-C_{u,wg}\right)+B_{wg}\left(C_{u,wg}-C_{u,u}\right)-\tilde{p}_u\left\{C_{nu,nu}\left(C_{u,u}-C_{u,wg}\right)+\right.\right.$$
$$\left.\left.+\left[\left(-C_{nu,nu}-C_{u,wg}\right)\frac{\partial \tilde{B}_u}{\partial \tilde{M}}+\left(C_{u,wg}-C_{u,u}\right)\frac{\partial \tilde{B}_{nu}}{\partial \tilde{M}}+\left(C_{nu,nu}+C_{u,u}\right)\frac{\partial \tilde{B}_{wg}}{\partial \tilde{M}}\right]\left(\bar{q}+B_{wg}\right)\right\}\right\}\bigg/D \qquad \text{(A.19)}$$

$$\frac{\partial \tilde{p}_{nu}}{\partial \tau}=\left\{\bar{q}\left(2C_{u,u}-4C_{u,wg}+2C_{wg,wg}\right)+B_{wg}\left(C_{u,u}-2C_{u,wg}+C_{wg,wg}\right)+\tilde{p}_u\left\{\left(C_{u,wg}^{\,2}-C_{u,u}C_{wg,wg}\right)+\right.\right.$$
$$\left.\left.+\left[\left(C_{wg,wg}-C_{u,wg}\right)\frac{\partial \tilde{B}_u}{\partial \tilde{M}}+\left(2C_{u,wg}-C_{wg,wg}-C_{u,u}\right)\frac{\partial \tilde{B}_{nu}}{\partial \tilde{M}}+\left(C_{u,u}-C_{u,wg}\right)\frac{\partial \tilde{B}_{wg}}{\partial \tilde{M}}\right]\left(\bar{q}+B_{wg}\right)\right\}\right\}\bigg/D \qquad \text{(A.20)}$$

$$\frac{\partial \tilde{p}_u}{\partial \tau}=\left\{2\bar{q}\left(C_{u,wg}-C_{wg,wg}\right)+B_{wg}\left(C_{u,wg}-C_{wg,wg}\right)+\tilde{p}_u\left\{C_{nu,nu}\left(C_{u,wg}-C_{wg,wg}\right)+\right.\right.$$
$$\left.\left.+\left[\left(-C_{nu,nu}-C_{wg,wg}\right)\frac{\partial \tilde{B}_u}{\partial \tilde{M}}+\left(C_{wg,wg}-C_{u,wg}\right)\frac{\partial \tilde{B}_{nu}}{\partial \tilde{M}}+\left(C_{nu,nu}+C_{u,wg}\right)\frac{\partial \tilde{B}_{wg}}{\partial \tilde{M}}\right]\left(\bar{q}+B_{wg}\right)\right\}\right\}\bigg/D \qquad \text{(A.21)}$$

Plugging (A.18)–(A.21) in (A.1) and using again the Slutsky decomposition, we finally get:

$$\frac{\partial \hat{B}_u}{\partial \tau}=\left\{2\bar{q}\left(C_{u,wg}^{\,2}-C_{u,u}C_{wg,wg}\right)+\tilde{p}_{nu}\left(C_{nu,nu}\left(C_{u,wg}^{\,2}-C_{u,u}C_{wg,wg}\right)\right)+\right.$$
$$+B_{wg}\left(C_{u,wg}^{\,2}-C_{u,u}C_{wg,wg}\right)+\left[\left(C_{nu,nu}C_{u,wg}+C_{nu,nu}C_{wg,wg}\right)\frac{\partial \tilde{B}_u}{\partial \tilde{M}}+\right.$$
$$\left.\left.+\left(C_{u,u}C_{wg,wg}-C_{u,wg}^{\,2}\right)\frac{\partial \tilde{B}_{nu}}{\partial \tilde{M}}+\left(C_{nu,nu}C_{u,u}-C_{nu,nu}C_{u,wg}\right)\frac{\partial \tilde{B}_{wg}}{\partial \tilde{M}}\right]\left(\bar{q}+B_{wg}\right)\right\}\bigg/D \qquad \text{(A.22)}$$

$$\frac{\partial \hat{B}_{nu}}{\partial \tau} = \left\{ \overline{q}\left(2C_{nu,nu}C_{u,u} + 2C_{nu,nu}C_{wg,wg} - 4C_{nu,nu}C_{u,wg}\right) + \tilde{p}_{nu}\left(C_{nu,nu}\left(C_{u,wg}{}^2 - C_{u,u}C_{wg,wg}\right)\right) + \right.$$

$$+ B_{wg}\left(C_{nu,nu}C_{u,u} + C_{nu,nu}C_{wg,wg} - 2C_{nu,nu}C_{u,wg}\right) + \left[\left(C_{nu,nu}C_{u,wg} + C_{nu,nu}C_{wg,wg}\right)\frac{\partial \tilde{B}_{u}}{\partial \tilde{M}} + \right.$$

$$\left. \left. + \left(C_{u,u}C_{wg,wg} - C_{u,wg}{}^2\right)\frac{\partial \tilde{B}_{nu}}{\partial \tilde{M}} + \left(C_{nu,nu}C_{u,u} - C_{nu,nu}C_{u,wg}\right)\frac{\partial \tilde{B}_{wg}}{\partial \tilde{M}}\right]\left(\overline{q} + B_{wg}\right)\right\} \bigg/ D \tag{A.23}$$

$$\frac{\partial \hat{B}_{wg}}{\partial \tau} = \left\{ 2\overline{q}\left(C_{u,wg}{}^2 - C_{u,u}C_{wg,wg}\right) + \tilde{p}_{nu}\left(C_{nu,nu}\left(C_{u,wg}{}^2 - C_{u,u}C_{wg,wg}\right)\right) + \right.$$

$$+ B_{wg}\left(C_{u,wg}{}^2 - C_{u,u}C_{wg,wg}\right) + \left[\left(C_{nu,nu}C_{u,wg} + C_{nu,nu}C_{wg,wg}\right)\frac{\partial \tilde{B}_{u}}{\partial \tilde{M}} + \right.$$

$$\left. \left. + \left(C_{u,u}C_{wg,wg} - C_{u,wg}{}^2\right)\frac{\partial \tilde{B}_{nu}}{\partial \tilde{M}} + \left(C_{nu,nu}C_{u,u} - C_{nu,nu}C_{u,wg}\right)\frac{\partial \tilde{B}_{wg}}{\partial \tilde{M}}\right]\left(\overline{q} + B_{wg}\right)\right\} \bigg/ D \tag{A.24}$$

If preferences are quasilinear (qL), (A.22)–(A.24) expressions simplify, and we can write:

$$\frac{\partial \hat{B}_{u}}{\partial \tau} = \left\{\left(2\overline{q} + B_{wg}\right)\left(C_{u,wg}{}^2 - C_{u,u}C_{wg,wg}\right) + \tilde{p}_{nu}\left(C_{nu,nu}\left(C_{u,wg}{}^2 - C_{u,u}C_{wg,wg}\right)\right)\right\} \bigg/ D \tag{A.22-qL}$$

$$\frac{\partial \hat{B}_{nu}}{\partial \tau} = \left\{\left(4\overline{q} + B_{wg}\right)\left(C_{nu,nu}C_{u,u} + C_{nu,nu}C_{wg,wg} - 2C_{nu,nu}C_{u,wg}\right) + \right.$$

$$\left. + \tilde{p}_{nu}\left(C_{nu,nu}\left(C_{u,wg}{}^2 - C_{u,u}C_{wg,wg}\right)\right)\right\} \bigg/ D \tag{A.23-qL}$$

$$\frac{\partial \hat{B}_{wg}}{\partial \tau} = \left\{\left(2\overline{q} + B_{wg}\right)\left(C_{u,wg}{}^2 - C_{u,u}C_{wg,wg}\right) + \tilde{p}_{nu}\left(C_{nu,nu}\left(C_{u,wg}{}^2 - C_{u,u}C_{wg,wg}\right)\right)\right\} \bigg/ D \tag{A.24-qL}$$

A.2.4 A change in the θ coefficient

Running the same computational exercise as before, but now holding constant all parameters except θ we finally get:

$$0 = \tilde{p}_{wg} + \frac{\partial \tilde{p}_{u}}{\partial \theta} + \frac{\partial \tilde{p}_{nu}}{\partial \theta} + \frac{\partial \tilde{p}_{wg}}{\partial \theta} \tag{A.2-θ}$$

$$\frac{\partial \tilde{B}_{u}}{\partial \tilde{p}_{u}}\frac{\partial \tilde{p}_{u}}{\partial \theta} + \frac{\partial \tilde{B}_{u}}{\partial \tilde{p}_{nu}}\frac{\partial \tilde{p}_{nu}}{\partial \theta} + \frac{\partial \tilde{B}_{u}}{\partial \tilde{p}_{wg}}\frac{\partial \tilde{p}_{wg}}{\partial \theta} + \frac{\partial \tilde{B}_{u}}{\partial \tilde{M}}\frac{\partial \tilde{M}}{\partial \theta} = \frac{\partial \tilde{B}_{wg}}{\partial \tilde{p}_{u}}\frac{\partial \tilde{p}_{u}}{\partial \theta} + \frac{\partial \tilde{B}_{wg}}{\partial \tilde{p}_{nu}}\frac{\partial \tilde{p}_{nu}}{\partial \theta} + \frac{\partial \tilde{B}_{wg}}{\partial \tilde{p}_{wg}}\frac{\partial \tilde{p}_{wg}}{\partial \theta} + \frac{\partial \tilde{B}_{wg}}{\partial \tilde{M}}\frac{\partial \tilde{M}}{\partial \theta} + \overline{q} \tag{A.3-θ}$$

$$\frac{\partial \tilde{B}_{nu}}{\partial \tilde{p}_u}\frac{\partial \tilde{p}_u}{\partial \theta}+\frac{\partial \tilde{B}_{nu}}{\partial \tilde{p}_{nu}}\frac{\partial \tilde{p}_{nu}}{\partial \theta}+\frac{\partial \tilde{B}_{nu}}{\partial \tilde{p}_{wg}}\frac{\partial \tilde{p}_{wg}}{\partial \theta}+\frac{\partial \tilde{B}_{nu}}{\partial \tilde{M}}\frac{\partial \tilde{M}}{\partial \theta}=\frac{\partial \tilde{B}_{wg}}{\partial \tilde{p}_u}\frac{\partial \tilde{p}_u}{\partial \theta}+\frac{\partial \tilde{B}_{wg}}{\partial \tilde{p}_{nu}}\frac{\partial \tilde{p}_{nu}}{\partial \theta}+\frac{\partial \tilde{B}_{wg}}{\partial \tilde{p}_{wg}}\frac{\partial \tilde{p}_{wg}}{\partial \theta}+\frac{\partial \tilde{B}_{wg}}{\partial \tilde{M}}\frac{\partial \tilde{M}}{\partial \theta\tau}+\bar{q} \quad \text{(A.4-}\theta\text{)}$$

$$\frac{\partial \tilde{M}}{\partial \theta}=\bar{q}\frac{\partial \tilde{p}_u}{\partial \theta}+\bar{q}\frac{\partial \tilde{p}_{nu}}{\partial \theta} \qquad\qquad\qquad\qquad\qquad\qquad\qquad\qquad\qquad \text{(A.5-}\theta\text{)}$$

Solving the system for the changes in the virtual magnitudes with respect to θ we get the following results:

$$\frac{\partial \tilde{M}}{\partial \theta}=\bar{q}\Bigg\{B_{wg}\left(-C_{nu,nu}-C_{u,u}\right)+\tilde{p}_{wg}\Bigg\{\ C_{u,wg}{}^{2}+C_{nu,nu}\ C_{u,wg}-C_{nu,nu}C_{wg,wg}-C_{u,u}C_{wg,wg}+ \qquad\qquad \text{(A.25)}$$
$$+\left[\left(C_{u,wg}-C_{nu,nu}\right)\frac{\partial \tilde{B}_u}{\partial \tilde{M}}+\left(C_{u,wg}-C_{u,u}\right)\frac{\partial \tilde{B}_{nu}}{\partial \tilde{M}}+\left(C_{nu,nu}+C_{u,u}\right)\frac{\partial \tilde{B}_{wg}}{\partial \tilde{M}}\right]B_{wg}\Bigg\}\Bigg\}\Bigg/D$$

$$\frac{\partial \tilde{p}_{wg}}{\partial \theta}=\Bigg\{B_{wg}\left(C_{nu,nu}+C_{u,u}\right)+\tilde{p}_{wg}\Bigg\{\ C_{nu,nu}\ C_{u,wg}-C_{nu,nu}C_{u,u}- \qquad\qquad\qquad \text{(A.26)}$$
$$-\left[\left(C_{u,wg}-C_{nu,nu}\right)\frac{\partial \tilde{B}_u}{\partial \tilde{M}}+\left(C_{u,wg}-C_{u,u}\right)\frac{\partial \tilde{B}_{nu}}{\partial \tilde{M}}+\left(C_{nu,nu}+C_{u,u}\right)\frac{\partial \tilde{B}_{wg}}{\partial \tilde{M}}\right]B_{wg}\Bigg\}\Bigg\}\Bigg/D$$

$$\frac{\partial \tilde{p}_{nu}}{\partial \theta}=\Bigg\{B_{wg}\left(C_{u,wg}-C_{u,u}\right)+\tilde{p}_{wg}\Bigg\{\ C_{u,wg}{}^{2}-C_{u,u}C_{wg,wg}+ \qquad\qquad\qquad\qquad \text{(A.27)}$$
$$+\left[\left(C_{wg,wg}-C_{u,wg}\right)\frac{\partial \tilde{B}_u}{\partial \tilde{M}}+\left(2C_{u,wg}-C_{u,u}-C_{wg,wg}\right)\frac{\partial \tilde{B}_{nu}}{\partial \tilde{M}}+\left(C_{u,u}-C_{u,wg}\right)\frac{\partial \tilde{B}_{wg}}{\partial \tilde{M}}\right]B_{wg}\Bigg\}\Bigg\}\Bigg/D$$

$$\frac{\partial \tilde{p}_u}{\partial \theta}=\Bigg\{B_{wg}\left(-C_{nu,nu}-C_{u,wg}\right)+\tilde{p}_{wg}\Bigg\{\ C_{nu,nu}\ C_{u,wg}-C_{nu,nu}C_{wg,wg}+ \qquad\qquad\qquad \text{(A.28)}$$
$$+\left[\left(-C_{wg,wg}-C_{nu,nu}\right)\frac{\partial \tilde{B}_u}{\partial \tilde{M}}+\left(-C_{u,wg}+C_{wg,wg}\right)\frac{\partial \tilde{B}_{nu}}{\partial \tilde{M}}+\left(C_{nu,nu}+C_{u,wg}\right)\frac{\partial \tilde{B}_{wg}}{\partial \tilde{M}}\right]B_{wg}\Bigg\}\Bigg\}\Bigg/D$$

Plugging (A.25)–(A.28) in (A.1) and using again the Slutsky decomposition, we finally get:

$$\frac{\partial \hat{B}_u}{\partial \theta}=\Bigg\{B_{wg}\left(C_{nu,nu}C_{u,wg}-C_{nu,nu}C_{u,u}\right)+\tilde{p}_{wg}\Bigg\{\ C_{nu,nu}\left(C_{u,wg}{}^{2}-C_{u,u}C_{wg,wg}\right)+ \qquad\qquad \text{(A.29)}$$
$$+\left[\left(C_{nu,nu}C_{u,wg}+C_{nu,nu}C_{wg,wg}\right)\frac{\partial \tilde{B}_u}{\partial \tilde{M}}+\right.$$
$$\left.+\left(C_{u,u}C_{wg,wg}-C_{u,wg}{}^{2}\right)\frac{\partial \tilde{B}_{nu}}{\partial \tilde{M}}+\left(C_{nu,nu}C_{u,u}-C_{nu,nu}C_{u,wg}\right)\frac{\partial \tilde{B}_{wg}}{\partial \tilde{M}}\right]B_{wg}\Bigg\}\Bigg\}\Bigg/D$$

$$\frac{\partial \hat{B}_{nu}}{\partial \theta} = \left\{ B_{wg}\left(C_{nu,nu}C_{u,wg} - C_{nu,nu}C_{u,u}\right) + \tilde{p}_{wg}\left\{ C_{nu,nu}\left(C_{u,wg}{}^2 - C_{u,u}C_{wg,wg}\right) + \right. \right.$$ (A.30)

$$+ \left[\left(C_{nu,nu}C_{u,wg} + C_{nu,nu}C_{wg,wg}\right)\frac{\partial \tilde{B}_u}{\partial \tilde{M}} + \right.$$

$$\left. \left. + \left(C_{u,u}C_{wg,wg} - C_{u,wg}{}^2\right)\frac{\partial \tilde{B}_{nu}}{\partial \tilde{M}} + \left(C_{nu,nu}C_{u,u} - C_{nu,nu}C_{u,wg}\right)\frac{\partial \tilde{B}_{wg}}{\partial \tilde{M}}\right]B_{wg}\right\}\right/ D$$

$$\frac{\partial \hat{B}_{wg}}{\partial \theta} = \left\{ B_{wg}\left(C_{nu,nu}C_{wg,wg} - C_{nu,nu}C_{u,wg} - C_{u,wg}{}^2 + C_{u,u}C_{wg,wg}\right) + \right.$$ (A.31)

$$+ \tilde{p}_{wg}\left\{C_{nu,nu}\left(C_{u,wg}{}^2 - C_{u,u}C_{wg,wg}\right) + \left[\left(C_{nu,nu}C_{u,wg} + C_{nu,nu}C_{wg,wg}\right)\frac{\partial \tilde{B}_u}{\partial \tilde{M}} + \right. \right.$$

$$\left. \left. + \left(C_{u,u}C_{wg,wg} - C_{u,wg}{}^2\right)\frac{\partial \tilde{B}_{nu}}{\partial \tilde{M}} + \left(C_{nu,nu}C_{u,u} - C_{nu,nu}C_{u,wg}\right)\frac{\partial \tilde{B}_{wg}}{\partial \tilde{M}}\right]B_{wg}\right\}\right/ D$$

If preferences are quasilinear (qL), these expressions simplify, and we can write,

$$\frac{\partial \hat{B}_u}{\partial \theta} = \left\{ B_{wg}\left(C_{nu,nu}C_{u,wg} - C_{nu,nu}C_{u,u}\right) + \tilde{p}_{wg}\left(C_{nu,nu}\left(C_{u,wg}{}^2 - C_{u,u}C_{wg,wg}\right)\right)\right\}\right/ D$$ (A.29-qL)

$$\frac{\partial \hat{B}_{nu}}{\partial \theta} = \left\{ B_{wg}\left(C_{nu,nu}C_{u,wg} - C_{nu,nu}C_{u,u}\right) + \tilde{p}_{wg}\left(C_{nu,nu}\left(C_{u,wg}{}^2 - C_{u,u}C_{wg,wg}\right)\right)\right\}\right/ D$$ (A.30-qL)

$$\frac{\partial \hat{B}_{wg}}{\partial \theta} = \left\{ B_{wg}\left(C_{nu,nu}C_{wg,wg} - C_{nu,nu}C_{u,wg} - C_{u,wg}{}^2 + C_{u,u}C_{wg,wg}\right) + \right.$$ (A.31-qL)

$$\left. + \tilde{p}_{wg}\left(C_{nu,nu}\left(C_{u,wg}{}^2 - C_{u,u}C_{wg,wg}\right)\right)\right\}\right/ D$$

A.2.5 A change in q^{-j}

Differentiating (A.2)–(A.5), holding constant all parameters except $\overline{q}$, we get:

$$0 = \frac{\partial \tilde{p}_u}{\partial \overline{q}} + \frac{\partial \tilde{p}_{nu}}{\partial \overline{q}} + \frac{\partial \tilde{p}_{wg}}{\partial \overline{q}}$$ (A.2-q^{-j})

$$\frac{\partial \tilde{B}_u}{\partial \tilde{p}_u}\frac{\partial \tilde{p}_u}{\partial \overline{q}} + \frac{\partial \tilde{B}_u}{\partial \tilde{p}_{nu}}\frac{\partial \tilde{p}_{nu}}{\partial \overline{q}} + \frac{\partial \tilde{B}_u}{\partial \tilde{p}_{wg}}\frac{\partial \tilde{p}_{wg}}{\partial \overline{q}} + \frac{\partial \tilde{B}_u}{\partial \tilde{M}}\frac{\partial \tilde{M}}{\partial \overline{q}} = \frac{\partial \tilde{Q}_{wg}}{\partial \tilde{p}_u}\frac{\partial \tilde{p}_u}{\partial \overline{q}} + \frac{\partial \tilde{Q}_{wg}}{\partial \tilde{p}_{nu}}\frac{\partial \tilde{p}_{nu}}{\partial \overline{q}} + \frac{\partial \tilde{Q}_{wg}}{\partial \tilde{p}_{wg}}\frac{\partial \tilde{p}_{wg}}{\partial \overline{q}} + \frac{\partial \tilde{Q}_{wg}}{\partial \tilde{M}}\frac{\partial \tilde{M}}{\partial \overline{q}} + 1$$ (A.3-q^{-j})

$$\frac{\partial \tilde{B}_{nu}}{\partial \tilde{p}_u}\frac{\partial \tilde{p}_u}{\partial \tilde{q}}+\frac{\partial \tilde{B}_{nu}}{\partial \tilde{p}_{nu}}\frac{\partial \tilde{p}_{nu}}{\partial \tilde{q}}+\frac{\partial \tilde{B}_{nu}}{\partial \tilde{p}_{wg}}\frac{\partial \tilde{p}_{wg}}{\partial \tilde{q}}+\frac{\partial \tilde{B}_{nu}}{\partial \tilde{M}}\frac{\partial \tilde{M}}{\partial \tilde{q}}=\frac{\partial \tilde{Q}_{wg}}{\partial \tilde{p}_u}\frac{\partial \tilde{p}_u}{\partial \tilde{q}}+\frac{\partial \tilde{Q}_{wg}}{\partial \tilde{p}_{nu}}\frac{\partial \tilde{p}_{nu}}{\partial \tilde{q}}+\frac{\partial \tilde{Q}_{wg}}{\partial \tilde{p}_{wg}}\frac{\partial \tilde{p}_{wg}}{\partial \tilde{q}}+\frac{\partial \tilde{Q}_{wg}}{\partial \tilde{M}}\frac{\partial \tilde{M}}{\partial \tilde{q}}+1 \qquad (A.4\text{-}q^{-j})$$

$$\frac{\partial \tilde{M}}{\partial q^{-j}}=1+\tilde{p}_u+\overline{q}\frac{\partial \tilde{p}_u}{\partial M}+\tilde{p}_{nu}+\overline{q}\frac{\partial \tilde{p}_{nu}}{\partial M} \qquad\qquad (A.5\text{-}q^{-j})$$

Solving the system for $\partial\tilde{M}/\partial\overline{q}$, $\partial\tilde{p}_u/\partial\overline{q}$, $\partial\tilde{p}_{nu}/\partial\overline{q}$, and $\partial\tilde{p}_{wg}/\partial\overline{q}$ we get the following results:

$$\frac{\partial \tilde{M}}{\partial \overline{q}}=\tilde{p}_u+\tilde{p}_{nu}+\left\{\ \overline{q}(C_{nu,nu}+C_{u,u})+\overline{q}(\tilde{p}_u+\tilde{p}_{nu})\left[(-C_{nu,nu}-C_{u,wg})\frac{\partial \tilde{B}_u}{\partial \tilde{M}}+ \right.\right. \qquad (A.32)$$

$$\left.\left.+(C_{u,wg}-C_{u,u})\frac{\partial \tilde{B}_{nu}}{\partial \tilde{M}}+(C_{nu,nu}+C_{u,u})\frac{\partial \tilde{Q}_{wg}}{\partial \tilde{M}}\right]\right\}\!\!\bigg/D$$

$$\frac{\partial \tilde{p}_{nu}}{\partial \overline{q}}=(\tilde{p}_u+\tilde{p}_{nu})\left\{\left(C_{wg,wg}-C_{u,wg}\right)\frac{\partial \tilde{B}_u}{\partial \tilde{M}}+\left(2C_{u,wg}-C_{u,u}-C_{wg,wg}\right)\frac{\partial \tilde{B}_{nu}}{\partial \tilde{M}}+ \right. \qquad (A.33)$$

$$\left.+\left(C_{u,u}-C_{u,wg}\right)\frac{\partial \tilde{Q}_{wg}}{\partial \tilde{M}}\right\}+\left(C_{u,u}-C_{u,wg}\right)\!\!\bigg/D$$

$$\frac{\partial \tilde{p}_{wg}}{\partial \overline{q}}=(\tilde{p}_u+\tilde{p}_{nu})\left\{\left(C_{nu,nu}+C_{u,wg}\right)\frac{\partial \tilde{B}_u}{\partial \tilde{M}}+\left(-C_{u,wg}+C_{u,u}\right)\frac{\partial \tilde{B}_{nu}}{\partial \tilde{M}}+ \right. \qquad (A.34)$$

$$\left.+\left(-C_{nu,nu}-C_{u,u}\right)\frac{\partial \tilde{Q}_{wg}}{\partial \tilde{M}}\right\}+\left(-C_{nu,nu}-C_{u,u}\right)\!\!\bigg/D$$

$$\frac{\partial \tilde{p}_u}{\partial \overline{q}}=(\tilde{p}_u+\tilde{p}_{nu})\left\{\left(-C_{nu,nu}-C_{wg,wg}\right)\frac{\partial \tilde{B}_u}{\partial \tilde{M}}+\left(-C_{u,wg}+C_{wg,wg}\right)\frac{\partial \tilde{B}_{nu}}{\partial \tilde{M}}+ \right. \qquad (A.35)$$

$$\left.+\left(C_{nu,nu}+C_{u,wg}\right)\frac{\partial \tilde{Q}_{wg}}{\partial \tilde{M}}\right\}+\left(C_{nu,nu}+C_{u,wg}\right)\!\!\bigg/D$$

Plugging (A.35)–(A.36) in (A.1) and using again the Slutsky decomposition, we finally get:

$$\frac{\partial \hat{B}_u}{\partial \overline{q}}=\left\{(\tilde{p}_u+\tilde{p}_{nu})\left[C_{nu,nu}\left(C_{wg,wg}-C_{u,wg}\right)\frac{\partial \tilde{B}_u}{\partial \tilde{M}}+\left(C_{u,u}C_{wg,wg}-C_{u,wg}^2\right)\frac{\partial \tilde{B}_{nu}}{\partial \tilde{M}}+ \right.\right. \qquad (A.36)$$

$$\left.\left.+C_{nu,nu}\left(C_{u,u}-C_{u,wg}\right)\frac{\partial \tilde{B}_{wg}}{\partial \tilde{M}}\right]+\left(C_{nu,nu}C_{u,u}-C_{nu,nu}C_{u,wg}\right)\right\}\!\!\bigg/D$$

$$\frac{\partial \hat{B}_{nu}}{\partial \overline{q}} = \left\{ (\tilde{p}_u + \tilde{p}_{nu}) \left[C_{nu.nu} (C_{wg.wg} - C_{u.wg}) \frac{\partial \tilde{B}_u}{\partial \tilde{M}} + (C_{u.u} C_{wg.wg} - C_{u.wg}^{\ 2}) \frac{\partial \tilde{B}_{nu}}{\partial \tilde{M}} + \right. \right. \tag{A.37}$$
$$\left. \left. + C_{nu.nu} (C_{u.u} - C_{u.wg}) \frac{\partial \tilde{B}_{wg}}{\partial \tilde{M}} \right] + (C_{nu.nu} C_{u.u} - C_{nu.nu} C_{u.wg}) \right\} \Big/ D$$

$$\frac{\partial \hat{B}_{wg}}{\partial \overline{q}} = \left\{ (\tilde{p}_u + \tilde{p}_{nu}) \left[C_{nu.nu} (C_{wg.wg} - C_{u.wg}) \frac{\partial \tilde{B}_u}{\partial \tilde{M}} + (C_{u.u} C_{wg.wg} - C_{u.wg}^{\ 2}) \frac{\partial \tilde{B}_{nu}}{\partial \tilde{M}} + \right. \right. \tag{A.38}$$
$$\left. \left. + C_{nu.nu} (C_{u.u} - C_{u.wg}) \frac{\partial \tilde{B}_{wg}}{\partial \tilde{M}} \right] + (C_{nu.nu} C_{u.wg} + C_{u.wg}^{\ 2} - C_{nu.nu} C_{wg.wg} - C_{u.u} C_{wg.wg}) \right\} \Big/ D$$

If preferences are quasilinear (qL), these expressions simplify, and we can write:

$$\frac{\partial \hat{B}_u}{\partial \overline{q}} = (\tilde{p}_u + \tilde{p}_{nu})(C_{nu.nu} C_{u.u} - C_{nu.nu} C_{u.wg}) \Big/ D \tag{A.36-qL}$$

$$\frac{\partial \hat{B}_{nu}}{\partial \overline{q}} = (\tilde{p}_u + \tilde{p}_{nu})(C_{nu.nu} C_{u.u} - C_{nu.nu} C_{u.wg}) \Big/ D \tag{A.37-qL}$$

$$\frac{\partial \hat{B}_{wg}}{\partial \overline{q}} = (\tilde{p}_u + \tilde{p}_{nu})(C_{nu.nu} C_{u.wg} + C_{u.wg}^{\ 2} - C_{nu.nu} C_{wg.wg} - C_{u.u} C_{wg.wg}) \Big/ D \tag{A.38-qL}$$

Appendix

B
COMPREHENSION INDEX

In each survey instrument there is a set of questions addressed to the interviewer: the follow-up section. The last follow-up questions ask interviewers for their opinion with respect to role of the language and visual material used in explaining the valuation exercise to the respondent. This information will help us to infer the overall comprehension of the survey by the respondents. We used a three-point Likert scale in both questions with 1 = 'very helpful', 2 = 'helpful' and 3 = 'of little help'. We define a comprehension index (CIX) of the pilot i (with $i = 1$, Lisbon metropolitan area; $i = 2$, Pousos, and $i = 3$, Ajuda) in the following way:

$$CIX^i = w_{language}\left(\sum_{n=1}^{N} fu^n_{language}\Big/N\right)^i + w_{visual}\left(\sum_{n=1}^{N} fu^n_{visual}\Big/N\right)^i \qquad (B.1)$$

where $fu^n_{language}$ and fu^n_{visual} represent scores on a three-point Likert scale evaluating, respectively, the role of language and the visual material in terms of the n respondent's ability to comprehend the questionnaire. The $w_{language}$ and w_{visual} define the relative weights that we allocate to the language and visual material. They reflect an evaluation of these two qualitative elements in terms of their importance for good comprehension of the survey. If we believe that the language is assumed to be the most important driving force underlying the overall comprehension of the survey, and that the visual material complements the written information, we can give the greatest weight to the language. We fixed $w_{language}$ at 0.75 and w_{visual} at 0.25. Bearing that in mind, we have the conditions to calculate condition (B.1) for both pilots: we get $CIX^{Pilot\ I} = 1.46$ and $CIX^{Pilot\ II} = 1.5$, that is, they remain approximately the same, despite the lower level of education of the respondents in the Pilot II sample.

Appendix
C
The Survey Instrument: Questionnaire and Visual Aid

There are 28 versions of the survey instrument – see Table C.1. The different survey versions differ according to the policy protection policy, the level of information, the payment vehicle and the bid cards for the willingness-to-pay questions. Our study considers three policy scenarios, corresponding to three subsamples: one subsample is characterized by preventing the introduction of a tourism development plan for the wilderness areas (WA) of the Alentejo Natural Park; the second subsample is characterized by preventing the introduction of a tourism development plan for the recreational areas (RA) of the Alentejo Natural Park; and finally, the third subsample is characterized by preventing the introduction of a tourism development plan for both the wilderness areas and recreational areas. The different policy scenarios are identified in Section B.1 of the survey.

With respect to the level of information, we can distinguish two scenario versions: in one the respondents are informed of the financial effort that the government is making in the Alentejo Natural Park as a protected area; in the other version this information is omitted from the questionnaire.

We used two payment vehicles: in one survey version we designed a national park tax and in a second survey version we designed a national voluntary contribution scheme. The two information scenarios and payment vehicles are identified in Section B.2 of the survey. Finally, we consider four bid cards. Each bid card is characterized by a set of discrete amounts of Portuguese escudos: an initial amount and higher (lower) follow-ups if the respondent accepts (refuses) the initial amount. The Portuguese escudo amounts are asked in the questions P-9, P-10 and P-11.

Table C.1: *Survey versions*

Scenario version	WA		RA		(WA + RA)		
Level of information	ON	ON	ON	ON	OFF	OFF	ON
Payment vehicle	TAX	VC	TAX	VC	TAX	VC	VC
P-9	1200	1200	1200	1200	1200	1200	1200
P-10	3600	3600	3600	3600	3600	3600	3600
P-11	600	600	600	600	600	600	600
	A1	B1	C1	D1	E1	F1	G1
P-9	2400	2400	2400	2400	2400	2400	2400
P-10	4800	4800	4800	4800	4800	4800	4800
P-11	1200	1200	1200	1200	1200	1200	1200
	A2	B2	C2	D2	E2	F2	G2
P-9	4800	4800	4800	4800	4800	4800	4800
P-10	9600	9600	9600	9600	9600	9600	9600
P-11	2400	2400	2400	2400	2400	2400	2400
	A3	B3	C3	D3	E3	E3	G3
P-9	9600	9600	9600	9600	9600	9600	9600
P-10	24000	24000	24000	24000	24000	24000	24000
P-11	4800	4800	4800	4800	4800	4800	4800
	A4	B4	C4	D4	E4	F4	G4

The Questionnaire (english version)

B1: Voluntary Contribution, Full Questionnaire

SURVEY:
Payment Instrument: VC
Scenario: 1
Card: I

Interviewer: _____   Parish: _____
Start: _____ End: _____   Municipality: _____

    Good-morning/good-afternoon/good-evening. My name is .... and I am working with the Survey Research Centre of the Portuguese Catholic University in a national survey of Portuguese families. We focus our attention on the study of public opinion on issues concerning economic development vs. environment protection.
    (PAUSE)

    Most of the questions ask about the attitudes and opinions of Portuguese families. There are no right or wrong answers. Completing the survey does not require any special education or skills: all material is read and carefully explained.
    (PAUSE)

> Your answers are strictly confidential. The collected data will only be used for statistical purposes and the name of your family will never be associated with your answers. Please think carefully about each question and give your best answer.

SECTION A

A.1
Portuguese citizens have been expressing different opinions with respect to the degree of importance regarding various social concerns existing in our country. I am going to read to you a list of some that we often hear about in the news.

P-1. For each one, I would like you to tell me whether you think it is 'very important', 'important', 'somewhat important' or 'of little importance' in terms of government action.
(ROTATE a-e; READ EACH ITEM ON THE LIST; CIRCLE ONE CODE BEFORE PROCEEDING TO THE NEXT ITEM)

		very important	important	somewhat important	of little importance	DO NOT READ	
						D/K	N/A
a.	Medical assistance and social security	1	2	3	4	99	999
b.	Environmental protection	1	2	3	4	99	999
c.	Public security	1	2	3	4	99	999
d.	Unemployment	1	2	3	4	99	999
e.	Quality of the public education system	1	2	3	4	99	999

We now turn your attention to environmental protection issues.
(PAUSE)

A.2
There are several sources of environmental pollution in Portugal. Unfortunately, the government cannot address all these sources at the same time. Therefore it is necessary to establish priorities.

P-2. Please state your opinion and indicate whether each of the following pollution sources should be 'very important', 'important', 'somewhat important' or 'of little importance' with respect to their priority for governmental action.
(ROTATE a-i; READ EACH ITEM ON THE LIST; CIRCLE ONE CODE BEFORE PROCEEDING TO THE NEXT ITEM)

		very important	important	somewhat important	of little importance	DO NOT READ D/K	DO NOT READ N/A
a.	Treatment of air pollution caused by factory chimney emissions	1	2	3	4	99	999
b.	Treatment of farmland pollution caused by the use of pesticides and fertilizers	1	2	3	4	99	999
c.	Controlling the noise caused by building construction, traffic and discos	1	2	3	4	99	999
d.	Conservation of animal and plant wildlife in their natural habitats	1	2	3	4	99	999
e.	Treatment of dangerous waste products caused by chemical factories	1	2	3	4	99	999
f.	Treatment of water pollution in the rivers and dams	1	2	3	4	99	999
g.	Protection of nature and conservation of the protected areas	1	2	3	4	99	999
h.	Treatment of air pollution caused by the cars	1	2	3	4	99	999
i.	Treatment of urban sewage and recycling of household waste	1	2	3	4	99	999

A.3

Despite the fact that Portugal faces several sources of environmental pollution, this questionnaire will only address nature conservation and protected areas issues.

(PAUSE)

P-3. Prior to this survey, had you, or anybody in your family, heard or read anything about the protected areas in Portugal?

1. YES -» P4
2. NO -» P6

DO NOT READ	
99.	D/K
999.	N/A

P-4. Which Area(s) or Park(s)?

____

–

____

–

[CODIFY]

P-5. Please check if the Alentejo Natural Park is mentioned

1. YES
2. NO

Portuguese law established in 1992 a national network of protected natural areas. The conservation of nature is the major goal. Today the network covers 31 sites, including a National Park. These areas are open spaces, with no entrance fee or restrictions on visiting hours. Nevertheless, the visitors are requested to follow a set of rules:

(READ ALL)

do not enter the nature reserves

do not leave trash around

do not collect plants, flowers and fruits   do not make fires
do not walk outside the paths and roads   do not camp

P-6. In your opinion, is the conservation of nature and protection of the Natural Areas 'an urgent problem', 'a problem for future generations' or, on the contrary, is it 'not a problem'?

(READ 1-3: ROTATE)

1. an urgent problem
2. a problem for future generations
3. is not a problem

DO NOT READ
99. N/O
999. N/A

SECTION B

B.1

Now I would like to call your attention to the Natural Area of Alentejo. This is the map that describes the Natural Area of Alentejo: it includes the municipalities of Sines, Odemira, Aljezur e Vila do Bispo.

SHOW MAP 1
INDICATE: MUNICIPALITIES

As you can see, it refers to a large area when compared to other Natural Protected Areas in Portugal.

SHOW MAP 2
INDICATE: YELLOW ZONE AND SHADOW AREAS

The Natural Area of Alentejo constitutes a good site for enjoying a set of recreational activities such as fishing, sailing, walking or just going for a picnic. The clearness of the ocean water and the quality of the sand make the Alentejo coastline an attractive place to go to the beach. The area offers a rich, historic setting of which the Infante Navigation School is the highlight.

SHOW: PHOTO 1
INDICATE: FORTALEZA DE SAGRES

The Natural Area of Alentejo is also the refuge for both animal and plant wildlife. In some cliffs along the coastline, it is possible for visitors to observe the white stork. This area is the natural habitat of some species seriously threatened in Portugal, namely the otter and the Iberian lynx. For the lynx, biologists estimate a population of just three or four individuals. The Alentejo Natural Area is also very rich in plants and flowers, especially in the remote sand-dunes.

SHOW: PHOTO 2
SHOW: PHOTO 3

> **SHOW: PHOTO 4**
> **SHOW: PHOTO 5**

B.2

In 1988 the Portuguese Government introduced a protection programme for the described area and in 1995 created the *Parque Natural do Sudoeste Alentejano e Costa Vicentina,* as an effective instrument for the conservation of this natural setting. The Alentejo Natural Park is constituted by two major areas or zones:

Wilderness Areas (*Áreas de Protecção da Natureza*);

Recreational Natural Areas (*Áreas Naturais de Ambiente Rural*);

In the Wilderness Areas the major objective is the protection of local biodiversity (animal and plant wildlife): all human access in this zone, including visitors, is restricted.

> **SHOW: PHOTO 6 (UP)**
> **INDICATE: MAP 6 (READ THE LEGEND)**

The Recreational Natural Areas are open to all visitors and recreational activities (for exapmle, fishing, going to the beach, walking or just picnicking) in a relaxed environment and in contact with nature. The local population is, in this zone, allowed to carry on tourism as long as it respects the environment.

> **SHOW: PHOTO 6 (DOWN)**
> **SHOW: MAP 6 (READ THE LEGEND)**   (PAUSE)

P-7. Have you, or anybody in your family, ever visited the Alentejo Natural Park?

1.	YES	-» P8
2.	NO	-» B3

DO NOT READ	
99.	D/K
999.	N/A

P-8. What was the principal reason that drew you there?
(READ 1-6: ROTATE)

		YES	NO
1.	Walking and sightseeing in the countryside	1	0
2.	Going to the beach	1	0
3.	Visiting the local villages and their historic heritage	1	0
4.	Going for fun holidays with friends, visiting local bars and discos	1	0
5.	Fishing and hunting	1	0

Other: _____

B.3
TOURISM DEVELOPMENT: SCENARIO DESCRIPTION

I would like to call to your attention the following situation. As we often hear in the news, the tourism industry has been showing a strong interest in promoting the commercial development of the Alentejo Natural Park. One of the proposals submitted by the tourism industry to the Portuguese government is summarily characterized by the urbanization of the wilderness areas for commercial and tourism development.

| **SHOW: PHOTOS 6-1** |
| **SHOW: MAP 6-1** |

As you can observe, with the commercial and tourism development of the WA, we assist the urbanization of the coastline with the construction of tourism-related infrastructures such as a marine infrastructure and hotels.

| **INDICATE: PHOTO 6-1 (UP)** |

With the commercial and tourism development of the WA, it is no longer possible to guarantee the preservation of the local biodiversity: species such as the Iberian lynx, the bald eagle and the otter will become extinct.

| **INDICATE: MAP 6-1 (UP)** |

This commercial and tourism development proposal does not directly interfere with the RA: the government will continue preserve of the recreational areas where visitors will still able to enjoy going to the beach in a relaxed environment.

| **INDICATE: PHOTO 6-1 (DOWN)** | |
| **INDICATE : MAP 6-1 (DOWN)** | **(PAUSE)** |

I will show again photos 6 so that you can compare the changes involved.

| **SHOW: PHOTOS 6 (UP and DOWN)** | **(PAUSE)** |

| **SECTION C** |

CV.1.1.

C.1
In the last three years the Portuguese government invested 560 million escudos in running the Alentejo Natural Park as a protected area. Nevertheless, such a budget is not sufficient to continue to guarantee to all Portuguese that there will not be any tourism development of the Park.

In order to continue guaranteeing to all Portuguese that there will not be any tourism development of the Alentejo Natural Park, the Park Management Agency, together with the national organizations for environmental protection, launched a national money raising campaign whose funds will be exclusively applied to keeping the Alentejo Natural Park free from any tourism development.

Please think about:

> Your current household income
> Your current household expenses
> The existence of other Natural Areas

P-9. Keeping these factors in mind, would your household agree to contribute a donation of 1200 escudos (or equivalently 100 escudos/month during one year) to protect the WA and in this way guarantee the non-extinction of local wildlife such as the Iberian lynx and the fishing eagle?

| 1. | YES | -» **P10** |
| 2. | NO | -» **P11** |

| 999. N/A | DO NOT READ | -» **P11** |

P-10. And would your household still be willing to contribute a donation of 3600 escudos (or equivalently 300 escudos/month during one year)?

| 1. | YES | -» **P111** |
| 2. | NO | -» **P111** |

| 999. N/A | DO NOT READ | -» **P111** |

P-11. And would your household already be willing to contribute a donation of 600 escudos (or equivalently 50 escudos/month during one year)?

| 1. | YES | -» **P111** |
| 2. | NO | -» **P111** |

| 999. N/A | DO NOT READ | -» **P111** |

P-111. Could you please now state the maximum that your household is prepared to contribute for the protection of the WA and in this way guarantee the non-extinction of local wildlife such as the Iberian lynx and the fishing eagle?

| 1. | _____ | -» **section D** |

DO NOT READ		
2. ZERO	-» **P12**
999. N/A	-» **P12**

C.2

P-12. Could you please tell us which is the principal reason why your household will not make any contribution?

(READ 1-8: ROTATE; REPEAT WHENEVER NECESSARY)

1.	I cannot afford to contribute so much money.
2.	I do not believe in the described national fund campaign.
3.	I prefer to spend that amount of money elsewhere.
4.	The proposed protection plan is not worth so much money.
5.	I do not agree with this type of question.
6.	The proposed protection plan is a break in the development of the region.
7.	I believe that this questionnaire is not the best approach to look at these issues.
8.	The protection of nature does not have a price.
9.	The protection of natural areas is a responsibility of the Portuguese government.

| 999. N/A | DO NOT READ |

SECTION D

D.1

P-13. Please let me know your household's opinion by answering whether you think that you completely agree, or you agree, or you sometimes agree and sometimes disagree, or you disagree or you completely disagree with each of the following statements.
(READ EACH ITEM ON THE LIST; ROTATE 1-26; CODE BEFORE PROCEEDING TO THE NEXT ITEM)
        5. I COMPLETELY AGREE
        4. I AGREE
        3. SOMETIMES I AGREE, SOMETIMES I DISAGREE
        2. I DISAGREE
        1. I COMPLETELY DISAGREE

code

1.	My family and I would have great pleasure in knowing that the SIC, RTP and TVI together have agreed to introduce in their TV schedule more documentary films about wildlife and its natural habitats.	_____
2.	My family and I think that the preservation of the Alentejo coastline is important because this is a place which all of us can visit and see very beautiful natural landscapes.	_____
3.	My family and I like to see the Portuguese government giving more support to the national organizations that are promoting work in the field of environment conservation.	_____
4.	My family and I think that the preservation of the Parks is important because these are privileged places where everybody may enjoy a walk or a picnic in a relaxed environment.	_____

Code:

5.	My family and I take great satisfaction in knowing that today it is guaranteed that our children, and future generations, will continue to be able to observe wildlife in its natural habitat.	_____
6.	Despite the fact that my family and I may never see an otter in its natural habitat, we will be very worried if the total population of otters in Portugal becomes extinct.	_____
7.	My family and I like to spend the weekends at home or going to the movies rather than going out for a walk in the countryside or by the beach.	_____
8.	Our family admires the individuals who, on a voluntary basis, participate in collecting donations for national programmes for social aid and solidarity.	_____
9.	My family and I take great pleasure in knowing that we are still able to visit villages in Alentejo that keep their true identity and their typical houses, façades and streets.	_____
10.	Despite the fact that my family and I may never see an Iberian lynx in its natural habitat, we are very happy to know that we have the guarantee that the lynx is kept safe from extinction in Portugal.	_____
11.	My family and I think that the preservation of the natural areas is important since they are privileged sites for recreational activities such as sightseeing or biking in a natural environment.	_____
12.	There are some funding campaigns to which my family and I feel very close and therefore we do not hesitate to contribute a donation.	_____
13.	Despite the fact that my family and I may never visit a Natural Park, we are very happy to see these natural areas protected so that other Portuguese citizens may also have the possibility to observe wildlife in its natural habitat.	_____
14.	My family and I think that the preservation of the Alentejo coastline is important because this is a privileged place where all of us may enjoy going to the beach in a relaxed environment and being in contact with nature.	_____
15.	It is difficult for me to decline my help to other individuals who, either in the streets or at my door, beg for charity.	_____
16.	Whenever I am approached by identified personnel, it is not hard to me to refuse to make a financial contribution to a national fund raising campaign.	_____
17.	The protection of the forests is very important because for Portugal they are a very important source of wealth.	
18.	With the increasing use of the media in our elementary schools as well as an increasing number of school visits to the zoo, it will no longer be important to take the children on educational trips to the Natural Areas.	_____
19.	Sometimes our particpation in national fund raising campaigns can be explained because we come under observation and feel 'socially-pressure' to contribute, and therefore we do not decline to make a contribution.	_____
20.	I am happy with myself whenever I give a financial contribution to national fund raising campaigns.	_____

Code:

21.	With Portuguese participation in the EU, the preservation of our national diversity is no longer so important since we are constructing a common and shared European culture.	_____
22.	Despite the fact that my family and I may never observe an eagle in nature, we take great pleasure in knowing that the eagles are kept safe from extinction.	_____
23.	My family and I like to contribute to good causes such as the protection of the environment, and whenever we can afford it, we do not decline our help to such fund raising campaigns.	_____
24.	Giving blood is giving life.	_____
25.	During the holidays, my family and I prefer to stay home or to go to the beach rather than to travel around Portugal visiting our traditional villages.	_____
26.	My family and I think that the preservation of the Alentejo coastline is important because in this way we are protecting the natural lifestyle of the local inhabitants, which belongs to our national identity.	_____

D.2
The final questions concern the characterization of your household.
P-14. Could you please tell me to which age group you belong?

1.	18–29	years		5.	60-69	years
2.	30–39	years		6.	+ 69	years
3.	40–49	years				
4.	50–59	years		999.	N/A	DO NOT READ

P-15. Could you please tell me which level of education applies to you?
(READ 1-6)

1. Less than 4 years of schooling
2. Elementary school (5-6 years of schooling)
3. High school studies: low level (7-9 years of schooling)
4. High school studies: technical school studies (10 to 11 years of schooling)
5. High school studies: higher level (12 years of schooling)
6. University studies

999. N/A | DO NOT READ

P-16. Respondent:

1.   Male   0.   Female

P-17. What is your current job?

1.	Employed	-»Job _____	-» P19	[CODIFY]
13.	Unemployed	-»P18	999. N/A	DO NOT READ	-» P19

P-18. Would you be interested in working for the tourism industry in the Alentejo Natural Area?

1.   YES   -» P19
2.   NO   -» P19

| 999. | N/A | DO NOT READ | -» P19 |

P-19. Could you please tell me in which category does your monthly household net income fall?

P-20. In which of the following activities have you, or your family, participated?

(READ A-F: ROTATE)

| | | Yes | No | do not read | |
				D/K	N/A
1.	Going to the beach	1	2	99.	999.
2.	Surfing, boating or sailing	1	2	99.	999.
3.	Biking	1	2	99.	999.
4.	Walking	1	2	99.	999.
5.	Camping	1	2	99.	999.
6.	Fishing or hunting	1	2	99.	999.

| SHOW CARD 1 |

P-21. During the last year, did you, or anybody in your family, make a donation to a national fund raising campaign (for example, *Operação Pirilampo, Liga Portuguesa Contra o Cancro, Bombeiros*)?

1.   YES   -» P22
2.   NO   -» P23

| 99. D/K | DO NOT | -» P23 |
| 999. N/A | READ | -» P23 |

P-22. How many times?

1.   Once   4.   Four or more times
2.   Twice
3.   Three times

| 999. D/K | DO NOT READ |

P-23. During the last year, did you, or anybody in your family, make charitable donations to the poor?

1.   YES   -» P24
2.   NO   -» P25

| 99. D/K | DO NOT | -» P25 |
| 999. N/A | READ | -» P25 |

P-24. How many times?

1.   Once   4.   Four or more times
2.   Twice

3.   Three times | 999. D/K | DO NOT READ |

P-25. During the last year, have you, or anybody in your family, given blood?

| 1. YES   -» P2 | 99. D/K | DO NOT | -» P27 |
| 2. NO   -» P27 | 999. N/A | READ | -» P2 |

P-26. How many times?

1. Once	4. Four or more times
2. Twice	
3. Three times	999. D/K DO NOT READ

P-27. Counting yourself, how many people live in your household? _____

P-28. Please indicate if you, or anybody in your family, is a member of the following organisations.
(READ 1-7; CIRCLE THE RIGHT ANSWER)

1.	National Geographic Society (or subscriber)
2.	Greenpeace or World Wildlife Fund (WWF)
3.	Quercus
4.	*Liga para a Protecção da Natureza*
5.	*Fundo de Protecção para os Animais Selvagens (FAPAS)*
6.	Scouts
7.	*Grupo de Estudo de Organização do Território e Ambiente (GEOTA)*
0.	Not a member of any organisation

Other _____

THANK RESPONDENT FOR THE CO-OPERATION
SAY GOODBYE

INTERVIEWER FOLLOW-UP

A. In your opinion how did the respondent understand the valuation question of the protection programme?

1. understood very well
2. understood
3. understood little
4. did not understand

B. In your opinion how important was the language, maps and photos in making this questionnaire better understood by the respondent?

		very important	important	somewhat important	of little importance
a.	language	1	2	3	4
b.	maps and photos	1	2	3	4

CESOP ADDITIONAL RECORD

Respondent's residential area:

1. Rural
2. Somewhat Rural
3. Somewhat Urban
4. Urban

Respondent's residence type:

1. Hut or degraded place
2. Low rank accommodation
3. Medium rank accommodation
4. High rank accommodation
5. Luxurious apartment or palatial house

The Questionnaire (Portuguese)

B1: Contribuição voluntária, questionário integral

contribuição voluntária

SONDAGEM
TIPO:
Instrumento: Contribuição Voluntária (CV)
Cenário: 1
Cartão: I

Freguesia: _____
Concelho: _____
Contexto: Rural / Pró-Rural / Pró-Urbano / Urbano

Entrevistador: _____
Início: _____ Fim: _____

Bom-dia/Boa-tarde/Boa noite. Chamo-me .... e estou a colaborar com o Centro de Estudos da UCP numa sondagem dirigida às famílias portuguesas.
(PAUSA)

Focaremos a nossa atenção no estudo da opinião pública sobre os temas:
Desenvolvimento Económico e Protecção do Ambiente em Portugal
(PAUSA)

Nesta entrevista todas as famílias podem participar, não há qualquer tipo de descriminação. O seu total preenchimento não requer quaisquer conhecimentos ou educação específicos por parte das famílias entrevistadas: todo o material apresentado é por nós explicado não sendo necessário a leitura de qualquer documento.
(PAUSA)

> **As suas respostas são confidenciais servindo apenas para fins estatísticos, pelo que lhe peço a sua colaboração e que responda o mais exactamente quanto possível a cada uma das questões**

A1.

Os portugueses têm vindo a expressar diferentes opiniões relativamente ao grau de importância de vários problemas económico-sociais existentes em Portugal.

P-1. Qual é o grau de importância (**muito importante, bastante importante, de alguma importância** ou **pouco importante**) que atribui às seguintes áreas de acção governamental?

(**Ler TUDO a-e: Rodar**)

NÃO LER

		muito importante	bastante importante	de alguma importância	pouco importante	s/ op/	s/ res/
a.	Assistência Médica e Segurança Social	1	2	3	4	99	999
b.	Protecção Ambiental	1	2	3	4	99	999
c.	Segurança Pública	1	2	3	4	99	999
d.	Combate ao Desemprego	1	2	3	4	99	999
e.	Qualidade do Sistema de Educação Pública	1	2	3	4	99	999

A2.

Foquemos agora a nossa atenção na protecção ambiental (**PAUSA**) Existem vários problemas de poluição em Portugal que não podem ser resolvidos todos ao mesmo tempo. Há portanto que estabelecer prioridades.

P-2. Peço-lhe que me dê a sua opinião dizendo-me qual o grau de prioridade (**muito urgente, bastante urgente, de alguma urgência** ou **pouco urgente**) na realização das seguintes acções de protecção ambiental.

(**Ler TUDO a-i: Rodar**)

Não Ler

		muito urgente	bastante urgente	de alguma urgência	pouco urgente	sem opi/	sem res/
a.	Tratamento da poluição do ar emitida pelas chaminés das fábricas	1	2	3	4	99	999
c.	Tratamento da contaminação dos solos produzida pelos herbicidas, insecticidas e fertilizantes	1	2	3	4	99	999
c.	Protecção do ruído produzido pelas obras de construção civil, trânsito e discotecas	1	2	3	4	99	999
d.	Conservação dos animais, plantas e seus espaços naturais	1	2	3	4	99	999
e.	Tratamentos dos lixos químicos perigosos produzidos pelas indústrias	1	2	3	4	99	999
f.	Tratamento da poluição das águas de rios e barragens	1	2	3	4	99	999
g.	Conservação da Natureza e preservação de espaços verdes	1	2	3 .	4	99	999
h.	Tratamento da poluição do ar produzida pelos automóveis	1	2	3	4	99	999
i.	Tratamento dos esgotos e reciclagem do lixo produzido em nossas casas	1	2	3	4	99	999

A3.
Ainda que Portugal enfrente vários problemas de protecção ambiental, esta sondagem focará apenas na Conservação da Natureza e Áreas Naturais Protegidas. **(PAUSA)**

P-3. Alguma vez ouviu ou leu alguma notícia sobre as Áreas Naturais Protegidas?

1.	SIM -» P4	99. Não se lembra	NÃO -» B1
2.	NÃO -» P6	999. Sem resposta	LER -» B1

P-4. Referente(s) a que Área(s) ou Parque(s)?

_____

–

_____   CODIFICAR

–

P-5. Verique se o Parque Natural do Alentejo foi mencionado   1. SIM

2. NÃO

(PAUSA)
A Lei Portuguesa consagra, desde 1992, uma rede Nacional de Áreas Protegidas. São hoje um total de 31 áreas, incluindo um Parque Nacional.

As Áreas Protegidas são espaços abertos, sem bilhete de entrada ou horário de funcionamento. A conservação da Natureza é o seu grande objectivo: existe portanto a necessidade de cumprimento de certas regras.
(Ler TUDO)

- não colher plantas, flores ou frutos
- não caminhar fora dos caminhos
- deitar o lixo nos locais apropriados
- necessária autorização para construção de novas casas e estradas
- acampar apenas nos parques autorizados
- não fazer lume

P-6. Na sua opinião a Conservação da Natureza e das Áreas Protegidas é um **problema imediato e urgente**, um **problema para as gerações futuras** ou, pelo contrário, **não constitui um problema**?
(Ler 1-3: Rodar)

1.	problema imediato e urgente	99. Não sabe	NÃO
2.	problema para as gerações futuras	999. Sem resposta	LER
3.	não contitui um problema		

B1.
Neste momento gostaria de focar a sua atenção na Área Natural do Alentejo.

| APRESENTAR MAPA 1 e MAPA 2 |

Este é o mapa que descreve a Área Natural do Alentejo: inclui os concelhos de Sines, Odemira, Aljezur e Vila do Bispo.
⇨ **INDICAR: CONCELHOS no MAPA 1**

Como pode aqui verificar trata-se de uma extensa área quando comparada com outras Áreas Naturais.
⇨ **INDICAR: ZONA EM AMARELO e ZONAS SOMBREADAS no MAPA 2**
(PAUSA)

Este é um bom local para a prática de um conjunto de actividades recreativas como a pesca, andar de barco, passear no campo ou fazer pic-nics. A transparência das águas e a qualidade da areia nas praias tornam a costa Alentejana um bom local para fazer praia. Existe também aqui um rico património histórico: destancando-se a escola de navegação no cabo de Sagres.

| APRESENTAR FOTO 1 |

⇨ **INDICAR: Ponta de Sagres no mapa e Fortaleza de Sagres)**
(PAUSA)

A Área Natural do Alentejo é o refúgio de um grande número de animais e plantas selvagens.

| APRESENTAR FOTOS 2-5 |

Entre as aves podemos aqui encontrar, por exemplo, a águia-pesqueira (ameaçada de extinção em Portugal) e ainda a cegonha branca.
⇨ **INDICAR: FOTO da Cegonha Branca**

Existem igualmente aqui algumas lontras e cerca de três linces ibéricos (espécies gravemente ameaçadas de extinção no nosso país)
⇨ **INDICAR: FOTO do Lince e da Lontra**

A área é igualmente rica em plantas e flores em especial na zona das dunas.
⇨ **INDICAR: FOTO das Dunas**

B2.
Em 1988 o Governo Português decretou a protecção de Natureza de tal Área Natural e em Julho de 1995 é criado o Parque Natural do Alentejo.
(PAUSA)
O Parque Natural do Alentejo tem duas grandes categorias de terrenos:

  1) áreas de protecção da natureza
  2) áreas naturais de ambiente rural

| APRESENTAR FOTOS 6 e MAPA 6 |

As Áreas de protecção da natureza: são zonas destinadas à protecção de animais e plantas no seu estado selvagem. O acesso dos visitantes é aqui condicionado.

⇨ **INDICAR: FOTO da Reserva perto de Odexeixe**
⇨ **LER: MAPA 6 com a Legenda da Reserva**
(PAUSA)

As Áreas naturais de ambiente rural: são zonas abertas aos visitantes, ao recreio e lazer num ambiente tranquilo e em contacto com a natureza. A população residente pode aqui praticar actividades agrícolas tradicionais e ainda um turismo respeitador do ambiente.

⇨ **INDICAR: FOTO da Praia Natural perto de Porto Covo**
⇨ **LER: MAPA 6 com a Legenda da Praia Natural)**
(PAUSA)

P-7. Alguma vez o(a) sr(a) ou alguém do seu agregado familiar **visitou** a esta Área Natural?

1. **SIM**   -» **P8**
2. **NÃO**   -» **B3**

99. Não se lembra   NÃO -» **D**
999. Sem resposta   LER   -» **D**

P-8. Qual foi o principal motivo que levou à sua visita?
(Ler 1-6: Rodar)

1. Passear pelo campo e ver as paisagens
2. Fazer praia
3. Visitar as vilas e os monumentos históricos

4. Ir a bares e discotecas
5. Caçar ou pescar
6. Outra _____

B3.
ALTERNATIVA: ABERTURA AO TURISMO
Chamava agora a sua atenção para s seguinte situação. A indústria hoteleira tem vindo a manifestar o forte interesse no sentido do crescimento do turismo de tal região do Alentejo. Uma das soluções propostas passa pela abertura das ÁREAS DE PROTECÇÃO DA NATUREZA ao turismo e urbanização dos seus terrenos.
(PAUSA)

APRESENTAR FOTOS 6-1 e MAPA 6-1

Como se pode observar com a urbanização das áreas de protecção da natureza, haverá a construção de uma marina, hoteis e aldeamentos turísticos.

Com tal construção não é agora possível garantir a preservação de animais e plantas selvagens: espécies como o lince ibérico e a águia pesqueira acabarão mesmo por desaparecer.

⇨ **INDICAR: FOTO da urbanização da Reserva perto de Odeceixe**
⇨ **LER: MAPA 6-1. Legenda da urbanização**

> Esta proposta não interfere directamente com as áreas naturais de ambiente rural: haverá a manutenção de zonas onde é ainda possível fazer praia, e outras actividades recreativas, num ambiente tranquilo e em contacto com a natureza.

⇨ **INDICAR: FOTO da Praia Natural**
⇨ **LER: MAPA 6-1. Legenda da Praia Natural**

⇨ **INDICAR novamente FOTOS 6 para fazer a comparação**

CV.1.I.
C1
O governo Português investiu nos últimos três anos 560.000 contos com o funcionamento do Parque Natural do Alentejo. Tal verba não é suficiente para continuar a garantir aos Portugueses que não haverá qualquer urbanização das Áreas de Protecção da Natureza. Assim, a Direcção do Parque em conjunto com organizações nacionais de protecção ambiente lançaram uma Campanha Nacional de angariação de fundos a reverter exclusivamente a favor da protecção do Parque.

Assim pense por favor:

- No rendimento e despesas correntes do seu agregado familiar;
- Na existência de outras áreas naturais;

P-9. Estaria o seu agregado familiar de acordo em fazer um donativo de 1200$00 (ou seja 100$00/mês durante um período de um ano) por forma a poder assegurar o não desaparecimento de plantas e animais selvagens como o lince ibérico e a águia pesqueira?

1. SIM   -» **P10**
2. NÃO   -» **P11**   **999.** Sem resposta   não ler   -» **P11**

P-10. E estaria disposto a contribuir com um donativo de 3600$00 (ou seja 300$00/mês durante um período de um ano)?

1. SIM   -» **P111**
2. NÃO   -» **P111**   **999.** Sem resposta   não ler   -» **P111**

P-11. E já estaria disposto a contribuir com um donativo de apenas 600$00 (ou seja 50$00/mês durante um período de um ano)?

1. SIM   -» P111
2. NÃO   -» P111   **999.** Sem resposta não ler -» **P111**

P-111. Então qual é seu valor máximo que está disposto a contribuir por forma poder assegurar o não desaparecimento de plantas e animais selvagens como o lince ibérico e a águia pesqueira?

1. _____   -» **D**
2. NADA/ZERO   não ler   -» **P12**   **999.** Sem resposta   não ler   -» **P12**

P-12. Qual o principal motivo que o levou a não contribuir para a preservação do Parque Natural do Alentejo.
(Ler 1-8: Rodar e Repetir se necessário)

1. Não tenho possibilidades para contribuir com tanto dinheiro

2. Não acredito na campanha de angariação de fundos

3. Prefiro gastar o dinheiro em outras coisas

4. A preservação do Parque não vale para mim tanto dinheiro

5. Não concordo com este tipo de perguntas

6. A preservação do Parque é um travão ao desenvolvimento da região

7. Penso que o inquérito não é a melhor forma de tratar este tipo de questões

8. A preservação da natureza não tem preço e portanto não aceito qualquer urbanização do
   Parque Natural

9. A preservação do Parque é da responsabilidade do Estado

999. Sem resposta   NÃO LER

D.

P-13. Diga-me a sua opinião a cada uma delas respondendo se **concorda totalmente**, ou se **concorda em parte**, ou se **nem concorda nem discorda, ou** se **discorda em parte** ou ainda se **discorda totalmente**.
(Ler 1-33: Rodar)

1.	Eu e a minha família teríamos grande satisfação em saber que a SIC, RTP e TVI juntos acordaram em alterar a grelha de programação com a introdução de mais programas e documentários sobre a vida animal selvagem	5. Conc. total. 4. Conc. part. 3. N Conc. N Disc. 2. Dis. part. 1. Disc. total.
2.	Eu e a minha família pensamos que preservação do litoral alentejano é importante porque este é um local que todos nós podemos visitar e observar paisagens de grande beleza natural	5. Conc. total. 4. Conc. part. 3. N Conc. N Disc. 2. Dis. part. 1. Disc. total.
3.	Eu e a minha família gostaríamos de ver o governo a prestar maior apoio às organizações que desenvolvem trabalho no domínio da protecção do ambiente	5. Conc. total. 4. Conc. part. 3. N Conc. N Disc. 2. Dis. part. 1. Disc. total.
4.	Eu e a minha família pensamos que a preservação dos Parques é importante pois estes são espaços onde todos nós podemos passear ou ainda fazer pic-nics num ambiente tranquilo e em contacto com a natureza	5. Conc. total. 4. Conc. part. 3. N Conc. N Disc. 2. Dis. part. 1. Disc. total.
5.	Eu e a minha família teriamos uma grande satisfação em saber que nos é garantido que os nossos filhos, e gerações vindouras, continuarão a ter a oportunidade de observar animais e plantas no seu estado selvagem	5. Conc. total. 4. Conc. part. 3. N Conc. N Disc. 2. Dis. part. 1. Disc. total.
6.	Ainda que nunca venha ver uma lontra em liberdade, o total desaparecimento da população de lontras em Portugal deixar-me-ia preocupado(a)	5. Conc. total. 4. Conc. part. 3. N Conc. N Disc. 2. Dis. part. 1. Disc. total.
7.	Eu e a minha família gostamos mais de aproveitar os fins de semana para ficar em casa ou ir até ao cinema do que sair e ir passear até ao campo ou praia	5. Conc. total. 4. Conc. part. 3. N Conc. N Disc. 2. Dis. part. 1. Disc. total.
8.	Nós em casa temos uma verdadeira admiração por todos os indivíduos que andam nas ruas a recolher donativos em peditórios nacionais de caridade social	5. Conc. total. 4. Conc. part. 3. N Conc. N Disc. 2. Dis. part. 1. Disc. total.
9.	Eu e a minha família temos uma grande satisfação em saber que ainda podemos encontrar e visitar lugares e vilas alentejanas com as suas ruas e casas típicas	5. Conc. total. 4. Conc. part. 3. N Conc. N Disc. 2. Dis. part. 1. Disc. total.
10.	Ainda que nunca venha ver um lince em liberdade, eu teria grande satisfação em saber que nos é garantido que o lince ibérico é salvo de perigo de extinção (=desaparecimento)	5. Conc. total. 4. Conc. part. 3. N Conc. N Disc. 2. Dis. part. 1. Disc. total.
11.	A preservação das áreas naturais é importante pois estas constitutem locais previlegiados de recreio (=andar a pé, brincar, andar de bicicleta) ou descanso em ambiente tranquilo e em contacto com a natureza	5. Conc. total. 4. Conc. part. 3. N Conc. N Disc. 2. Dis. part. 1. Disc. total.
12.	Existem certos peditórios com os quais eu e minha família nos sentimos verdadeiramente solidários e por isso não hesitamos em contribuir com um donativo	5. Conc. total. 4. Conc. part. 3. N Conc. N Disc. 2. Dis. part. 1. Disc. total.

13.	Ainda que eu nem a minha família nunca visite um Parque Natural, nós teríamos grande satisfação em ver estas áreas a serem protegidas e assim ter a garantia que os outros portugueses possam observar animais e plantas no seu estado selvagem	5. Conc. total. / 4. Conc. part. / 3. N Conc. N Disc. / 2. Dis. part. / 1. Disc. total.
14.	Eu e a minha família pensamos que preservação do litoral alentejano é importante porque este é um local que todos nós podemos visitar e aí fazer praia em ambiente tranquilo e de grande beleza natural	5. Conc. total. / 4. Conc. part. / 3. N Conc. N Disc. / 2. Dis. part. / 1. Disc. total.
15.	É difícil recusar a ajuda a mendigos que na rua, ou de porta em porta, andam a pedir esmola	5. Conc. total. / 4. Conc. part. / 3. N Conc. N Disc. / 2. Dis. part. / 1. Disc. total.
16.	Ainda que solicitado por pessoal identificado, não me é difícil recusar a contribuição com um donativo para um peditório nacional	5. Conc. total. / 4. Conc. part. / 3. N Conc. N Disc. / 2. Dis. part. / 1. Disc. total.
17.	A protecção da nossas florestas é importante pois a madeira constitui para Portugal importante fonte riqueza	5. Conc. total. / 4. Conc. part. / 3. N Conc. N Disc. / 2. Dis. part. / 1. Disc. total.
18.	Com uma maior divulgação de programas sobre a vida animal nas escolas e um crescente número de excursões das crianças ao jardim zoológico, não serão tão necessárias as visitas de estudo aos parques naturais	5. Conc. total. / 4. Conc. part. / 3. N Conc. N Disc. / 2. Dis. part. / 1. Disc. total.
19.	Por vezes a nossa ajuda em peditórios nacionais é justificada pois ao sermos observados por outras pessoas sentimo-nos envergonhados e por isso não negamos a nossa contribuição	5. Conc. total. / 4. Conc. part. / 3. N Conc. N Disc. / 2. Dis. part. / 1. Disc. total.
20.	Fico contente comigo próprio quando posso contribuir com um donativo ou uma esmola	5. Conc. total. / 4. Conc. part. / 3. N Conc. N Disc. / 2. Dis. part. / 1. Disc. total.
21.	Com a entrada de Portugal para a CE, a preservação da nossa diversidade não é hoje tão importante pois todos caminhamos agora para uma cultura Europeia comum	5. Conc. total. / 4. Conc. part. / 3. N Conc. N Disc. / 2. Dis. part. / 1. Disc. total.
22.	Ainda que eu nunca veja uma águia em liberdade, teria grande prazer em saber que nos é garantido que a águia é salvaguardada de extinção (=desaparecimento)	5. Conc. total. / 4. Conc. part. / 3. N Conc. N Disc. / 2. Dis. part. / 1. Disc. total.
23	Eu e minha família gostamos de contribuir para boas causas tais como a proteção do ambiente, e sempre que podemos, participamos com o nosso donativo em peditórios nacionais	5. Conc. total. / 4. Conc. part. / 3. N Conc. N Disc. / 2. Dis. part. / 1. Disc. total.
24.	Dar sangue é dar vida	5. Conc. total. / 4. Conc. part. / 3. N Conc. N Disc. / 2. Dis. part. / 1. Disc. total.
25.	Durante as férias eu e a minha família preferimos ficar por casa do que visitar vilas e outros lugares à descoberta da beleza do país	5. Conc. total. / 4. Conc. part. / 3. N Conc. N Disc. / 2. Dis. part. / 1. Disc. total.
26.	Eu e a minha família pensamos que preservação do litoral alentejano, dos usos e costumes dos seus habitantes, é importante porque estamos assim a salvaguardar a nossa identidade nacional	5. Conc. total. / 4. Conc. part. / 3. N Conc. N Disc. / 2. Dis. part. / 1. Disc. total.

E. Passemos agora ás últimas questões.

P-14. Que idade tem ?

1.	20–29	anos
2.	30–39	anos
3.	40–49	anos
4.	50–59	anos

5.	60–69	anos
6.	+ de 69	anos

999. Sem resposta   NÃO LER

P-15. Qual o seu nível de instrução escolar?
(Ler 1-7)

1. Intrução primária (ou ler e escrever)

2. Ensino Básico

3. 9° ano de escolaridade

4. Curso geral dos liceus ou curso complementar (11° ano)

5. Curso técnico professional (12° ano)

6. Licenciatura ou bacharelato

999. Sem resposta   NÃO LER

P-16. Sexo do inquirido.

1. Homem   **2.** Mulher

P-17. Qual a sua situação profissional?

1. Empregado (a)   -»Profissão _____ -» P19   [CODIFICAR]

13. Desempregado(a)   -»P18

999. Sem resposta   não ler -» P19

P-18. Estaria interessado/a em vir a trabalhar na indústria hoteleira no sudoeste Alentejano?

1. SIM   -» P19
2. NÃO   -» P19   **999.** Sem resposta   NÃO LER   -» P19

P-19. Qual dos seguintes escalões melhor traduz o rendimento líquido mensal da sua família?

APRESENTAR FICHA 6	**Recordo que o Centro de Estudos da UCP garante rigorosamente:**

1) **a confidencialidade dos seus dados**
2) **dados apenas servem para fins estatísticos**

1. Menos de 75 contos
2. De 75 a 149 contos
3. De 150 a 299 contos

4. De 300 a 450 contos
5. De 451 a 599 contos
6. De 600 a 799 contos

7. De 800 a 1200 contos
8. Mais de 1200 contos

999. Não responde   NÃO LER

P-20. Quais das seguintes actividades a sua família já praticou?

(Ler a-f: Rodar)

		Sim	Não	n/sab	n/ resp
				Não Ler	
a.	Ir à praia	1	2	99	999
b.	Fazer surf ou andar de barco	1	2	99	999
c.	Andar de bicicleta	1	2	99	999
d.	Passear a pé	1	2	99	999
e.	Acampar	1	2	99	999
f.	Pescar ou caçar	1	2	99	999

P-21. No ano passado, alguma vez você ou alguém da sua família contribuiu para peditórios nacionais (por exemplo, Operação Pirilampo, Liga Portuguesa Contra o Cancro, Bombeiros)?

1. SIM   -» **P22**
2. NÃO   -» **P23**

99. Não se lembra   NÃO   -» **P23**
999. Sem resposta   LER   -» **P23**

P-22. Quantas vezes?

1. Uma vez
2. Duas vezes
3. Três vezes

4. Quatro ou mais vezes

999. Sem resposta   NÃO LER

P-23. No ano passado, alguma vez você ou alguém da sua família deu esmola aos mendigos?

1. SIM   -» **P24**
2. NÃO   -» **P25**

99. Não se lembra   NÃO   -» **P25**
999. Sem resposta   LER   -» **P25**

P-24. Quantas vezes?

1. Uma vez
2. Duas vezes
3. Três vezes

4. Quatro ou mais vezes

999. Sem resposta   NÃO LER

P-25. No ano passado, alguma vez você ou alguém da sua família deu sangue?

1. SIM   -» **P26**
2. NÃO   -» **P27**

99. Não se lembra   NÃO   -» **P27**
999. Sem resposta   LER   -» **P27**

P-26. Quantas vezes?

1. Uma vez	**4.** Quatro ou mais vezes
2. Duas vezes	
3. Três vezes	**999.** Sem resposta NÃO LER

P-27. Contando consigo, **quantas pessoas** constituiem o seu agregado familiar? _____

P-28. Por favor indique se o(a) sr(a) ou alguém no seu agregado familiar é membro (ou foi) de alguma das seguintes organizações.

1. National Geographic Society (ou assinante da revista)

2. Greenpeace ou World Wildlife Fund (WWF)

3. Quercus

4. Liga para a Protecção da Natureza

5. Fundo de Protecção para os Animais Selvagens (FAPAS)

6. Escuteiros

7. Grupo de Estudo de Organização do Território e Ambiente (GEOTA)

8. Outra _____

0. Não é membro de qualquer organização

MUITO OBRIGADO PELA SUA COLABORAÇÃO
DESPEDIR-SE

F. *Follow-Up:* **observações sobre a entrevista**
RESPOSTAS DO ENTREVISTADOR

1. Çomo pensa que o entrevistado percebeu a proposta da doação (ou imposto) destinado à preservação do Parque Natural?
   (Por favor anote com um círculo o número correspondente à sua resposta)

   1. percebeu muito bem
   2. percebeu bem
   3. percebeu pouco
   4. percebeu muito pouco

2. Na sua opinião qual o papel do seguinte material para uma boa compreesnsão da sondagem? (Por favor anote com um círculo o **número** correspondente à <u>sua</u> resposta)

		Muito importante	bastante importante	pouco importância	nada importante
a.	linguagem	1	2	3	4
b.	mapas e fotos	1	2	3	4

The Questionnaire (english version)

B1: National Tax, WTP referendum question

The Portuguese government invested in the last three years 560 million Escudos in running the Alentejo Natural Park as a protected area. Nevertheless, such a budget is not sufficient to continue guaranteeing to all Portuguese that there will not be any tourism development of the Park. In order to continue guaranteeing to all Portuguese that there will not be any tourism development of the Alentejo Natural Park, the government proposes a referendum regarding the introduction, only for a period of one year, of the National Park Tax. Its revenue will be exclusively applied to keep the Alentejo Natural Park free from any tourism development. All Portuguese households would have to pay the tax if the majority votes in favour.

Please think about:

> Your current household income
> Your current household expenses
> The existence of other Natural Areas

P-9. Keeping these factors in mind, if the tax amount to be paid was 1200 escudos (or equivalently 100 escudos/month during one year) to protect the WA and this way guarantee the non-extinction of local wildlife such as the Iberian lynx and the Fishing Eagle, how would your household vote?

1.   VOTE IN FAVOUR   -» **P10**
2.   VOTE AGAINST   -» **P11** | **999.** N/A | DO NOT READ | -» **P11** |

P-10. And how would your household vote if the tax amount to be paid was 3600 escudos (or equivalently 300 escudos/month during one year)?

1.   VOTE IN FAVOUR   -» **P111**
2.   VOTE AGAINST   -» **P111** | **999.** N/A | DO NOT READ | -» **P11** |

P-11. And how would your household vote if the tax amount to be paid was 600 escudos (or equivalently 50 escudos/month during one year)?

1.   VOTE IN FAVOUR   -» **P111**
2.   VOTE AGAINST   -» **P111** | **999.** N/A | DO NOT READ | -» **P11** |

P-111. Could you please now state the maximum tax amount that your household is prepared to pay for the protection of the WA and in this way guarantee the non-extinction of local wildlife such as the Iberian lynx and the fishing eagle?

1.   _____   -» **section D** | DO NOT READ |
                                            | 2.   ZERO   -» **P12** |
                                            | 10. N/A   -» **P12** |

The Questionnaire (portuguese)

B1: Imposto Nacional de Parques, referendo

O Governo Português investiu nos últimos três anos 560.000 contos com o funcionamento do Parque Natural do Alentejo. Tal verba não é suficiente para continuar a garantir aos Portugueses que não haverá qualquer urbanização das Áreas de Ambiente Rural. Assim, o Governo propõe um referendo sobre a introdução, e apenas durante o periodo de um ano, do Imposto Nacional de Parques. A sua receita fiscal reverterá exclusivamente a favor da Protecção do Parque do Alentejo. Todos os agregados familiares portugueses terão de o pagar se a maioria das famílias votar sim à sua aplicação.

⇨ **se houver ? : rúbrica a adicionar ao valor anual do IRS das famílias**

Assim pense por favor:

*   No rendimento e despesas correntes do seu agregado familiar;
*   Na existência de outras áreas naturais;

P-9. Se por forma a poder assegurar o não desaparecimento de plantas e animais selvagens como o lince ibérico e a águia pesqueira o montante de imposto a aplicar for 1200 escudos (ou seja, 100 escudos/mês durante um período de um ano) como é que votaria?

1.	VOTO A FAVOR	-» P10	
2.	VOTO CONTRA	-» P11	999. Sem resposta não ler -» P11

P-10. E se o montante de imposto a aplicar fosse 3600 escudos (ou seja, 300 escudos/mês durante um período de um ano) como é que votaria?

1.	VOTO A FAVOR	-» P111	
2.	VOTO CONTRA	-» P111	999. Sem resposta não ler -» P111

P-11. E se o montante de imposto a aplicar fosse apenas 600 escudos (ou seja, 50 escudos/mês durante um período de um ano) como é que votaria?

1.	VOTO A FAVOR	-» P111	
2.	VOTO CONTRA	-» P111	999. Sem resposta não ler -» P111

P-111. Então qual é o valor máximo de imposto que está disposto a contribuir por forma a assegurar o não desaparecimento de plantas e animais selvagens como o lince ibérico e a águia pesqueira?

1.	_____	-» DM	
2.	NADA/ZERO	não ler -» P12	10. Sem resposta não ler -» P12

The Visual Aid

MAP 1: ALENTEJO NATURAL AREA

MAP 2: ALENTEJO NATURAL AREA IN PORTUGAL

PHOTO 1: INFANTE NAVIGATION SCHOOL

PHOTO 2: WHITE STORK NEST

PHOTO 3: IBERIAN LYNX

PHOTO 4: AN OTTER

PHOTO 5: THE DUNES

PHOTO 6

PROTECTION OF THE ALENTEJO NATURAL PARK

UP: Wilderness Areas

DOWN: Recreational Areas

MAP 6

PROTECTION OF THE ALENTEJO NATURAL PARK

Wilderness Areas

PHOTO 6-UP:
RESERVE near Odeceixe

Protection and non-extinction guarantee of $\begin{cases} \text{otter and lynx} \\ \text{stork} \\ \text{dunes} \end{cases}$

Recreational Areas

PHOTO 6-DOWN:
BEACH near Porto Covo

Open air in contact with nature $\begin{cases} \text{picnics} \\ \text{trekking} \\ \text{rural turism} \end{cases}$

PHOTO 6-1

WILDERNESS AREAS OPEN TOURISM DEVELOPMENT

UP: Urbanization of the Wilderness Areas

DOWN: Recreational Areas

MAP 6-1

WILDERNESS AREAS OPEN TOURISM DEVELOPMENT

Urbanization of the Wilderness Areas

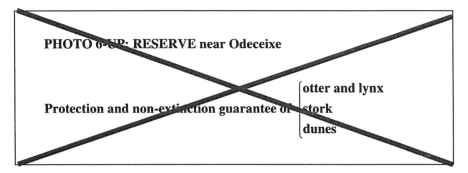

PHOTO 6-UP: RESERVE near Odeceixe

Protection and non-extinction guarantee of {otter and lynx / stork / dunes}

Protection of Recreational Areas

PHOTO 6-DOWN: BEACH near Porto Covo

Open air in contact with nature {picnics / trekking / rural turism}

PHOTO 6-2

RECREATION AREAS OPEN TOURISM DEVELOPMENT

UP: Wilderness Areas

DOWN: Urbanization of the Recreational Areas

MAP 6-2

RECREATION AREAS OPEN TOURISM DEVELOPMENT

Wilderness Areas

PHOTO 6-UP: RESERVE near Odeceixe

Protection and non-extinction guarantee of $\begin{cases} \text{otter and lynx} \\ \text{stork} \\ \text{dunes} \end{cases}$

Urbanization of the Recreational Areas

PHOTO 6-DOWN: BEACH near Porto Covo

Open air in contact with nature $\begin{cases} \text{picnics} \\ \text{trekking} \\ \text{rural turism} \end{cases}$

PHOTO 6-3

WILDERNESS AREAS and RECREATION AREAS OPEN TOURISM DEVELOPMENT

UP: Urbanization of the Wilderness Areas

DOWN: Urbanization of the Recreational Areas

MAP 6-3

WILDERNESS AREAS and RECREATION AREAS OPEN TOURISM DEVELOPMENT

Urbanization of the Wilderness Areas

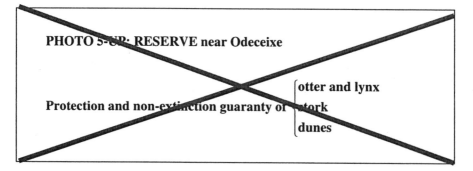

PHOTO 5-UP: RESERVE near Odeceixe

Protection and non-extinction guaranty of stork

otter and lynx

dunes

Urbanization of the Recreational Areas

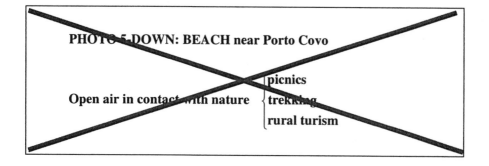

PHOTO 5-DOWN: BEACH near Porto Covo

Open air in contact with nature

picnics

trekking

rural turism

| CARD 1 |

(READ EACH INTERVAL;
REPEAT WHENEVER NECESSARY:
   A) YOUR ANSWERS ARE CONFIDENTIAL;
   B) INFORMATION ONLY USED FOR STATISTICAL PROPOSES;

1.	Under 75 000
2.	+ 75 000 and - 149 000
3.	+ 150 000 and - 299 000
4.	+ 300 000 and 450 000
5.	+ 451 000 and 599 000
6.	+ 600 000 and 799 000
7.	+ 800 000 and 1 200 000
8.	+ 1 200 000

Appendix
D
PUBLIC OPINION WITH RESPECT TO GOVERNMENT POLICY ISSUES

The initial survey question asks the respondents to rank the different areas of governmental policy action according to their priority.[115] Despite the fact that 70% of the respondents consider the environmental protection as a 'very important' government policy area, we can verify that unemployment, medical assistance and social security areas constitute the most important areas of government action. In the last two places, but not far from the front-ranking positions, we find Public Education and Security policy areas – see Table D.1.

Table D.1: *Public opinion regarding government policy programmes (%)*

	Very important	Important	Somewhat important	Of few importance	Index*
Unemployment	79.0	15.0	3.3	1.0	18.7
Medical assistance, social security	79.9	15.3	3.2	0.7	18.6
Environment protection	70.2	21.1	5.9	1.2	17.9
Public education	71.0	21.0	4.5	1.2	17.8
Public security	69.5	22.1	5.2	1.3	17.7

* Note: In order to be able to compute the index, different scores are assigned to each possible response: 20 to 'very important'; 15 to 'important'; 10 to 'somewhat important' and, finally, 5 to 'of few importance'.

In the second question the respondents were asked to state their opinion about different government areas for environmental protection. A complete breakdown of the responses is presented in Table D.2. According to the survey responses, and respective index results, we can classify the governmental areas for environmental protection into four categories of priority action. water pollution and toxic waste top the ranking of priorities of the Portuguese households. As a matter of fact, they are the only areas that are considered as 'very important' by more than 70% of the respondents. In a second category of priority, we find domestic waste recycling, nature and wildlife conservation policy areas. Air pollution from factories and

---

[115] We used a four Likert scale: 'very important', 'important', 'somewhat important' and 'of little importance'.

Table D.2: *Public opinion regarding government actions at environmental level (%)*

	very important	important	somewhat important	of few importance	index
Water pollution	74.3	20.0	3.3	1.0	18.2
Toxic waste	72.8	20.0	4.4	1.2	18.1
Domestic waste recycling	65.0	24.1	8.6	1.0	17.5
Nature conservation	63.2	26.3	7.6	0.8	17.4
Conservation of wildlife	57.7	28.4	11.1	1.3	17.0
Air pollution from factories	56.9	26.6	13.1	1.4	16.8
Farmland pollution	49.3	30.3	15.0	2.2	16.0
Air pollution from cars	54.2	14.2	14.2	2.9	14.5
Noise pollution	36.7	26.3	26.0	8.6	14.3

farmland Pollution share the third priority position. As the least important areas of environmental action we have the air pollution from cars, an issue typically associated with major cities like Lisbon, and noise pollution. These scored relatively low, when compared with the remaining areas, and may be interpreted as a 'non-priority' policy areas in terms of government action.

Appendix
E
INFORMATION CONTEXT: MULTIVARIATE REGRESSION ANALYSIS

The parametric estimation results confirm that the information context is not statistically relevant in explaining the stated WTP amount. As we can observe in Table E.1 the information 'on' (dummy) variable has a p-value lower than 10%. In Chapter 11 we return to the multivariate regression analysis of the stated WTP answers and explain in detail the different explanatory variables.

Table E.1: *(WA + RA) Valuation function*

Parameters		Estimate	St. Error	P-value
Factor scores	'use'	0.162	0.11	0.14
	'warmglow'	0.240*	0.11	0.04
	'existence'	0.233*	0.11	0.04
Area (dummy)	'rural'	0.017	0.29	0.95
	'urban'	0.094	0.18	0.61
Age (dummy)	20s	0.774*	0.40	0.05
	30s	0.655*	0.36	0.07
	40s	0.428	0.35	0.23
	50s	0.221	0.33	0.51
	70s	−0.601	0.42	0.15
Occupation (dummy)	Executives	−0.565	0.53	0.29
	Scientists	−1.520*	0.54	0.00
	Technicians	−0.124	0.42	0.77
	Administrative	−0.269	0.42	0.52
	sales services	−1.040*	0.43	0.01
	farmers & fishers	−2.690*	0.28	0.03
	Craftsmen	−0.173	0.39	0.66
	assembly workers	0.045	0.60	0.94
	unskilled workers	−1.380*	0.58	0.01
	Housekeepers	−0.312	0.36	0.39
	working students	−1.000	0.78	0.20
Education (dummy)	primary (freq.)	−0.529	0.59	0.37
	Primary	−0.762	0.52	0.14
	secondary: low	−0.776	0.49	0.11
	secondary: high	−0.263	0.50	0.61
	University	0.865*	0.51	0.09
Information context (dummy)	information 'on'	0.057	0.20	0.78
	payment vehicle	−0.349	0.24	.15
	net income	0.018	0.08	.82
	household	0.098	0.08	.23
	protest	−1.385*	0.27	.00
Intercept (β)		8.259		
Scale (σ)		1.566		
Log-Likelihood		−573.110		

Notes: * significant at 10%. Reference group: respondent in her 60s who completed a medium level of secondary studies and is now retired.

F.1 Motivation factor model

In a matrix notation, and for all individuals, we may rewrite equation (10.1) as:

$$\mathbf{av} = \Lambda \mathbf{f} + \Xi \tag{F.1}$$

where

$$
\underset{(M \times J)}{\mathbf{av}} =
\begin{bmatrix}
av_{1,1} - \overline{av}_1 & av_{1,2} - \overline{av}_1 & \cdots & av_{M,J} - \overline{av}_1 \\
av_{2,1} - \overline{av}_2 & av_{2,2} - \overline{av}_2 & \cdots & av_{2,J} - \overline{av}_2 \\
\vdots & \vdots & & \vdots \\
av_{M,1} - \overline{av}_M & av_{M,2} - \overline{av}_M & \cdots & av_{M,J} - \overline{av}_M
\end{bmatrix}
\tag{F.2}
$$

captures the matrix giving the answers of the sample respondents on the 26 attitudinal items as presented in the instrument survey; and:

$$
\underset{(3 \times J)}{\mathbf{f}} =
\begin{bmatrix}
f_{u,1} & f_{u,2} & \cdots & f_{u,J} \\
f_{nu,1} & f_{nu,2} & \cdots & f_{nu,J} \\
f_{wg,1} & f_{wg,2} & \cdots & f_{wg,J}
\end{bmatrix}
\tag{F.3}
$$

captures the matrix of factor scores giving the position of the sample respondents on the three motivation functions. The factor scores (a scalar) give the 'position' of the respondents on the underlying motivation functions. Furthermore,

$$\Lambda_{(M\times3)} = \begin{bmatrix} \lambda_{1,u} & \lambda_{1,nu} & \lambda_{1,wg} \\ \vdots & \vdots & \vdots \\ \lambda_{M,u} & \lambda_{M,nu} & \lambda_{M,wg} \end{bmatrix} \tag{F.4}$$

captures the matrix of factor loadings showing the correlations between the answers on the 26 items and the position of the respondents on the three motivation functions. Finally,

$$\Xi_{(M\times J)} = \begin{bmatrix} \phi_{1,1} & \phi_{1,2} & \cdots & \phi_{M,J} \\ \phi_{2,1} & \phi_{2,2} & \cdots & \phi_{2,J} \\ \vdots & \vdots & & \vdots \\ \phi_{M,1} & \phi_{M,2} & \cdots & \phi_{M,J} \end{bmatrix} \tag{F.5}$$

captures the matrix of the residual terms.

Bearing in mind the A1–A5 premises, we may re-write the covariance of our motivation factor model as:

$$\Sigma \equiv \text{cov}(\mathbf{av}) = E(\mathbf{avav'})$$

$$= E\big[(\Lambda\mathbf{f} + \Xi)(\Lambda\mathbf{f} + \Xi)'\big], \quad \text{with A5}$$

$$= \Lambda E(\mathbf{ff'})\Lambda' + E(\Xi\Xi'), \quad \text{with A1, A3 and A4}$$

$$= \Lambda \text{cov}(\mathbf{f})\Lambda' + \text{cov}(\Xi), \quad \text{with A2}$$

$$= \Lambda\Lambda' + \Omega$$

that is:

$$\Sigma \equiv \Lambda\Lambda' + \Omega \tag{F.6}$$

F.2 Estimation method

The first step consists of attempting to find an estimator $\hat{\Lambda}$ that will approximate the fundamental expression (F.6) with $\mathbf{S}$ – the sample correlation matrix – in place of Σ, that is:

$$\mathbf{S} \cong \hat{\Lambda}\hat{\Lambda}' + \hat{\Omega} \tag{F.7}$$

The objective is to estimate the communalities, that is, $\hat{\Lambda}\hat{\Lambda}'$, such that the underlying motivational structure is able to reproduce these correlations as well as possible. Having previously chosen the SMC, we will proceed to factor $\mathbf{S}$ into $\mathbf{S} = \hat{\Lambda}\hat{\Lambda}'$. For that we use the spectral decomposition, that is:

$$S = CDC'$$ (F.8)

where C is an orthogonal matrix constructed with the normalized eigenvectors of S ($CC' = I$) and:

$$D = \begin{bmatrix} \Delta_1 & 0 & \cdots & 0 \\ 0 & \Delta_2 & \cdots & 0 \\ \vdots & \vdots & & \vdots \\ 0 & 0 & \cdots & \Delta_{26} \end{bmatrix}$$ (F.9)

where $\Delta_1, \Delta_2, ..., \Delta_{26}$ are the eigenvalues of S. To finish factoring $S = CDC'$ into the form $\hat{\Lambda}\hat{\Lambda}'$, and since the eigenvalues of the positive definite matrix S are all positive, we can factor D into $D = D^{\frac{1}{2}}D^{\frac{1}{2}}$ where:

$$D^{\frac{1}{2}} = \begin{bmatrix} \sqrt{\Delta_1} & 0 & \cdots & 0 \\ 0 & \sqrt{\Delta_2} & \cdots & 0 \\ \vdots & \vdots & & \vdots \\ 0 & 0 & \cdots & \sqrt{\Delta_K} \end{bmatrix}$$ (F.10)

Therefore we may rewrite (F.8) as

$$\hat{\Lambda}\hat{\Lambda}' = S = CDC' = \left(CD^{\frac{1}{2}} \right)\left(CD^{\frac{1}{2}} \right)$$

However we do not define $\hat{\Lambda} = \left(CD^{\frac{1}{2}} \right)$ because $CD^{\frac{1}{2}}$ is a (26x26) matrix, while we are looking for $\hat{\Lambda}$, with a (26×3) dimension – this factor structure will be submitted to formal testing. In this context, we define D_3 as containing the largest three eigenvalues and C_3 containing the corresponding eigenvectors. Therefore we estimate Λ by:

$$\hat{\Lambda} = \left(C_3 D_3^{\frac{1}{2}} \right)$$ (F.11)

Finally, and in irder to find a frame of reference where the factors are more interpretable, the estimated matrix $\hat{\Lambda}$ will be submitted to a rotation and $\hat{\Lambda}^* = \hat{\Lambda}T$ (where T is orthogonal) will be obtained. Since $TT' = I$, the rotated loadings provide the same estimate of the covariance matrix, that is, $\mathbf{S} \cong \hat{\Lambda}^* \hat{\Lambda}^{*\prime} + \hat{\Omega} = \hat{\Lambda} \mathbf{T} \mathbf{T}' \hat{\Lambda}' + \hat{\Omega} = \hat{\Lambda} \hat{\Lambda}' + \hat{\Omega}$ preserving, therefore, the initial communalities. We propose the varimax method as the selected orthogonal rotation procedure because this method is characterized by seeking rotated loadings that maximize the variance of the squared loadings in each column of $\hat{\Lambda}^*$. Therefore it attempts to make the loadings either large (in absolute value close to one) or small (close to zero) so as to help the interpretation of the motivational structure.

Appendix
G
WARMGLOW PAYMENT VEHICLE CROSS EFFECT: ESTIMATION RESULTS

As we can observe in Table G.1 the cross-effect warmglow-payment vehicle does not play a relevant role in explaining the stated WTP amount. As it shows, the respective p-value is lower than 10%.

Table G.1: *Valuation function*

Parameters	WA programme			RA programme			(WA + RA) programme		
	Est.	Sd. Er.	p-val.	Est.	Sd. Er.	p-val.	Est.	Sd. Er.	p-val.
Use/recreation	0.088	0.12	0.48	0.290*	0.13	0.02	0.167	0.11	0.12
Warmglow	0.475*	0.19	0.01	0.346*	0.16	0.04	0.153*	0.12	0.00
Existence	0.438*	0.12	0.00	0.249*	0.14	0.08	0.295*	0.11	0.01
Rural	0.400	0.33	0.23	-1.020*	0.37	0.00	0.061	0.29	0.83
Urban	0.141	0.23	0.55	0.357	0.22	0.10	0.100	0.18	0.58
20s	0.699	0.48	0.14	1.466*	0.50	0.00	0.774*	0.40	0.05
30s	0.948*	0.49	0.05	1.442*	0.46	0.00	0.619*	0.36	0.08
40s	0.268	0.48	0.57	0.917*	0.44	0.04	0.455	0.35	0.20
50s	0.235	0.41	0.57	0.955*	0.41	0.01	0.222	0.33	0.56
70s	-0.370	0.47	0.44	0.039	0.45	0.93	-0.562	0.42	0.18
Executives	0.909	0.68	0.18	-1.001	0.63	0.11	-0.483	0.53	0.36
Scientists	0.333	0.58	0.57	-0.320	0.59	0.59	-1.430*	0.54	0.00
Technicians	0.003	0.50	0.99	-0.737	0.48	0.12	-0.053	0.42	0.89
Administrative	0.747	0.50	0.13	-0.736	0.46	0.11	-0.189	0.42	0.65
Sales services	-0.884*	0.51	0.09	-0.474	0.46	0.31	-0.970*	0.43	0.02
Farmers & fishers	0.248	0.72	0.73	-1.030	0.68	0.40	-2.620*	0.27	0.03
Craftsmen	0.326	0.47	0.49	-0.603	0.46	0.19	-0.083	0.39	0.83
Assembly workers	-1.013	0.61	0.10	0.074	0.59	0.90	0.162	0.60	0.78
Unskilled workers	0.030	0.66	0.96	-0.682	0.61	0.26	-1.230*	0.58	0.03
Housekeepers	-0.279	0.45	0.53	-0.750*	0.45	0.09	-0.235	0.41	0.52
Working students	-1.658*	0.87	0.05	-0.324	0.77	0.67	-0.939	0.77	0.22
Primary (freq.)	0.062	0.62	0.92	0.254	0.60	0.67	-0.503	0.58	0.39
Primary	1.048*	0.52	0.04	0.323	0.47	0.49	-0.787	0.51	0.12
Secondary: low	1.257*	0.51	0.01	0.211	0.45	0.21	-0.762	0.48	0.11
Secondary: high	0.962*	0.53	0.07	-0.067	0.44	0.87	-0.272	0.50	0.58
University	1.099*	0.45	0.02	0.018	0.54	0.97	0.839	0.51	0.10
Payment vehicle	-0.101	0.20	0.62	-0.390*	0.19	0.05	-0.329	0.20	0.11
Vc × warmglow	0.125	0.27	0.65	0.213	0.24	0.37	0.166	0.17	0.16
Net income	0.162*	0.09	0.09	0.291*	0.10	0.00	0.166	0.16	0.72
Household	-0.135	0.11	0.23	-0.092	0.09	0.33	0.088	0.08	0.28
Protest	-1.780*	0.31	0.00	-2.020*	0.32	0.00	-1.441*	0.27	0.00
Intercept (β)	6.585			6.880			8.210		
Scale (σ)	1.291			1.195			1.554		
Log–Likelihood	-304.96			-278.71			-570.18		

Notes: * significant at 10%. Reference group: respondent in her 60s who completed a medium level of secondary studies and is now retired.

BIBLIOGRAPHY

Agresti, A. (1990) 'Analysis of Ordinal Categorical Data', John Wiley, New York, US.

Akaike, H. (1973) 'Information Theory and an Extension of the Maximum Likelihood Principle', in B. Petrov and B. Csake (eds), *Second International Symposium on Information Theory*, Akademai Kiado, Budapest.

Alberini, A. (1995) 'Optimal Designs for Discrete Choice Contingent Valuation Surveys: Single–bound, Double–bound and Bivariate Models', *Journal of Environmental Economics and Management*, 28, 287–306.

Andreoni, J. (1988) 'Privately Provided Goods in a Large Economy: the Limits of Altruism', *Journal of Public Economics*, 35, 57–73.

Andreoni, J. (1989) 'Giving with Impure Altruism: Applications to Charity and Ricardian Equivalence', *Journal of Political Economy*, 97, 3, 1447–1458.

Andreoni, J. (1990) 'Impure Altruism and Donations to Public Goods', *Economic Journal*, 100, 464–477.

Arndt, J. and E. Crane (1975) 'Response Bias, Yea Saying and the Double Negative', *Journal of Marketing Research*, 12, 218–220.

Arrow, K.J. (1951) 'Social Choice and Individual Values', John Wiley, New York, US.

Asher, H.B. (1976) 'Causal Modelling', *Sage University Papers*, Quantitative Applications in Social Sciences, Sage, Beverly Hills, California.

Bateman, I.J., I.H. Langford, K.G. Willis, R. Kerry and G.G. Garrod (1993) 'The Impacts of Changing Willingness to Pay Question Format in Contingent Valuation Studies', *CSERGE Working Paper*, University of East Anglia and University College London.

Becker, G.S. (1965) 'A Theory of Allocation of Time', *Economic Journal*, 75, 493–517.

Becker, G.S. (1976) 'The Economic Approach to Human Behaviour' Chicago University Press, Chicago, US.

Becker, G.S. (1993) 'Nobel Lecture: The Economic Way of Looking at Behaviour', *Journal of Political Economy*, 101 (3), 385–409.

Bennett, J.W. (1984) 'Using Direct Questioning to Value the Existence Benefits of Preserved Natural Areas', *Australian Journal of Agricultural Economics*, 28, 136–152.

Bergland, O. (1997) 'Valuation of Landscape Elements Using Contingent Valuation Methods', *paper presented at the Eight Annual Conference of the EAERE*, Tilburg University, The Netherlands.

Bergstrom, J.C., J.R. Stoll and A. Randall (1989) 'The Impact of Information on Environmental Commodity Valuation Decisions', *American Journal of Agricultural Economics*, 685–691.

Bergstrom, T., L. Blume and H. Varian (1986) 'On the Private Provision of the Public Good', *Journal of Public Economics*, 29, 25–49.

Bishop, R.C. (1980) 'Endangered Species: an Economic Perspective', *Transactions if the 45th North American Wildlife and Natural Resources Conference*, Wildlife Management Institute, Washington DC.

Bishop, R.C. and T. A. Heberlein (1979) 'Measuring the Value of Extramarket Goods: are Indirect Measures Biased?', *American Journal of Agricultural Economics*, 926–930.

Bishop, R.C. and T. A. Heberlein (1990) 'The Contingent Valuation Method', in Johnson, R.L. and G.V. Johnson (eds), *Economic Valuation of Natural Resources: Issues, Theory and Applications*, Social Behaviour and Natural Resources Series, Boulder, CO, and Oxford.

Bjornstad, D.J., and J.R. Kahn (eds) (1996), *The Contingent Valuation of Environmental Resources; methodological issues and research needs*, New Horizons in Environmental Economics, Edward Elgar, Cheltenham, UK.

Bockstael, N.E., K.E. McConnell and I. Strand (1991) 'Recreation', in J.B. Braden and C.D. Koldstad (eds) *Measuring the Demand for Environment Quality*, Elsevier Science Publishers, North–Holland.

Boman, M. and G. Bostedt (1995) 'Valuing the Wolf in Sweden', *Report No. 110, Swedish University of Agricultural Sciences*, Department of Forest Economics, Umeå.

Bohm, P. (1972) "Estimating the Demand for Public Goods: an Experiment", *European Economic Review*, 3, 110-130.

Bowker, J.M. and J.R. Stoll (1988) 'Use of Dichotomous Choice Nonmarket Methods to Value the Whooping Crane Resource', *American Journal of Agricultural Economics*, 70, 327–381.

Boyle, K.J. (1990) 'Dichotomous Choice, Contingent Valuation Questions: Functional Form Is Important', *North–eastern Journal of Agriculture and Resource Economics*, 19 (2), 125–131.

Boyle, K.J., M.P. Welsh and R.C. Bishop (1993) 'The Role of Question Order and Respondents Experience in Contingent–Valuation Studies', *Journal of Environmental Economics and Management*, 25, S80–S90.

Boyle, K.J., W.H. Desvousges, F.R. Johnson, R.W. Dunford and S.P. Hudson (1994) 'An Investigation of the Part–Whole Biases in Contingent Valuation Surveys', *Journal of Environmental Economics and Management*, 27, 64–83.

Braden, J.B. and C.D. Koldstad (eds) (1991) *Measuring the Demand for Environment Quality*, Elsevier Science Publishers.

Braden, J.B., C.D. Koldstad and D. Miltz (1991) 'Introduction, Summary and Conclusions', in J.B. Braden and C.D. Koldstad (eds) (1991) *Measuring the Demand for Environment Quality*, Elsevier Science Publishers, North–Holland, 3–16 and 323–330.

Brookshire, D.S. (1997) 'Heterogeneous Preferences, Special Interests and the Voluntary Provision of Public Goods', *paper presented at the Eight Annual Conference of the EAERE*, Tilburg University, The Netherlands.

Brookshire, D.S., R.C. d'Arge and W.D. Schulze (1981) 'Experiments in Valuing Public Goods', in *Advances in Applied Econometrics*, vol.1, 123–172, JAI Press.

Brookshire, D.S., L.S. Eubanks and A. Randall (1983) 'Estimating Option Prices and Existence Values for Wildlife Resources', *Land Economics*, 59, 1–15.

Cameron, T.A. (1988) 'A New Paradigm For Valuing Non-Market goods Using Referenda Data: Maximum Likelihood Estimation by Censored Logistic Regression', *Journal of Environmental Economics and Management*, 15, 355–379.

Cameron, T.A. (1991) 'Interval Estimates of Non-market Resource Values from Referendum Contingent Valuation Surveys', *Land Economics*, 67 (4), 413–21.

Cameron, T.A. and M. D. James (1987) 'Efficient Estimation Methods For Closed-ended Contingent Valuation Surveys', *American Journal of Agricultural Economics*, 269–276.

Carson, R.T. (1991) 'Constructed Markets', in J.B. Braden and C.D. Kolstad (eds), *Measuring the Demand for Environment Quality*, University of California, North–Holland.

Carson, R.T. (1997) 'Contingent Valuation Surveys and Tests of Insensitivity to Scope', in R.J. Kopp et al. (eds), *Determining the Value of Non-marketed Goods*, Kluwer Academic Publishers, The Netherlands.

Carson, R.T. and R.C. Mitchell (1993a) 'The Value of Clean Water: the Public's Willingness to Pay for Boatable Fishable and Swimmable Quality Water', *Water Resources Research*, 29 (7), 2445–2454.

Carson, R.T. and R.C. Mitchell (1993b) 'The Issue of Scope in Contingent Valuation Studies', *American Journal of Agricultural Economics*, 75 (5), 1263–1267.

Carson, R.T. and R.C. Mitchell (1995) 'Sequencing and Nesting in Contingent Valuation Surveys', *Journal of Environmental Economics and Management*, 28, 155–173.

Carson, R.T., W.M. Hanemann and R.C. Mitchell (1986) 'Determining the Demand for Public Goods by Simulating Referendums at Different Tax Prices', *San Diego Department of Economics Working Paper*, University of California.

Carson, R.T., R.C. Mitchell, W.M. Hanemann, R. J. Kopp, S. Presser and P. A. Ruud (1992) 'A Contingent Valuation Study of Lost Passive Use Values Resulting from the *Exxon Valdez* Oil Spill', *Report prepared for the Attorney General of the State of Alaska*, Washington.

Carson, R.T., L. Wilks and D. Imber (1994a) 'Valuing the Preservation of Australia's Kakadu Conservation Zone', *Oxford Economic Papers*, 46 (5), 727–49.

Carson, R.T., J. Wright, N. Carson, A. Alberini and N. Flores (1994b) *A Bibliography of Contingent Valuation Studies and Papers*, Resource Damage Assessment Inc., La Jolla, CA.

Carson, R. T., Groves T. and M. J. Machina (1999) 'Incentive and Informational Properties of Preferences Questions', *paper presented at the plenary session of the 9th Annual Conference of the European Association of Environmental and Resource Economists*, Oslo, Norway.

Champ, P.A. (1994), 'Nonmarket Valuation of Resource Amenities: A Validity Test of the Contingent Valuation Method', *Ph.D. dissertation*, University of Wisconsin.

Champ, P.A., R.C Bishop, T.C. Brown and D.W. McCollum (1997) 'Using Donation Mechanism to Value Nonuse Benefits From Public Goods', *Journal of Environmental Economics and Management*, 33, 151–162.

Ciriacy–Wantrup (1947) 'Capital Returns from Soil Conservation Practices', *Journal of Farm Economics*, 29, 1180–1190.

Commission of the European Communities (1992) 'Europeans and the Environment in 1992', *Eurobarometer 37.0*, Brussels, Belgium.

Cooper, J.C. (1993) 'Optimal Bid Selection for Dichotomous Choice Contingent Valuation Surveys', *Journal of Environmental Economics and Management*, 24, 25–40.

Cooper, J.C. (1994) 'A Comparison of Approaches to Calculating Confidence Intervals for Benefit Measures from Dichotomous Choice Contingent Valuation Surveys', *Land Economics*, 70 (1), 111–22.

Cornes, R. and T. Sandler (1984) "Easier Riders, Joint Production and Public Economics", *Economic Journal*, 94, 580-598.

Cornes, R. and T. Sandler (1986) *The Theory of Externalities, Public Goods and Club Goods*, Cambridge University Press, New York.

Cornes, R. and T. Sandler (1994) 'The Comparative Static Properties of the Impure Public Good', *Journal of Public Economics*, 54, 403–421.

Cronin, F. J. (1982) 'Valuing Nonmarket Goods Through Contingent Markets', Report to US EPA, Washington.

Cropper, M.L. and A.M. Freeman III (1991) 'Environmental Health Effects', in J.B. Braden and C.D. Koldstad (eds) *Measuring the Demand for Environment Quality*. Elsevier Science Publishers, North–Holland.

Cummings, R.G., D.S. Brookshire and W.D. Schulze (1986) *Valuing Environmental Goods: a State of the Art Assessment of the Contingent Valuation Method*, Rowman and Allenheld, New Jersey.

Cummings, R.G., P.T. Ganderton and T. McGuckin (1994) 'Substitution Effects in CVM Values', *American Journal of Agricultural Economics*, 76 (2), 205–214.

d'Arge, R.C. (1985) 'Environmental Quality Benefits Research for the Next Five Years: Some Observations and Recommendations', *Report to the US EPA*, Washington DC.

Davis R.K. (1963) 'The Value of Outdoor Recreation: an Economic Study of the Maine Woods', Ph.D. dissertation, Department of Economics, Harvard University.

Deaton, D. (1997) *The Analysis of Household Surveys: a Microeconomic Approach to Development Policy*, Johns Hopkins University Press, Baltimore, MD.

Desvousges, W.H., F.R. Johnson, R.W. Dunford, K.J. Boyle, S.P. Hudson and K.N. Wilson (1993a) 'Measuring Natural Resource Damages with Contingent Valuation: Tests of Validity and Reliability', in J. A. Hausman (ed.), *Contingent valuation: a Critical Assessment*, Contributions to Economic Analysis, North–Holland, New York, US.

Desvousges, W.H., A.R. Gable, R.W. Dunford and S.P. Hudson (1993b) 'Contingent Valuation: the Wrong Tool to Measure the Passive–use Values Losses', *Choices*, 2nd quarter, 9–11.

Desvousges, W.H., S.P. Hudson, and M.C. Ruby (1996) 'Evaluating CV Performance: Separating the Light from the Heat', in D.J. Bjornstad and J.R. Kahn (eds), *The Contingent Valuation of Environmental Resources; methodological issues and research needs*, New Horizons in Environmental Economics, Edward Elgar, Cheltenham, UK.

Diamond, P.A. (1996) 'Testing the Internal Consistency of Contingent Valuation Surveys', *Journal of Environmental Economics and Management*, 30, 337–347.

Diamond, P. A. and J. A. Hausman (1994) 'Contingent Valuation: Is Some Number Better than No Number?', *Journal of Economic Perspectives*, 8 (4), 45–64.

Diamond, P.A., J.A. Hausman, G.L. Leonard and M.A. Denning (1993) 'Does Contingent Valuation Measure Preferences? Experimental Evidence', in J. A. Hausman (ed.), *Contingent valuation: a Critical Assessment*, Contributions to Economic Analysis, North–Holland, New York, US.

Duffield, J.W. and D.A. Patterson (1991) 'Inference and Optimal Design for a Welfare Measure in Dichotomous Choice Contingent Valuation', *Land Economics*, 67 (2), 225–239.

Dupuit, J. (1844) 'On the Measurement of the Utility of Public Works', *Annales des Ponts et Chausées*, 2nd series, volume 8; reprinted in D. Munby (ed.) *Transport: Selected Readings*, Harmondsworth, Penguin Books, 1968.

Ehrenfield, D. (1988) 'Why Put a Value on Biodiversity?', in E.O. Wilson (ed.), *Biodiversity*, Washington, National Academy Press, 212–216.

Farquaharson, R. (1969) Theory of Voting, Yale University Press, New Haven, CN.

Feenstra, J.F. (1984) 'Cultural Property and Air Pollution', Ministry of Public Housing, Physical Planning and the Environment, The Netherlands.

Fischhoff, B. and L. Furby (1988) 'Measuring Values: A Conceptual Framework for Interpreting Transactions with Special Reference to Contingent Valuation of Visibility', Journal of Risk and Uncertainty, 1, 147–184.

Freeman, A.M. III (1979) 'Approaches to Measuring Public Goods Demands', *American Journal of Agricultural Economics*, 61, 915–920.

Friedman, D. and S. Sunder (1994) *Experimental Methods: A Primer for Economists*, Cambridge University Press, New York, US.

Gibbard, A. (1973) 'Manipulation of Voting Schemes: a General Approach', *Econometrica*, 41, 587–601.

Green, J. R. and J. J. Laffont (1978) 'A Sampling Approach to Free Riding Problem', in A. Sandmo (ed.), *Essays in Public Economics*, Lexington Books.

Gregory, R., S. Lichtenstein and P. Slovic (1993) 'Valuing Environmental Resources: a Constructive Approach', *Journal of Risk and Uncertainty*, 7, 177–197.

Groves, R.M. (1989) 'Survey Errors and Survey Costs', John Wiley, New York, US.

Halstead, J.M., A.E. Luloff and T.H. Stevens (1992) 'Protest Bidders in Contingent Valuation', *Northeastern Journal of Agriculture and Resource Economics*, 21 (2), 160–169.

Hammack, J. and G.M. Brown (1974) *Waterfowls and Wetlands: Towards a Bioeconomic Analysis*, John Hopkins University Press for Resource for the Future, Baltimore, MD, US.

Hanemann, M.W. (1984) 'Welfare Evaluations in Contingent Valuation Experiments with Discrete Responses', *American Journal of Agricultural Economics*, 66, 332–341.

Hanemann, M. W. (1994) 'Valuing the Environment Through Contingent Valuation', *Journal of Economic Perspectives*, 8 (4), 19–43.

Hanemann, M.W., J. Loomis and B. Kanninen (1991) 'Statistical Efficiency of Double–bounded Dichotomous Choice Contingent Valuation', *American Journal of Agricultural Economics*, 73 (4), 1255–1263.

Hanley, N.D. (1988) 'Using Contingent Valuation to Value Environmental Improvements', *Applied Economics*, 40, 541–549.

Hanley, N. and J. Milne (1996) 'Ethical Beliefs and Behaviour in Contingent Valuation Surveys', *Journal of Environmental Planning and Management*, 39 (2), 255–72.

Hanley, N.D. and C.L. Spash (1993) *Cost–Benefit Analysis and the Environment*, Edward Elgar, Cheltenham, UK.

Hanley, N., C.L. Spash and L. Walter (1995) 'Problems in Valuing the Benefits of Biodiversity Protection', *Environment and Resources Economics*, 5 (3), 249–272.

Harman, H.H. (1976) *Modern Factor Analysis*, Chicago University Press, Chicago, US.

Harrison, G.W. and B. Kriström (1995) 'On the Interpretation of Responses in Contingent Valuation Surveys', in P-O. Johansson, B. Kriström and K.G. Mäler (eds), *Current Issues in Environmental Economics*, Manchester University Press, Manchester.

Hatcher, L. (1994) *A Step–by–Step Approach to Using the SAS System Factor Analysis and Structural Equation Modelling*, SAS Institute, Cary, US.

Hausman, D.M. (1993) 'Taking Ethics Seriously: Economics and Contemporary Moral Philosophy', *Journal of Economic Literature*, 671–731.

Hausman, J.A. (ed.) (1993), *'Contingent valuation: a Critical Assessment'*, Contributions to Economic Analysis, North–Holland, New York, US.

Hausman, J.A. and P.A. Diamond (1993) 'On Contingent Valuation Measurement of Nonuse Values', in J. A. Hausman (ed.), *Contingent valuation: a Critical Assessment*, Contributions to Economic Analysis, North–Holland, New York, US.

Hausman, J.A., G.K. Leonard and D. McFadden (1993) 'Assessing Use Value Losses Caused by Natural Resource Injury', in J. A. Hausman (ed.), *Contingent valuation: a Critical Assessment*, Contributions to Economic Analysis, North–Holland, New York, US.

Herriges, J.A. and J.F. Shogren (1996) 'Starting Point Bias in Dichotomous Choice Valuation with Follow–Up Questioning', *Journal of Environmental Economics and Management*, 30, 112–31.

Hicks, J. R. (1943) 'The Four Consumer Surpluses', *Review of Economic Studies*, 11 (1), 31–41.

Hoehn, J. P. and J. B. Loomis (1993) 'Substitution Effects in the Valuation of Multiple Environmental Programs', *Journal of Environmental Economics and Management*, 25, 56–75.

Hoehn, J.P. and A. Randall (1987) 'A Satisfactory Benefit Cost Indicator from Contingent Valuation', *Journal of Environmental Economics and Management*, 14, 226–247.

Hoehn, J. P. and A. Randall (1989) 'Too Many Proposals Pass the Benefit Cost Test', *American Economic Review*, 79, 544–551.

Hoevenagel, R. (1992) 'An Assessment of Contingent Valuation Surveys', in S. Navrud (ed.), *Pricing the European Environment*, Scandinavian University Press, Oslo, 177–94.

Hoevenagel, R. (1994) 'The Contingent Valuation Method: Scope and Validity', *Ph.D. dissertation*, Institute for Environmental Studies, Vrije Universiteit, Amsterdam, The Netherlands.

Hoevenagel, R. (1996) 'The Validity Of The Contingent Valuation Method: Perfect And Regular Embedding', *Environmental and Resource Economics*, 7 (1), 57–78.

Hoevenagel, R. and J.W. van der Linden (1993) 'Effects of different descriptions of the Ecological Good on Willingness to Pay Values', *Ecological Economics*, 7 (3), 223–237.

Holmes, T. P. and R.A. Kramer (1995) 'An Independent Sample Test of Yea-saying and Starting Point Bias in Dichotomous–choice Contingent Valuation' *Journal of Environmental Economics and Management*, 29, 121–32.

Hutchinson, W.G., S.M. Chilton and J. Davis (1995) 'Measuring Non–use Value of Environmental Goods Using the Contingent Valuation Method: Problems of Information and Cognition and the Application of Cognitive Questionnaire Design Methods', *Journal of Agricultural Economics*, 46 (1), 97–112.

Imber, D., G. Stevenson and L. Wilks (1991) 'A Contingent Valuation of the Kakadu Conservation Zone', Resource Assessment Commission Research Paper no.1.

Instituto Nacional de Estatística (1992) *Censos 91*, Lisboa, Portugal.

Jakobsson K. M. and A. K. Dragun (1996) *Contingent Valuation and Endangered Species*, UK, Edward Elgar, Cheltenham, UK.

Johansson, P.O., B. Kriström and H. Nyquist (1994) 'Optimal Designs, Spikes and Risks', *Working Paper*, Stockholm School of Economics.

Johansson, P.O., B. Kriström and K–G Mäler (eds) (1995) *Current Issues in Environmental Economics*, Manchester University Press, Manchester.

Johnson, N.L and S. Kotz (1970) *Continuous Univariate Distributions*, 2, John Wiley, New York, US.

Johnson, R.L. and G.V. Johnson (eds) (1990) 'Economic Valuation of Natural Resources: Issues, Theory and Applications', *Social Behaviour and Natural Resources Series*, Boulder, CO and Oxford.

Judge, G.G., W.E. Griffiths and R.C. Hill (1985) *The Theory and Practice of Econometrics*, John Wiley, New York.

Kahneman, D. (1986) 'Valuing Environmental Goods: an Assessment of the Contingent Valuation Method', in R.G. Cummings, D.S. Brookshire and W.D. Schulze (eds), *Valuing Environmental Goods: a State of the Art Assessment of the Contingent Valuation Method*, Rowman and Allenheld, N. Jersey.

Kahneman, D. and J.L. Knetsch (1992a) 'Valuing Public Goods: the Purchase of Moral Satisfaction', *Journal of Environmental Economics and Management*, 22, 57–70.

Kahneman, D. and J.L. Knetsch (1992b) 'Contingent Valuation and the Value of Public Goods: Reply', *Journal of Environmental Economics and Management*, 22, 90–94.

Kaiser, H. F. (1960) 'The Application Of Electronic Computers To Factor Analysis', *Educational and Psychological Measurement*, 20, 141–151.

Kalton, G. (1983) 'Introduction to Survey Sampling', *Sage University Papers*, \Quantitative Applications in Social Sciences, Sage, Beverly Hills, California.

Kanninen, B.J. (1993a) 'Design of Sequential Experiments for Contingent Valuation Studies', *Journal of Environmental Economics and Management*, 25, Part 2, S1–S11.

Kanninen, B.J. (1993b) 'Optimal Experimental Design for Double–Bounded Dichotomous Choice Contingent Valuation', *Land Economics*, 69 (2), 138–46.

Kanninen, B.J. (1995) 'Bias in Discrete Response Contingent Valuation', *Journal of Environmental Economics and Management*, 28, 114–125.

Kemp, M.A. and C. Maxwell (1993) 'Exploring a Budget Context for Contingent Valuation Estimates', in J. A. Hausman (ed.), *Contingent valuation: a Critical Assessment*, Contributions to Economic Analysis, North–Holland, New York, US.

Kim, J.O. and C.W. Mueller (1990) 'Factorial Analysis: Statistical Methods and Practical Issues', *Sage University Papers*, Quantitative Applications in Social Sciences, Sage, Beverly Hills, California.

Kirkland, W.T. (1988) 'Preserving the Whangamarino Wetland: an application of the Contingent Valuation Method', *M.Ag.Sc. Thesis*, Massey University, Palmerston North, New Zealand.

Kopp, R.J., W.W. Pommerehne and N. Schwarz (1997) *Determining the Value of Non–Marketed Goods*, Studies in Risk and Uncertainty, Kluwer Academic Publishers, The Netherlands.

Kriström, B. (1990) 'A Non–Parametric Approach to the Estimation Of Welfare Measures in Discrete Response Valuation Questions', *Land Economics*, 66, 135–139.

Krutilla, J.V. (1967) 'Conservation Reconsidered', *American Economic Review*, 57, 777–786.

Lancaster, K.J. (1966) 'A New Approach to Economic Theory', *Journal of Political Economy*, 74, 134–157.

Lancaster, K.J. (1971) *Consumer Demand: a New Approach*, Columbia University Press.

Lehmann E.L. (1975) *Nonparametrics: Statistical Methods Based on Ranks*, Holden–Day, San Francisco.

Likert, R. (1967) 'The Method of Constructing an Attitude Scale', in Fishhbein (ed.), *Readings in Attitudes Measurement*, 90–95. Originally in *Archives of Psychology*, 140, 44–53, Columbia University Press.

Loomis, J.B. (1989) 'Test–Retest Reliability of the Contingent Valuation Method: a Comparison of General Population and Visitor Responses', *American Journal of Agricultural Economics*, 71 (1), 76–84.

Loomis, J.B. (1990) 'Compare Reliability of the Dichotomous Choice and Open–ended Contingent Valuation Techniques', *Journal of Environmental Economics and Management*, 18, 78–85.

Loomis, J. B. (1994) 'Review of: the Economic Value Of Biodiversity', *Journal of Economic Literature*, 33 (4), 2026–2027.

Loomis, J.B., M. Lockwood and T. DeLacy (1993) 'Some Empirical Evidence on Embedding Effects in Contingent Valuation of Forest Protection', *Journal of Environmental Economics and Management*, 24, 45–55.

Loomis, J.B., A.G. Caban and R. Gregory (1994) 'Do Reminders of Substitutes and Budget Constraints Influence Contingent Valuation Estimates?', *Land Economics*, 70 (4), 499–506.

Lunander, A. (1998) 'Inducing Incentives to Understate and to Overstate within the Open–ended and the Dichotomous–choice Elicitation Format', *Journal of Environmental Economics and Management*, 35, 88–102.

Maddala, G.S. (1983) *Limited Dependent and Qualitative Variables in Econometrics*, Econometric Society Monographs, Cambridge University Press, New York, US.

Marshall, A. (1920) *Principles of Economics: An Introductory Volume*, London: Macmillan.

Mattsson, L. and B. Kriström (1987) 'The Economic Value Of A Moose As A Hunting Object', *Scandinavian Forest Economics*, 29, 27–37.

McClelland, G., W.D. Schultze, J.K. Lazo, D.M. Waldman, J.K. Doyle, S.R. Elliot and J.R. Irwin (1992) 'Methods For Measuring Non–Use Values: A contingent valuation study of groundwater cleanup', US EPA Agreement CR#–815183.

McFadden, D. and G.K. Leonard (1993) 'Issues in the Contingent Valuation of Environmental Goods: Methodologies for Data Collection and Analysis', in J. A. Hausman (ed.), *Contingent valuation: a Critical Assessment*, Contributions to Economic Analysis, North–Holland, New York, US.

Ministério do Ambiente e Recursos Naturais (MARN) (1995a) Decreto Regulamentar n. 26/95 de 21 de Setembro, Diário da República, série B, n. 219.

Ministério do Ambiente e Recursos Naturais (MARN) (1995b) Decreto Regulamentar n. 33/95 de 11 de Dezembro, Diário da República, série B, n. 284.

Ministério do Emprego e Segurança Social (MESS) (1994) *Classificação Nacional das Profissões*, Instituto do Emprego e Formação Profissional, Lisbon, Portugal.

Milgrom, P. (1993) 'Is Sympathy an Economic Value? Philosophy, Economics, and the Contingent Valuation Method', in J. A. Hausman (ed.), *Contingent valuation: a Critical Assessment*, Contributions to Economic Analysis, North–Holland, New York, US.

Mitchell, R.C. and R.T. Carson (1989) *Using Surveys to Value Public Goods: The Contingent Valuation Method*', Resources for the Future Washington DC, US.

Mitchell, R.C. and R.T. Carson (1993) 'Current Issues in the Design, Administration, and Analysis of Contingent Valuation Surveys', *San Diego Department of Economics Working Paper*, University of California.

National Oceanic and Atmospheric Administration (NOAA) (1993) 'Report of the NOAA Panel on Contingent Valuation', *Federal Register*, 58 (10), 4601–4614.

Navrud, S. (ed.) (1992) *Pricing the European Environment*, Scandinavian University Press, Oslo, Norway.

Navrud, S. (1999) *Assessment of Environmental Valuation Reference Inventory (EVRI) and the Expansion of Its Coverage to the EU*', European Commission, DG XI, Brussels, Belgium.

Norton, B.G. (1982) 'Environmental Ethics and Nonhuman Rights', *Environmental Ethics*, 4, 17–36.

Norton, B.G. (1988) 'Commodity, Amenity and Morality the Limits of Quantification in Valuing Biodiversity', in E. O. Wilson (ed.), *Biodiversity*, Washington, National Academy Press, 200–205.

Nunes, P.A. (1997) 'Avaliação Económica do Parque Natural do Sudoeste Alentejano e Costa Vicentina: abordagem contingente', *Statistical Report*, Centro de Estudos e Sondagens de Opinião, Universidade Católica Portuguesa.

Nunes, P.A. (1998a) 'Avaliação Económica do Parque Natural do Sudoeste Alentejano e Costa Vicentina: abordagem contingente', *Relatório Final – Protocolo de Colaboração com o Instituto de Conservação da Natureza*, Center for Economic Studies, Catholic University of Leuven.

Nunes, P.A. (1998b) 'Non–parametric testing procedures and parametric model specifications of the stated WTP responses from a CV survey in Portugal', *paper presented at the XIIth World Congress of the International Economic Association*, August, Buenos Aires, Argentina.

Palmquist, R.B. (1991) 'Hedonic Methods', in J.B. Braden and C.D. Koldstad (eds) *Measuring the Demand for Environment Quality*, Elsevier Science Publishers, North–Holland.

Pearce, D.W. and A. Markandya (1989) *Environmental Policy Benefits: Monetary Valuation*, OECD, Paris.

Pearce, D.W. and D. Moran (1994) *The Economic Value of Biodiversity*, Earthscan Publications, London, UK.

Pethig, R. (ed.) (1994) *Valuing the Environment and Measurement Issues*, Kluwer Academic Publishers, The Netherlands.

Plano Nacional da Política de Ambiente (1995) *Acções Programáticas Específicas do Ministério do Ambiente e Recursos Naturais*, Ministério do Ambiente e Recursos Naturais (MARN), Lisboa, Portugal.

Ootegem, L. (1994) 'An Economic Theory for Private Donations', *Ph.D. dissertation*, Faculty of Economics, Catholic University of Leuven.

Portney, P.R. (1994) 'The Contingent Valuation Debate: Why Economists Should Care?', *Journal of Economic Perspectives*, 8 (4), 3–17.

Randall, A. (1988) 'What Mainstream Economists Have to Say about the Value of Biodiversity', in E. O. Wilson (ed.), Biodiversity, Washington, National Academy Press, 217–223.

Randall, A. (1991) 'Total and Non-use Values', in J.B. Braden and C.D. Kolstad (eds), *Measuring the Demand for Environmental Quality*, Elsevier Science Publishers, North–Holland.

Randall, A., B. Ives and C. Eastman (1974), 'Bidding Games for Valuation of Aesthetic Environmental Improvements', *Journal of Environmental Economics and Management*, 1, 132–149.

Randall, A., J.P. Hoehn and D.S. Brookshire (1983) 'Contingent Valuation Surveys for Evaluating Environmental Assets', *Natural Resources Journal*, 23 (3), 635–48.

Ready, R.C. and D. Hu (1995) 'Statistical Approaches to the Fat Tail Problem for Dichotomous Choice Contingent Valuation', *Land Economics*, 71 (4), 491–99.

Rencher, A.C. (1995) *Methods of Multivariate Analysis*, John Wiley New York, US.

Rockel, M.L. and M.J. Kealy (1991) 'The Value Of Nonconsumptive Wildlife Recreation In The United States', *Land Economics*, 67 (4), 422–34.

Römer, A.U., and W.W. Pommerehne (1992) 'Germany and Switzerland', in S. Navrud (ed.), *Pricing the European environment*, Scandinavian University Press, Oslo, Norway.

Rosen, S. (1974) 'Hedonic Prices and Implicit Markets: Differentiation in Pure Competition', Journal of Public Economy, 82, 34–55.

Rowe, R. D., R. d'Arge and D. Brookshire (1980) 'An Experiment on the Economic Value of Visibility', *Journal of Environmental Economics and Management*, 7, 1–19.

Rowe, R.D., W.D. Schulze, W.D. Shaw, D. Schenk, and L. Chesnut (1991) 'Contingent Valuation of the Resource Damage Due to the Nestucca Oil Spill', *Final Report*.

Rummel, R. J. (1979) *Applied Factor Analysis*, Northwestern University Press, Evanston, IH.

Sagoff, M. (1980) 'On the Preservation of Species', Columbia Journal of Environmental Law, 7, 33–67.

Samples, K.C. and J.R. Hollyer (1990) 'Contingent Valuation of Wildlife Resources in the Presence of Substitutes and Complements', in R.L. Johnso and G.V. Johnson (eds) *Economic Valuation of Natural Resources: Issues, Theory and Applications*, Social Behaviour and Natural Resources Series, Boulder, CO, and Oxford.

Samples, K.C., J.A. Dixon and M.M. Gowen (1986) 'Information Disclosure and Endangered Species Valuation', *Land Economics*, 62 (3), 306–312.

Samuelson, P. (1954) 'The Pure Theory of Public Expenditure', *Review of Economics and Statistics*, 36(4), 387–389.

Satterthwaite, M. (1975) 'Strategic-proofness and Arrow Conditions: Existence and Correspondence Theorems for Voting Procedures and Welfare Functions', Journal of Economic Theory, 10, 187–217.

Schkade, D.A. and J.W. Payne (1993) 'Where Do the Numbers Come from? How People Respond to Contingent Valuation Questions', ', in J. A. Hausman (ed.), *Contingent valuation: a Critical Assessment*, Contributions to Economic Analysis, North–Holland, New York, US.

Schkade, D.A. and J.W. Payne (1994) 'How People Respond to Contingent Valuation Questions: A Verbal Protocol Analysis of Willingness to Pay for an Environmental Regulation', *Journal of Environmental Economics and Management*, 26, 88–109.

Schokkaert, E., (1980) 'Modelling Consumer Preference Formation', *Ph.D. dissertation*, Faculty of Economics, Catholic University of Leuven.

Schokkaert, E. and L. van Ootegem (1990) 'Sen's Concept of the Living Standard applied to the Belgian Unemployed', *Recherches Economiques de Louvain*, Université Catholique de Louvain, Belgium.

Schulze, W.D., R.D. Rowe, W.S. Breffle, R. Boyce and G. McClelland (1993) 'Contingent Valuation of the Natural Resource Damage Due to Injuries to the Upper Clark Fork River Basin', *Final Report to the State of Montana*, Boulder, CO, US.

Seip, K. and J. Strand (1992) 'Willingness to Pay for Environmental Goods in Norway: A Contingent Valuation Study with Real Payment', Environmental and Resource Economics, 2(1), 91–106.

Siegel, S. and N.J. Castellan (1988) *Nonparametric Statistics for the Behavioral Sciences*', 2nd edition, McGraw–Hill, New York.

Sinden, J.A. (1988) 'Empirical Tests of Hypothetical Bias in Consumers' Surplus Surveys', *Australian Journal of Agricultural Economics*, 32, 98–112.

Smith, V.K., (1991) 'Household Production Function and Environmental Benefit Estimation', in J.B. Braden and C.D. Koldstad (eds) '*Measuring the Demand for Environment Quality*', Elsevier Science Publishers, North–Holland.

Smith, V.K. (1992) 'Arbitrary Values, Good Causes and Premature Verdicts', *Journal of Environmental Economics and Management*, 22, 71–89.

Smith, V.K. (1993) 'Natural Resource Damage Liability: Lessons from Implementation and Impacts on Incentives', *Resources for the Future Discussion Paper*, 44, 94–101.

Smith, V.K. (1994) 'Resource Evaluation at a Crossroads', *Resources for the Future Discussion Paper*, 68, 94–106.

Stigler, G. J. and G. S. Becker (1977). 'De Gustibus non est Disputatum', *American Economic Review*, 67, 76–90.

Stiglitz, J. E. (1988) *The Economics of the Public Sector*, W.W. Norton, New York, US.

Stoll, J. and L. A. Johnson (1984) 'Concepts of Value, Non–market Valuation and the Case of the Whooping Crane', *Transactions if the 45th North American Wildlife and Natural Resources Conference*, WMI, Washington DC.

Stukat, K.G. (1958) *Suggestibility: a Factorial and Experimental Analysis*, Wiksell Stockholm, Sweden.

Swanborn, P.G. (1993) *Schaaltechnieken*, 3rd Edition, Boom, Amsterdam, The Netherlands.

Thompson, S.K. (1992) *Sampling*, John Wiley, New York, US.

Thomson, G.H. (1951) *The Factorial Analysis of Human Ability*, London University Press, London.

Turnbull, Bruce W. (1976) 'The Empirical Distribution Function with Arbitrarily Grouped, Censored and Truncated Data', *Journal of the Royal Statistical Society*, B38, 290–295.

Tversky, A. and D. Kahneman (1973) 'Availability: a Heuristic for Judging Frequency and Probability', *Cognitive Psychology*, 5, 207–232.

United States Department of Interior (USDI) (1989), 'District of Columbia Circuit Court of Appeals, re–interpretation of the Comprehensive Environmental Response, Compensation and Liability Act of 1986'.

Van der Veer D. and C. Pierce (1986) *People, Penguins and Plastic Trees: Basic Issues in Environmental Ethics* Wadsworth, Belmont, US.

Varian, H.R. (1990) *Intermediate Microeconomics: a Modern Approach*, W.W. Norton, New York, US.

Walsh, R.G., J.B. Loomis and R.A. Gillman (1984) 'Valuing Option, Existence, and Bequest Demands for Wilderness', *Land Economics*, 60, 14–29.

Whitehead, J.C. and G.C. Blomquist (1995) 'Do Reminders of Substitutes and Budget Constraints Influence Contingent Valuation Estimates? Comment', *Land Economics*, 71 (4), 541–43.

Whitehead, J.C., P.A. Groothuis and G.C. Blomquist (1993) 'Testing for Non–response and Sample Selection Bias in Contingent Valuation: Analysis of a Combination Phone/Mail Survey', *Economics Letters*, 41 (2), 215–20.

Wiestra E. (1996) 'On the Domain of Contingent Valuation', *Ph.D. dissertation*, Twente University, The Ntherlands.

Wilcoxon, F. (1945) 'Individual Comparisons by Ranking Methods', *Biometrica*, 1, 80–83.

Willig, R.D. (1979) 'Consumer's Surplus Without Apology', *American Economic Review*, 66 (4), 589–597.

Wilson, E.O. (1994) *The Diversity of Life*', Penguin, Harmondsworth, UK.

Woo, L.G. (1996), 'Out of Site, Out of Mind: A Contingent Valuation Analysis of the Siting of a Sanitary Landfill', University of North Carolina.

World Bank Report (1990) *Mexico Forestry and Conservation Sector Review: Substudy of Economic Valuation of Forests*, World Bank, New York, US.

Index

251